THE MORAL AND POLITICAL
STATUS OF CHILDREN

The Moral and Political Status of Children

edited by

DAVID ARCHARD

and

COLIN M. MACLEOD

OXFORD

UNIVERSITY PRESS

OXFORD
UNIVERSITY PRESS

Great Clarendon Street, Oxford OX2 6DP

Oxford University Press is a department of the University of Oxford.
It furthers the University's objective of excellence in research, scholarship,
and education by publishing worldwide in

Oxford New York

Auckland Bangkok Buenos Aires Cape Town Chennai
Dar es Salaam Delhi Hong Kong Istanbul Karachi Kolkata
Kuala Lumpur Madrid Melbourne Mexico City Mumbai Nairobi
São Paulo Shanghai Singapore Taipei Tokyo Toronto
and associated company in Berlin

Oxford is a registered trade mark of Oxford University Press
in the UK and in certain other countries

Published in the United States
by Oxford University Press Inc., New York

© the several contributors 2002

The moral rights of the author have been asserted
Database right Oxford University Press (maker)

First published 2002

British Library Cataloguing in Publication Data

The moral and political status of children: new essays/edited by David Archard,
Colin M. Macleod.
p.; cm.
Includes bibliographical references.
1. Children's rights. 2. Children—Social conditions. I. Archard, David. II. Macleod,
Colin M. (Colin Murray), 1962–
HQ789.M667 2002   305.23—dc21   2002018839
ISBN 0–19–924268–2

1 3 5 7 9 10 8 6 4 2

Typeset in Minion by
Cambrian Typesetters, Frimley, Surrey
Printed in Great Britain
on acid-free paper by
T.J. International Ltd.,
Padstow, Cornwall

Contents

Contents

Notes on Contributors

David Archard has been Reader in Moral Philosophy at the University of St Andrews since 1995 and is Director of the Centre for Ethics, Philosophy and Public Affairs. He is the author of several books including *Children, Rights and Childhood* (1993) and *Sexual Consent* (1998), and many articles in social, political, legal, and applied moral philosophy. He is a member of the editorial boards of *Philosophical Quarterly, Journal of Applied Philosophy, Res Publica,* and *Contemporary Political Theory*.

Barbara Arneil is an Associate Professor in the department of political science at the University of British Columbia. Her research interests include liberal democratic thought, feminist theory, and most recently the role of children in democratic theory and practice. Her publications include *John Locke and America* (OUP, 1996), and *Feminism and Politics* (Blackwell, 1999).

Samantha Brennan is Associate Professor of Philosophy at the University of Western Ontario. Her research interests are in moral and political philosophy within particular interests in moral rights, the debate between consequentialism and deontology, family justice and children's rights, and feminist approaches to ethics. She is an executive editor of the *Canadian Journal of Philosophy*. She has co-authored a number of papers on children's rights with Robert Noggle. Her home page can be found at *http://publish.uwo.ca/~sbrennan*.

Harry Brighouse is Professor of Philosophy at the University of Wisconsin, Madison, and Professor of Philosophy of Education at the Institute of Education, University of London. He is the author of *School Choice and Social Justice* (OUP, 2000) and is currently thinking about the place of the family in liberal theory.

Shelley Burtt taught political philosophy at Yale University from 1987 to 1998 and is the author of *Virtue Transformed: Political Argument in England, 1688–1740* (Cambridge University Press, 1992). She has written recently on issues of genetic testing, parental rights, fœtal abuse, and the legal treatment of corporal punishment. Her essay on 'Comprehensive Educations and the Liberal Understanding of Autonomy' will be published in a collection edited by Walter Feinberg and Kevin McDonough.

Eamonn Callan is Professor of Education and Associate Dean at the Stanford University School of Education. He is the author of *Creating Citizens: Political Education and Liberal Democracy* (OUP, 1997), and many articles and chapters in the philosophy of education.

Joe Coleman is an Assistant Professor of Political Science at Bucknell University. His research focuses on education, school reform, and the politics of children, and has appeared in *Ethics*. He also has a forthcoming article on school choice in *The School Field*.

James Griffin is White's Professor of Moral Philosophy Emeritus at Oxford University. He is the author of *Well-Being: Its Meaning, Measurement, and Moral Importance* (OUP, 1986) and *Value Judgement: Improving Our Ethical Beliefs* (OUP, 1996), and is now writing a book on human rights.

Colin M. Macleod is Associate Professor of Philosophy at the University of Victoria, Victoria, British Columbia. He is the author of *Liberalism, Justice, and Markets: A Critique of Liberal Equality* (OUP, 1998).

Véronique Munoz-Dardé is Senior Lecturer in Philosophy at University College London (Department of Philosophy), where she has taught since 1994. She is the author of *La Justice sociale: Le Liberalisme egalitaire de John Rawls*. She has published articles in the areas of contractualism, distributive justice, and liberalism. Her essays in this volume is part of a larger project on the subject of contractualism and distributive justice.

Robert Noggle is Associate Professor of Philosophy at Central Michigan University. He has published articles on personal autonomy, manipulative actions, moral motivation, value theory, and utilitarianism in *American Philosophical Quarterly*, *Philosophical Studies*, *Canadian Journal of Philosophy*, *Utilitas*, and *Social Theory and Practice*. He is working on a book on personal autonomy, a study of the moral status of children (in collaboration with Samantha Brennan with whom he has co-authored a number of papers on children's rights), and the debate between consequentialism and deontology.

Hillel Steiner is Professor of Political Philosophy at the University of Manchester and a Fellow of the British Academy. He is the author of *An Essay on Rights* (1994) and co-author of *A Debate Over Rights: Philosophical Enquiries* (with Matthew Kramer and Nigel Simmonds, 1998). He is also co-editor of *The Origins of Left-Libertarianism: An Anthology of Historical Writings* and *Left-Libertarianism and its Critics: The Contemporary Debate* (with Peter Vallentyne, 2001). His current research includes the application of libertarian principles to global, and to genetic, inequalities.

Peter Vallentyne is Professor of Philosophy at the Virginia Commonwealth University. He has written on the metaphysics of laws and properties, moral dilemmas, the moral status of children, issues in egalitarianism, and a wide variety of issues in consequentialist moral theory. He edited *Contractarianism and Rational Choice: Essays on the Work of David Gauthier* (1991) and co-edited (with Hillel Steiner) *The Origins of Left-Libertarianism: An Anthology of Historical Writings* (2001) and *Left-Libertarianism and Its Critics: The Contemporary Debate* (2001). He is currently writing a book on left-libertarianism (which combines self-ownership with egalitarianism).

1

Introduction

David Archard and Colin M. Macleod

Philosophical Views of Children: A Brief History

Feminist philosophers and historians of ideas rightly point out in criticism of the canon that women do not really figure within the classic texts of moral and political philosophy. Women are deprecated for their failings, mentioned only in passing, simply ignored, or absorbed within the household whose head is the husband. Something similar may be said to be the case with children. Children have not been the subject of any extended philosophical discussion until recent years. When philosophers of the past have talked about children it has not been in any organized or concentrated fashion, and their scattered comments have not offered any systematic, positive characterization of the status of the child and of childhood.

Two ideas of children are nevertheless to be found in the history of moral and political philosophy. Not exactly competing ideas, nevertheless they point in very different directions, and yet each has continued to exert an influence on our thinking about the child. The first idea is that children are simply the property of their parents. Or if not precisely a thing to be owned, none the less the child is, in some sense, an extension of the parent. Aristotle compares the sovereignty of a man over his chattels to that of a father over his child, and concludes that a child 'until it reaches a certain age and sets up for itself' is 'as it were part of himself', that is the parent (Aristotle 1984: 5. 6. 1134[b]).

In the modern period few, if any, are prepared openly to defend the view that children are their parents' property. The libertarian, Jan Narveson, does think parents have property rights over their offspring but argues that these are severely constrained by a public interest in the welfare and actions on others of the future adults these children will become (Narveson 1998: 272–4). However, some contemporary philosophers have been happy to characterize children as, if not exactly things to be owned, then certainly mere extensions of their parents. Robert Nozick, for instance, describes children as 'part of one's substance . . . part of a wider identity you have' (Nozick: 1989 28).

The second idea is that children are proto- or incomplete adults. They are not yet possessed of the powers and capacities that characterize human beings proper. This idea has some important negative implications. Drawing on Aristotle's view of the child as an unfinished human being, children are viewed in privative terms for what they are not rather than positively for what they are in themselves. They are seen as 'becoming' rather than 'being'. Furthermore, the passage into maturity is essentially one from inadequacy—vulnerability, weakness, dependence, ignorance, passivity—into the achievements of age—security, strength, independence, knowledge, and agency.

This idea provides an obvious foundation for the exercise of constrained parental paternalism. It is constrained in two senses. It must be exercised for the good of the child and its exercise lasts only for so long as the child is incapable of making its own choices. A child, in its incapacity, needs to be cared for and yet as it matures the need for parental authority diminishes. John Locke elegantly expressed the thought in the following terms. As children 'grow up to the use of reason', 'the rigour of government' may be 'gently relaxed' (Locke 1960: § 41).

Grotius, for example, who is sometimes mistakenly cited as having viewed children as their parents' property, in fact distinguished a number of periods in a child's life. During the first period of 'imperfect judgement', 'all of the actions of the child are under the control of the parents'. In the succeeding period, 'when judgement has now matured', a child's actions are not subject to the parents' rule, although, since the child remains at home, parental control is proper if some important family matter is at stake. In the final period children has acquired full judgement and has withdrawn from the family (Grotius 1925: 2. 5).

The idea that a child progressively acquires the abilities of an adult is the predominant contemporary one. Nevertheless the proprietarian view provides a plausible if repugnant alternative account of why parents have rights over their children, and both the paternalistic and proprietarian views can be found in our thinking about parental rights (Montgomery 1988). One obvious reason for the influence of the proprietarian story is that it locates parental rights in the natural fact of generation. It is because parents produce their own children that they have rights in respect of them. John Locke famously offered a defence of private property by means of self-ownership and the exercise of one's labour. Yet he struggled to resist the conclusion that, since children are undoubtedly the fruits of their parent's labour, they must be thought of as their parent's property. His arguments to the contrary are unpersuasive (Nozick 1974: 288–9).

The contemporary neo-Lockean, Hillel Steiner, blocks the unpalatable conclusion by arguing that children are *not* fully the fruit of their parents' labour since they require natural resources in the form of genetic information transmitted from previous generations (Steiner 1994: 248). Others have argued that one cannot own what is itself self-owning and inasmuch as a child is, or at least becomes, self-owning it cannot thus be owned by its parents (Becker 1977: 38–9).

If children are not the legitimate holdings of their producers, how are parents warranted in exercising authority over them? Thomas Hobbes believed that children are in 'absolute subjection' to parents who may 'alienate them . . . pawn them for hostages, kills them for rebellion, or sacrifice them for peace' (Hobbes 1994: 23. 8). Yet he also thought that this dominion did not derive from generation, but rather 'from the Childs Consent, either expresse, or by other sufficient arguments declared' (Hobbes 1968: part 2, ch. 20). Hobbes is one of the earliest defenders of the important view that the authority of one person over another is rooted in the consent or will of the latter. It should be no different with parental authority. Yet, of course, there are notorious difficulties with the principle that legitimate authority rests on consent, and there are additional and perhaps insuperable difficulties in understanding how children could give their consent, even in retrospect, to parental authority.

Some have sought to ground parental rights in a duty of care. Kant, who denied that a child is a thing to be owned by its parents, believed that those who have brought a child into the world thereby 'incur an obligation to make the child content with his condition so far as they can'. And it is '(f)rom this duty there must necessarily arise the right of parents to *manage* and develop the child' (Kant 1996: 64–5). What has been called the 'priority thesis—that any parental rights derive their warrant, and scope, from the morally prior duty of care—remains an influential idea (Blustein 1982). However, many others have been driven to the conclusion that parents have no rights over children, although they most certainly do have duties of care.

Current Thinking about Children

The idea that children themselves have rights is a very modern one. This is because the very idea of rights in general is itself modern, and the thought that children as a group deserve to have extended to them all the rights possessed by adults dates from the 1970s (Farson 1974; Holt 1975). Similarly thinking about what is owed to children as a matter of justice can be attributed to the influence of John Rawls's *A Theory of Justice* (Rawls 1971). For the most part, contemporary discussion of these and other matters related to the moral and political status of children has been sporadic and limited. The proponents of child liberation drew attention to the possibility that children should be viewed as distinct subjects for political theory and practice. Yet the liberationists' extremely problematic assimilation of adults and children was so easily refuted that they had little impact on the research agenda of mainstream political theory.

While it is true that Rawls can be credited with inspiring discussions of the moral and political status of children, his own work is generally inattentive to the topic. Among leading figures of contemporary political philosophy, Rawls's neglect of this topic is by no means anomalous. In the highly influential work of Robert Nozick, Ronald Dworkin, David Gauthier, and Michael Walzer we find no sustained discussion of how the moral and political status of children should be understood or what the implications of considering children directly might have for the shape of a defensible theory. Even important feminist contributions that rightly contest the neglect of the family in contemporary theory, such as Susan Okin's *Justice, Gender, and the Family* (Okin 1989), have surprisingly little direct discussion of the status of children.

Recently, however, there has been an increased interest in exploring the moral and political status of children with the resources provided by contemporary developments in moral and political theory. This interest has been propelled by a realization by scholars of the gaps in recent theory but also by more general political developments and legal controversies. The changing character of the family (for example, the decline of the 'traditional' family) in Western nations and increased awareness of problems faced by children (such as, poverty, abuse, juvenile delinquency) have placed issues concerning children squarely on the public agenda. Similarly, the enormous explosion of interest in cultural politics has been accompanied with greater awareness of the way children are implicated in the social reproduction of cultural, religious, and national identity. The public and academic debate about such matters is often characterized by sharply divergent claims about the putative rights, responsibilities, and entitlements of children, parents, and the state. At the same time the adoption in 1989 by the United Nations General Assembly of the Convention on the Rights of the Child and its ratification by over 120 countries has provided a powerful, and influential, legal instrument for our understanding of the status of the child.

In all this there seems to be a trend towards taking children seriously as distinct subjects of moral and political theory who have complex and evolving interests. The basic idea that children must be viewed as developing beings whose moral status gradually changes now enjoys near universal acceptance but the implications of accepting this position are more complex than they once appeared. It no longer seems possible to posit a simple harmony between the interests of children and those charged with the responsibility of rearing them, such that the exercise of authority over children during their development of maturity can be viewed as a fairly straightforward matter. Instead the challenge is to deepen our understanding of children's interests and to explore how the conceptualization of children's interests affects the character of the moral claims they have.

The Book

The chapters in this book address various dimensions of this challenge. Although the precise emphasis in each chapter varies, the overall collection is animated by a concern with four principal interrelated but distinguishable themes. These are rights, autonomy, education, and distributive justice.

Rights

The recognition that a being has moral rights is one powerful way of signalling that it has an important kind of moral status in virtue of which special protections or entitlements, not granted to other beings, are legitimately extended to it. Children undoubtedly have some kind of special moral status. Everyone agrees that ensuring that the basic needs of children are adequately met is a particularly urgent moral requirement. Similarly, we reserve our strongest moral condemnation for those who deliberately or negligently harm children. A natural way of giving expression to the moral urgency associated with the claims of children is to suppose that they have rights. Yet the attribution of rights, whether moral or legal, to children is fraught with controversy. In the view of some theorists, the very vulnerabilities and incapacities that seem to ground the moral urgency of children's claims disqualify them as proper rights-bearers. Advocates of the so-called choice theory of rights place particular emphasis on the relation between rights and personhood. The primary and appropriate functions of rights are the recognition and protection of the person qua autonomous agent. Since children, at least infants, lack the capacities requisite for autonomy on which the very concept of a right is allegedly predicated, it makes no sense, however well-intentioned this might be, to ascribe rights to children.

This line of argument is pursued by James Griffin. Through an analysis that focuses on the development of the human rights tradition, Griffin argues that the language of human rights is best reserved for beings capable of agency. Less restrictive conceptions of rights, such as those that link rights to the protection of needs, lead to a proliferation of rights of a sort that dilutes the normative importance of rights. Griffin maintains that denying that infants have rights need not diminish the moral significance of their claims to care. The absence of a right need not signal diminished moral importance.

Harry Brighouse's examination of children's rights displays greater sympathy for the rival interest theory of rights. On this approach, the primary function of rights is the protection of fundamental interests. Since children undeniably have fundamental interests that merit protection, it is perfectly sensible to attribute rights, especially welfare rights, to them. As Brighouse points out, the interest theory need not be hostile to the accommodation of rights that protect agency because, at least in the case of adults, there is a strong connection between the protection of agency and the promotion of

welfare. The welfare interests of adults and children are sufficiently comparable to warrant the recognition of similar welfare rights for both children and
adults. However, the agency rights that are sensibly attributed to adults cannot
be attributed to children because children initially lack and only gradually
develop the kind of capacities for agency that are necessary for agency rights.
Brighouse's analysis provides a basis both for vindicating the ideas that children have rights but that the purported rights of children to culture, religion,
and free expression are ill conceived.

Samantha Brennan shares Brighouse's willingness to attribute some rights
to children and she emphasizes the significance of the gradual development of
autonomy in children for understanding the character of their rights.
However, Brennan resists the suggestion that the interest theory can provide a
satisfactory general analysis of rights. Instead, she argues that the often posed
dichotomy between the interest and choice model of rights can obfuscate a
proper understanding of children's rights. Rather Brennan defends a gradualist model in which the grounds for attributing rights to a being change in
response to the development of autonomy. Rights for children initially function to protect their interests but, as they develop into full-fledged
autonomous choosers, rights function to ensure that their choices, even those
that do not serve their welfare, are respected.

A different dimension of the issue of children's rights concerns the efficacy
of rights discourse in advancing the well-being of children. Most proponents
of children's rights contend that broad political and legal recognition of children's rights actually advances the well-being of children. However, it is sometimes argued that even well-intentioned emphasis on the importance of
protecting rights can have the perverse consequence of undermining the
interests of those whose rights are championed. This theme is explored by
Barbara Arneil who contends that the excessive faith that liberal theorists have
had in the power of rights and rights discourse can have deleterious consequences for children. As vulnerable and dependent beings, children need to be
nurtured with love and affection in a setting in which intimate relationships
between parents and children can flourish. Arneil contends that a rights-
focused discourse is conceptually ill-equipped to accommodate the importance of establishing and supporting caring relationships and thus provides an
inadequate way of conceptualizing the claims of children. Drawing on work
by Carol Gilligan and others, Arneil suggests that an ethic of care, emphasizing responsibilities over rights, provides a better way of conceptualizing and
responding to the interests of children as children instead of as proto-adults.

Autonomy and Education

An issue closely allied to debates about children's rights concerns the status of
children as beings who initially lack capacities for autonomous self-direction
but who can acquire these capacities as they mature. The fact that children

initially lack autonomy clearly does not deny them status as moral agents but it does affect our understanding of their status as moral agents. Whereas competent adults are generally permitted to direct their own lives as they see best, huge portions of children's lives are subject to the authoritative decisions of adults, especially their guardians. The authority that parents and other adults can legitimately exercise over children is constrained. It is obvious, for instance, that parents are obligated to exercise their authority in ways that are commensurate with promoting the interests of their children. Yet various difficult puzzles arise when an effort to articulate the nature and basis of such authority is made, especially when attention is focused on the stake children have in becoming autonomous. Various facets of this broad issue are addressed in this book.

Robert Noggle's chapter examines the salient features that distinguish the moral status of children and adults. Noggle argues that cognitive incompetence cannot adequately explain the special character of children's moral status. One problem is that children remain subject to some parental authority even after the age at which they can be characterized as having a general cognitive deficit. Noggle argues that because children lack preference structures that are sufficiently stable over time they are not 'temporally extended agents'. In virtue of this fact, children should be viewed as 'special agents'. Parents are charged by the moral community with the responsibility of fostering the development of temporally extended agency and other related moral capacities that Noggle identifies as a sense of decency and a value system. The parameters of parental authority are delineated by determining what sort of upbringing best assists children in acquiring the capacities that facilitate their transition from 'special agents' to full and well-functioning members of the moral community.

A different but related vantage to that of Noggle's considers the relation between autonomy and the leading of a good life. All decent parents seek to rear their children in ways that contribute to their children leading genuinely good lives. Eamonn Callan considers what role the promotion of autonomy in children has in advancing the laudable aim of parents. Callan is particularly interested to assess a familiar liberal claim that grounds the value of autonomy promotion in the instrumental contribution autonomy makes to securing our interest in leading a good life. Callan accepts the broad importance of autonomy to leading a good life and thus he shares the liberal antipathy to ways of rearing children that threaten to stunt or impair children's capacities for autonomy. However, Callan argues that a common liberal construal of the way in which autonomy contributes to the leading of a good life is defective. The liberal 'instrumental' defence of autonomy emphasizes the fallibility of our judgements about goodness and the consequent importance of being able to revise our conceptions of the good in response to considerations that suggest they are mistaken. The mistake that

Callan detects in the liberal instrumentalist argument is its one-sided focus on ensuring that children develop capacities for *revision* of their conceptions of the good. According to Callan, a deeper understanding of autonomy requires us also to heed the importance of fostering the capacities that will permit rational *adherence* to a conception of the good. Once the importance of this dimension of autonomy is appreciated, the liberal enthusiasm for ensuring that children are exposed to diverse influences requires reassessment. Exposing children to a diverse but shallow secular public culture might not facilitate goodness-enhancing autonomy in a way that is superior to the more insular strategies of religious minorities whose child-rearing practices are critiqued by liberals.

The character of the education that children receive is obviously an important determinant of their life prospects. It has an impact not only on cognitive and moral development, including the acquisition of autonomy, but also on the very identity of children. It is not surprising, therefore, that there are heated debates over the prerogatives that different stakeholders, such as the state, cultural communities, parents, and children, have in shaping the form and content of education. The principal focus of discussion in the two chapters of this book that address educational matters is on the role of education in the inculcation of values.

The social reproduction of distinct cultural groups depends on the cross-generational transmission of values, languages, and traditional practices that distinguish different cultures. It is common for both parents and cultural communities to claim that they may legitimately undertake educational measures designed to ensure that their children come to have a particular cultural identity. David Archard critically assesses three possible justifications of this purported prerogative: a group strategy, a parenting strategy, and familial strategy. He argues that first two strategies are problematic because they fail to grapple adequately with various aspects of children's independent moral status. Thus groups may not legitimately view children merely as vehicles for the realization of their preference to perpetuate a way of life. And parents cannot view their children as mere extensions of themselves whose identities they are entitled to shape as they see fit. Archard sees greater promise in the familial strategy that emphasizes the value to children of sharing a way of life, based around shared values, with their family. However, this strategy provides a limited account of the actual extent to which parents may mould the identity of their children. Archard argues that it is only by directly assessing children's stake in becoming autonomous that a full picture of parental prerogatives to shape identity can be established. On this matter, Archard argues that parental prerogatives are limited by the importance that attaches to ensuring children acquire a 'sufficient' degree of autonomy. But given the analysis of autonomy favoured by Archard, one that parallels some aspects of Callan's view, the pursuit of multicultural policies of a suitably nuanced variety is not foreclosed by recognition the importance of accommodating children's interests.

Joe Coleman's chapter broaches the issue of moral standing of adolescents. Whereas young children lack the moral powers that Rawls calls a conception of the good and a sense of justice, the same easy assumption cannot be made about teenagers closer to the age of majority. Coleman presents a review of psychological data that suggests that such adolescents often display a degree of moral and cognitive maturity that closely parallels that of adults who, unlike their teenage counterparts, enjoy full citizenship rights. Coleman alleges that recent discussions amongst liberal theorists concerning the importance of civic education have failed to appreciate the significance of this finding. The principal issue concerns the legitimacy of mandatory schemes of civic education that are aimed at equipping children with the capacities required for responsible citizenship. Liberals, whether of the comprehensive or political variety, typically endorse compulsory civic education for younger persons but they reject the idea that adults can be subjected to compulsory civics lessons or required to demonstrate competency about civic matters as a condition of enjoying full citizenship rights. Coleman suggests that this differential treatment of adults and adolescents is usually justified by appeal to the supposed incapacities of the latter. But the suggestion that adults routinely possess citizenship capacities that younger persons lacks is not substantiated by the data. Coleman argues that an 'authority-oriented' approach to civic education of the sort that is linked to the claim that younger persons lack capacities and are thus subject to authority of educators must be abandoned. In its place, Coleman urges the adoption of a more democratic, 'participation-oriented' approach that is predicated on the idea of students and educators as equals. In Coleman's view, it is not that democratic schooling is more effective than a highly disciplinary approach to civic education in inculcating civic virtue. Rather democratic schooling is a requirement that flows from according younger persons the respect that justice requires.

Justice

The final cluster of essays examines different ways in which consideration of children should affect our understanding of justice, particularly matters of distributive justice. There is, of course, considerable controversy over how the basic but abstract requirements of distributive justice are to be understood. Even within the broadly egalitarian conceptions of justice represented in the chapters in this volume there is substantial theoretical diversity. None the less, with respect to the issue of the best theoretical accommodation of children within theories of justice, there are some common themes. First, the interests of children, and the entitlements to resources and opportunities to which these interests may give rise, require direct consideration from the point of view of justice. The justice-based claims of children cannot simply be subsumed under the claims of their parents or families. Second, although children, in virtue of the immaturity of their moral powers, may reasonably be treated differently from other members of the moral community, they none the less stand as equal members of the moral community. The ideal of justice that requires equal consideration of interests extends directly to the equal consideration of children's interests. Third, a children-sensitive theory of justice pays particular attention to ways in which the allocation of resources to children affects their life prospects. A theory of justice must be centrally concerned with ensuring that the ways in which children are treated by parents, guardians, the community, and the state are commensurate with them *all* having at least decent life prospects.

The determinants of a child's life prospects are varied and complexly interrelated but there seems to be an important distinction between what Hillel Steiner calls a person's 'initial genetic endowment' and 'post-conception inputs' such as nutrition and education. Inequalities in life prospects can arise out of differences in the character of either. Steiner's chapter explores how differences in natural endowment that can give rise to inequalities should be addressed. He approaches this matter from a left-libertarian perspective in which a principle of self-ownership is taken to be morally fundamental. A self-owning person is, according to Steiner, entitled to their natural abilities and the products that are generated by exercise of those abilities. As a consequence, self-ownership forbids coercive transfers of products between persons aimed at reducing inequality. Steiner's question is whether it is permissible to pursue measures aimed at reducing inequalities in natural ability levels. One important influence on ability level is the quality of the post-conception inputs a person receives during childhood. Steiner claims that children have an enforceable claim against the adults who are responsible for creating them to resources sufficient to ensure the development of children's abilities to a minimum level. Thus a child who suffers a cognitive deficit due to the failure of her parent to feed her well is entitled to recover damages from the negligent parent. If parents are responsible for the provision of adequate 'post-conception' inputs, can they also be held responsible for ensuring that a child's genetic endowment meets some adequate threshold? Steiner argues that the response to this problem is profoundly affected by developments in genetic science. Prior to the recent advances in genetic science, it seemed incoherent to suppose that parents could be held liable for the poor quality of a child's basic genetic endowment. This was because, simplifying matters somewhat, personal identity could not survive any changes in genetic endowment. A child could not complain that its parents failed to provide an adequate genetic endowment because any changes to the genes of the would-be complainant would have resulted in the creation of entirely different person. However, Steiner argues that with the revolution in genetic science it is now possible to effect genetic changes without altering identity. If this is so, then children can, in principle, claim a right against 'genetic-disablement'.

Peter Vallentyne's chapter examines the problem of how justice should respond to concern about the life prospects of children from a slightly different angle. Individuals who voluntarily elect to procreate seem to have special duties *vis-à-vis* their offspring and other members of the community whose lives can be affected by the introduction of new human beings. Vallentyne challenges the assumption that procreators have extensive *special* duties to their progeny. His provocative conclusion is that the duties of procreators to their offspring are surprisingly limited. Procreators fully discharge their duties to their children by merely ensuring that the children they create have lives that are worth living. However adults, in general, also have fairly extensive justice-grounded duties to children. Thus Vallentyne endorses the view that adults have a shared duty to ensure that children enjoy an equal opportunity to lead a good life. Such a position imposes significantly fewer constraints on the elimination of inequality between children than Steiner's view does. Procreators' duties to others are potentially more demanding than might usually be supposed. Here procreators have a duty to ensure that their children do not violate the rights of others, including their equality rights. On Vallentyne's view, procreation is a risky business in the sense that one's offspring might create disadvantages for others either by violating their rights or by diminishing their equality-grounded entitlements. Those who create risk for others must accept liability and provide suitable compensation for any risk that ripens into an actual harm. Procreators are, on Vallentyne's theory, even responsible for providing compensation for disadvantages caused for others by their adult children.

Although there is no necessary connection between procreation and the rearing of children, it is common for procreators to create families as well as offspring. We know that the life prospects of children can be influenced in both positive and negative ways by their familial circumstances and this familiar observation provides the point of departure for the chapters by Véronique Muñoz-Dardé, Shelley Burtt, and Colin Macleod. Macleod's chapter explores and seeks to resolve a tension between a liberal egalitarian conception of distributive justice and the family. Contemporary liberal theory now seems committed to the development of an account of distributive justice that is appropriately sensitive to considerations of individual responsibility. Such an account can be invoked to show why certain economic inequalities are not unjust providing they reflect the choices made in a position of initial equality by mature, responsible adults. By contrast, inequalities that arise because of the influence of arbitrary factors of social or natural contingency are unjust. At the same time, liberal theory is sympathetic to preservation and protection of the institution of the affective family in which relations between parents and children are characterized by displays of partiality. A problem arises here because parents typically care more about their own children than other children and those who have prospered (for example, through their diligent pursuit of economic opportunities) often seek to confer special economic and social advantages on their children. The inequality between children of different families that can result from such forms of partiality is inconsistent with the principle that condemns arbitrariness in the distribution of resources and opportunities. In responding to this problem, Macleod argues that children's access to resources and opportunities should not be significantly determined by parental entitlement to resources and, in cases of conflict, the goal of securing a fair share of resources for children takes priority over ensuring that resource distribution amongst adults tracks responsibility. Recognizing the priority of the justice-based entitlements of children does not entail abandonment of the family as an institution for rearing children. But, on Macleod's view, justice does require the establishment of social institutions and policies that impose constraints on the way in which parents can permissibly express their partiality for their children.

Véronique Muñoz-Dardé tackles the problem of how considerations of responsibility are relevant to the crafting of a theory of distributive justice that adequately recognizes the claims of children. She contrasts two perspectives on justice. One asks individuals directly to bear the costs of their own choices; the other asks them to do so only once background conditions of justice have been established by fair institutions. She favours the latter, Rawslian, perspective. The family, nevertheless, presents a difficulty for this account of justice, since its existence seriously limits the realization of a principle of equality of opportunity. Muñoz-Dardé believes that the family in some form must exist if any society is to be just and thus concludes that this principle of equal opportunity cannot have lexical priority in a theory of justice.

Burtt's chapter is less expressly concerned with matters of distributive justice but it retains a focus on the contribution that families can make to advancing the interests of children. Recent sociological studies, primarily in the United States, have established a connection between the traditional two-parent nuclear family and positive outcomes for children raised in them. Many recent commentators, who Burtt dubs the 'new familists', have suggested that this evidence supplies good justification for public policy measures aimed expressly at promoting this type of traditional family structure. However, Burtt identifies various reasons for disputing the policy recommendations of the new familists. The success of the traditional family structure arguably has less to do with its intrinsic superiority over other family structures than to the fact that many other institutional arrangements are structured in ways that advantage the nuclear family. Also those who favour exclusive promotion of the traditional family do not adequately address the problem that nurturing children within the nuclear family typically depends upon a sexist division of domestic labour. In a different vein, Burtt points out that the recommendations of the new familists are demographically infeasible. Within contemporary industrial societies, there is too much diversity in existing family structures to warrant exclusive promotion of the traditional family. The general inadequacies of the new familist position points to the need to develop what Burtt calls a 'critical theory of family structure'. Such a theory identifies the developmental needs of children and examines the ways in which various family structures can function, in concert with other social institutions, to meet these needs. Such a theory does not preclude the possibility that some family structures are genuinely superior to others. However, the theory of family structure outlined by Burtt shows that it is very doubtful that the traditional family has the unique virtues attributed to it by the new familists.

Further Issues

No collection of essays on children can hope to be comprehensive and deal with all the issues that might be raised. Moreover no introduction could provide a full guide to all the questions that need to be asked by moral and political philosophers about children and childhood. However, two matters not discussed at length in the chapters of this book are worth briefly sketching. Doing so indicates a programme of possible future work and also marks out the boundaries, along with the associated assumptions, of existing work. One matter is the status of the child, the other is the role of the state.

By the status of the child is meant not its moral or political status but rather the question of how we should define a child. To define childhood chronologically in terms of age seems inadequate. For what is important is not that a child is a human being below a certain specified age but rather—as has been suggested—that a child is someone lacking certain capacities—cognitive, conative, and of character—whose possession distinguishes the state of adulthood. Yet we cannot define a child solely in terms of its lack of adult capacities. For some who are of an adult age lack these capacities—the severely mentally disabled, for instance. These persons are not properly described as 'children'. Or at last they are so only metaphorically. 'Childlike' seems a more appropriate description.

Is then a child a human being to be defined as someone who *in virtue of their age* lacks the capacities that adults normally, and as a general rule, possess? That may be so, though some will still maintain that saying even this begs a crucial question. There are further questions. Do children, also in virtue of their age, possess features and characteristics that their adult counterparts lack? Wonderment before the world and an innocence that is not simply an ignorance suggest themselves as some of these putative characteristics. Is the distinction between adulthood and childhood a natural one that is roughly unchanged across cultures, or are there significantly distinct ways in which the two differ according to society and time?

Again the single contrast between childhood and adulthood might suggest that there are only two internally undifferentiated categories of human being. But this is evidently mistaken. At least in the West we have for some years distinguished between 'infants', 'young people', 'teenagers', and 'adolescents', to use just some of the terms available to us. These terms might be argued to be the means of providing a more fine-grained characterization of childhood. But at the same time they press against the simple opposition of child and adult. For it is clear that an adolescent is more of an adult than a very young infant, who is correspondingly more of a child. To the extent that this is so it is harder to maintain that all children should be treated morally and politically in quite different ways from all adults. At the very least it seems plausible to argue that any discussion of the moral and political status of the child should be grounded in a logically prior agreement on who should be counted a child.

What about the role of the state? The state has long been regarded as *parens patriae*, literally the parent of the nation. In this role the state, and its representatives, act as guardians in the last instance of the interests of those unable by reason of their weakness, vulnerability, or incapacity to defend or advance their own. The state, thus, fulfils a parental duty of care towards the very young within its jurisdiction. It does so when those entrusted in the first instance with discharging duties of parenthood fail to do so. For this reason the state in modern Western countries enacts and enforces child protectionist laws and policies, those for instance dealing with parental abuse, cruelty, and neglect.

But does the state also have an independent set of interests of its own in respect of children? There is one very important reason for thinking that it does. This is that the state should secure the conditions for the reproduction of its institutions and their essential social, political, economic, and cultural preconditions. For instance, the state must surely ensure that the future population size of its citizenry does not become so great nor so small as to threaten the continued existence of society. It may be appropriate then, as in China, for the government to limit the number of children a family may have or, by direct contrast, to set in place incentives that encourage procreation. The state also has an interest—at least in a democratic polity—in ensuring that its future citizens are equipped with the capacities necessary to participate in the effective and stable governance of their society. It may also have an interest in guaranteeing that these same citizens are motivated by a sense of justice, that is, a willingness to play their part in supporting institutions regulated by principles of justice.

Now it is of course moot what capacities and dispositions are necessary if the future citizenry are to play the stipulated role and how much is thus required by way of regulation of a citizen's upbringing and education. However it is surely at least true that the state cannot remain indifferent to how children within its jurisdiction are reared and that its interest in this matter is not exclusively a question of the public protection of the children's interests. The state is not simply *parens patriae*. If this is so there are interesting questions of how to balance the various claims that can be made on behalf of child, parent, and state. This fact will have its most obvious ramifications in the field of education.

Concluding Comment

In most parts of the world, there is a lamentable distance between the moral and political status children have in theory and the treatment they receive in practice. The most basic needs of too many children in the world routinely go unmet, with the result that many thousands of infants perish each year. Many of those who survive infancy can look forward to a childhood characterized by poverty, disease, violence, and illiteracy. Malnutrition contributes to over a half of under-5 deaths in developing countries. More than 130 million children of school age in developing countries have no access to basic education; 250 million children have to work, often in hazardous and exploitative conditions; 540 million children worldwide—one in four of all children—live in dangerous and unstable situations (UNICEF 2000).

The life prospects of children in affluent nations are generally much better but even here there are alarming numbers of children who are neglected, abused, or unfairly deprived. By any plausible moral standard, these are serious moral failings. They point not only to the relevance of further philosophical examination of the status of children but particularly to the urgency reforming the various social and political practices that neglect the claims of children so egregiously. Taking children seriously requires better theory and better practice.

Following the practice of many authors and editors, we have decided to donate all our editorial royalties from this book to Save the Children, an organization which does an excellent job in promoting and protecting the welfare and rights of children throughout the world.

The editors have supplied a brief guide to suggested further reading. This guide lists some of the major general writings in moral and political philosophy, as well as background material in the major areas covered by the chapters.

I

Children and Rights

2

Do Children Have Rights?

James Griffin

Do Children Have Rights?

Of course, children have legal rights. But do they also have human rights? Or do they, at least, have something closely analogous to human rights—namely, general moral rights that children have simply in virtue of being children? One cannot answer these questions unless one knows, as one might put it, the existence conditions (Sumner 1987: 10–11) of these various kinds of rights, conditions that allow one to say that the right in question exists and what its content is.

Let me start with the existence conditions of human rights. I can only baldly state what, to my mind, is the best account of them, without justifying it. But, in compensation, the account I shall propose is not at all eccentric and, indeed, seems to be the dominant account in the human rights tradition.

The Human Rights Tradition

A term with our modern sense of 'a right' emerged in the late Middle Ages, probably first in Bologna, in the work of the canonists, experts (mainly clerical) who glossed, commented on, and to some extent brought system to the many, not always consistent, norms of canon and Roman law (Robinson, Fergus *et al.* 1994). In the course of the twelfth and thirteenth centuries the use of the Latin word *ius* expanded from meaning a law stating what is fair to include also our modern sense of 'a right', that is, a power that a person possesses to control or claim or do something (Tierney 1997: *passim* but e.g. 42–5). For instance, in this period one finds the transition from the assertion that it is a natural law (*ius*) that all things are held in common and thus a person in mortal need who takes from a person in surplus does not steal, to the new form of expression, that a person in need has a right (*ius*) to take from a person in surplus and so does not steal (Tierney 1997: 72–3). The prevailing view of the canonists is that this new sort of *ius*, a right that an individual has, derives from the natural law that all human beings are, in a specific sense, equal: namely, that we are all made in God's image, that we are free to act for reasons, especially for reasons of good and evil. We are rational agents; we are, more precisely, moral agents (Dagger 1989: 298–301).

This link between our freedom and the dignity of our status became a central theme in the political thought of all subsequent centuries. Pico della Mirandola, an early Renaissance writer who studied canon law in Bologna in 1477, gave an influential account of the link. God fixed the nature of all other things but left man alone free to determine his own nature. It is given to man 'to have that which he chooses and be that which he wills' (Pico della Mirandola 1998: 3). This freedom constitutes, as Pico calls it in the title of his best known work, 'the dignity of man'.

This same link between freedom and dignity was at the centre of the early sixteenth-century debates about the Spanish colonization of the New World. Many canonists argued emphatically that the American natives were undeniably moral agents and, therefore, should not be deprived of their autonomy and liberty, which the Spanish government was everywhere doing. The same notion of dignity was also central to political thought in the seventeenth and eighteenth centuries, when it received its most powerful development at the hands of Rousseau and Kant. And this notion of dignity, or in any case the word 'dignity', appears in the most authoritative claims to human rights in the twentieth century. The United Nations says little in its declarations, covenants, conventions, and protocols about the grounds of human rights; it says simply that human rights derive from 'the inherent dignity of the human person',[1] but the most plausible interpretation of this use of 'dignity' is that it is still the Enlightenment use.

An Account of Human Rights

The human rights tradition does not lead inescapably to any particular account of human rights. There can be reasons to take a tradition in a new direction or to break with it altogether. None the less, the best account is, I should say, very much in the spirit of the tradition and goes like this.

Human life is different from the life of other animals. We human beings reflect; we form pictures of what a good life would be and try to realize these pictures. This is what we mean by a characteristically *human* existence. It does not matter if some animals have more of our nature than we used to think, nor that there might be intelligent creatures elsewhere in the universe also capable of deliberation and action. So long as we do not ignore these possibilities, there is no harm in continuing to speak of a characteristically 'human' existence. And we value our status as human beings especially highly, often more highly even than our happiness.

Human rights can then be seen as protections of our human standing, our personhood. And we shall understand personhood better by analysing agency into its components. Being an agent involves, first, assessing and choosing one's own course through life (autonomy). One's choice must be real: so, second, one must have at least minimum education and information to know what the possibilities are. Having chosen one's course, one must, third, be able to follow it; one must have at least the minimum resources and capabilities that it takes. And, fourth, others must not stop one from pursuing, within limits, what one sees as a good life (liberty).

It is already clear that the generative capacities of the notion of personhood are great. We have a right to life (without it personhood is impossible), to security of person (for the same reason), to a voice in political decision (a key exercise of autonomy), to free expression, to assembly, and to a free press (without them the exercise of autonomy would be a sham). It also generates, I should say (though this is hotly disputed), a positive freedom, namely to a right to minimum learning and material resources needed for a human existence, that is, for more than mere physical survival.

But personhood cannot be the only ground for human rights. It leaves many rights too indeterminate. For example, we have a right to security of person. But what does that exclude? Would it exclude forcefully taking a few drops of blood from my finger to save the lives of many others? Perhaps not. To up the stakes, would it also not exclude forcefully taking one of my kidneys? After all, the few weeks it would take me to recover from a kidney extraction would not deprive me of my personhood. Where is the line to be drawn? The personhood consideration on its own will not make the line determinate enough for practice. And if a proposed right cannot become a practicable claim that one person can make upon another, then it will not be a right. That degree of determinateness must be among the existence conditions for rights. To fix a sufficiently determinate line we should have to introduce considerations such as these. Given human nature, have we left a big enough safety margin? Is the right too complicated to do the job we want it do? Is the right too demanding? And so on. We must consider how human beings and their societies actually work. So, to make the right to security of person determinate enough we need another ground, call it practicalities.

Human Infants

So much for what seems to me the best account of human rights. Human infants (and animals and human foetuses and the severely mentally handicapped and sufferers from advanced Alzheimer's disease) are not agents. Do they not then have human rights?

Human agents have a kind of natural equality: they all have the capacities to reflect and choose and act, and once above a certain threshold any further difference in the degree to which they have these capacities is irrelevant to their having human rights. This means that distinctions between man and woman, black and white, highly educated and little educated—in fact, all distinctions but for agent and non-agent—are similarly irrelevant. But it is not clear how to regard the distinction between infant and adult. As John Locke put it, '*Children*, I confess are not born in this full state of *Equality*, though they are born to it' (Locke 1988: ch. 6, §55). On the one hand, infants are not agents. On the other, they will grow into agents, and that must itself be a reason for special concern for them. If agency attracts the protection of rights, why not then *potential* agency?

Locke's remark nicely captures a widespread intuition: infants are born *to* personhood and thereby to a certain moral status. Is not this status quite important enough for us to gloss the personhood account to include potential as well as actual persons? I said earlier that I am inclined to include certain welfare rights among human rights—namely, a right to minimum material provision. And the rationale that I would offer is that, if agency is so specially valuable, then some of that value must get transferred to what is a necessary condition for it. That thought would seem to lie behind not only a right to minimum provision but also a right to life. It is also a necessary condition for my now being an agent that no one did away with me while I was an infant. The trouble with this argument, if it were generalized, is that it would prove altogether too much. It is also a necessary condition of my now being an agent that my parents did not decide to abort me, and did not decide to use contraceptives when I was in fact conceived, and did not decide not to have more children before I was conceived, and so on. The rights of an agent do not transfer to *any* necessary condition for the existence of that agent.

It is true that there are various ways in which one could try to stop this backward proliferation of rights. One could say that one violates rights only if, in the first place, there is someone around to hold the rights. Whose rights would have been violated if my parents had decided not to have a third child? One might say that, so far as human beings go, we need to have at least a fertilized egg on the scene before we have something that could even conceivably have rights. But let me concentrate on the case for infants' having rights. In many parts of our moral life we regard infants as members of 'the human moral community'—to use a vague phrase. For instance, we regard deliberately killing an infant as murder, just as we do deliberately killing an innocent human being of any other age, and exceptions to that judgement will be extremely rare. But does their membership in the human moral community also carry human rights? Well, one might say that the reasons for making them members are reasons for making them nothing short of full members.[2] But that seems not to be so. Our tradition grants them protection of their lives, but not, say, the vote. If 'full membership' means having all the powers and protections of any other member, then the tradition is wise not to grant full membership. And from the idea of mere 'membership' alone, it is hard to deduce anything determinate—particularly whether infants are rights-holders.

The word 'potential' can have different senses in this context. A 'potential' agent can be a being who will, with some degree of probability, become an agent—a probability ranging from slight possibility to high likelihood. But, again, a foetus, a zygote, perhaps even an egg and sperm on course to fertilization would all be potential agents and so rights-holders; on this line of thought, they would all have, for example, a right to life. Or a 'potential' agent can be a member of a species a characteristic mature example of which is an agent. This second sense would then bring into the class of potential agents beings who never will be agents: for example, a severely mentally handicapped infant, an infant with extreme spina bifida who will die within a few months of birth. It would also, as before, bring into the class foetuses, zygotes, and so on. Think of an extreme case of those who would now be included: an anencephalic baby. Such a case raises acutely the question why we should want to put moral weight on features of the species instead of on features of individuals. If agency is the source of the values protected by rights, why should we accord these protections to beings who are not, and never will be, agents? Though there are good reasons to accord anencephalic babies respect not far from that given to normal babies, they are not reasons to accord them, despite their condition, the values of agency.

I think that the best case for regarding infants as rights-holders is this. We have not yet seen at all clearly how the second of my two existence conditions for human rights—namely, practicalities—works. The personhood condition gives us a right only to the sort of security of person, for instance, that is necessary to one's having a recognizably human existence. Would it stop the state from forcibly taking one of my kidneys? Not obviously, as I remarked earlier, because the few weeks that I should need to recuperate would hardly destroy my human standing. But the personhood condition does not, on its own, give us enough to make the line defining the right to security of person determinate enough for it to set up effective claims on others and so, as I said earlier, for us to say that a right yet exists. Practicalities have to come into play. For instance, governments are altogether too prone to interfere in individual lives. The lines defining 'personhood' are, of course, very fuzzy, and if governments exploited this fuzziness to intrude deep into our lives, we should have lost too much of what we value highly, even if our defence ultimately succeeded. We need a safety-margin. And we need a clear line, so that there is minimum fuzziness to exploit. Maybe the practicalities ground suggests a protection against the forcible extraction of *any* body parts or fluids, even though the personhood ground, in first delivering an indeterminate form of a right to security of person, itself does not.

I think it is plausible that the practicalities ground will have such an effect: that is, that the narrowing effect of the personhood ground will often to some extent be reversed by a broadening effect from the practicalities ground. There is a similar problem about the determinate line to be drawn around the category of 'agents'. When does a human being become an 'agent'? At age 7? 15? 18? The fixing of the boundary is not just a theoretical issue: it is an immensely important social one. It is tempting, even, to abandon the notion 'human agent' rights and go back to talking simply about 'human' rights. The broader class of 'human beings' is a lot more easily identified than the class of 'human agents'. And a justification for that move might be found not in abstract moral theory but in practicalities.

Still, I think that we should not do it. What human rights could an infant have? The right to free expression? To worship? Of the well established rights, the only one that it even makes sense to attribute to an infant is the right to life. And of more recently proposed rights—say, the ones to be found in the United Nations *Convention on the Rights of the Child*—the only others that it makes sense to attribute to an infant (as distinct from a child) are a right to the protection and care necessary for well-being and a right to development 'to the maximum extent possible'.[3] The justification that the *Convention* offers for special care for children is, plausibly enough, their vulnerability, and certainly their vulnerability imposes substantial obligations on us not imposed by those able to look after themselves.[4] The question, though, is whether these obligations are connected to a human right. Not all weighty obligations are: our obligation not to be generally nasty to people is not. Both of the rights suggested by the *Convention* stand in need of considerable clarification. Care necessary for what level of well-being? And do we really want to recognize a duty to ensure a child's development 'to the maximum extent possible'? That would mean developing every single talent and ability a child has to the last degree. But that is a thoroughly dubious policy for raising sane and healthy children, let alone a duty we have to a child, let alone a claim that a child can make on us by right. This right, as formulated in the *Convention*, is more well-meaning than well-conceived; it is probably better to see it as a right simply to development. But then the same question arises here too: to what level of development?

What we need in order to answer these questions is what I have been calling an account of human rights. Reference to the greater vulnerability of children is not enough. Animals, foetuses, and embryos produced *in vitro* not all of which will be implanted are all highly vulnerable, but few of us would say that they all have a right to life, well-being, and development. What would that account of human rights be?

Need Accounts of Human Rights

This is the place to pause and reflect upon a major alternative to the personhood account. If one thinks that infants (and perhaps also human beings in an irreversible coma and animals and so on) have rights, then one might well want to explore the idea that rights are based, not on personhood, but on some especially fundamental needs. Infants (and human beings in an irreversible coma and so on) certainly have needs.

Statements of need are always of the form: x needs a in order to ϕ. An element needs a free electron to conduct electricity; a terrorist needs cool nerves to plant a bomb.[5] The first task for a need account is to specify the kind of need that grounds human rights. The plausible proposal is that human rights are grounded in 'basic' human needs. The idea of a 'basic' human need is this. One can distinguish adventitious needs that persons acquire in virtue of their choosing one particular goal rather than another (if I were to decide to plant a bomb, I should need cool nerves) from needs that arise from goals that in a sense are not chosen but are characteristic of human life generally. As human beings, we need food simply in order to survive. Though in special circumstances survival can become subject to choice, in normal circumstances it is not; survival is, rather, what human life characteristically aims at. Human beings, as such, need air, food, water, shelter, rest, health, and companionship. A basic human need, we might say as a first attempt at definition, is what human beings need in order to avoid ailment, harm, or malfunction—or, to put it positively, what they need to function normally.[6]

We should obviously have to go well beyond this initial definition to make the notion of a basic need determinate enough to provide a satisfactory explanation of human rights. Is interesting work a basic need? Well, without it, alienation, a kind of social pathology, results. Is education? Well, without it, one's intellect will atrophy. And how much education is a basic need?

This is merely to point out work that a need account still has to do, not to make an objection to it. But there seem to me to be reasons to doubt that this further work can be satisfactorily done. The need account is, I think, pointed in the wrong direction. Its central notion is that of normal functioning. The paradigm case would be the normal functioning of the human body and mind. To that idea of normal functioning we could add a description of characteristic human roles or tasks in order to give content to the notion of 'function'. Now, as an account of basic needs this is an attractive, if still fairly primitive, proposal. But basic needs, so understood, do not make a promising account of human rights. My human right would be violated if on some occasion I were to be denied freedom of religious observance. But is it at all plausible to think that I should then be ailing, that my body or mind would be malfunctioning? That gets the malfunction in the wrong place. What is functioning badly is my society. The idea of health, mental and physical, may be central to a useful notion of basic needs, but it is the wrong place to be looking for an explanation of human rights. It is too narrow. One could stretch it, but, as I think the example of freedom of religion shows, we should have in the end effectively to abandon the idea of health and replace it with a quite different one.

There is a closely related point. If we were to have a human right to anything needed to avoid ailment and malfunction, then human rights would be in danger of becoming implausibly lavish. I could then demand by right that society devote resources, if it had them, to curing any ailment I had, however slight, and to correcting any malfunction I experienced, however unimportant. But nearly everyone accepts that, on the contrary, there comes a point where ailments and malfunctions become so trivial that they do not create, by right, a demand upon others to remedy them. When we have the sniffles, we ail. We all have minor psychological hang-ups that sometimes cause us to malfunction. But it is deeply counterintuitive that ailments such as those give us a right, even an easily overridable one, to a cure. Perhaps, if a society were well-off and the sniffles or these minor hang-ups could be cured by a fairly cheap pill, then the national health service ought to provide it. It is hard to find in the need account resources to draw the line we want here.[7]

There is a further problem. More than just human beings can ail and malfunction; so can foetuses, embryos *in vitro*, sperm, eggs, animals, and plants. A need account would have either to accept the consequence that they too have rights to life and development or to explain why it is not a consequence.

So far I have mentioned ailment and malfunction, which are only two of the three terms that I used earlier to define 'basic' human need. The third term is 'harm': a basic human need, one could say, is what is needed to avoid harm (Feinberg 1973: 111 and Wiggins 1987: 10; the remarks in the text apply also to Wiggins's idea of a life's being 'blighted'). But that, too, is far from enough. Foetuses, embryos *in vitro*, and so on can also be harmed. And harm specifically to human beings extends far beyond any plausible ground for human rights. One can harm someone by being continually nasty to them; in fact, one can often do them more harm that way, which is no violation of their rights, than one can by denying them some minor liberty, which would be. What a need account has to explain is what kinds of harms violate rights. The explanation cannot simply be that they are *major* harms, as the last example shows. It is a quality of harm that we are after, not a quantity. And ideally, in order to accord more with the tradition of human rights, the harm should have something to do with what is special about *human* life.[8]

The need account loses just that link to the human rights tradition. As we saw earlier, the tradition grounds rights in our human status, in what is peculiar to being human and that other familiar forms of life lack. But most basic human needs are not special to human life; they overlap with the basic needs of many other species.

All of that said, I must not exaggerate the difference between the need account and my personhood account. To my mind, the personhood account generates a positive right to the minimum provision necessary to support life as an agent, which is substantially more than what is needed simply to support life. So my personhood account too faces the difficulties of compiling and justifying a list of basic needs. My account can therefore be seen as a kind of need account: what is needed to function as an agent. What is needed will be air, food, water, shelter, rest, health, companionship, education, and so on. There will clearly be great overlap between the lists that emerge from these two accounts. And if the need account spells out the notion of 'normal functioning' by appeal to the especially basic roles in a characteristic human life— say, parent, householder, worker, and citizen (Braybrooke 1987)—then the convergence of the two lists will be still greater. But the lists will not be the same. The personhood account is more focused and exclusive in the role it specifies: what is needed to function as an agent.

A Class of Rights on their Own?

Perhaps it is wrong to treat children's rights, as I have done so far, as a species of human rights. I mentioned at the start that they might instead form a class of rights on their own, general moral rights that children have simply in virtue of being children—analogous to human rights, but no more.

If a child had these rights in virtue of being a child, then we should need some grasp of what it is about children that attracts this strong protection. That is, we should need to know the existence conditions of this class of general moral rights. The United Nations cites children's vulnerability. But zygotes, embryos, foetuses, and indeed many forms of animal life are vulnerable, but we do not regard that feature as sufficient for their having rights.

The most plausible proposal is that the existence condition is their being potential persons. That they are both potential agents and vulnerable explains, no doubt, the especially strong obligations we feel to them. But for the reasons I gave earlier they do not seem to be the existence conditions for a narrow enough class of rights. There is, admittedly, a whiff of stipulation in this conclusion, which I shall come back to in a moment.

Infants and Children

The personhood account of human rights still seems to me the most promising one we have. Therefore, it seems to me best to reserve the term 'human rights' for agents.

That then leaves us the large problem of settling the boundary disputes about when a human being is an agent. When is a person capable of autonomous choice? In the natural development of a child, the capacity appears in stages, and therefore respect for the child's autonomy should (ideally) increase in parallel stages. But parents and schools and governments face all of these difficult definitional problems already—for instance, in deciding when, and to what degree, paternalism is justified (say, in determining how much weight to put on a child's wishes in a custody decision in a divorce).

What seems to me clear is that children, as opposed to infants, are capable of agency. So my scepticism about infants' rights does not extend in any whole-scale way to children's rights. I should certainly have no doubts about many children's having rights on the definition of a 'child' employed in the United Nations *Convention on the Rights of the Child*: namely, anyone under legal majority (so in most places anyone under 18). But children are capable of some degree of agency much younger than that. The autonomy of children of only a few years has often to be respected, and they rightly think that their dignity is affronted if it is not. We should see children as acquiring rights in stages—the stages in which they acquire agency (for helpful discussions of how they might acquire rights in stages, see Archard 1993: chs. 5 and 6; Wellman 1997).

So I am inclined to conclude that human rights do not extend to infants, to patients in an irreversible coma or with advanced Alzheimer's, or to the severely mentally defective. And if they do not extend to them, it is hard to find a case for extending them to foetuses. This conclusion is compatible with our none the less having weighty obligations to members of all of these classes. And this conclusion about rights is, in part, a decision to keep the language of rights for a different, narrower, clearer, moral domain. There is bound to be an element of stipulation in any account of human rights. But does this not seem the best stipulation?

Notes

1. To be found in the Preambles to the *International Covenant on Economic, Social, and Cultural Rights* and the *International Covenant on Civil and Political Rights*, both adopted by the General Assembly of the United Nations in 1966.
2. That is what Loren E. Lomasky says (1987: 202, but see generally chs. 7 and 8). His problem is the same as mine, because he too makes agency central to having rights: 'Project pursuers enjoy rights in virtue of being project pursuers' (p. 152). Contrary to me, he thinks that children, including infants, are rights-holders. 'Children have rights (against adults) if and only if there are goods-for-the-child that others have reason to acknowledge and respect' (p. 161). But this does not distinguish children from animals, who, Lomasky thinks, do not have rights. 'If their [children's] care were morally optional, usually forthcoming from concerned adults but not demanded from any, then children could be highly regarded accoutrements of the moral community, but they would not be rights-holders' (pp. 164–5). This would distinguish animals from children, only if we could distinguish the kind of 'demand' that rights represent from the ordinary kind of demand that morality makes—say, the demand not to be cruel to animals. This has always seemed to me a difficult job. And respect for animals is not 'morally optional' either; *that* cannot be the basis of the distinction. Rights-holders are not merely duty-attracters. Lomasky later says that infants are, while animals and foetuses are not, *full* members of the moral community. On that, see the text. He also puts much weight on this as a necessary condition for being a right-holder:

'those who are in a position to act on the being in question, for good or ill, have reason to acknowledge it as an individual meriting their respect' (p. 196). Though Lomasky, in an interesting discussion of the moral significance of birth, makes some case for distinguishing children from foetuses (roughly that with birth we form attachment to infants), it is less clear how it distinguishes children from much-loved family pets.

3. Arts. 3(2), 6(2). Given the Covenant's definition of a 'child', it is clear that the rights it lists apply also to infants. 'For the purposes of the present Convention, a child means every human being below the age of eighteen years, unless under the law applicable to the child, majority is attained earlier.' *Convention on the Rights of the Child*, United Nations, adopted by the General Assembly 1989.

4. Preamble.

5. I borrow these examples from a discussion of needs in Griffin 1986: 41 (and I originally borrowed the first example from Garrett Thomson). For a fuller development of some of the points in this section see ibid., ch. 3, sects. 2–6.

6. See e.g. Braybrooke 1987: a 'criterion' of a basic need is its being something 'essential to living or to functioning normally' (p. 31). Later he says more fully that the 'criterion' for inclusion on the list of basic needs and for the level of satisfaction required 'is being indispensable to mind or body in performing the tasks assigned to a given person under a combination of basic social roles, namely the roles of parent, householder, worker, and citizen. If what is thus indispensable is not supplied, the person's functioning in these tasks is deranged' (p. 48). See also Thomson 1987.

   'Basic need' is a technical term and so has to be defined. Though the definitions vary, most are close to Braybrooke's. See eg. Wiggins 1981: 209, 'basicness is a question of the conceivability or difficulty ... of arranging or re-arranging matters so that a person can dispense with x ... without his life or activity being blighted'. For a more finely developed vocabulary see Wiggins and Dermen 1987: §§8 and 9; besides the *basicness* of needs they distinguish their *gravity, urgency, entrenchment*, and *substitutability*.

7. Of course, one should not require the need account on its own to have the resources to solve all problems about morality's becoming 'implausibly lavish'. Other parts of morality might serve to keep morality from becoming too demanding or too generous: e.g. general motivational constraints on human action which limit obligations. But general constraints do not provide enough help here; they do not, for instance, explain why there comes a point where ailments and malfunctions become too trivial to create a right to a cure.

   Braybrooke discusses the problem that endless medical demands create for a basic needs account in Braybrooke 1987: ch. 8.3. He thinks these medical demands constitute 'a breakdown in the concept of needs' (p. 294). 'In the end, there is no way out of acknowledging that nothing already present in the concept of needs saves the need for medical care from becoming a bottomless pit' (p. 301). That said, Braybrooke rightly goes on to insist that this and certain other breakdowns do not weaken the case for according a dominant role to basic human needs in social decision.

   David Wiggins says that he answers this objection (1987: §17, 38 n. 45): 'for purposes of a social morality S that is actually lived and succeeds in proposing to agents shared concerns that they can make their own, there is an *abstract claim right or entitlement to x under conditions C* just where *x is something the denial or removal of which under conditions C gives (and can be seen as giving) the person denied or deprived part or all of a reason, and a reason that is avowable and publicly sustainable within S, to reconsider his adherence to the norms of reciprocity and cooperation sustained by S. . . . A social morality cannot of course give any partic-ular person a guaranteed title to wealth, health, happiness, or security from ordi-nary misfortune. But equally it must not be such as to threaten anyone who is to be bound by it that it will bring upon him or any other individual participants, as if gratuitously, the misfortune of having his vital interests simply sacrificed for the sake of some larger public good' (p. 31–3).

Wiggins's answer goes in two different directions, in a way that makes it an unclear guide to what we should say e.g., about a society's not mounting a crash programme to find a cure for AIDS. AIDS sufferers might well see themselves as having their literally 'vital' interests 'sacrificed for the sake of some larger public good' (such as keeping a few more paintings in the UK and out of the clutches of the Getty), and they might well think that society's turning its back on them, as many of them saw it, gives them simple reason to reconsider their 'adherence to the norms of reciprocity and cooperation sustained by S'. But then they might instead think that even such a vital interest as life gives them no 'guaranteed title to . . . health'. Wiggins's emphasis seems to be more on the first line of thought. The three principles that he sees as the basis of rights (p. 34) he later describes as 'scarcely more than the preconditions of man's securing their own survival in their own way, or in the best way relative to their circumstances' (p. 39). And later still he says that '*it is pro tanto unjust* if, among vital interests actually affected by such [social] interventions, the greater strictly vital need of anyone is sacrificed in the name of the lesser interests of however many others' (p. 43).

8. There are ways of elaborating accounts to try to meet some of these objections. For instance, one could introduce a measure for the importance or urgency of a need—say, the more the need is already met the less important or urgent it becomes. For instance, the more a society meets the demands of health the less urgent the remaining demands of health become. T. M. Scanlon (1975) developed this line of thought. But though this elaboration of the need account may have some plausibility as a basis of social choice (a society has devoted enough of its resources to health, and the demands of art and education are now more impor-tant), it lacks plausibility as a basis for human rights. After a certain amount of investment in health, further investment may no longer be especially important. But important for whom? Presumably, for society. But it would certainly be highly important for those people who will die because the society could, but has decided not to, mount a crash programme to find a cure for AIDS. But human rights are claims that individuals can make against others, including their society. This elab-oration of the need account, though it may have its purposes, takes it away from the entitlements that reside in each individual, and so takes it away from relevance to human rights.

3

What Rights (if Any) do Children Have?

Harry Brighouse

The Convention on the Rights of the Child, which was signed by most existing nation-states, assigns to children a vast array of rights, which it is the obligation of parents, and signatory states, to protect. The Convention has been enormously influential on the thinking of policy-makers, welfare agencies, non-governmental organizations, and even child welfare workers, especially in the developed world, concerning the proper place of children in the political order, and the duties of governments toward children. The rights it accords to children include the right to 'a name' and to be registered immediately after birth (Articles 7 and 8); extensive rights to health and health services (Article 24); the right to an education directed at 'the development of the child's personality, talents, and mental and physical abilities to their fullest potential' and the 'preparation of the child for responsible life in a free society, in a spirit of understanding, peace, tolerance, equality of sexes, and friendship among all peoples, ethnic, national and religious groups, and persons of indigenous origin' (Article 29); the right to be cared for by appropriate authorities when separated from their parents (Articles 20 and 21) and the rights to freedom of expression, religion, and association (Articles 13, 14, and 15).

The convention is motivated by the best of intentions, and it is reasonable to think that its implementation is, broadly speaking, to the good. But there is something very strange about thinking of children as bearers of rights. The liberal model for the attribution of rights is of a competent rational person, who is better positioned than any other feasible assignee to judge what is in his or her interests, and is therefore guaranteed freedom to act on what she judges to be the best reasons for action. We have rights because they allow us to make of our lives what we will—make them truly our own, as it were. The further an agent departs from the liberal model of the competent rational person, the less appropriate it seems to be to attribute rights. But children depart far from this model, and depart further the younger they are.

Does this mean that the convention is fundamentally flawed? The question of what rights we have fundamentally, or morally, is distinct from that of which rights we should be legally granted. Some legal rights do not reflect fundamental rights (at least in any straightforward way) but are none the worse for that: the right to drive an automobile, or to import sushi, for example. So even if children had no fundamental rights it might still be appropriate to attribute to them many legal rights. In the first part of this chapter I shall examine three arguments that children lack fundamental rights. I shall then argue that it is generally illuminating to think of children as bearers of welfare rights, but not, usually, as bearers of agency rights. I shall then examine the structure of the welfare and agency interests children have, and how they are related to one another. In the final part I shall look at three particular rights, asserted by the Convention, concerning agency, the rights to religion, freedom of expression, and culture, and explain why children do not have those rights. Not only do they not have those rights fundamentally, but I shall conjecture that attributing those rights to them legally endangers their interests, because it will tend to lead to subordinating their interests in religion expression and culture to those of their parents.

The Child-Centred Rejection of Children's Rights

There are two ways of challenging the idea that children have rights. The first and historically dominant way, is to take an adult-centred stance and say either that children do not have the kind of status that justifies our giving their interests protection in terms of rights or that the rights of adults are so extensive that they exhaust the terrain—and children's interests can be protected only in so far as doing so is compatible with the rights of adults. So, for example, in thinking about the value of the family, parents and their rights take centre stage and while it is assumed that recognizing parents' rights promotes the good of children, the good of adults is the justification for the claimed rights.

I shall not consider this strategy, because it is thoroughly implausible. Much more interesting and plausible is the child-centred strategy, which acknowledges children's interests to be central, but claims, that for various reasons, granting children rights is an inappropriate means to protect those interests. The child-centred strategy is more plausible because it does not assume that there is some stage in a normal person's life in which their moral status changes from lesser to greater: it accepts that moral status does not naturally change, and that children, like adults, count as separate persons who count equally, but says that that status requires different protective mechanisms depending on the competences and situation of the person.

The first argument I want to consider is that thinking of protecting children's interests fundamentally in terms of rights inevitably leads to the neglect of some of their most fundamental interests. Onora O'Neill (1989) argues that taking 'rights as fundamental in looking at ethical issues in children's lives we

... get an indirect, partial and blurred picture', and 'quer[ies] whether children's positive rights are best grounded by appeals to fundamental (moral, natural, human) rights' (O'Neill 1989: 187).

She points first to the distinction between perfect and imperfect obligations, arguing that the latter cannot be captured by rights talk:

> Sometimes we are required to perform or omit [some type of action] for all others. Sometimes we are required to perform or omit this type of action for specified others. Sometimes we are required to perform or omit an act for unspecified others, but not for all others ... obligations of the third sort cannot plausibly be thought of as having corresponding rights. (O'Neill 1989: 189)

This is so because, although agents have no latitude over whether to perform or omit the pertinent act, we do have some discretion over whom should be the beneficiary of that performance or omission. For example, the obligation to be kind to strangers is not the obligation to be kind to all strangers, nor to be kind to specified strangers, only to be kind to some. No particular stranger has a claim on our kindness. If I am in a hurry to get back to my wife's bedside as she gives birth, I fall down on no obligation by refusing a lift to a stranger who needs to get to the other side of town: and I can fulfil the obligation of kindness to strangers by helping out another stranger, even though his need is no greater, when my own legitimate concerns press upon me less urgently.

But much of what every child needs in order to have what is due to them is nothing they have a right to from any particular person, or from all people. As O' Neill puts it '[The] obligation [to be kind and considerate in dealing with children—to care for them—and to put ourselves out in ways that differ from those in which we must put ourselves out for adults] may bind all agents, but is not one that we owe either to all children ... or merely to antecedently specified children' (1989: 190). Furthermore, 'the obligations of roles such as parent or teacher or social worker are commonly taken to require more than meeting those rights that are institutionalised with the role' (1989: 190). 'Cold, distant or fanatical parents and teachers, even if they violate no rights, deny children the "genial play of life": they can wither children's lives. Children can hardly learn to share or show what Burke called "the unbought grace of life" if we are concerned only with their enforceable claims against others' (1989: 192–3).

This argument certainly impugns thinking of what is owed to children *solely* in terms of rights. But it does not impugn rights talk with respect to children altogether. It seems reasonable to think that each child has a right to some level of education. The ultimate authority charged with guaranteeing this right is presumably the state. The state is the guarantor of last resort: its duty is to ensure those institutional arrangements which most reliably ensure that every child gets the appropriate level of education. This may require that it provide schools itself, or may just require that it provide (or fund) schooling at the margins, for those children whose parents either cannot or will not pay for the education themselves. Similarly it seems reasonable to think that each child has a right to a high level of care. Parents, furthermore, have the obligation to provide this: but if the parents fall down the state must step in: it is, again, guarantor of last resort.

As O'Neill observes, any parent who refrains from doing anything more than the child has a right against her to do, will be failing to discharge all the obligations of parenthood. And the child will be better off, and the relationship better and more fulfilling, if the parents' attitude toward his relationship to the child is one of a loving caring relationship, not as a merely right- or even obligation-based set of interactions. But this, morally full, relationship, is compatible with her seeing the child as having some specific rights which he is required to observe, and which he is in a uniquely suitable position to protect. Rights need not vie with love and care in a relationship—they can instead shape the relationship in which love has a proper place.

There is an analogy here with the role of rights in a marital relationship in shaping that relationship (though there is also an obvious disanalogy). Michael Sandel, in his criticism of liberalism's reliance on rights talk, makes an analogy with the family, and claims that rights will replace affection because 'to invoke the circumstances of justice is simultaneously to concede, implicitly at least, the circumstances of benevolence, or fraternity, or enlarged affection' (Sandel 1982: 32): if the family members see themselves as rights-holders this will loosen the bonds of affection which bind their fates together. But there is no reason for this to be so. True, if they persistently assert their rights against one another, the bonds of affection will break down (though whether the rights-assertion is cause or effect is open to question). But a great deal of rights-thinking does not involve the assertion of rights. It involves waiving one's rights; neglecting one's own interests for those of others; noticing that rights-holders have refrained from asserting their rights out of affection, or consideration for one's interests; regarding others as rights- holders and so respecting their rights even though one's own selfish interests are thereby harmed. These aspects of rights-holding affect marital relationships, at least mature ones in which the participants regard themselves truly as equals, quite profoundly. Waiving what one regards oneself as having a right to willingly, or enthusiastically, is a meaningful and intimate gesture which would be unavailable absent rights-holding within the relationship. Similarly one sometimes recognizes that one's partner has a right to, and deeply wants, something from one, and while one recognizes that they would willingly waive that claim, out of love, or concern, or an interest in maintaining the equality within the relationship, one does not ask them for the waiver, and sometimes one even does not present the opportunity for the waiver: this again is a valuable gesture within the relationship (see Tomasi 1991).

The disanalogy is obviously that the gesture of waiving one's right (against one's parents) is not available to children, since they do not yet have the conceptual or emotional resources to give that action the meaning it has when carried out amongst adults. But seeing one's child as a right-holder against one, and taking that to heart, will both constrain and shape one's actions with regard to the child. Some things that would merely be good for one's child, but to which they have no right, one refrains from—because as a separate person one also has one's own interests which one should pursue. Other things that would merely be good, but to which they have no right, one does do. But those things to which one knows they have a right, one does, without regard to one's own interests. It is not that one could be a good parent while only observing the child's rights; but that one can be a good parent without doing everything that will be good for them, and cannot be a good parent without doing those things to which they have a right.

O'Neill also makes a second, more political, critique of the idea of children's rights. She notes that a central purpose of the grand declarations of rights, from the Declaration of the Rights of Man to the Universal Declaration of Human Rights, and more recent campaigns for minority rights and women's rights, was to make a statement of the morally *de jure* equality of persons, and to encourage persons whose *de facto* status is less than equal to assert their equal status. 'The rhetoric of rights disputes established powers and their categories, and seeks to empower the powerless; it is the rhetoric of those who lack power, but do not accept the status quo. Those who claim their rights deny that the powers that be may define who they are, what they may do, or what they are entitled to' (O'Neill 1989: 201). So the women's rights movement encourages women to be independent and to change the conditions that make them vulnerable. Rights cannot have this function for children, because the vulnerability and dependence of children is not an ameliorable artifice of unjust social institutions: it is a natural feature of their biological condition. The way for children to overcome their dependence and vulnerability is not to assert their rights or think of themselves as rights-holders but, as O'Neill puts it, to 'grow up' (O'Neill 1989: 204).

Again, her point is correct, but I do not think it impugns children's rights even as having an important political function. Even if there were no political function of children's rights talk, the critique would have power only if children's rights talk systematically *misled* people into neglecting the facts of children's vulnerability, dependence, and inabilities. I shall argue that the implementation of some specific purported children's rights may indeed do this, but I see no reason to think that they would do so in general. But there is, indeed, a function of the rights talk which infuses the great human rights documents, in addition to that mentioned by O'Neill, which function is well played by declarations of children's rights. Not only does rights talk remind and exhort the lesser placed to assert their equality, it also reminds and exhorts the better placed to withdraw their assertions of superiority. The call for women's rights functions not just to encourage women to claim their rights, but also to encourage men to grant them, to think of women as people whose interests count as much as do men's. The human rights documents speak to the powerful as follows:

You may indeed have superior power. But this fact does not authorise you to use that power to your own advantage. In some cases you must attempt to relinquish that power. But in others, in which it cannot be relinquished, you must understand that the person in your power is a rights-bearer, one whose interests count for as much as yours. When you use your power with respect to that person you are morally bound to attend first to their, and only after that to your own, interests.

In the cases of women, and members of dominated ethnic groups, such an exhortation implies that over time the bearer of greater power should return it to its proper holder, the rights-bearer. But where, for whatever reason, such transfer is impossible, or, as in the case of children, is prohibited by other moral considerations, it reminds the power-holder that the interests of the subject of power, and not only those of its holder, should guide them in using the power. Animal rights talk appears to have had something like this function: guiding people to treat animals in a way that at least takes account of the animals' interests and not just those of the people treating them.

This, possibly lesser, function of rights attributions, in contrast to the one O'Neill discusses, is of great significance with respect to children. It draws the attention of governments, welfare agencies, and parents to the independent standing of the child, and the centrality of her interests in determining policy, intervention, and her upbringing respectively. In an era when talk of children's rights is more or less taken for granted this may seem trivial, the more central task being to determine what those interests are and to act on them; but it is very new that children's interests have systematically been taken seriously by governments and welfare agencies and that the patriarchalist legacy of the pre-modern age has been seriously challenged. Erik Olin Wright has pointed out that the popular rhetoric (as opposed to the theoretical justification) behind even most of the most extreme parental rights talk appeals, most fundamentally, to the interests of the children ('We parents have the right to raise our children without external interference because we know best what is good for our children').

A third objection to a certain conception of children's rights comes from Robert Goodin and Dianne Gibson. Goodin and Gibson identify two theoretical models of rights. On the first, the choice theory, what it is to have a right is to have a legally respected choice: 'rights holders may either stand on their rights, demanding the treatment that is by rights due to them, or else they may waive that rightful treatment' (Goodin and Gibson 1997: 185–203 at 186). On this theory the inappropriateness of considering children rights-bearers is obvious: because they are not competent choosers, are vulnerable, and are dependent, children (especially young children) cannot make choices about whether to claim or waive their rights 'they lack the requisite autonomy, in the moral much more importantly than the merely physical sense of the term. Their will is unformed or deformed, their judgement deficient or impaired' (Goodin and Gibson 1997: 187). The idea is, of course, not that children are literally unable to choose: from a fairly early age one can ask a child which of two or three things they want to do, and they will formally make a choice. But children often do not grasp the ramifications, for them or for others, of the choice they make. This is true even of very simple decisions (what and whether to eat for lunch; how long and with whom to play after lunch; how early to go to bed), let alone decisions about whether to waive or claim their rights.

Goodin and Gibson claim, though, that on an alternative model of rights it would be appropriate ascribe rights to children. On the interest theory of rights

> it does not matter that rights-holders are not in a position to assert rights . . . . what it is to be a right-holder . . . is merely to be a direct intended beneficiary of someone else's duty-bound performance . . . . All that is strictly required [to be a right-holder] is that one have interests which are recognisable by others who are duly empowered, by the moral community more generally, to press those claims on one's behalf. (Goodin and Gibson: 188)

For adults, to be sure, we often need to know their preferences, or at least something about them, to know what their interests are. But for children, even young children to whom no long-term preferences can reasonably be ascribed, we can identify publicly articulatable interests which make no references to their contingent preferences: needs for shelter, care, nutrition, education, etc. Enshrining these in legal—and even fundamental moral—rights can make sense.

Agency Rights and Welfare Rights

Goodin and Gibson's suggestion is that the purpose of fundamental moral rights is to protect our fundamental interests as persons: to guarantee the claim of each person to those things without which an acceptable life is usually not possible. For children nearing maturity and for most adults, one of these things is choice. Our lives are profoundly affected by big decisions, such as whom and whether to marry, when and whether to have children, where to live, which of our talents to develop, which of our vices to battle at a particular time, and small decisions, such as what to have for breakfast, how many layers of clothing to wear, which novels to take on holiday. In order for these projects and activities to be rewarding—to enhance our well-being—we usually need to identify with them from the inside. For this to be the case we usually need to have played some role in the authorship of the decision: choice is a powerful mechanism for inducing the identification normally required for the execution of a decision to serve our interests. So our lives will usually go better if we have some considerable say in the authorship of those decisions than if we have none. This is not to deny that such decisions are always taken in circumstances not of our own choosing, nor to deny that many of them are taken in negotiation with others (we do not choose whether and whom to marry unilaterally). But choice is not the single fundamental matter involved in having rights: rights protect funda-mental interests, which for all people who have a developed capacity for choice includes a good deal of choice, and for all who have a capacity for choice that can be developed includes the interest in developing and being able to exercise that capacity.

   If we see rights as functioning to protect fundamental interests, it is easier to see that it is appropriate to attribute them to children. There are, as Goodin and Gibson say, interests which can be publicly articulated and attributed to all children: the interests in shelter, education, basic health care, and to be cared for by a loving adult, for example. If children cannot claim the rights that protect these interests, as they cannot when they are young, this does not count against their being rights: it simply indicates that when the state institutionalizes the rights, it must clearly specify who are the trustees for which interests, and devise mechanisms for holding them accountable. But the rights it makes sense for us to attribute to children on this, interest-based, view of rights, are all of a certain kind. They are what we might call, following Amartya Sen, welfare rights (rights which pertain directly to well-being) rather than what we might call agency rights, rights which involve their bearers in making choices about how to act. The reason it makes sense to attribute these rights to children is exactly the reason that on the choice model it made little sense to attribute rights to children alto-gether: they are not, and can be publicly shown not to be, competent choosers, and so are not yet capable of assessing how to act on matters concerning their own well-being or that of others.

   How does this distinction between welfare and agency rights help with our thinking about children? Welfare rights are rights to certain sources of well-being, which sources are taken not to be distinctive at all but to be, broadly, the same for all. Health, and pursuant to that some level of health care provi-sion, are needed by all, whatever their distinctive life-plan. Some degree of education is required for people to chose between options in life and (more importantly for current purposes) to pursue most plans of life. Without a subsistence level of income, and access to shelter, it is impossible to pursue a worked-out plan of how to live—the starving man lives hand to mouth, not according to a plan. Our interest in these particular contributions to our well-being is very urgent—urgent enough to justify our claim to a right: and it can only be said that a right has been provided (for adults) if the state provides strong guarantees of access to these goods.

Welfare rights justify themselves. The starving man is starving: one does not need to point to some further absence in his life which is consequent on his starving to justify the claim that he is suffering a remediable loss of welfare. But welfare rights are also valuable for the exercise of agency rights (and many other things). If we are focused on meeting our urgent needs, we lack time, energy, and attention for other pursuits. Having them guaranteed frees us up to pursue our interests in agency.

Furthermore, the agency rights of adults have implications for the institutionalization of their welfare rights. For example, even though it is publicly knowable that a particular medical procedure has a very high likelihood of benefiting some adult, it is not permissible to override their preference not to have the procedure. This is because among the agency rights adults have are the rights to forgo, for whatever reason, particular sources of welfare. Adults have a conception of their own good, which they have the agency right continually to review and pursue: if, in the light of this conception, an adult judges that a particular general source of welfare will not in fact, all things considered, enhance their welfare, she is permitted to waive the right to that source: many welfare rights are waivable, as a matter of agency right.

Why do adults have the agency rights to waive many of their welfare rights? The answer is simple. It is because in general, for mature and competent persons, their sense of identification with their own life, and the activities involved in it, is more central to their overall well-being than any particular source of well-being on offer. It is better for them, usually, to pursue an activity with which they identify than one which goes against the grain of their fundamental commitments, even if the latter is, in some sense, objectively better. This may not always be true—and there are some theorists like Thomas Hurka (1997) who deny it—but it is usually true, and the state is not capable of being well-informed about those particular instances when it is false (if it ever is) and so should act as if it is true. The agency right to waive particular welfare rights can thus be explained in terms of its contribution to the agents' welfare.

Children's Rights

So the relationship between the agency and welfare rights of adults is complex. On the interest model, agency rights are vital because of their indirect contribution to well-being, rather than because choice is given an intrinsic value of its own. The contribution of agency rights to welfare depends on the assumptions that adults can choose with some level of competence, and that for them having choice is a powerful mechanism for inducing identification with the activity chosen.

But children combine three features which combine to make them unlike adults. Children are profoundly dependent on others for their well-being, because they cannot meet their own needs (emotional, physical, developmental), or negotiate the obstacles in the social world in such a way that their needs will be met. They are also (for this reason) profoundly vulnerable to the decisions of others. Even if those on whom they are dependent are highly reliable with respect to their welfare, whenever something goes wrong it is normally because the decisions of another have failed. Children also, unlike other persons who are dependent and vulnerable, have the capacity to develop the capabilities to meet their own needs, those very needs for which they are dependent on others. The combination of these three features make children unique. The very old, the severely cognitively disabled, and domestic animals share the first two conditions of children, but not the third. That children combine these characteristics forces us to look more closely at the content of their interests and the structure of whatever rights they may have in the light of those interests. (It is true that people in comas, like children, share the three characteristics. But what must be done to develop their capabilities is quite different—the aim is to restore normal functioning, not to develop it. Some people may argue that the comatose have at least the opportunity to have expressed their preferences concerning treatment while comatose in the light of their mature conception of the good. I am sceptical of this: so-called advance directives, depending they do on judgements about one's response to extreme and unknown hypothetical situations, lack the authority that the response to actual situations has.)

So far I have distinguished between welfare and agency rights, and claimed that (for adults) both sets of rights are best explained by the interest model. Now I want to distinguish two kinds of interest people have: immediate interests and future interests. One's immediate interests are one's interests in what happens to one in the present. So for example, I have an immediate interest in having shelter, food, moderate wealth, a relatively clean environment, enjoying intimacy with my family, being able to do the day-to-day work involved in my job. Of course, I give differential weights to these different interests, but attach some weight to them all. My future interests are vaguer: I have an interest in having a comfortable retirement, in being able to travel to see my children and their children, in being able to exercise when old. Again I attach different weight to these interests, and different weight to them than to my immediate interests. There may be conflict within and across both sets of interests, and the weighting I attach to the interests will affect the choices I then make. Some discount the future a great deal, attaching overwhelming weight to their immediate interests; others discount the future much less, and forgo opportunities for welfare in the present in order to have greater likelihood of welfare in the future.

Figure 1 shows the kinds of interests adults have.

Immediate Welfare	Immediate Agency
Future Welfare	Future Agency

Figure 1

Notice that:

- Present agency interests cannot be properly protected without some welfare interests being met. For example, it is distracting to be underfed and under-sheltered: those in great material need have less choice concerning with whom they will associate, and less opportunity to deliberate responsibly about public political matters.
- Future agency interests are not different in kind from the present—they are just temporally different. Our religion, our voting intentions, our associations, may change in response to our choices and judgements, but the ways we make those choices and judgements, and the psychological resources available to us in making them, do not normally change fundamentally over time. Similarly for present and future welfare interests: even though we do anticipate having different basic needs in our later life, we are equipped in younger adulthood to anticipate what they will be and to prepare for and insure against them.
- If adults had the right sort of upbringing, they can be presumed to be autonomous. So protecting agency rights is vital: it lets them be the judge of (*a*) how to use their agency rights and (*b*) how to protect their future agency and welfare interests and current welfare interests.

The taxonomy in Figure 1 also holds for children's interests. But there are important differences between their case and that of adults.

First, their future welfare and agency interests differ radically in kind from their immediate interests. Take welfare first. A child's immediate welfare interests include a loving and secure relationship with her parents: this is at the centre of her immediate welfare in a way that no particular relationship is at the centre of her welfare in the future. Her vulnerability ensures that she needs specific agents to protect her; but in the future she will need to be able to protect herself. She needs to be provided for, not to provide for herself. Even such things as nutritional needs and sleep needs change radically between childhood and adulthood, and in ways that children do not understand well.

Second, the immediate agency interests of children differ a great deal from those of adults, that is from their own future agency interests. Very young infants have few immediate agency interests at all. They need constant care, supervision, nutrition, interaction with others, and sleep. As children grow older, their immediate agency needs change—in order to get immediate enjoyment and fulfilment they need to be able to express themselves, and make choices within a restricted range. It is important that they get to choose their friends, and whether to play with them (as long as they are prevented from playing all the time, and also prevented from refraining from socializing with others altogether). They must not feel themselves to have no control over their diet, but it is also vital, not just for their long-term well-being, but for their short-term enjoyment, that their choice is restricted somewhat (ten ice creams at a single sitting does not enhance their short-term enjoyment—nor, at least for many young children, does a ten-hour TV marathon). These restrictions do not damage their immediate agency interests in the way that they do those of adults: appropriate restrictions imposed by another person do not imply a lack of respect for her agency. Very young children, furthermore, do not even take them to imply a lack of respect for their agency, although, of course, as they age this changes, and in modern open societies they are likely to feel slighted by restrictions some time before they are right to feel that way.

Another difference, though, is that protecting the immediate interests of the child is insufficient to protect her developmental, and hence future, agency interests. Her key developmental agency interest is in being able to become an adult who can make her own choices consistent with her own welfare, someone with, as Rawls puts it, a developed capacity for a sense of justice and for a conception of the good, including the capacity rationally to revise her conception of the good—that is, someone who has an adult's capacity for agency. This requires more than the mere indulgence of her immediate agency interests: she must be taught to be able to empathize and sympathize, reason about principles, think about moral rules, discipline her own behaviour. There is at least a potential conflict between her immediate welfare and agency interests on the one hand (enjoying herself, doing what she wants) and her developmental agency interests.

An objection, suggested to me by Colin Macleod, might be raised here. Macleod expresses scepticism that a welfare-grounded reason can be found for developing a sense of justice, because a well-developed sense of justice often requires (and inclines) us to act against our own welfare interests. I have two responses to this. First, in fact, in a reasonably well-ordered society it is important for our own welfare that we are able to understand what justice requires and, for the most part, act on it; because there are fairly serious costs to acting unjustly, in terms of both legal and social sanctions. These are not the most important reasons for acting justly, but they are reasons, and they are grounded in the welfare of the agent. I do not, however, think that this response is compelling in a society that is far from well-ordered and I do not have a well-thought-out account of why individuals should have a sense of justice in a radically unjust society. Second, at the base of our welfare interests is an interest in living a life that is actually good: and injustice on our part detracts from the goodness of our lives.

Children are not well placed, themselves, to protect their future welfare and agency interests, or their immediate welfare interests, for two reasons. First, they are not independent: they are dependent both physically and emotionally on very particular other people, whom they have not chosen: usually their parents, siblings, and, if they are fortunate, a more extended family. The extent of this dependence can easily be underestimated, because most children become moderately well-functioning adults, and it is quite hard to determine at what point parenting becomes so bad as that children's needs are not met to some basic threshold. But dependent they are: children who are thoroughly neglected in the first few years of life can never become even minimally competent speakers of natural languages, can never function effectively in human society, and appear to lack even the basic elements of a flourishing life. Second, with respect to their future interests, children are not well-informed. They do not have more than partial conceptions of what their future interests will be. We can distinguish here between two kinds of future interests: particular interests and universal interests. Their particular interests are those which depend on the conception or conceptions of the good they will come to have in adulthood; their universal future interests are those they will share with all others regardless of their conceptions of the good. Their particular interests are unknown to them because they do not yet have a conception of the good, and do not know what their conceptions of the good will be. Even if they did know what their conception was going to be, this would give them very limited information about their future particular interests: lacking a developed sense of how social interaction works and of their own place in the social order, it is hard for them to know what their particular interests conceptions support.

Their universal future interests, those which are not dependent on their particular conceptions of the good, are similarly hard for them to know. Children lack a conception of what it is to be a sexual being, of what it is to negotiate intimate personal relationships as an equal, of what it is to be responsible for the welfare of another, and of what it is to be responsible for their own welfare. Yet vivid ideas of these things are essential for an understanding of what one's interests are as an adult. The relationship between children's interests is represented in Figure 2.

I should flag here that what I say is true of young children. As children age, if they are well brought up, what I have said is ever less true of them, until, eventually, it is no more true of them than of normal adults. This has implications for what counts as a good upbringing: children must be given increased responsibility for themselves and others in order to come to have a conception of it—they must be allowed at the right ages (which will differ from child to child) more independence. Ill-raised children, of course, may well continue to lack the experience from which they can acquire the conceptual and emotional resources required to understand their interests.

Could it be objected that adults, too, lack a vivid conception of every possible eventuality? In their young adulthood, for example, they have only a very

Immediate Agency Interests (Determined by service to future agency interests, especially personal autonomy. Include increasing opportunities for agency as child ages).	Future Agency Interests (Personal autonomy, ability to act on conception of the good, whatever that is).
Immediate Welfare Interests (Shelter, nutrition, loving care, etc. Serve, but also valuable independently of, future interests. Include increasing opportunities for agency as child ages).	Future Welfare Interests Particular (depends on mature conception of good) Universal (independent of mature conception of good)

Figure 2

dim conception of the likely outcomes in old age. No one embarking on a (first) marriage fully understands the moral and emotional commitments they are making. Most people start rearing children with little prior experience of the responsibilities involved, and without full appreciation of the future joys and setbacks their children will give them. The differences between adults and children is one of degree not one of kind: so how can it justify the difference in structure of rights?

First, there are two important differences. Children under the age of 6 normally lack basic abilities to reason: they cannot, for example, understand that addition and subtraction are converse of one another, they do not have a conception of proportion, and only have an elementary notion of time. They also lack basic abilities of self-command which most adults have mastered: the ability to defer gratification emerges around this age, but takes some time to develop fully. As I have said, this is a difference between young children and adults, and is one that erodes as the child ages. The second difference is that adults, unlike children, are equipped to entertain the possibilities, and to gauge which are the relevant possibilities to consider and entertain. They have many avenues for accessing help in considering possibilities and how to deal with them: novels, advice, the ability to identify experts—plumbers, doctors, parents, policemen, etc. This allows them to prepare for many of the likely eventualities that will befall them. Children by contrast have only their parents, by and large. The resources available for them increase dramatically as they grow older (as long as their parents are responsible): but this is as they near adulthood, and their situation becomes more like that of adults.

Furthermore adults have, or at least have access to, self-knowledge which enables them to negotiate opportunities to their own advantage. Sometimes they fail to do this, because of weakness of the will, bad luck, imperfect knowledge, or other adverse conditions; or because they conscientiously prioritize the advantage of others over their own. But in general they have the resources to understand and pursue their own advantage in action, where children often do not. It is not only concerning the life-shaping matters that children lack these resources, but also relatively minor matters. They do not understand, for example, that if they forgo lunch they will be ill-tempered in the afternoon; or that if they get too cold they will want to stop playing and return inside; that rough playing with the dog will trigger an asthma attack. These are matters where they lack the simple understanding of how their bodies work, or the basic self-knowledge most adults have, or, in some cases, the self-discipline which enables them to weigh costs and benefits to their own short-term advantage.

Even if these differences are a matter of degree, they are a matter of great degree, and that may suffice to generate a difference in the structure of their rights. In discussing the model of rights attributions to adults I have repeatedly used the notions of competence and rationality, the idea being that adults who are competent and rational are properly granted agency rights, including the right to make choices over how to pursue their welfare interests. But competence and rationality are matters of degree: the idea is that there is a threshold of competence and rationality above which it is appropriate to grant these agency rights, but below which it is not. The existence of a threshold does not mean that what is at issue is not a matter of degree; it just makes it appropriate to treat someone above the threshold qualitatively differently than someone below it. (Of course, there are hard questions about where the threshold is, and given that those questions are hard, there are other hard questions about what to do with those persons whose competence and rationality are near but probably below the threshold.)

What is the upshot of the foregoing discussion? It seems quite plausible to attribute to children rights which protect their standard welfare interests, and these rights do not differ fundamentally in structure from the welfare rights we properly attribute to adults. They are hard and fast protections of the immediate interests of the children; assertions that these interests must be protected no matter what. What does differ between the case of adult's and child's welfare rights is the agent charged with exercising the right. In the case of the adult it is the adult: within the law she makes choices concerning how and whether to pursue her own welfare interests. In the case of children's welfare rights, the designated right-exercising agent is someone other than the bearer of the right. This is because the reasons that support coincidence of agent with bearer in the case of adults—that the bearer is well-acquainted with her needs, and that in order for outcome to enhance her welfare she must endorse it—are absent. The designated agents are instead, others, well-acquainted with the needs of the child: usually it will be appropriate to divide the agency between parents and welfare agencies of the state.

But for the same reasons that it is appropriate to divorce the agent from the bearer in the case of welfare rights, it is generally inappropriate to ascribe agency rights to children, at least to young children. Agency does not play the same role as with adults in determining their welfare interests, and yielding to their choices in the way that rights would require jeopardizes their developmental and future agency interests. Parents are obliged to assist them in developing their capacities for agency, which process requires that they give children multiple opportunities for agency. But neither they nor the state should guarantee agency rights.

Children's Purported Rights to Culture, Religion, and Expression

My conclusion is that it is perfectly sensible and illuminating to attribute fundamental welfare rights to children, but not, usually, sensible or illuminating to attribute fundamental agency rights to them. In this section I shall argue, further, that legal agency rights are often inappropriate for children. To illustrate I shall consider three purported rights, all asserted in the convention: the child's right to their own culture, a child's right to freedom of religion, and a child's right to freedom of expression.

But before that, I should make two caveats. The first caveat is that children cannot come to be competent agents without some experience of agency. They must have the experience of choice before it makes sense for them to be seen as having the right to choice. I do not think this justifies children's agency *rights*: instead what it justifies is an obligation on parents (and the agencies of the state) regularly to introduce children, as they age, to situations in which they can make choices, and in which they are not fully protected from the consequences of their decisions. As they get older they should be protected ever less from the consequences of their choices, until, on the cusp of being rights-holders, they should be protected from consequences no more than adults are. The point here is that those responsible for the education and upbringing of the child must be guided by these considerations: and hence the child can be said to have a right to an upbringing that prepares her for competent agency (which will include many opportunities for agency) but not to have agency rights.

The second caveat is that there are different areas of decision-making in our lives, and each individual achieves competence in different areas at different speeds. Statutory law in many countries does not designate a single age of majority, but designates different ages as those for achievement of different rights. The rights to marry, to have sexual intercourse, to vote, to drink alcohol, to stand for office, and to drive an automobile are separate rights, the exercise of which require different skills and competences, and it is reasonable for them to be granted at slightly different ages (I don't mean to endorse the particular ages at which states grant these rights, some of which seem odd at best). I am not arguing, in particular, that there is some sudden age at which all children become full adults, at which point all should have all the agency rights of adulthood. Some agency rights can reasonably be thought to kick in early, others later.

Now let me turn to some particular agency rights. First, the right to one's own culture. Article 30 of the convention says the following:

In those States in which ethnic, religious or linguistic minorities or persons of indigenous origin exist, a child belonging to such a minority or who is indigenous shall not be denied the right, in community with other members of his or her group, to enjoy his or her own culture, to profess or practice his or her own religion, or to use his or her own language.

(Note that the convention makes no mention of the correlative rights of children who belong to a majority culture. I assume this is not because such children are not thought to have these rights, but because it is thought that their purported rights will be politically secure without the protection of the convention.)

What does it mean to say that an *adult* has a right to her own culture? It means that the government may not interfere with her cultural practices (as long as they do no harm to non-consenting others) and that it must protect her practices from the interference of others. Cultural practices include forms of religious worship, forms of linguistic communication, performance in and attendance at artistic endeavours, choices of cuisine, sport, and many more apparently trivial personal habits. Adults have this right because these kinds of activity are intrinsic to their expressing their personal commitments and even their personality. The cultural practices are their own because they have committed to them against a background in which it was possible to reject them, to embrace alternative cultural practices instead, and their right includes the right, still, to embrace other practices instead of or as well as these. If an adult belongs to a group it is because she has chosen to belong to it, either by gravitating to it away from that into which she was born, or by not gravitating away from that into which she was born: so in protecting the group the state protects the individuals (as long as it does not restrict, and does not allow groups to restrict, the availability of exit).

But for children the world is open in a way that it is not to adults. The openness of their world is reflected in the fact that we may not consider them burdened by the culture in which they are raised. They have not yet had the opportunity to embrace the cultural practices in which they were raised against a background of choice—it is the culture in which they are being raised but it has not yet been made their own.

Furthermore children are raised in families, by their parents (sometimes adoptive, more often biological). For children, they are members of groups not by choice, or by having refrained from choosing to leave, but because their parents belong to the group. Consider the likely effects of treating them as if the culture in which they are raised is 'their own'. To do so burdens them with that culture because, unlike adults, they do not have the liberty to explore alternatives at their own will. Whereas the right to one's own culture is liberatory for an adult, it can be burdensome for a child, whose cultural choices are likely primarily to reflect the personalities and interests of other people (their parents) rather than their own. In some, maybe many, happy cases they may grow into the culture—it may suit their personalities and interests very well. But in some cases it will not; a culture which places a taboo on homosexual practices will never suit well someone who is homosexual; a culture which promotes a restrictive gendered division of labour will ill-suit many girls and women who have intellectual or leadership capacities which they will have few or no opportunities to develop (see Okin, 1998, 1999 for an elaboration of the tension between the interests of women (and hence girls) and the claims of minority (and majority) cultures to cultural protection).

A different understanding of the child's right to their own culture is hinted at by the English wording of the text: that parents must allow the child (since it must not be denied the right) to enjoy the culture of the group to which the child ascriptively 'belongs' regardless of their own (the parents') preferences. Imagine a Korean parent in North America, for example, who wants her child to become immersed in mainstream American culture to minimize the risk that they will not develop the cultural understandings that provide access to many of the opportunities mainstream Americans enjoy. Or a Native American parent who moves away from the reservation in order to remove their child from the dangers posed by desperate poverty, and thus deprives her child of the community with whom he can practise and enjoy the indigenous culture. This reading of the right would deny the parents the freedom to make those choices for their children. Though hinted at by the wording this is clearly not the intent of the article, and rightly so. To guarantee the right, on this reading, the state would need invasive access to the internal life of the family, and would have to intervene in the relationship without any justification in terms of the immediate or developmental interests of the child. The minority or indigenous community has no special claim on the child against the preferences of the parent, and the child has no interest in participating in a community which her parent has, for whatever reason, left.

A third understanding of the right to one's own culture could be advanced: that it implies that children have the same rights with respect to culture as adults do. It is deeply implausible to claim that children have this right. Imagine the institutional consequences. No one (including their parents) would be permitted forcibly to prevent them attending any legal cultural event; no one could force them to attend one; they would have free choice over what and when to eat; which classes to take in school: the difficulty of, and opportunity costs of learning, another language might influence their choice over whether to adopt them as part of their cultural outlook, just as it does for adults. To grant children an adult's right to culture would be unenforceable, since the state could not possibly investigate every complaint (or even a small fraction of the complaints) of force within the family. But it would, again, jeopardize the family as an institution, to the detriment of the developmental interests of children.

None of this is to argue that children have no interest in being raised so that they can have a secure sense of belonging in some community. David Archard has suggested an argument for children's right to their own culture which is worth looking at. The argument says that children have an interest in acquiring an identity which is not grounded in choice: this is valuable both instrumentally, because it enables them unselfconsciously to negotiate the conflicts within their culture, and intrinsically because it provides them with a sense of 'effortless belonging'. The most straightforward way of providing them with such an identity (and it has to be provided for them because they cannot provide it for themselves) is to pick out certain contingent features—like race, or native language, or neighbourhood of birth, or ethnicity of parentage—and tie the culture they acquire to that or those features. So they will come to have a richer life overall if they are raised in and into the culture of their parents.

On the most natural reading of this argument, it reflects the first interpretation above of what counts as the child's culture—it is the parent's culture. I agree with the argument that a sense of secure belonging is valuable, and that some degree of induction into one's surrounding culture is needed for that sense of belonging. But I do not believe we should sanctify this interest with the protection of a right.

First, if a child has a right to induction into their parents' culture (that is, if the first understanding is the right one), this wrongly restricts the discretion of the parent over their child's cultural exposure. The parent may have been raised in, and continue to practise, the local culture, but, recognizing the deep flaws in that culture, or recognizing the harm that culture will do to their own child's personal development, may aspire to expose their child to different cultural influences. Certain 'macho' subcultures in American society are bad for almost everyone who participates in them—if my son is particularly sensitive, or particularly aggressive, I may judge that he is better off being shielded from this culture, even if I myself am so imbued in the culture that I cannot help participating in it. I may judge this to be the case even if the cost of doing so is that he will always feel somewhat alienated from his cultural surroundings (and, maybe, alienated somewhat from me).

While it is important that many of the unchosen sources of identification that ground our identities be difficult, or costly, to revise, the interests children have in having such identities is sufficiently (if not excessively) protected by simply assigning their parents a substantial role in their upbringings. There is no need for an additional right to 'their own' culture. For some of us it is vital for our long-term well-being that we be able to throw off some of the unchosen parts of our identities. Most of the cultures in the history of the world, including most contemporary cultures, are both sexist and contain strong taboos against homosexuality. These elements of their cultures are acquired by almost everyone raised in them, and for most women and homosexuals it is essential to their well-being that they be able to cast off these aspects of their identities—it is also helpful if others (heterosexuals, men) cast off these aspects too. A cultural policy devoted to the well-being of each person will seek merely adequate protection of the interest in acquiring unchosen, difficult to shrug off, identities, and will seek simultaneously to ensure that each individual has the emotional and intellectual resources to revise their identities to be congruent with their own personalities. A 'right to their own culture' for children, I am claiming, gives excessive protection to the first interest, and insufficient to the second (see Brighouse 1998 for a more detailed explanation of what the second interest consists in and how it would be protected best).

Turn now to Article 14, which asserts that: 'States Parties shall respect the right of the child to freedom of thought, conscience and religion' and 'States Parties shall respect the rights and duties of the parents and, when applicable, legal guardians, to provide direction to the child in exercise of his or her right in a manner consistent with the evolving capacities of the child'. The article gives explicit licence to the parent to direct the child's use of the right. This is a funny kind of right: in what sense is one's conscience, or religious exercise, free, if another person's will directs it? What appears to be a right for one person turns out to be a licence for another to direct that person. And it is hard to see, for the reasons invoked above, how else this purported right could be understood. Young children cannot reasonably be thought of as having their own religious commitments—their expressions of commitment almost invariably reflect those of their parents or some other authority figures. They simply do not have the complexity of belief or the wherewithal to evaluate reasons for belief that lend authenticity to their expressions of commitment. Again, alternative understandings of the right analogous to those of the right to one's own culture mentioned above might be asserted, but they would fall for similar reasons. It is just not clear how the notion of a right illuminates anything about the moral circumstances of the child.

Consider, finally, Article 13: 'The child shall have the right to freedom of expression; this right shall include freedom to seek, receive and impart information and ideas of all kinds, regardless of frontiers, either orally, in writing or in print, in the form of art, or through any media of the child's choice.' Again, remember that the child is (according to the Convention as well as to common moral understandings) to be raised in the family. Her parents, reasonably and unavoidably, have a great deal of control over the information she will receive (and hence be able to impart). It is important for the developing child to have some licence to express herself, but that expression should rarely be taken as reflecting their personalities or commitments as they would for adults. Young, and even much older, children, are often 'trying out' expressions, to find out what they mean or what their effects will be. Their ability to learn requires that they have space to give expression to thoughts and ideas, which is a prerequisite for developing the skills of rational reflection and enquiry, but in doing so they are not, to use a useful metaphor, 'expressing themselves'.

Concluding Comment

I have argued that children's agency interests are structured quite differently from those of adults. I have argued that this difference, in combination with children's vulnerability and dependence on adults, makes it inappropriate to think of them as bearers of fundamental agency rights, and unwise to attribute to them at least some of the legal agency rights declared in the Convention. There is room within my account for the idea that children may properly be granted agency rights which are correctly distinguished from those of adults, and when the age at which the right kicks in is clearly specified. For example, babies are obviously not consulted in child custody arrangements after a divorce, even though their interests are properly given great weight; 10 year olds, by contrast, may have a right to have not just their interests, but also their preferences, taken into consideration. But, unlike adults, whose preferences over their own arrangements should be taken to be authoritative, in the case of the 10 year old the judge should only take the child's preference into account, and should prioritize their interests if she judges that there is a deep discrepancy between the two.

I am not arguing, then, that children should be completely controlled by their parents, just that they should be somewhat, and to the extent that they are they cannot be said, sensibly, to have the agency rights which adults have (in fact I develop a fairly strict account of the limits of parental authority over education in Brighouse 2000). The action of the state, and the division of authority devised by it over the upbringings of children should be designed to safeguard their immediate welfare rights and their prospective autonomy. Indeed, I suspect that granting some legal agency rights to young children in the form suggested by the Convention actually jeopardizes their prospective autonomy by giving parents too much effective control over the development of their rational capacities and their access to information.

None of this is to say that children should not have a good deal of freedom of expression or of choice to engage in cultural or religious practices. Nor is it to say that parents should not have a good deal of say over what practices their children engage in or how they are raised. Parents should have a good deal of say, and children should have a good deal of freedom—and as the child gets older the balance between the two should shift from one favouring the control of the parent to one favouring the freedom of the child. But the language of agency rights, in contrast with that of welfare rights, does not usually illuminate what children need.

Note

Thanks are due to David Archard and Colin Macleod for comments on a previous draft, to Peter Vallentyne for comments on another work which prompted some of these thoughts, and to Lynn Glueck and Erik Olin Wright for typically illuminating discussions.

4

Children's Choices or Children's Interests: Which do their Rights Protect?

Samantha Brennan

The philosophical debate regarding children's rights has, understandably, focused on the question of whether children *have* rights. Philosophers writing about children's rights have paid little or no attention to the *kinds of rights* children arguably possess. Participants in the debate have bypassed ongoing and important debates between rights theorists regarding the nature of rights. Instead, more attention has been paid to children's moral status. I think the assumption has been that we can decide whether children have rights and then leave it to rights theorists to sort out what rights are. Once this is settled we can simply recognize children as possessing rights with the same nature and structure as adults. I argue that this assumption is mistaken and that paying attention to children can usefully inform debates about the kinds of rights there are.

Whether any particular kind of being—children, animals, or environmental objects such as mountains or trees—has rights is a different sort of substantive debate about rights. It is an important debate but one I leave aside for the purposes of this chapter. My main goal in this chapter is to respond to what is often thought to be the main philosophical block to the possibility of children possessing rights–the claim that rights properly understood protect choices. Responding to this objection only shows that it is possible for children to have rights. In itself it is not an argument for the further claim that children do, in fact, have rights.[1]

This chapter has four parts. First, I introduce in very general terms the debate between the choice conception of rights and the interest conception of rights. Second, I set out to show that the structure of the debate surrounding children's rights has hampered moral theorists from making real progress on the issues. Third, I aim to see what the debate regarding children's rights looks like if we reframe the debate to take account of the differences between interest and choice theories of rights. Fourth, I argue that considerations regarding children and their characteristics are important at the foundational level.

Thinking about children might help us make progress in the seemingly intractable debate between the interest theory and the choice theory of moral rights. I defend the view that rights can protect either choices or interests and that what determines which is protected in a particular case depends upon the nature of the being who is the holder of the right. The model I will suggest makes the most sense is the gradualist one, according to which children change through the process of intellectual, emotional, and moral development from being the sort of creatures whose interests are protected by rights to being the sort of creatures whose rights protect their choices.

The Concept of a Right

What are rights? What function do they serve? Rights do two things. First, they serve as protections for individuals. Second, they place constraints on the behaviour of moral agents. These two ideas are linked. The way in which individuals are protected is just by constraining the behaviour of others. Noting that one can describe the requirements facing a moral agent from the point of view of the person who has a right, Shelly Kagan puts it this way: '(W)e can say that if there is a constraint of some sort governing how agents are to treat a given person, then that person has a right not to be treated in that way' (1998: 172). On some views about rights, there is an explanatory asymmetry between having a right and the constraint on the behaviour of others, because it is the existence of the right which explains the existence of a constraint on the behaviour of others and not the other way round.

Lesley Jacobs, for example, writes that at the core of the concept of a right is the idea that rights warrant respect from others and can be the basis of making claims against them (1997: 54). It is a debate within rights theory just how central the notion of claiming is to a proper understanding of the concept of a right. Some think that claiming is not part of the core concept at all and that we can describe the concept more neutrally in terms of the obligations a right imposes. The main worry with thinking of 'claiming' as emblematic of the concept of a right is that it seems that not all those who look as if they are rights-bearers are in a position to make or press claims. Not just children fall into this category, for so too do the elderly, the disabled, and the very ill.[2] The defender of the centrality of 'claiming' may respond by drawing a distinction between the activity of claiming and the more objective notion of 'having a claim'. 'Having a claim', like 'having a reason', can be so even if the subjective element of the person's recognizing it or being able to act on it is missing. Likewise, one can have a moral claim even if there is no court of complaint to lodge the claim and even if the person with the claim is not able to make it herself.

We can go on to ask about the nature of the obligation rights impose. In what way are the actions of others constrained because of my rights? There are two traditional answers to this question and a lively debate continues between advocates of the competing views. On the one hand, there are those who argue that the function of rights is to protect the *choices* of the right-bearer. On the other hand there are those who argue that rights serve to protect the *interests* of the right-bearer. Note that the concept of a right (generically construed in terms of protections and constraints) is compatible with either a choice-protecting or an interest-protection conception. Indeed, it is also compatible with a mixed conception involving both choices and interests.[3]

Advocates of the choice conception of rights point to property rights as a paradigm example of rights protecting a choice. My right in something I own gives me the ability to control the fate of thing owned. I can keep it, sell it, throw it away, paint it purple, etc. The right consists in the protection of my choices regarding the owned object. Such protections need not be absolute. The choice conception is consistent with either thinking that rights protect my choices in all circumstances, no matter what else is at stake for others, or with the view that rights have thresholds and can justifiably be infringed when enough is at stake for others (Brennan 1995b). For example, my property rights normally entail that I can choose to lend my car to others or not but if a police officer is chasing down a suspect she may justifiably make use of my car without my permission. This is true also in wartime and other circumstances in which a great deal hangs in the balance. In cases of rights with thresholds, what the right would protect is a range within which I am free to choose. Once the rights threshold has been surpassed—say if there is enough at stake for others—my right could justifiably be infringed. This is perfectly compatible with saying that beneath the threshold the right serves to protect choice.

Advocates of the interest conception, of course, have their own favourite examples. Consider the rights which protect me from physical assault. This right is thought to be fundamentally about protecting my interests, not my choices, since I am not free to allow others to break my legs or kill me. Or at least I am not free to do so when such an action would substantially set back my interests. I can allow a surgeon to break my leg in order to reset a broken bone properly. On the interest conception I can allow others to bring about my death, say in a case of assisted suicide, if it is the case that my death would be a good thing for me. The assisted suicide case makes clear that what is called the interest conception actually includes some consideration of choice, for interest is not sufficient to justify killing me if I am able to have a say in the matter. So it is not that consent is irrelevant. Rather it is that consent on its own is insufficient. The action in question must also not set back my interests. Thus, my consent is not normatively decisive if I am allowing my leg to be broken as part of an initiation rite into a secret society or cult. In the case of physical assault, it seems clear that rights protect me even against my own ill-advised choices. Of course there are some problematic grey zone cases which fall somewhere in the middle. Personally I wonder about the moral legitimacy of boxing though I recognize my reaction to the sport is extreme. Even fans and defenders of boxing might baulk at a reality TV show which featured fights to the death with million dollar stakes.

However, it is equally clear that some rights do protect my choices even if I make choices not in my own interest. Returning to the property case, I can give away my home or sell my car for a dime, no matter how foolish such actions would be. In these sorts of cases the only sort of challenge to the legitimacy of the transaction one could raise would concern my decision-making abilities, that is, my rational capacity to consent. But this is a procedural concern, not a substantive one, since it focuses on my ability to choose rather than the content of my choices. So which is it, do rights protect my choices or do they protect my interests? There are numerous responses advocates of either competing conception can make to the other's favoured examples. The interest theorist can claim that in the property case choice is a way of protecting their interests, for example. But if we protect the interest by protecting the choice in this instance, why not also in the cases involving one's body?

Now it may be that our intuitive responses to these sorts of cases are not to be trusted. Perhaps there is nothing wrong, morally speaking, with consensual fights to the death. So one response to such cases consists in denying the validity of our moral intuitions or their relevance to deciding the issue at hand. Are there responses which seek to uphold the intuitive judgement that our rights do not protect choices such as the choice to risk one's own life in games of combat? One such response draws on the idea that rights are not absolute even when the benefits at stake are those belonging to the right-bearer herself.[4] We might also argue that legal restrictions against such activities are justified even in the face of valid moral rights which protect such choices. This argument would, in its most plausible form, focus on the circumstances in which such choices are made and raise worries about the legitimacy of consent in such contexts. For example, if most applicants for a US television version of 'Battle to Death for a Million Bucks' turned out to be very poor with sick family members in need of expensive medical therapies this ought to sound alarm bells about coercion.

But before we end up too far embroiled in debates between the choice theorist and the interest theorist, I want to return us briefly to somewhat duller territory. That is, I want to make a few clarifying remarks regarding what the debate between the choice conception and the interest conception is not about. It is not primarily a debate over which sorts of rights there are, positive or negative. Many of the examples given by benefit theorists are rights to some good or other, and most rights given as examples by choice theorists are negative rights. However, protecting my choices may sometimes require others to do something and securing my interests may sometimes require nothing more than leaving me alone. Likewise, this debate is not primarily about the foundations of rights, though some proponents of the positions discussed hold the views they do because of commitments at the foundational level. There is a related debate concerning the nature of the foundations of rights but it is not what is at stake in this debate. Instead, the choice conception and the interest conception are put forward as competing accounts of what rights *are*, as analyses of what it is for a thing to be a right. They offer competing accounts of the necessary and sufficient condition of a thing's being a genuine right.

To recap, according to the choice theory, all rights consist in the protection of an individual's choice. What is central to a thing's being a genuine right is the ability it confers upon the right-bearer to waive or demand its enforcement. According to the interest theory, all rights consist in the protection of an individual's interests. Thus, the choice theory will deny that a right's potential to protect an interest of an individual is sufficient for an individual to hold the right in question and the interest theory will deny that a right's potential to protect an individual's choice is sufficient for an individual to hold the right in question (Kramer *et al.* 1998: 62).[5]

As analyses of a concept, the choice theory and the interest theory set out to do two things. The first task is descriptive, getting it right about what we mean by rights. In this mode, analysts of a concept ask 'Is *this* how we use the term or is *that* how we use it?' But there is also a second task. Having arrived at a correct analysis, we are now in a position to sort out correct usages of the term from the incorrect, to sort out purported instances of rights into the genuine and the spurious.

In the volume *A Debate over Rights: Philosophical Inquiries*, Matthew Kramer, Nigel Simmonds, and Hillel Steiner take on this issue of the choice theory versus the interest theory of rights, with Simmonds and Steiner arguing for the choice theory and Kramer advocating on behalf of the interest theory. What is interesting in this collection of essays and rejoinders is only partly the debate about the nature of rights. It is also noteworthy for another debate which cuts across the first. How is the debate between the choice theory and the interest theory to be decided? What sorts of considerations are relevant? Kramer and Steiner argue that the relevant considerations are purely formal. No substantive moral or political views can inform our judgement about which account of rights is correct. Or at the very least these evaluative assumptions should be kept to an absolute minimum. In the next section of the chapter we will see how this view, combined with the choice conception, leads Steiner and some other choice theorists to deny that children have rights.

The Argument from Choice to No Rights for Children

What is the connection between the debate regarding what it is that rights protect and the debate over whether children have rights? Arguing against the choice, or will, theory, Matthew Kramer writes:

One of the most arresting theses to which the Will Theory commits its upholders is the verdict that children and mentally incapacitated people have no rights. Because infants and mentally infirm people are both factually and legally incompetent to choose between enforcing and waiving their claim against others, and because children older than infants are legally incompetent and sometime factually incompetent to engage in enforcement/waiver decisions they hold no powers to make such decisions. Now, given that the Will Theory insists that claims must be enforceable and waivable by claim-holders if the claims are to count as rights, it leads to the conclusion that the young and the mad do not have any rights. (Kramer *et al.* 1998: 69)

Neil MacCormick similarly argues against the choice theory of rights on the grounds that it cannot accommodate children's rights. MacCormick uses the rights of children as a 'test case' to demonstrate the adequacy of competing theories of rights. MacCormick proceeds from what he calls a 'simple and barely contestable assertion: at least from birth, every child has a right to be nurtured, cared for, and if possible, loved until such a time as he or she is capable of caring for himself or herself' (1982: 154–5). He argues that we must either abstain from ascribing rights to children or abandon the choice conception of rights. His own position is that we should abandon the choice theory.

But the argument sometimes goes the other way. Some of those who argue against the existence of children's rights do so by appeal to the choice theory of rights. Wayne Sumner, for example, writes that 'on any plausible analysis of agency the choice model will deny rights, on logical grounds, to inanimate objects, plants, non-human animals, fetuses, infants, young children and the severely mentally handicapped' (1987: 203). Since Sumner thinks the role of rights play is protecting one's ability to manage one's life for oneself, it is, he thinks, no great shock that people or things who lack the ability to be self-planners also lack rights. Of course, it does not follow from the denial of rights that there are no moral obligations owing to children, only that the correct explanation of these duties cannot rest in their possessing rights.[6]

This is yet another instance of the phenomenon that one person's modus ponens is another person's modus tollens, for it is argued either that:

1. If the choice theory of rights is correct, then children cannot have rights.
2. The choice theory of rights is correct.
3. Children cannot have rights.

Or that:

1. If the choice theory of rights is correct, then children cannot have rights.
2. Children do have rights.
3. The choice theory of rights is not correct.

Both arguments assume that it follows from the choice theory that children cannot have rights but they disagree about what conclusion we should draw from this. What is the argument for the shared premiss, premiss 1? What about the choice theory of rights precludes children from having rights? It cannot be that children are unable to make choices. This is true with infants and very young toddlers but children beyond age 2 not only make choices but are able to communicate very loudly just what those choices are. ('I want to wear the dirty dinosaur t-shirt inside out.'[7]) Notice that, in the quotation from Kramer, he switches from 'infants' to 'young children' and then again to 'the young'. If the inability to choose were the only reason that the choice theory blocked children from having rights, then only infants would be left without rights. Another issue Kramer raises is the legal competence of children to enforce their rights. However, legal competence is a bit of a red herring if it is moral rights we are talking about. The language of moral rights is often posed as a criticism of existing standards of legal justice. Further, we can imagine steps the legal system might take to allow children to pursue their claims. There are, in some states and provinces, advocates for the mentally and phys-ically disabled. In Ontario, for example, there is a provincially appointed and paid Children's Lawyer who represents the interests of children in a variety of cases where their interests are thought to diverge from other parties involved in a legal dispute.[8] While the official mandate of the Children's Lawyer is framed in terms of children's interests, one could imagine a more activist version still which allowed children to initiate legal proceedings or otherwise pursue their choices in legal matters.

It seems to me that the main reason speaking against rights which protect children's choices is that often children do not choose well or wisely. There are two ways to think of this problem, one which focuses on the end results of children's choices and another which looks at their process of choosing. The difficulty cannot lie just in the content of their choices since adults too frequently make bad choices. The problem must be with children's capacity for choosing. Here choosing cannot just mean 'stating a choice' since children can state choices. There is more to choosing than merely stating a choice. It is in the process by which the choice is made that children go wrong.

In *Against Equal Rights for Children* (1992) Laura Purdy argues that chil-dren are lacking in rationality, the capacity for long-term planning, and in self-control. She is against assigning equal rights to children, on the grounds that so doing would not protect children's interests (given the inferior ratio-nality and self-control of children). Purdy does not take up the distinction between the choice conception of rights and the interest conception of rights but her work is relevant to the debate, for her argument against equal rights for children rests on children's inability to make good choices. Rights like those of adults, if assigned to children, will fail to protect children's interests. Purdy's main opponent is the child libertationist who thinks of children as having all the same rights as adults. Nothing in Purdy's work suggests that children cannot have rights which protect their interests. Purdy's own 'protective rights' fall into this category. Once one considers the possibility that children might have rights which protect their interests, it follows from this view that it is impossible for the assignment of children's rights to go against their interests.

It is the 'Equal' in the 'Equal Rights' of Purdy's title that I think needs emphasis. In the case of adults Purdy assumes that their rights protect choices and thus if children had rights equal to those of adults they would have rights that protected their choices.[9] Purdy distinguishes her position from the stronger no-rights-at-all-for-children view. Purdy's claim is that, if one accepts that there is at least one protective right which restricts children's liberty, which applies only to children and not to adults, then one has rejected the equal-rights-for-children thesis. And so we can accept all of her arguments regarding the ways in which children's choosing can go wrong and still allow that children have rights. In the end it turns out to be consistent with Purdy's view then that children might have rights that protect their interests.

Purdy is not alone thinking about children's rights without addressing the distinction between choice-protecting rights and interest-protecting rights. Howard Cohen, a child-libertarian defender of children's rights, constructs his defence in terms of children's abilities to 'borrow capacities' in order to make choices (Cohen 1980). Children can and do have rights on Cohen's view but the abilities required to exercise those rights must be borrowed from others. Just as an adult engages an accountant to do her books, so too children engage those with right-bearing skills to assist in the exercise of their rights. And so Cohen agrees with Purdy that children lack some of the capacities required to be a right-bearer (where rights protect choices) but he thinks that this is no impediment to assigning them rights. Where needed they can borrow the abilities of others to choose. Cohen's work also assumes that rights protect choices and thus begs the question against interest theory. Cohen's defence of children's rights is weak because of this and I find it striking that it is Cohen's version of rights-for-children upon which most critics of children's rights draw.

How is it that children make bad choices? Let me describe two sorts of ways that children's choosing goes wrong. First, children's choices frequently fail to reflect stable, long-term preferences. The child who loves skating today may hate it tomorrow; the child who will only wear purple today will tomorrow only wear pink; and so on. Second, the ways in which children change represent a gradual change to becoming the sort of being who is able to have stable, long-term preferences and can reflect critically and rationally upon them. Consider what the moral world would be like if children remained children— that is, if there were beings about with permanent and varied rational capacities. In such a world the problem of what to do about children's choices would be a different sort of problem. Our worries with children are partly concerns about identifying the right unit for moral protection: the person the child is now or the person the child will become. Lumping entirely for the future person seems to ignore the very real person in front of us now. Rights protect persons but is that the person-at-a-time or the person-over-a-life-time?[10] With adults, where rights protect choices, we make this a problem for theorists of rational choice to decide and for rational choosers to decide for themselves, but we do this assuming that adults have pretty stable interests over a lifetime. With children, even if we do favour the future person it is not clear we do that best by ignoring the current person's expression of prefer-ences. We want to teach our children to be good choosers and we do that, in part, by letting them try out the business of choosing.

In recognition of the balancing we do between young children and the adults they will become, Hugh LaFollette draws a distinction between two different kinds of autonomy—descriptive autonomy and normative auton-omy. In the case of children 'descriptive autonomy' refers to children's voli-tional and intellectual abilities and 'normative autonomy' concerns questions of how parents and the state ought to treat children (LaFollette 1999: 139). This distinction allows LaFollette to account for the phenomenon of treating children autonomously even when they lack some of the relevant abilities, for, on his view, it is a mistake to equate normative autonomy with descriptive autonomy. LaFollette advocates granting children 'circumscribed normative autonomy' for reasons similar to the ones I have presented. He writes: 'We must train children to become autonomous, and that requires, among other things, that we treat them in some respects as if they already were autonomous' (1999: 139).

LaFollette's model of autonomy gradualism shares certain features with the rights gradualism I am advocating. His model of circumscribed autonomy contains different stages of autonomy for children, ranging from administered autonomy (in this case the choices are more apparent than real since the parent is always ready to step in) to minimally constrained autonomy (here the parents step in from time to time but only infrequently and the parents are willing to allow their child to make more serious errors and live with the results) (1999: 149). This model works well for parents and other close care-givers but not so well for freedoms which require the state's protection. As parents we allow our children to take on freedoms and responsibilities and then evaluate how they are faring, but such evaluation may be beyond the scope of government institutions. Thus, some legal rules may need to be applied on the basis of coarse lines even if the moral facts are more complex.

Consider the case of teenage children and alcohol consumption. Setting a drinking age at 18, 19, or 21 will inevitably be too restrictive for some young adults, given their cognitive and emotional abilities, but not restrictive enough for others. Still, the state must draw a line somewhere and thus the result is that individuals who were too young to drink one day can buy out the liquor store the next. Parents can enjoy a more individualized and nuanced approach, such as allowing a child to choose wine with family meals at one age, and then supervised consumption of alcohol with friends at another, adjusting the rules to fit the child and the circumstances. Significantly, parents often undertake this process prior to the point of the legal drinking age to prepare their child for the right to purchase and consume alcohol. The option of setting rules more restrictive than the state laws does not exist in most places since the legal age for drinking is equivalent to or surpasses the age at which children can simply leave home. What we want to see as parents is that our children are ready to make choices of their own. This is a sensitive business and it is an aspect of parenting fraught with the possibility of error—too much interference and protection and our children do not learn to take risks or to chance failure, too little and they make some very bad choices which affect their lives for years to come. Parents need to balance the child's status as chooser and future chooser against what is at stake for the child.

Children's Rights and Children's Choices

What is the alternative to conceiving of children's rights solely in terms of protected choices? Well, children's rights might also protect their interests. As an example, consider children's rights regarding education. One main component of education rights for children consists in the right to some standard of education or other. Such a right is primarily about protecting children's interests, not their choices. A child has the right to an education but such a right does give the child choices about whether or not to undertake the process of education. But as a child matures and acquires the capacity to choose, children's educational rights may well also protect their choices. The change in what the right protects occurs gradually, over time, and will depend on the local context. To the horror of many parents, children at a certain grade level are often free to choose their own courses—to drop mathematics in favour of cultural studies, to drop all physical education courses in favour of more free time for friends. At another stage, children, now young adults, are given the right to end their schooling altogether.

Wayne Sumner, arguing from the perspective of the choice theory, recognizes that since the capacities to plan and choose are acquired gradually, so too children acquire rights in a gradual fashion. As I have discussed, parents may choose to give children certain freedoms on a trial basis and re-evaluate later how well they fared exercising this freedom. But the choice theory would seem to commit us to the view that, prior to this acquisition of choosing skills, children have no rights. This seems to me to be false. I see no difference between an adult and a child when it comes to rights against physical harms.[11] And I am not so bothered that a justification of *that* right may have to proceed in terms of interests, for this was true also of adult right-bearers. Adult right-bearers, recall, cannot waive altogether their right not be harmed when doing so would be very much against their interests. Of course, one could always say that one had waived this right but the point is that, in some cases, doing so would have no moral force. This is true also of the very young child who says he waives his rights to an education.

The picture I prefer is one in which children move gradually from having their rights primarily protect their interests to having their rights primarily protect their choices. This reflects the transition of the child from being a creature whose interests are of moral concern, and hence deserve the protection of rights, to being a creature who can choose for herself. A child's right to education is one example of how a right can change its content from protecting interests to protecting choices. We could also apply the gradualist account to a child's right to care and nurturance which for very young children is a right protecting a child's interest in being well loved and cared for. For older children the right plausibly protects some elements of choice for the child in terms of who provides the care. If the gradualist account of rights is correct, then children and adults will both be protected by rights but there will be important differences between the rights of adults and the rights of children in terms of what it is the right protects.[12]

The Gradualist View Defended

How might one defend the gradualist view? Neil MacCormick argues for the reconciliation of choice-protecting rights and interest-protecting rights through a commitment to a common foundation for rights of both sorts. If the true role of rights is to promote or protect the interests of persons, argues MacCormick, then rights will sometimes protect interests directly and rights will sometimes protect choices. Whether a right protects one's interests or one's choices will depend on which form of protection best advances one's interests. Rights protect choices when having one's choices protected is just what is in one's interest and rights protect interests directly when it is having those interests protected, rather than one's choices, that best promotes one's interests.

It is no surprise that having interest protection as a goal will lead to interest-protecting rights. But why would interest protection lead to choice protecting rights? The utilitarian-liberal defence of rights which protect choices is that adults typically do a better job of choosing for themselves than having others choose for them. According to this line of argument, choice-protecting rights are justified on instrumental grounds. Choices are protected as a means to promoting interest advancement. MacCormick attributes this line of reasoning to Mill and presents it as an explicitly liberal account of rights. Children, then, are an exception to a general rule, for children, along with the mentally incapacitated, are not the best judges of what is in their interests (MacCormick 1982: 165).

I worry about this strategy for grounding rights claims generally. Part of my concern is that the protection of interests does not seem to me to be the correct way to ground rights claims. It seems like the wrong sort of foundation. I am also worried that it is not likely to be a successful foundation for rights since it just seems to me to be false on many issues that people best promote their own welfare by choosing for themselves. However, the consequentialist defender of the gradualist account of rights need not rely on MacCormick's argument. There may be consequentialist reasons for protecting adults' rights to choose other than the claim that individuals are the best judge of what is in their interests.

The second consequentialist line of argument for the gradualist account of rights is compatible with the claim that people are not always the best judges of their interests. Indeed, while I have separated these arguments out into three distinct strands, it is common for consequentialist defenders of rights to rely on more than one of these arguments. Instead of focusing on the value of autonomous choosing in terms of its success in promoting interests, the second argument notes that people most always care about choosing for themselves. Mature persons usually have an independent desire to choose for themselves that is consistent with it being true that people in fact make choices that go against their other interests. We would rather make our own mistakes, in some cases, than have someone else choose for us, even if that other party would do a better job. (For example, the argument in favour of arranged marriages that they have higher rates of success is rarely convincing. Whether or not the claim is right, and by what standard success is measured, the argument seems beside the point. In the arena of personal relationships we place a high value on making our own choices even if we think that there is a greater chance we will make mistakes.) The independent desire to choose for oneself tips the scale in favour of rights which protect choices being the best way to protect the interests of adult persons. Again, this will depend on the truth of certain claims about persons and choosing. In order to see if this view can bear the weight of accounting for rights which protect choices we will need to know (at least) how strong the desire for choosing for oneself usually is, how far adults get it wrong when they do make choices which do not reflect their interests, and how to weigh the relative importance of these two factors. Again, this seems to me to be a shaky foundation from which to make claims about rights.

The third consequentialist line of argument for the gradualist account of rights counts choosing itself as part of what is good for persons, whether or not individual persons believe this to be so. On this way of thinking choosing is not only valuable on instrumental grounds, it is also an intrinsic good, valuable whether or not a person desires to make his or her own choices and whether or not it leads to the enhancement of an individual's subjective welfare in other ways. On this view, choosing is good in itself and is not merely worthy of protection, on instrumental grounds. In what sense would choosing be good for persons if it did not help advance their other desires and it is not valued for its own sake? The account of interests which included choosing in this way would have to be a fairly objective version of interests, where what is good for me is at quite a far remove from what I want for my life. My sense is that this kind of argument will not suit consequentialists who focus on welfare as the thing to be maximized. Again, I worry about grounding rights on consequentialist foundations. This worry remains even when the consequentialism includes an objective account of the good to be promoted.

To recap, MacCormick's view about children's rights is a gradualist one in that children will progress from having their interests protected by rights to having their choices protected as they become better able to judge what is in their interests. However, MacCormick's account of why rights work in this way depends upon a consequentialist grounding for rights and I have raised worries about each of the three ways in which a consequentialist might argue for choice-protecting rights. So while I find the outcome of MacCormick's reconciliation of the two kinds of rights attractive, I have worries about the consequentialist strategy of grounding rights in the promotion of interests.

The formalists in the debate between the interest theory and the choice theory will not like MacCormick's proposed solution either. Here is the worry: participants in the debate between the interest theory and the choice theory claim that what they are offering are competing analyses of the concept of a right, competing accounts of what it is for a thing to be a right. It is claimed that this debate is independent of foundational considerations regarding what it is that grounds any particular assignments of rights. But MacCormick's proposed solution moves the debate to a different level for, on his account of the interest theory, interests are not themselves what rights protect. Instead, most of the time rights will protect choices and the consideration of interests plays a very different role. So MacCormick's answer works but I am not sure it counts as an answer to the original problem. It succeeds by broadening the scope of the debate between the interest theorist and the choice theorist.

How then might we proceed? My own suggestion retains the focus on choice and choosing but looks at children as would-be choosers. We can view the transition from childhood to adulthood as the gradual transition from being the sort of being who has interests but not the ability to protect them oneself to becoming a full-fledged autonomous chooser. We can think of the infant and the rational, mature adult at two ends of this extreme but many of the interesting questions and issues arise with children whose abilities are in between. One way debates about children's rights can go wrong is by failing to pay sufficient attention to the messy but morally important stages of middle childhood. This transition is never complete for even in the case of fully autonomous adults there are some choices their rights do not protect (as in the case in which a great deal of one's welfare is at issue).

Some worries remain. A feature of the gradualist account is that rights protect children's interests. Now young children are not the only sorts of creatures with interests but not the ability to choose well for themselves. Animals too fall into this category. Indeed, this suggests a common line of criticism against the interest theory of rights. Some charge that the interest theory is too expansive, assigning rights willy-nilly, wherever interests exist, and thus cheapening the currency of rights claims. Since my gradualist account also allows for the protection of interests by rights, this charge could be levelled at it as well. I think there are two different, but both plausible, lines of response one might give. First, it may be that animals also deserve to have their interests protected by rights. This does not seem so controversial if one thinks about the interests animals have in not experiencing pain and suffering. Second, it may be that the future of children as fully autonomous persons is enough to distinguish between animals and children. That is, it may be that the reason we protect children's interests with rights is because of the status they enjoy as future autonomous choosers. This would draw a line between most children and animals. I say 'most' because of the existence of children whose future does not hold autonomous choosing. There are children with severe disabilities who will need their interests, rather than their choices, protected for their entire lives. I am reluctant to deny that such children are rights-bearers. Hence, my own inclination is to extend interest-protecting rights to all children and animals. I think that is where the assignment of rights ends since I do not think that environmental objects—trees, mountains, rivers, etc.—have interests, but the argument for that claim would take us far beyond the scope of this chapter.

Another feature of my gradualist account is that the rights of adults protect their choices. As children acquire the ability to choose, their rights will change from protecting interests primarily to protecting primarily choices. But what is so special about choice? I expressed some nervousness earlier about the claim that choosing is part of a person's objective good. I was even more sceptical of the claim that people do a good job of choosing in terms of successfully promoting their interests. If choice is not good for persons, then what makes it worthy of the special treatment of rights? I think this question gets the issues backwards. It is not that choice is special. Rather, the way we must treat other rational adults involves a set of constraints which follows from the sort of creatures we are. Asking about the goodness of choosing puts the ball too squarely in the consequentialist's court. Not all questions about ethics reduce to questions about value. As Judith Thomson puts it: 'There is more to morality than value: there are also claims. And it is not because a claim infringement has a negative value that we ought not to infringe claims. We ought not to infringe claims—when we ought not to infringe them—because of what a claim is' (1990: 148).

Conclusion

I hope to have shown in this chapter that the relationship between the debate between the choice theory of rights and the interest theory of rights and the debate concerning whether children have moral rights is not as simple as participants in these debates have assumed. In place of both the interest theory and the choice theory, I have suggested a gradualist conception of rights which includes protections for interests and choices. What do we say to the existence of both rights which protect choices and rights which protect interests? Since both the choice theory of rights and the interest theory purport to be offering necessary and sufficient conditions for the having of a right, it seems as if one of the two accounts must be wrong. If I am right that rights can protect choices and interests, then neither account is correct. Thinking about the case of children makes it clear to me that rights can protect interests even if rights for adults almost always protect choices.

In the final section of the chapter I presented some considerations in support of a gradualist conception. This included an examination of MacCormick's interest theory and the presentation of an alternative account. What is the difference between my gradualist view and MacCormick's? The main difference is that I do not want to say that choosing gets protected because of our interests—either our interests in choosing for its own sake or because we do a better job advancing our interests when our choices are protected. What my view has in common with MacCormick's is the idea that children move from having rights which protect their interests to having rights which protect their choices. The end result is that, although I think children have rights, I also think that the kind of rights children possess are significantly different in nature than the rights of adults.

Notes

I have many people to thank for their helpful comments on drafts of this chapter in its various stages. First, I need to thank Robert Noggle for his comments on very early drafts. I would also like to thank the audience at the Atlantic Region Philosophical Association meeting, particularly Sandra Bartky, Richmond Campbell, and Nathan Brett. Thanks also to Alistair Macleod for asking good, hard questions at the meeting of the North American Society for Social Philosophy where this chapter was read and to the editors of this volume, Colin Macleod and David Archard for their thoughtful questions and comments. Thanks are due as well to the Social Sciences and Humanities Research Council of Canada for funding the larger research project—'The Moral Status of Children and the Moral Limits of Parenting: A Threshold Rights Approach to Matters of Family Justice'—of which this chapter is part.
  1. A complete argument for the strong claim that children have rights and an account of the substantive content of children's rights is part of a larger project I am undertaking with Robert Noggle. See Brennan and Noggle 1997.

2. Joel Feinberg (1970) is the best known defender of the centrality of the activity of claiming to the possessing of a right. Elizabeth Wolgast (1987) details the criticism I have just sketched.

3. Peter Vallentyne suggested the possibility of the mixed conception.

4. See my 'Paternalism and Rights' (1994) for a general discussion of the question of how benefits to the right-bearer count towards overriding the same right bearer's right.

5. See Kramer *et al.* 1998: 62 for a statement of these in terms of necessary and sufficient conditions.

6. It is odd, I think, to find Sumner (1987) drawing the conclusion that children do not have rights from a commitment to the choice conception. The move strikes me as both under-motivated and theory-serving. Sumner is a welfare consequentialist. While consequentialists are not shy of theory-serving it is usually only in the case of consequentialism itself. All other components of their moral theories are usually justified on the basis of their contribution to the best results.

7. It is this very phenomenon—with my own then 3-year-old daughter—that made me think there might be a market in buttons which read 'I chose my own clothes today.'

8. 'The Children's Lawyer of the Ministry of the Attorney General is responsible for representing children under the age of 18 with respect to their personal and property rights in the administration of justice. As provided for by law, the Office of the Children's Lawyer investigates, advocates, protects and represents the personal and property rights and obligations of persons, usually minors, under a disability at law in proceedings before the courts and tribunals of Ontario. Lawyers within the Office represent children in various areas of law, including child custody and access disputes, child protection proceedings, estate matters and civil litigation. Social workers prepare reports for the court in custody/access proceedings and may assist lawyers appointed by the Children's Lawyer to represent children in custody/access proceedings.' From the website of the Children's Lawyer, http://www.attorneygeneral.jus.gov.on.ca/html/OCL/oclhome.htm.

9. Purdy herself thinks people have misread the book when they view it as opposed to rights for children. The main aim of the book, writes Purdy, is to try to show that there are important morally relevant differences between children (defined generically) and adults (personal correspondence). Thinking about Purdy's book as focused in this way makes it less controversial. I also fear it makes it less interesting.

10. See Robert Noggle's chapter in this volume for further discussion of this issue. Noggle describes children as 'persons in progress'.

11. Sandra Bartky has raised the issue of whether children's rights ought to be stronger than a similar right held by an adult given that the long-term impact of negative treatment on children is likely to be much greater than the impact on an adult right-bearer. This point connects nicely with my view that the strength of rights can vary with the potential harm to the right bearer were the right infringed. See Brennan 1985*a*. If Bartky's claim is correct, and my view about the strength of rights is correct, then we have good reason for supposing that children's rights are stronger than similar rights held by adults.

12. Joel Feinberg's 'A Child's Right to an Open Future' (1980)—an important contri-

bution to the contemporary debate about children's rights—argued that both children and adults have rights but that some of them differed in kind. Adult-only rights include the right to vote, to drink alcohol, to choose and practise one's own religion. There are also, on Feinberg's account, rights which both children and adults possess, such as the right not to be physically harmed. None of this is particularly controversial. Feinberg's main contribution was to argue that there are rights children possess in virtue of their status as children, 'rights in trust' or 'anticipatory autonomy rights' which protect the child's ability to make choices in the future.

5

Becoming versus Being:
A Critical Analysis of the Child in Liberal
Theory

Barbara Arneil

Liberal theory's main concern at its inception was to create citizens of a state rather than subjects of a king. The change of status is critical, and within such a theoretical context, children play an important role. If one is subject to the king, based on patriarchal authority, there is little distinction to be drawn between adult and child in political theory, for both are equally subject to the arbitrary and absolute rule of the monarch. As seventeenth-century theorists began to challenge this notion of absolute rule in favour of the citizen who consents to authority as the basis of political power, it became necessary to distinguish between those who have the rational capacity to consent to political authority and those who do not. One important distinction to be drawn was between the rational adult citizen and the non-rational child. Unlike other groups who lacked the reason to be citizens (servants, slaves, and wives), children of citizens ultimately have the potential to *become* citizens, as they develop their rational capacities, and ultimately enjoy the rights of citizenship. In this regard they are unique amongst those individuals barred from citizenship. Moreover they constitute a central challenge to patriarchy, because if children of citizens eventually grow up and enjoy the rights of citizenship, the authority of the father must, by definition, be limited. The subject child, *becomes* the adult citizen.

Thus, the role children play in early liberal theory is one of citizens in waiting, human beings who do not yet possess the necessary attributes of citizenship, namely reason, autonomy, and the capacity for having authority over oneself, but will possess them in the future. As such, children are potential bearers of rights, which they may exercise only when they have reached the age of reason. They are not ends in themselves but rather creatures in the process of development. If there is one word that might summarize the role of children in early liberal theory, it is that of 'becomings' rather than 'beings'.

Conceiving of children as 'becomings' with the potential rights of citizenship has enormous implications for the ways in which liberal theory has developed in relation to children, up to and including the introduction of children's rights theories. We shall begin by examining the very foundations of liberal theory in John Locke's *Two Treatises of Government*.[1] In his challenge to patriarchal authority we find the origins of both the child as 'becoming' and *subject* to the authority of his/her parents and an embryonic notion, through the doctrine of natural rights, of the child as *citizen*, or 'being'.

The Child as 'Becoming' in Liberal Theory

Becoming, as G.W.F. Hegel first noted, encompasses the contradictory notions of 'being' and the negation of 'being' simultaneously (Hegel 1967). Children in early liberal theory, as becomings, exhibit both of these characteristics. To the extent that they are *potential* rights-bearing citizens, with a kernel of rationality, they are beings; to the extent that they are irrational creatures they are the negation of their future adult forms. These contradictory states exist simultaneously within the developing child, as he/she progresses from the latter to the former. There are three aspects to the idea of 'becoming' that we shall explore in more depth. Becoming, almost by definition, is defined by the end product, by the particular 'being' that one is to become. Anything described as 'becoming' is being viewed from the perspective not of what it currently is, but what it will be in the future. Thus the first aspect of children in liberal theory which must be examined is the specific end to which they are directed, namely the nature of liberal citizenship. The second aspect of becoming is the process by which one reaches that end goal, a subject largely subsumed under theorizing about education. The third aspect of 'becoming' is the scope of children included and excluded by the process. Each of these aspects, *the end product, the process,* and *the scope* of 'becoming' will be analysed in turn.

The End Product of Becoming

For Locke, children are used to undermine the patriarchal theory of authority defended by Sir Robert Filmer, who famously argued, in his defence of an absolute monarchy, that the child is subject to his father for his entire life, as the Englishman is absolutely subject to the monarch. Locke will make the case that both forms of authority are limited, the former is limited by the age of the child, the latter by the natural rights of the governed. For Locke, as the child reaches the age of reason and *becomes* an adult, he is no longer subject to his father.[2] The *product*, for Locke, is the rational citizen or property owner, who has the reason and knowledge to consent to the authority of the state to pass laws and collect taxes. Locke explicitly states that the objective of child development, under the parent's tutelage, is 'the use of Reason, or a state of

Knowledge wherein they may be suppose capable to understand that rule, whether it be the law of nature or the municipal law of their country they are to govern themselves by: Capable . . . to . . . live, as Free-men under that Law'. Only when one is rational can one exercise the right to liberty and property. Thus, rights are inextricably linked to the capacity for reason, and any interest in the development of the child is consequently focused on their emerging rationality.

An important aspect of viewing children from the perspective of the citizens they are about to become is that they are defined in terms of what they lack. Children, in Locke's *Two Treatises*, are described alternatively as existing 'in the *imperfect* State of Childhood' (as opposed, presumably to the 'perfect' state of adulthood), or in a 'nonage' (ii. 58). Such descriptions are familiar to feminist critics of Western political thought. If male adults are taken as the reference or end point from which to measure women and children, it is not surprising that both groups are found wanting. More importantly, children are not simply defined as *lacking* certain qualities in the descriptions above; they are constructed as the *opposite or negative form* or the adult. Children ultimately function as a mirror in liberal theory within which to reflect a negative image of the positive adult form.

The Process of Becoming

Given the focus on intellect and 'reason', it is not surprising that the main process by which the citizen is created in liberal thought is *education*. Ultimately, education becomes the central focus of Locke's political theory, and much liberal theory (and practice) to follow, with regard to children. Education continues to be the major way in which the liberal state and child intersect, and perhaps the only way in which the liberal state is universally involved in children's lives. The obligations of parents and society to children are often simply reduced to their education. John Eekelaar comments: 'While children are resident with their parents, the law imposes no duty on the parents to fulfill the develomental interests, apart form ensuring their education' (1986: 173). This singular focus on education creates a tendency in contemporary liberal democracies for childen's interests, as a whole, to be represented by Ministers and Ministries of Education within the state. The public education system is the foundation around which the public 'care' of children is built. Thus, one can find 'after-school' care for the hours outside of school time, a patchwork of pre-school care for children not yet in school, and 'school preparedness' touted as the most valuable goal of nursery education.[3]

Locke argues, consistent with the objectives of child development discussed above, that the main duty of parents towards their children is education towards rational autonomy. 'The Power than that Parents have over their Children arises from that Duty which is incumbent on them, to *take care* of their Offspring during the imperfect state of childhood. *To inform the Mind,* and govern the Actions of their yet ignorant nonage, till Reason shall take its place' (ii. 58; my emphasis).

It is critical to recognize in this quotation that Locke transforms 'taking care' of children to 'informing the mind'. Locke believes that education of the mind is the *key* responsibility of the father, although it may be delegated to others. 'The first part then of Paternal Power, or rather duty . . . is Education . . . [but] a Man may put the Tuition of his Son in other hands' (ii. 69). Thus, at the very foundation of liberal theory, the *care* of *children* is translated, by Locke, to mean the *education* of *sons*. This seemingly simple and obvious translation (at least to Locke) has profound implications for all subsequent liberal theory. The question of how to care for children (beyond educational needs) is lost to liberal theory from this point onwards. The development of children beyond the intellectual dimension (namely physical, social, or emotional development), or the extent to which the state might be concerned with their care, is simply written out of liberal theory at its inception. It is not that Locke is unaware of the broader caring and development needs of children. Rather, given that the singular objective is to produce 'rational citizens', the process of producing such creatures makes such questions simply, but utterly, irrelevant to liberal political theory.

Other forms of care are excluded from liberal analysis on three grounds, all linked to the original foundations of liberal citizenship. First, the broad care of children was of no concern to early liberal thinkers because it belonged to the private, as opposed to public sphere. Thus while education had a public interest element, caring for children (especially pre-school age children) was a domestic matter. Secondly, the care of children was an organic or 'natural' phenomenon, the result of instinct, and therefore of little political interest. In other words, politics and education are worlds constructed through reason and language, cultural phenomena that need to be theorized in order to be properly constituted. Childcare, on the other hand, is a natural phenomenon that just happens according to instinct (in particular maternal instinct). Finally, the care of children fell outside of political theory because it was a largely female occupation. While men and boys need to be concerned with politics and education respectively, women's main concern was with domestic care. It is assumed, therefore, that girls, as future care-givers (as opposed to citizens) do not need to be educated or trained. The extent to which the public world of autonomous citizens engaged in pursuit of their own personal projects is dependent upon this invisible world of dependents and care-givers is simply left aside. All of these aspects of caring have, to a greater or lesser degree, survived through to the present day.

The separation between a public world of rights-bearing citizens and a domestic sphere of non-rights-bearing care-givers and their dependants is a critical distinction which has been analysed at length by feminist commentators (Pateman, 1988; Arneil, 2000). While early liberal thinkers initially ignored the domestic sphere, more recently, attempts have been made to break down this divide. Liberal feminists have used rights to empower women, arguing that the public sphere must be expanded to include women as citizens. More recently, children's rights theorists have made the same claims on behalf of children. Both of these schools of thought attempt to transcend the organic, domestic, and mainly female sphere of care-giving by expanding the scope of citizenship and autonomy to include those previously excluded. The problem, as we shall see, is that the private sphere of care and the interdependent relations within it, are fundamentally different from the rights-based ethic of the public world of the male citizen. As the latter transcends the former, the ethic of care and the relations between dependants and their care-givers is simply subsumed within the larger ethic of liberal justice without any consideration of what is lost as a result.

The Scope of Becoming

Finally, given the focus on rationality and autonomy as the goals of development, and education as the process by which to get there, children who are visible in liberal theory are limited to those of a school age. If you are pre-rational (as is the case with infants and pre-school children) you are of little interest to liberal theory and, as we shall see, the theorization of children's rights, particularly as it applies to the right of autonomy. The idea of becoming means that you have begun a process, that you share at least a modicum of what constitutes the full being of adult citizenship. Infants as irrational creatures are thus seen as pre-becomings or the full negation of the adult being. Infants are literally and metaphorically non-existent in liberal theory.

Children as Becomings: Conclusions

At the heart of liberal theory's treatment of children as 'becomings' are three central problems. The first is that, from Locke onwards, liberal theory has never looked at the political world from the perspective of the child, as beings in his/her own right from the point of birth. Instead, children have been used as tools through which the specific end products of particular liberal theories of politics may be explored. Thus, children are defined as future citizens, and are of increasing interest to the liberal theorist the closer they are to the age of reason. The specific goals of citizenship shape the way in which children are constructed, and the care of children begins and ends with their education to these ends. Ultimately, the individual child is largely a tool to illuminate the nature of the autonomous adult citizen by providing the perfect mirror within which to reflect the negative image of the positive adult form.

The second problem is the underlying view of society. Children are excluded as 'beings' from the larger community exactly because they do not have the entrance requirements necessary to belong to the political sphere. The liberal political community is actually an association. One must join the association by consenting to its rules and authority. In this sense the 'becoming' child is literally no part of the community to which he/she is born, until the hypothetical *moment* he/she is considered rational and can consent to its authority. Locke explicitly argues: 'a child is born a subject of no country or government. He is under his father's tuition and authority till he come to the age of discretion, and then he is a free man, *at liberty what government* he will put himself under, what body politic he will unite himself to' (ii. 118). This is a critical point, because political theories built on rights conceptualize the individual as a discrete entity (even in the case of a child) and the relations between people as contracts of mutual consent. Thus not only is the child a distorted image of the adult in liberal theory, but he/she is excluded at birth from belonging to this community until he/she can consent to it.

The third problem is the conception of the state. If individual rights are the basis upon which society is built, then the state's primary obligation is to preserve those rights. The state's role is either non-interference in the private sphere or to be the enforcer of contracts and rights. The state is thus fundamentally an authority to be circumscribed by such rights and contracts, to be engaged only when it is required by conflicts arising between individuals, and to intervene in the private sphere only as a last resort. Such a conception of the state, inherent in a theory based on rights, is problematic when applied to dependants and their care-givers, who will naturally see the state more as a potential resource than threat.

The goal, as stated at the outset, of Locke's political theory and liberal thought as a whole is to change the status of the individual from that of a subject to a citizen through the vehicle of rights. While adults are citizens, and children remain subjects in Locke's theory, the child enjoys the potentiality of citizenship. Children's rights theorists, who wish, in turn, to change the status of children and make them citizens, necessarily build upon this foundation, and the transcendence of the private sphere of care and dependence by the public sphere of autonomy and rights. By choosing the vehicle of rights to express children's needs, such theories ultimately import the conceptualization of the individual, state, and society implicit in liberal theory, as shall be discussed.

The Child as 'Being': Children's Rights Theories

Children's rights theorists have attempted to overcome the status of children as 'becomings', arguing that children, like adults, are 'beings' or in Kantian terms 'ends in themselves'. The underlying goal of these theories is highly laudable: to change the status of children and thereby improve their lives. While there are many different ways of looking at children's rights, most analysts make some kind of distinction between social and economic rights (to nurturance, care-taking, or provision and protection), *and* civil or political rights (to self-determination, liberation, autonomy, or participation) (Freeman 1983; Franklin and Franklin 1996; Wald 1979; Eekelaar 1986; Rogers and Wrightsman 1978; Archard 1993). I have broken my analysis of rights into three sets: the rights to provision, protection and autonomy. Taken together the first two sets of rights are the most basic for the child. Unlike the traditional Lockean rights, they *demand* the involvement of authorities in children's lives and consequently do not change the status of the child in relation to these authorities. Autonomy is the key to changing the status of children and consequently their transformation into 'beings'. Through the concept of autonomy, children's rights theorists most fully embrace the conceptualization of the individual, society and state described in early liberal theory. The implications of each of these sets of rights, the degree to which they are good tools for expressing children's needs, and the extent to which they improve children's lives will be explored at the conclusion of this section.

The Right to Provision

The first set of 'rights', to the provision of basic needs, such as food, shelter, adequate care and education, is unlike the more traditional liberal rights that serve to constrain or check authorities in individuals' lives. The right to provision *demands* the involvement of the state in a child's life. This basic distinction between political rights that constrain, and social or economic rights that expand the state has been explored by Isaiah Berlin in his famous article on positive and negative freedoms (Berlin 1969). Put simply, a negative right (consisting of political freedoms) *constrains* the state from interference; a positive right (to social goods) *requires the involvement of the* state to fulfil such rights. The positive nature of such rights has several consequences.

Given that some governments are unable or unwilling to expend resources as required by the right to provision, such social rights claimed on behalf of children are often seen as moral aspirations rather than enforceable entitlements. As Michael Wald comments: 'these claims generally are not for things traditionally thought of as legal "rights" . . . Courts cannot order that the world be free of poverty or that all children have adequate health care' (1979: 261). They are 'ideal' or what some have called manifesto rights, exactly because they cannot be made enforceable in the same way as negative rights. To put it bluntly, it is easier for courts to enforce the obligation for governments *not* to act than to enforce them *to act*, which is the essential difference between a negative and positive right, respectively.

It has been argued, however, that social rights could (and should) be enforced in the same way that political rights are, through a properly constituted court of law (Schabas, 2000). The question immediately arises as to whether or not courts should play the same role in relation to social rights as they do to political rights, and what the implications would be. Let us consider a child's right to basic necessities. A court, faced with the petition of a child who argued that his/her level of social assistance was a violation of his/her basic social rights, might judge that the state in question should be required to spend a given amount of money on specific welfare programmes for families with children. Enforcement of children's rights to provision could ultimately create a court-enforced legislative agenda for children. At first glance, such an idea seems appealing for it would harness the energy of both the court and the state in fulfilling the most basic requirements of children. However, it raises profound questions for a liberal democratic society that need to be addressed.[4]

First, a court-enforced right of provision would shift the political debate about the best way to care for our children from parliament to the courts, and consequently from citizens and their representatives to lawyers and their clients. Second, it would be impossible for a government to make the (currently popular) argument that the state should *not* be in the business of guaranteeing an income to families or that certain people should be denied welfare in order to force them to work. Such political solutions would be struck down by a court of law that must *require* the state itself to guarantee income, where the family fails to do so. Whether or not one agrees with such political views is not the point. The question is rather whether such views, embraced for example by Clinton's welfare reforms, should be permanently excluded from political debate by a court that must enforce a set of rights? My point here is that the decision as to whether or not social and economic rights entail an increased role of the state in children's lives is largely a political debate; one which should leave all options on the table, and involve all citizens and their representatives in the discussion. Enforcement, through a court of law, has the potential to curtail such possibilities and ultimately may limit our capacity to meet the needs of children and their parents over the long term.

A second consequence of the positive nature of these rights (that governments or parents *must act*, as opposed to refraining from acting) is that they are probably better expressed directly as obligations of these authorities than as derivative obligations from a more fundamental set of rights. Freeman concedes: 'Much talk about rights is really talk about obligations and that perhaps it might be better if the sort of discussion found in the "manifesto literature" were couched in terms of duties rather than by reference to rights' (1983: 37). As Onora O'Neill argues, if obligations are only derivatives of rights, there may be certain kinds of important obligations to children, what O'Neill calls imperfect obligations, which cannot be expressed through a corresponding right. As such, if rights are taken as the starting-point of children's interests, such imperfect obligations will be left unexpressed (1989: 190–1). One crucial example that she gives is the obligation to be 'kind, considerate and involved' in our interactions with children. It is hard for 'rights based approaches to fully account of ways in which children's lives are particularly vulnerable to unkindness, lack of involvement cheerfulness or good feeling. Their lack may be invisible from the perspective of rights' (p. 192). O'Neill's point is that providing children with the basics of life is a necessary but not sufficient condition of 'caring' for children. They also require a disposition from adults that is caring, attentive and kind: an imperfect obligation that may be absolutely fundamental to the well-being of a child but nearly impossible to express as a positive right.

Finally, *children's* social and economic rights are unique because, unlike autonomous adults, they *must* depend on others for their basic needs. This set of 'rights', it can be argued, takes us in a direction diametrically opposed to traditional liberal rights: underpinning, even expanding the strength of the dual authorities of parents and states in children's lives. Thus, the right to provision not only does not change the status of children or empower them; it actually reinforces the power of adults, exactly because it recognizes children as dependent on their good will. Wald comments:

> Providing children with adequate income or health care does not entail giving them more autonomy of self-determination, quite the opposite. Demands for such rights recognize that children cannot provide for themselves and need the care and guidance of adults. Thus, these claims might be better thought of as protections due, rather than rights of, children. (1979: 261)

Indeed, some commentators argue that the emphasis on this set of rights actually *increases* the power of the adult over the child. 'Welfare rights to care and education . . . strengthens the hold that adults have over children' (Wyness, 2000: 5–6) and Wald and Wyness both compare the right to provision with the rights to autonomy, where the former reduces and the latter increases the power of children. Ultimately, therefore, this set of rights, as fundamental as they are to the child's well-being, does not change, from the point of view of a children's rights theorist, the status of the child as a 'becoming' and subject to the dual authorities in his/her life. Another set of rights must be included to overcome their continuing status as subject.

The Right to Protection

The second set of children's rights, to protection from abuse, neglect, exploitation, and danger, *also* supports the authority of the family, and most particularly the state in children's lives. The state takes on the role of monitor to watch whether 'adults, especially parents, are actually harming children' (Wald 1979: 262). So much of the language in reference to the 'protection' rights of children is loaded with policing/state imagery of standards, surveillance, intervention, and intrusion. Freeman's own description of this set of rights concludes: 'All states set some standards for parental conduct. They are usually pitched minimally. The norm is parental autonomy, rather than state intervention. Recent events have, however, led to an increased state monitoring of the adequacy of parental care' (1983: 44).

Children's rights theorists are often the strongest advocates for the state as a monitor, intervening in the private sphere in order to take tough punitive measures against parents who abuse their children. While the idea of constraining an arbitrary or abusive power is consistent with liberal rights, the support for an increasingly powerful state to interfere in private family relations is not. The reconciliation of these two conflicting aims within liberal thought results in a particular relationship between parents and the state. In keeping with the liberal foundation of 'rights', the state steps in only when family relations have broken down, in order to police the family. This has one very important implication: namely, to put the family and the state in an adversarial relationship to each other. The liberal state is reactive and often punitive in its approach to children and their families. Parents, in turn, rather than seeing the state as a supportive agency available before problems arise, tend to see social welfare agencies as the enemy who become involved, by definition, only when they fail. Moreover, these agencies often carry with them the threat of criminal proceedings and courts. Once again children's needs, defined as rights, are ultimately mediated through an adversarial and hostile system of enforcement in a court of law.

Finally, this second set of rights, like the first, does not change the status of the child in relation to the authorities in his/her life. Franklin and Franklin comment: 'Rights to protection do not involve any changes to the status of children or offer them any greater autonomy or independence from parents or other adults; indeed on consequence of protection rights may be in some, but certainly not all cases, be to diminish autonomy rights' (1996: 100. See also Wald 1979: 263). The child's status remains that of a subject or 'becoming'.

Let us turn to explore the set of rights that does seek to change the status of the child, namely autonomy rights, which is therefore essential to children's rights theories. While the first two sets of right may be necessary, by themselves they are not sufficient to a fully developed theory of children's rights. This final set of rights involves both a call for greater autonomy for the child in the public sphere, and greater participation rights in the private sphere of the family. These rights are rooted in the early liberal attack by Locke on patriarchal authority, namely the notion that the child has some kind of potentially equal status to that of the adult (as opposed to the subordinate relationship implied by paternalism). The emphasis in the Hegelian dialectic shifts from the negation of being to being itself. At the heart of this last set of rights, therefore, is the attempt to change the status of children, from that of becoming to being, of subject to citizen.

The Right to Autonomy

Children's rights theorists' primary interest is ultimately in this category of rights, for one central reason. The rights to provision and protection, as already discussed, can all too easily be addressed within a traditional liberal framework, even within a paternalistic framework. As has been suggested, such rights do nothing to change the status of or empower children. Only through the notion of autonomy is the child given full expression as a 'being' or citizen rather than a 'becoming' or subject. Freeman comments:

To respect a child's autonomy is to treat that child as a person and as a rights-holder . . . it is clear that we can do so to a much greater extent than we have assumed hitherto . . . If we are to make progress we have to recognize the moral integrity of children. We have to treat them as persons entitled to equal concern and respect. (1992*b*: 65)

Thus, underlying children's rights theories is a sense that progress can be measured to the extent that society has moved from a recognition of the first two sets of rights to this third set of rights, both in the past and in the future. Freeman comments on this historical shift amongst child rights theorists: 'The emphasis shifted from protection to autonomy, from nurturance to self-determination, from welfare to justice' (1992*a*: 3). The first phase of protection and provision rights, he claims, was embraced by the 1959 UN Declaration of the Rights of Children. Freeman concludes that these 'rights' should not be seen as true 'liberties' at all. 'Although the preamble to the Declaration refers to rights and freedoms, the ten principles set out in it do not embrace children's liberties (or freedoms) at all' (1992*a*: 4). Other theorists argue that this trajectory also provides future direction to children's rights advocates. 'Hope must surely be that in ten years time there will be a fourth phase in the development of the Children's Rights Movement. In this next phase, children will be the key political actors, seeking to establish . . . their right to participate in a range of settings which extend beyond the social and welfare arenas' (Franklin and Franklin 1996: 111).

Michael Freeman defines autonomy as 'the idea that persons as such have a set of capacities that enables them to make independent decisions regarding appropriate life choices' (1992*b*: 64). Autonomy is the freedom to make choices over one's life, a freedom that is restricted for children by both parents and the state. Children's rights theorists argue that children's autonomy can only be recognized if they are given greater freedom to choose. Child liberationists, like Richard Farson and J.C. Holt, would claim that children should be as free as adults to choose their actions (Farson 1978; Holt 1975). As such, the only constraint on children would be the classical liberal restraint, applied in equal measure to adults, that one's actions cannot harm the rights or freedoms of another. Most children's rights theorists, however, would argue that, while children's freedom to choose and participate in decisions over their own life should be increased, the critical question in defining the level of autonomy for the child is their rational maturity. Unlike the rights of provision and protection, which embrace all of the various needs of children, the right to autonomy embraces a conception of children focused on their rational capacity.

Thus, autonomy rights for children return us to the underlying view of adults and children first articulated by John Locke in early liberal thought. The difference of course, is that children are perceived to be far more like adults than what Locke had originally suggested. By incorporating this model of child development into their theories, however, children's rights theorists import the same problems associated with the end product, process, scope, and view of the *polis* described earlier in Lockean theory. Let us examine these parallels in detail.

The end product for children's rights theorists, like Locke, is rationality. Thus, Freeman argues that intervention in children's decision-making is justified 'only to the extent necessary to obviate immediate harm [the classical liberal criterion], *or to develop the capacities of rational choice* [of] *the individual*' (1992*b*: 67). The 'capacity for rationality' argument is often expressed in terms of 'tacit' consent, namely the parent has tacit consent to intervene, because a fully rational adult would approve of the decision being made on his/her behalf as a child. Freeman summarizes this approach:

The question we should ask ourselves is: what sort of action or conduct would we wish, as children, to be shielded against on the assumption that we would want to mature to a rationally autonomous adulthood and be capable of deciding on our own system of ends as free and rational beings? (1992*b*: 67; see also Eekelaar 1992: 229)

Consequently, the process, like early liberal theory, is also focused on rational capacity. Competency to make decisions is measured by the extent to which the child can intellectually distinguish between choices. An example of this narrowly intellectual version of maturity would be the outrage of the British National Council of Civil Liberties 'at the fact that the brightest maths student of modern times is not permitted to vote'. As Judith Hughes comments: '[this anger is] comically misplaced. Being good . . . at mathematics is not dependent upon being mature; acting with political authority is' (1989: 46). Thus, the development of the child is often seen in narrow and instrumental terms, dictated by the requirements of adult liberal citizenship. There is no room in these theories for the organic or multifaceted nature of maturation, and the care required beyond education to guide this process.

Thirdly, the emphasis on autonomy by children's rights theorists limits the scope of their interest. Like Locke's 'pre-becomings', the infant or pre-schooler's interests have very little bearing on any discussion of autonomy rights. In both cases, the focus on rationality and adult rights allows a single-sentence dismissal of early childhood, as an area covered under the first two sets of rights. Some more radical theorists take a different tack and attempt to widen the scope of adulthood to include even very young children, but in all of these cases, the underlying premiss remains. Adults (and their autonomy) are the referent points from which children's rights shall be measured. The category of 'children' is expanded or contracted in accordance with the extent to which one sees rational capacity as a precondition for autonomous choices.

Finally, at the heart of the right to autonomy is a particular associational vision of human relations. In the associational model of politics, as first articulated in early liberal theory, individuals agree to join together for the purposes of mutual benefit. Entry into such an associational society is premissed on the notion of consent. Thus, Locke famously argued that children were *not* subject to the government they were born under until they reached the age of maturity and consented to this rule (ii. 18). It is this associational view of society, first introduced by Locke, which continues to underpin children's autonomy rights. The implications for children of an associational view of both the *polis* and family shall be considered in turn.

The associational view of society implies that people must consent in order to join and give authority to the state. Initial consent is the foundation of liberal theories from Locke to John Rawls. In each case the consent must be freely given by rational beings or, in the case of children, beings that have the capacity for rationality. The main problem with this view of society is that it excludes anybody who does not have the requisite skills to join, namely rationality. An alternative view of the *polis* would eliminate any kind of entrance requirements and create a community that incorporated all people, regardless of their capacity to consent. Thus, unlike Locke's associational *polis*, the community would include children from birth, and not wait for their consent to make them full members. Hughes comments: 'we clearly need to drop this obsession with initial consent . . . [and allow for] the beginning of a notion of community rather than association; one which has no need of entry qualifications but within which freedom and autonomy are partly discovered and partly created' (1989: 40–1).

A second implication of the associational view of society is the underlying supposition that it is made up of individuals, each with particular interests that can be analytically separated from those of other individuals. Indeed, society is ultimately no more than the aggregate sum of these interests, expressed as rights. Such a conceptualization of society tends to disaggregate individuals and groups of people from one another. Thus, it is necessary to separate analytically children from both their families and wider society. John Eekelaar comments: '[Children's] interests must be capable of isolation from the interests of others', most particularly parents' interests' (1986: 169). This analytical separation of the child from his/her community, while necessary to a rights theory based on interests, is difficult to reconcile with the dependent nature of children and the symbiotic character of their relationship to their care-givers. Indeed, the child suddenly looks suspiciously like the 'unencumbered individual', which lies at the heart of the communitarian critique of liberal thought (Sandel 1982; MacIntyre 1981; Taylor 1979). Waldron summarizes this general point of view:

The 'unencumbered' individual [is] free to shrug off his communal allegiances whenever he chooses. The relatively unaffectionate and formalistic language of rights and contract theory is said to be an expression of his essential detachability from affective commitments; its formalism expresses the facts deemed most important about his moral status, without reference to any content of community. (1993: 375)

If the 'unencumbered' individual is difficult to sustain when theorizing about adults, it is even more problematic when applied to a child. For children are even less detachable, even more in need of affective commitments, and affected in a more profound way by the context and culture within which they live and mature. Thus Sandel concludes about the unencumbered individual of liberal thought: 'To imagine a person incapable of constitutive attachments is . . . to imagine a person wholly without character, without depth' (1982: 179). Sandel's conclusion may hold true for an adult but for a child the issue goes far beyond character and depth to survival and growth. Exactly because children are dependent and growing beings, they can *only* be viewed as connected, in a constitutive sense, to their families and cultures. Thus, if one wishes to include children in society before they are autonomous, and to the extent that one sees children as particularly *encumbered* individuals, then the vision of the *polis* better suited to children is that of community rather than association, as shall be discussed in the next section.

Let us turn and consider the application of this concept of association to the other kind of 'societies' children find themselves in: families. It is possible to think of the negative rights of autonomy, as constitutive of family relations, producing what might be called the 'associational family'. By making rights constitutive, the family is conceived of as a society of rights-bearing self-interested individuals whose relations with one another are based on a complex series of claimed rights and obligations. The extent to which the family should be seen as an association of individuals as opposed to a community, and the degree to which the liberal democratic ethos of political life should be applied to the private sphere, is an important discussion, with enormous implications for children.

However, I would like to examine a narrower, and more challenging case made for the need for autonomy rights in the family, namely, that rights are nothing more than a fallback position should the ties of affection, care, and kinship fail. In this version, rights need not be constitutive of family life but can serve as an insurance policy should the affectionate bonds break (Waldron 1993; Archard 1993). This is the case Jeremy Waldron makes: 'I will consider how much of that attack would be mitigated or refuted if liberals were to concede that the structure of rights is not constitutive of social life, but is instead to be understood as a position of fallback and security in case other constitutive elements of a social relationship ever come apart' (1993: 374).

At first glance, this view of rights as an insurance policy seems to reconcile the need to retain the primary bonds of affection and care within the family with the requirements of justice that individuals are treated fairly. Waldron uses the break-up of the family through divorce as his example of when it becomes critical to apply rights to family relations.

Rights serve two purposes at such a juncture. The first is to ensure the provision of care and support. 'The function of matrimonial law, with its contractual formulas and rigid rights and duties . . . is to provide a basis on which ties of love can be converted into legal responsibilities in the unhappy situation where affection can no longer be guaranteed' (Waldron 1993: 382). The second purpose is to allow individuals to start new relations without being oppressed by existing bonds of family or community. 'The structure of impersonal rules and rights not only provides a background guarantee; it also furnishes a basis on which people can initiate *new* relations with other people even from a position of alienation from the affective bonds of existing attachments and community. Impersonal rules and rights provide a basis for new beginnings' (Waldron 1993: 376).

This view of rights is consistent with its Lockean foundations: leave the private sphere alone, unless there is a fundamental conflict or breakdown that requires intervention by the state. In some ways this version of rights as a fall-back to the (assumed) private, harmonious family is even more damaging to children's interests than the constitutive view of rights. By definition, this theory of rights envisions the family being left to itself *unless* there is such a drastic problem that the state must intervene. To put it another way, the issue of 'affection' is considered to be apolitical, either it is there naturally or it is not. Consistent with early liberal theory's demarcation of the domestic, female, natural sphere of care as something beyond the world of politics, no consideration is given to how the state or society might support, in any number of ways, familial affection or care, before the breakdown occurs. The state's purpose is explicitly to *enforce rights,* namely the right to care and support *after* the fact. Thus, the state, and ultimately the court of law, gets involved in families and children's lives only *after* the breakdown occurs, rather than being proactively involved in the care of children prior to that point. A constitutive rights theory of the family could, theoretically at least, involve the state, in the form of the child's representative, in the family prior to the actual breakdown. Such a scenario would introduce other kinds of issues but leaving children in bad family situations until the point of legal proceedings would not be one of them, as is the case with the 'insurance' policy scenario.

Secondly, this notion of rights introduces not only the state but also the courts into the lives of children and their parents, as they negotiate their rights in relation to each other during a time of crisis. Family law, as Waldron points out, is based on a set of contractual rights. If you are to enforce rights, you need to have a court of law to back them up. As it stands presently, divorce proceedings often involve two lawyers representing the interests of the husband and wife in an adversarial system of adjudication in which each tries to best the other, in order to secure the most favourable splitting of the assets and spousal support. The process becomes even more divisive and emotional when children are involved, especially where they are used to inflict pain on the other party. If one were truly to represent the rights of the child within the court, it would seem to follow that he/she should also have independent counsel. Indeed, Freeman argues that failure to include the child's right to independent representation in the UN Convention is a major failing. (1992*a*: 5). However, the idea that the provision of a lawyer to a child during his/her parents' divorce proceedings, which follows naturally from the Waldron insurance thesis, is a progressive step in the advocacy of children's interests is indicative of the poverty of this approach to real children's lives in such difficult emotional circumstances. To put children in an adversarial forum (which notoriously exacerbates differences and conflict between family members) is already highly questionable. To then suggest that such a situation would be improved if only the child had his/her own lawyer fails to recognize the dependency of the child within the family, before, during, and most importantly *after* the court hearing is over. The objective, from the child's point of view, is not simply to ensure his/her interests are recognized but, as far as possible, that the caring and affectionate relations between him/herself and other family members are sustained. Institutions must be specifically designed with such ongoing care as an objective if such proceedings are to fulfil this need.

This brings us to Waldron's second purpose in asserting the need for rights as an insurance policy for the family, namely, it would allow individuals to 'leave' an oppressive situation. Archard comments on this idea in relation to children: 'It may be important for a child to know that it does rightfully belong to a public realm with its rules, rights and duties and is not just the member of a private, if loving community' (1993: 93). Given the 'insurance policy' thesis, it is important to note that we are explicitly talking about when that loving community fails. In this situation, knowing that there is a public realm 'of rules, rights and duties' would be of little comfort. The point is that unlike adults, children do not have the same capacity to simply 'initiate new relations with other people . . . from a position of alienation' (Waldron 1993: 376). It is the very nature of children that they live in relationships with their parents which, barring extreme situations, they cannot leave. Thus, in the case of divorce they do not have the choice to leave both parents. Rather they often must *choose* between the two. To take children's views into consideration is, of course, an important part of the decision-making process in custody cases. However, to put children in the position of choosing between parents, the ultimate act of autonomy within the family (consistent with Locke's notion that children may ultimately choose the authority which governs over them) is unjust for two reasons. To ask children to resolve this issue, when the break-up of any marriage is the result of decisions made by the adults, is to place the burden of responsibility on the wrong shoulders. Secondly, it fails to recognize once again that the family is not just individuals living together in an association but a set of deep and intimate relations, which the child, as a dependant, must remain within even after he/she has been forced to reject one or other of his/her parents.

The Rights of Children: Conclusion

Children's rights theorists have very good reasons for advocating rights for children. Rights are ultimately moral trump cards (Dworkin 1978). If you want to take children's needs and interests seriously, and make claims on their behalf that will compete with any other moral claims, it is necessary to make such claims in the language of rights. It is clear that any non-rights moral claim simply does not carry the same weight in contemporary moral or political debate. Avigail Eisenberg comments: 'Rights function to protect the most important and basic values. Rights "trump" other non-rights claims that conflict with them. A central characteristic of liberal democracy is that it is committed to protecting rights first before addressing non-rights claims' (2001: 163).

Children's rights theorists' ultimate goal is to improve children's lives. Rights are seen as the moral trump cards or best tools to achieve this end. 'We can and must believe that the state of childhood will be *improved* if we are prepared to take children's rights more seriously' (Freeman 1992b: 53). It is this assumption, that rights lead to an improved life for children, that I wish to challenge. Rights have certainly been used by different groups of adults to change their status *and thereby* improve their lives. For example, liberal feminists and civil rights workers in the USA have used rights to empower and improve the lives of women and African Americans, respectively. We should not, however, assume that the same holds true for children, because children are different, their needs are unique to the particular nature of their existence, and the approach of the 'authorities' (namely their care-givers) take to their emerging independence is different. As O'Neill comments: 'The crucial difference between . . . childhood dependence and the dependence of oppressed social groups is that childhood is a stage of life, from which children normally emerge and are helped and urged to emerge by those who have most power over them' (1992: 39).

Most importantly, while the concept of 'rights' has been extraordinarily elastic, it cannot escape its origins. Nor can the theorists who use it to anchor their claims. As such, a rights-based argument is ultimately concerned with a change in status for the individual, a state committed to the principles of both non-interference and enforcement (when necessary) of rights and contracts, and a society constituted by associational relationships of mutual self-interest. The nub of the problem is this: while rights theorists, building upon a liberal framework, ultimately believe that the fight to improve children's lives is progressing the further we move from 'nurturance' to 'self-determination' (or from social and positive rights to political and negative rights), it is clear that if one takes children's need to care seriously, we are moving in the opposite direction, namely from a focus on the right to liberal autonomy (and the conceptualization of the individual, state, and society which accompanies it) to a reconceptualized understanding of the need for (and responsibility to) care. In each of the different sets of rights that we examined, the underlying liberal constructs often proved to be obstacles in meeting this need to care and ultimately, therefore, stood in the way of improving the lives of children and their care-givers.

Thus, in the case of the first two sets of rights: expressing children's most fundamental need to care as an indirect obligation of the rights to provision and protection, the care of children is limited to providing for and protecting them, without any reference to the need of children to affection, kindness, and attention (a caring disposition) in fulfilling these obligations. Such imperfect obligations are inexpressible in the language of rights. Secondly, both of these rights are shaped and limited by the liberal foundations upon which they are built. The state either does not 'interfere' at all *or* intervenes in the private sphere of families only after the fact, in order to *enforce* the right to care. Rights necessarily construct the state in this role of fallback position and, ultimately, enforcer through the courts. The family, in turn, is put in a defensive position in relation to the state. Rights also construct the family as an association rather than a community, particularly when the need to support and nurture ongoing relations is needed the most by children, at the point of family breakdown. It is ironic that this most fundamental issue of care would be expressed in an *indirect* fashion focused as much on the *curtailment* of the state in relation to the family and the family in relation to the child's autonomy as in a *direct* fashion which would *enable* these two 'authorities' to work together to best meet children's needs.

Rights appear, at least at first glance, to fit more easily with the final concept considered, namely autonomy. But it is within this third set of rights that we were most fully returned to the world of the adult citizen first described by John Locke. With the focus on adolescence over infancy, rationality, and the underlying conceptualization of society and family as associational, this set of rights imports the end product, process, and scope of liberal theory into its own conceptualisation of children. Ultimately, by expanding the scope of autonomy simply to include children within the parameters of adult liberal citizenship, children's rights theorists move children further along the liberal scale of 'becoming'. In Hegelian terms, they are seen as more 'beings' than the negation of beings as first conceptualized by John Locke, but 'becomings' none the less. Thus, where early liberal theory used children to be a mirror within which the negative image of a positive adult form could be reflected, children's rights theorists use the same mirror to reflect an albeit positive, but smaller and shakier image of those same autonomous adult selves.

An Alternative View: Children and the Ethic of Care

An alternative starting-point would be to leave the mirror aside, and begin instead with the child, and consider what characterizes his/her existence as a 'being' in his/her own right, not in relation to a future self but as he/she exists now. Children and childhood have existed for as long as human beings have been around. Too much has been made of the 'constructed' nature of children in recent theories (Aries 1962; Freeman 1983; Stephens 1995). There are, of course, different conceptions of childhood based on one's historical, cultural, and geographical location (Archard 1993), but there remain certain universal truths about children which defy time and space. The first is that children, at least initially, are completely dependent on others for survival. This dependency, and the correlating need for care, is a universal characteristic of childhood.

A second universal characteristic of children is that they grow to maturity. The difference between the concept of 'growth' and 'becoming' is the more open, organic, and multifaceted nature of the former. Growing is an organic process, involving social, emotional, and intellectual development that does not easily submit to the liberal language of individualism, rights, autonomy, and association, to the either/or questions required by an associational view of either society or the family: is one rational or irrational, can one consent or not consent? Children are dependent and independent, rational and irrational at the very same time, to varying degrees, at different points in the day as well as throughout their young lives. In turn, caring for children does not fit neatly into categories of liberal thought. Where rights advocates see the world through a filter of power and authority (either one is a subject or a rights-bearing citizen), and authority figures treat those under their authority as one or the other, the care-giver's role fits uneasily into such a dichotomous world-view. For unlike the authority figures (who were the targets of early liberal theory) that wanted adults to remain as perpetual subjects in their kingdom, care-givers, in principle, are committed to supporting a child's emerging independence.

If we begin with children, as children, and not constructed reflections of an adult citizen, the central issue that we are faced with, therefore, is not authority, status, and rights (as we find in liberal theory), but 'care'. How do we best care for our children, who should do it, and what are the theoretical principles that should guide us? By asking this question, we reintroduce the domestic, female, and natural sphere first demarcated to be outside the concerns of political theory in Locke's *Two Treatises of Government* into our analysis. Incorporating this sphere back into liberal theory will necessarily challenge both the dichotomous foundations upon which it has been built, and the vision of a world constituted by self-seeking autonomous actors to which it aspires.

In an article which otherwise argues that the questions posed by considerations of liberal justice and care are not as dramatically different as some would have us believe, Will Kymlicka concludes that in the case of dependants, liberal theories of justice and rights are profoundly inadequate: 'Justice theorists have constructed impressive edifices by refining traditional notions of fairness and responsibility. However, by continuing the centuries old neglect of the basic issues of child rearing and care for dependants, these intellectual achievements are resting on unexamined and perilously shaky ground' (1990: 285). Kymlicka provides a simple suggestion at the end of his analysis on the application of liberal theories of rights and the ethic of care: 'Should we say that care applies to relations with dependents, while justice applies to relations with autonomous adults?' (1990: 284). Let us use this as a starting-point for our alternative view. What would an ethic of care applied to children look like? What would the implications be for the role of the family and state in children's lives in a liberal democracy? Ultimately, would this model help to improve children's lives in ways that rights doctrines cannot?

Carol Gilligan first articulated an ethic of care in opposition to a liberal-based ethic of justice based on rights:

In this conception, the moral problem arises from conflicting responsibilities rather than from competing rights and requires for its resolution a mode of thinking that is contextual and narrative rather than formal and abstract. This conception of morality as concerned with the activity of care centres moral development around the understanding of responsibility and relationships, just as the conception of morality as fairness ties moral development to the understanding of rights and rules. (Gilligan 1982: 19)

Since Gilligan's initial definition, there has emerged considerable literature expanding upon the care/justice divide (Tronto 1993; Larrabee 1993; Clement 1996; Kymlicka 1990). Exactly how these two principles of morality relate to each other is a difficult but important discussion. My argument, as applied to children, is nicely summarized by the title of Annette Baier's article on care theory: 'The Need for More than Justice' (1987*b*). Baier argues that while justice is *a* social value of great importance, she takes issue with the claim, made by John Rawls, that justice is the *first* virtue of social institutions. Similarly, I am arguing that, while rights are valuable, particularly in adult relations, they are not sufficient as moral principles underpinning our relations to children. As Tronto comments: 'I do not mean to destroy or undermine current moral premises, but simply to show that they are incomplete' (1993: 157).

The first element in an ethic of care as applied to children would be the primacy of responsibilities and obligations over rights and rules. Even children's rights theorists agree that the basic rights to provision are the most important to children (Eekelaar 1986: 171) and these rights are best expressed as obligations (Freeman 1983: 37). Beyond the simple obligations to provide and protect, such an approach to dependent children would better express the need for provision and protection to be done with 'kindness and consideration' (O'Neill 1992: 26–8) or 'attentiveness' (Tronto 1993: 127–31) towards children. In the first instance, expressing children's needs as obligations would allow us to articulate this 'imperfect' obligation, but as well an ethic of care would focus the relationship between parents and states on this goal through a mutually supportive rather than adversarial relationship. For example, an ethic of care would not divide the care of children between the parents to *fulfil*, and the state to *enforce*, as liberal rights theory does. Rather the orientation of an ethic of care is a proactive, problem-solving one in which the activity of care is fundamental (Gilligan 1982: 19; Tronto 1993: 242) and the relationship of care-givers is worked out with each of the parties looking to what aspects of care it might best provide. While parents may be best suited for both the intimate day-to-day care based on affection and the overarching guardianship of the child as a full human being, the state could complement these activities with more instrumental forms of care. States focused not simply on the need to provide and protect, but also the need for care and consideration, would necessarily support parents, as necessary, from the outset. Some have argued that such an approach to children is an idyllic view of the family and children, and ignores the possibility of abuse or neglect (Archard 1993; Waldron 1993). On the contrary, by taking care as the fundamental objective of both families and states, this model would attempt to help parents, through a myriad of different kinds of support, who might be likely either to abuse or neglect their children before it gets to that point. Put concretely, an adequately funded day-care system, parent resource centres, and in-home care services could provide as useful a set of tools in solving the problem of child abuse or neglect as child-welfare officers.

The critical difference is the scope and orientation of the state. The state's notion of obligation to children would not begin and end with the ministries of education and social welfare. Rather it might entail a Ministry of Children, which would encompass all children and their families from birth onwards, with their full range of developmental needs. The state's care of children, from the point of view an ethic of care, would not be a fall-back position, but a proactive integrated set of services available to parents and their children, even before the need arises. As a result, the distinction now made between school-aged and pre-school children would be redrawn. All children, *especially* young ones, require care. Parents often feel more burdened the younger the child is. Policy proposals like the 'comprehensive, integrated and coherent early childhood service' suggested by Peter Moss and Helen Penn (1996) would fit very nicely into such a model of a state based on care.

The second element in an ethic of care would be to reconceptualize both families and society as communities rather than associations. The unencumbered 'self' of liberal thought is particularly hard to sustain for a child. Liberals argue, as discussed, that it is critical for the individual, including the child, to have the autonomy to separate (at least analytically if not physically) from his/her community. 'It is a good thing that modern men and women feel able to distance themselves from, reflect on, and consciously embrace or repudiate any or all of the relations that constitute their history' (Waldron, 1993: 389). As communitarians have argued, the unencumbered self of liberal thought fails to account fully for the communal attachments that are constitutive of the individual. (Sandel 1984). The child even more than the adult is dependent on these attachments, and his/her context for the expression and development of the 'self'. Recognizing this constitutive self makes it not only possible but also necessary to take more seriously the ongoing relations between individuals, both within the family and society at large.

The third element in an ethic of care, which grows out of a recognition of community, is the emphasis on connectedness or relations between people. Children's relationships to others, particularly adult care-givers, are critical to their well-being. The state should do everything it can to support and nurture these relationships. This is particularly true when there is a breakdown in the family, by reason of divorce. By approaching the question of separation and custody from the point of view of an ethic of care, rather than children's rights, the connections between people and their dependence on one another is emphasized. Like Gilligan's Amy, the solution that one searches for takes into consideration not only the interests of all the parties (particularly children) but also how to minimize the damage done to the relationships of all involved (particularly the one between parents and child). This orientation would push us away from the adversarial system of family law as it is currently practised to a more mediation and counselling oriented approach. The alternatives to a system of rigidly defined individual rights and adversarial courts could be numerous, from forms of mediation and conciliation to a Family Court.[5]

The fourth element of an ethic of care as applied to children would be to take seriously the activity of care-giving of children within both the public and private spheres, and the reconceptualization of autonomy that would entail. As feminist commentators and care theorists have argued, it is problematic to apply the notion of autonomy not only to children, *but equally to* those who are looking after them. Kymlicka comments: 'For [liberal] justice not only presupposes that we are autonomous adults, it seems to presuppose that we are adults *who are not care-givers for dependents*. Once people are responsible for attending to the (unpredictable) demands of dependents, they are no longer capable of guaranteeing their own predictability' (1990: 285). The traditional picture of autonomy is the free pursuit of one's projects. Baier argues that an ethic of care, 'makes autonomy not even an ideal . . . a certain sort of freedom is an ideal . . . but to "live one's own life in one's own way" is not likely to be among the aims of persons' (Baier 1987a: 46). Thus autonomy for adults must be tempered by this recognition of the need for and responsibility to care on all of society's members.

Traditionally, the responsibility for the care-giving of children (beyond that of education) is assumed to rest on people (largely women) 'choosing' to do so in the private sphere. As more women have entered the public sphere, the responsibility for care-giving has shifted onto the welfare state. Both of these assumptions are problematic. As Baier comments on the former: 'A moral theory . . . cannot regard concern for new and future persons as an option charity left for those with a taste for it. If the morality the theory endorses is to sustain itself, it must provide for its own continuers, not just take out a loan on a carefully encouraged maternal instinct' (1987a: 53). As for the latter, both Jeremy Waldron and Michael Ignatieff assume that in a fully developed liberal welfare state, care will somehow be managed by the state, while autonomous individuals continue to pursue their projects. Waldron comments: 'Although we may not care for [dependants] on a face to face basis, we both provide impersonal structures to enable them to take care of themselves and respond collectively and impersonally as a society to the rights that they have to our support' (1993: 381).

Ignatieff concurs: 'It is this solidarity amongst strangers, this transformation through the division of labour of needs into rights and rights into care [mediated through the state] that gives us whatever fragile basis we have for saying that we live in a moral community' (1984: 9–10). This conceptualization of 'care', based on the liberal primacy of autonomy and rights, simply sets aside care-giving as something done outside of the realm of autonomous actors. If we take care-giving seriously, it will necessarily change the concept of autonomy which lies, as has been discussed, at the heart of liberal theory and children's rights doctrines. Kymlicka concludes:

> The whole picture of autonomy as the free pursuit of projects formed in the light of abstract standards presupposes that care for dependent others can be delegated to someone else, or to the state. . . . [Under an ethic of care] the commitment to autonomy is not a commitment to staking out ground for the pursuit of personal projects, free from the shifting needs of particular others, but is rather a commitment to meeting those needs in a courageous and imaginative way . . . Any more expansive notion of autonomy can only come at the price of abandoning our responsibilities. (1990: 285)

Thus, in the same way that rights are seen to be fundamental constraints on everyone's actions in an associational model of adults, so to the need for care, likewise, should be a fundamental moral constraint on all adults within a community, and not just one choice amongst many that a particular autonomous individual adult may make, nor left as the responsibility of the welfare state.

Conclusion:

Ultimately, liberal thought, including children's rights theories, is concerned with a change in status for the individual. Locke wished to make adult subjects into citizens; children's rights theorists similarly wish to transform children from 'becomings' into 'beings'. The language of rights suits this purpose perfectly. For rights are ultimately a means to express a particular view of the individual and his/her relationship to the family, state, and society as a whole. The heart of liberal and rights theory is the rational autonomous individual with society as an association, and the state as the enforcer of the rights of the individual to guarantee their equal status as citizens. In applying this model to children, children's rights theorists use a tool devised for a different kind of being with a different set of interests and needs. Thus, while the rights theorists hoped to overcome the early liberal theorists' construction of children as 'becomings', by adopting the same model of autonomous adult citizens with which to measure children, such theories simply move children further along the same scale of becoming. While rights have evolved and adapted over time they are still the products of their historical origins. In using them for new groups of people, including children, rights theorists cannot escape this legacy. As a result, rights theories do not see children as children. They are still not 'beings' in their own right but small adults who can be measured by the extent to which they are autonomous, and others in their lives can ultimately be judged by the degree to which they do not interfere in their freely chosen ends. This vision, of course is tempered by a commitment to the rights of provision and protection, but these rights (to care) are always seen as a stepping stone, a necessary foundation to the more highly developed rights to autonomy and self-determination.

Within the critique of such a vision of children's rights is an alternative view of moral and political theory, which was sketched out at the end of this chapter. Beginning with the child as a dependent creature that grows to maturity, an ethic of care overcomes some of the difficulties associated with the liberal/children's rights approaches. It views the child's development in holistic terms, going beyond the capacity for rationality. Each child is included, from infancy to adolescence, and the state's role goes beyond both education and social welfare to a fully integrated set of services focused on the child's need for care and the parent's responsibility for care-giving. The rights to provision and protection would be expressed more directly as the obligation to care, with the state acting as a proactive, enabling, and supportive force in parents' lives, rather than as either an insurance policy or enforcer. And the child's growth towards an independent adulthood would be seen as an organic process that unfolds within the context of a multitude of interdependent relationships within both the family and society at large. Such a vision would truly embrace children as full beings.

Notes

1. All future references will include the treatise and paragraph source from John Locke, *Two Treatises of Government* (Cambridge: Cambridge University Press, 1989).
2. I use the masculine pronoun because Locke is explicitly referring to sons of citizens when he discusses children in his political theory.
3. In Feb. 1999, the British Education Minister Margaret Hodge introduced a curriculum for nurseries and playgroups, including guides for children as young as 3. The explicit purpose of the curriculum was to make children more 'school ready'. In other words, it is the Education Ministry that is reaching further and further down into early childhood. These guidelines were devised by the British Qualifications and Curriculum Authority. Nick Tate, chief executive of the QCA, comments on the new guidelines: 'High quality early years education is firmly established as one of the conerstones of the Government's determination to raise standards in education'. *The Express* 20 Feb. 1999), 2.
4. I expand on this in more detail in Arneil (2000), my reply to William Schabas.
5. Not surprisingly, children's rights theorists are sceptical of such alternative systems of 'justice'. See Freeman (1983: 229–33).

II

Autonomy and Education

Humanism and Education

6

Special Agents:
Children's Autonomy and Parental Authority
Robert Noggle

Introduction and Preliminaries

Virtually all reasonable people hold that children are persons, and not, for example, pets or property. Normally, we think of persons as beings who can and should run their own lives, yet children are neither expected nor allowed to run their own lives. We tell them what to eat, when to bathe, where to sleep. We make them attend school and do homework. We forbid them from hitting their siblings or pulling the dog's tail. Moreover, we think that parents have the legitimate *authority* to issue commands of these sorts, and that coercion is at least sometimes justified to ensure compliance. But if children are persons, then parental authority over them requires some justification to show why it is not simple—albeit well-meaning—oppression of the weak by the strong. In this chapter, I will address the question of the nature and justification of parental authority. I will ignore the (important) question of who should have this authority, or whether biological parents have any inherent claim to it.

Parental authority is not, of course, the only component of the parent–child relationship. A full specification of that relationship would include each of the following components:

(1) *A Parental Duty* to promote the interests and protect the rights of the child;
(2) *Parental Discretion* in deciding how to carry out these duties and (limited) freedom from outside interference in doing so, provided that they are doing a reasonably decent job and neither neglecting nor abusing the child;
(3) *Parental Authority* to issue commands to the child and to exercise some coercion to enforce them, provided that they are not unreasonable, abusive, or harmful to the child or her important long-term interests.

A common and promising theory about the nature and justification of the parent–child relationship holds that it is a form of fiduciary or trustee relationship. Examples of fiduciary relationships include the relationship of trustee to owner, physician to patient, lawyer to client, and manager to stock-holder. The fiduciary model of the parent–child relationship attempts to assimilate the morally problematic parent–child relationship to a relationship that does not seem morally problematic.

There is a lot to be said for the fiduciary model of the parent–child relationship. The parent–child relationship does bear a strong formal resemblance to the fiduciary relationship. For in both cases, we have a principal and an agent, and the agent is charged with protecting the rights and promoting the interests of the principal. So we have an analogue of parental duty. Furthermore, both relationships provide some insulation from outside interference. Physicians, lawyers, etc. use their discretion in carrying out their fiduciary duties (relatively) free from outside interference. So we have an analogue of parental discretion. Also, the rationale for the fiduciary relationship seems analogous to that of the parent–child relationship. Fiduciary relationships make possible an agent's borrowing the capacities of an expert in some particular endeavour. I lack the capacity to practise law or medicine, or to run the business I own, so I empower an expert to do these things for me. It seems natural, then, to think of the child as borrowing more widely from the capacities of the parent in order to compensate for the (many) capacities that she needs but does not yet have (see Cohen 1998).

In addition, the fiduciary model of the parent–child relationship has important activist implications. For the fiduciary agent's 'discretion rights' to use her best judgement in doing her job are purely a function of her undertaking the relevant fiduciary duties. Although this feature of the fiduciary model provides parents with some (limited) rights to exercise discretion free from outside interference in family matters, it makes the existence and continuation of these parental rights contingent upon the parent's fulfilling her obligations to promote the child's interests and protect the child's rights (see Brennan and Noggle 1997).

The fiduciary model of the parent–child relationship seems right—as far as it goes. However, the traditional fiduciary relationship lacks any clear analogue to parental authority. The physician or lawyer does not have authority over the patient or client in the way that the parent is typically thought to have (at least limited) authority over the child. The physician or lawyer may not compel her patient or client to comply with her advice, however sound it may be: the patient or client may disregard it for any reason—or none at all. Parents, however, seem to have some authority to enforce compliance with their directives.

Of course one possible way to respond to this problem without rejecting the fiduciary model would be to deny the legitimacy of parental authority, and thus to argue that the parent–child relationship is morally legitimate only when it is strictly analogous to the traditional fiduciary relationship. Such a position—which would be a form of radical child liberation—might be justified if we could find no justification for parental authority.[1] However, I shall attempt to show that it is possible to justify at least some version of parental authority, and thus to show that the parent–child relationship, to this extent at least, is and should be unlike typical fiduciary relationships.

Now one might be tempted to think that we can do this within the context of the fiduciary model simply by claiming that children suffer from global cognitive deficits. These deficits, one might claim, render children globally incompetent and thus necessitate an unlimited, global fiduciary relationship in which the child must surrender to the fiduciary agent's (parent's) authority. One might suggest that when cognitive incompetence is only local—as when an otherwise competent adult lacks the capacity to manage her stock portfolio—the fiduciary agent's authority to make decisions for the principal is limited by the overriding authority of the principal herself. A competent principal retains ultimate authority to reject or accept the fiduciary agent's advice and override her decisions. But when incompetence is global then we might think that the principal lacks the capacities to make such decisions, and to exercise competent judgement about whether to override the fiduciary agent's decisions. Thus we might claim that *competent* principals retain authority over their agents, but that children are principals who suffer from *global incompetence*, and who must therefore submit to the authority of their parents, who act as fiduciary agents for them.

While I think that this suggestion is on the right track, it is not adequate as it stands. For while infants and very young children might well suffer from the kind of generalized cognitive incompetence that would clearly render any person incompetent, it is a gross exaggeration to claim that older children suffer from the kind of global cognitive deficit that would, *in and of itself*, make a person a legitimate candidate for paternalistic authority. Though they may be less intelligent or less wise than most adults, adolescents do not (normally) suffer from such profound cognitive deficits. In fact, an adolescent often has quite formidable cognitive capacities, and may possess better reasoning skills (and maybe even more knowledge) than some perfectly competent adults. The level of cognitive functioning of the typical adolescent is quite a bit above the threshold that seems reasonable for attributing competence to an adult. Yet we generally think that it is legitimate for parents to continue to exercise considerable authority over adolescent children. The problem is that parental authority seems to outlast the global cognitive deficits that characterize infancy and early childhood. While good parenting probably involves minimizing the resort to parental authority when dealing with adolescents, most of us think that parents nevertheless retain that authority at least into the middle to late adolescence of their children, when the cognitive capacities of the child may have progressed to the level of many competent adults.

It appears, then, that if we are to explain why children—including older children—lack the same authority *vis à vis* their parents that adult principals have over *their* fiduciary agents, then we must locate some difference between children and adults, and that difference must be more than just cognitive capacity. My suggestion is that there is a much more profound difference between children and adults that affects how they are able to relate to other persons as moral beings. Indeed, I will suggest that children lack the fully developed capacity for the kind of moral agency that allows adults to interact with other moral agents on equal terms. Now I certainly do not deny that children are persons, and that as such, they have moral standing that entitles them to moral concern and consideration by adults. That is, they are 'moral patients' who are entitled to receive moral concern from other persons. However, I will suggest that children lack important aspects of moral *agency*, and that this prevents them from relating to the community of moral agents in quite the same way that adults can.[2] Adults are, in effect, full members of the community of moral agents, while children are prospective or probationary members of the moral community.

Before proceeding, I should say a bit about the moral community. I take it that the moral community consists, roughly, of the kind of community that is proper for a group of moral agents. Any complete and detailed theory of what a moral community is would have to answer very difficult and tendentious questions about how, exactly, moral agents should live and interact together. Such a project is far too large for the present chapter, so I will not defend a set of necessary and sufficient conditions for something's being a moral community. Instead, let us say that a moral community is that community formed by moral agents getting along according to whatever moral and political principles turn out to be justified. Thus contractarian readers are invited to define 'moral community' as the set of signatories to the (actual or hypothetical) social contract, Kantian readers are invited to define it as the Kingdom of Ends, utilitarians may define it as the group of persons acting according to whatever social and legal rules are utility-maximizing, and so on.

What reason is there to think that children are not ready to join such a community? Although I do not deny the importance of the fact that children have less fully developed cognitive capacities than adults, we have just seen that this difference does not separate children from adults as clearly as we (adults) might like to think. It seems to me that a far more profound difference between children and adults is that children have not yet formed fully stable 'moral selves'. Their preference structures are in a state of flux, and they have not yet fully developed an evaluative compass and internalized the moral norms necessary for harmonious interaction with other moral agents. These differences do not rob children (or at least post-infant children) of agency altogether, for children are capable of the deliberate, intentional, and (more or less) rational pursuit of goals that seems to be the hallmark of simple agency. But simple agency does not by itself include certain capacities that seem necessary for full participation in the moral community.

I will argue that the institution of the parent–child relationship—including parental authority—can be seen as a morally legitimate response to the fact that children are 'special agents', who have simple agency but who have not (yet) fully developed moral agency. Its purpose is, in effect, to bridge the gap between the special agency of childhood and the full-fledged moral agency required for full citizenship in the moral community. Such a relationship is deeper and more radical than fiduciary relationships in which both principal and agent are already full members of the moral community.

The key to all of this is the difference between simple agency and moral agency. The main criterion for simple agency is the ability to engage in the rational, intentional, and deliberate pursuit of goals. (I don't pretend that the analyses of the terms 'rational', 'intentional', and 'deliberate' are simple or obvious, but that is not my concern here.) Moral agency requires more than mere agency. It also requires temporal extension, and something like what John Rawls calls the 'two moral powers': a sense of justice and a capacity to develop and pursue a conception of the good (1993: 19–21). By 'temporal extension' I simply mean the capacity and desire of an agent to see herself as persisting over time, to take into consideration her long-term interests and needs, and to formulate and pursue long-range projects. I take having what Rawls calls a 'sense of justice' to involve having a set of internalized norms of moral decency that allows one to get along with others without arousing their (legitimate) moral indignation. An agent who lacks such norms cannot be fully integrated into the moral community as a full member, for the norms of moral decency constitute a sort of 'rule-book' for the moral community. The second Rawlsian 'moral power' is the capacity to have a conception of the good; I take this to involve the ability to construct and act according to a relatively stable set of values, goals, and fundamental concerns that give the agent direction in living not only as an impulse-driven creature, but as a reflective moral agent.

Thus a moral agent is, at minimum, an agent who sees herself—and her interests and projects—as persisting through time, and who can reflect on her present preferences in light of her own future interests, her own system of personal values and fundamental concerns, and the norms of moral decency. Such an agent has what we might call moral autonomy, for she has the capacity to transcend mere desire and act according to prudence and to personal and moral values.[3]

Temporal Extension

A person displays simple *agency* when she sets and deliberately pursues some goal, or deliberately provides for her immediate needs and interests. A person displays *temporally extended agency* when she has and pursues a set of goals that remain fairly stable over time, or when she provides for both her short- and long-term interests and needs. Temporally extended agents see the goals and projects of their future selves as their own goals and projects; they see their future happiness and pain as their own. They identify with their future selves.

Children typically lack the degree of temporal extension that most adults have. There are two main reasons for this. First, adults typically have a fairly stable preference structure that is organized around a fairly stable set of fundamental concerns and core values. These consist of a person's deepest values, her most fundamental commitments and attachments, and what Bernard Williams calls 'ground projects': those goals, plans, and relationships that give meaning and purpose to her life (Williams 1976; compare Frankfurt 1988 and Richards 1986). Often, these values and concerns are tied to the person's deepest beliefs about the world, and in particular to whatever religious, philosophical, or metaphysical doctrines she holds. A person's core values and fundamental concerns not only form the foundation for much of the person's preference structure, but they also constitute a person's *value system*. In the same way that a person's most basic beliefs constitute a 'conceptual scheme' that provides a cognitive framework for understanding the world, so her most basic concerns provide an evaluative framework for guiding her actions and choices within it.[4] They form much of the background against which the moral agent evaluates her present preferences—their existence allows her not only to *want*, but to *value*.

Normally, adult core values and fundamental concerns are relatively stable, changing fairly little in the short run, and changing in a relatively orderly way in the longer run. For the most part, these changes occur when the adult sees that some of her core values and fundamental concerns are incompatible with others, and attempts (perhaps subconsciously) to adjust them to form a more coherent value system. Over time, such gradual adjustments can add up to fairly radical transformations. However, such a transformation can still be seen as the intelligible unfolding or logical evolution of a single 'moral self'— a single locus of agency that is temporally extended through time and which retains its identity through these relatively orderly incremental changes. One implication of this fact is that, for most adults most of the time, we can predict with reasonable accuracy that most of their core values and fundamental concerns will persist at least into the medium-term future.[5]

Infants and very young children do not have what we could call commitments, values, or projects at all. The infant's motivational system is better described as a set of biological drives, together with whatever pre-social impulses are acquired soon after birth. These drives and impulses comprise the totality of the infant's motivational system—to the extent that she is an agent at all, the infant is an impulse-driven, primarily biological agent.

Later the child begins to develop preferences that are less grossly biological. However, most of the young child's not purely biological preferences are simple and fleeting. Some of them may persist, continue to develop, and even-

tually form part of her fully developed and relatively stable identity as a reflective social and moral agent.[6] Nevertheless, it is difficult to tell whether any
particular non-biological preference will be important—or even present at
all—in the adult into whom the child will grow. This lack of stability in the
child's preference structure makes her agency far less temporally extended
than that of an adult. Although adult preferences do change, changes to an
adult's most basic values and most fundamental concerns are generally infre-
quent, far less radical, and far more gradual and orderly than those of the
child. Abrupt and radical changes are a part and parcel of childhood, whereas
they are unusual events for adults.

Second, the adult has extensive first-hand *experience* of radical changes to her
own preferences and concerns that took place as *she* grew up. The experience of
living through the radical changes that characterize childhood allows her to
appreciate the fact that her present desires are not absolutely fixed, and that her
future interests will be just as much her own as her present ones. The experience
of not wanting now what she desperately wanted before affords the adult some
'reflective distance' on her own current desires. This in turn allows her to appreciate the wisdom of at least some preference-neutral prudential planning, like
keeping one's options open, developing a wide variety of skills and capacities,
and storing up goods that will be useful for a wide variety of purposes.

Thus children are typically less temporally extended than adults because
their (not merely biological) concerns, goals, and preferences are in flux, and
because they have not had enough experience with their own growth to realize how radical—and how inevitable—the coming changes will be. This fact
goes a long way towards explaining why children need adults as fiduciary
agents. For the parent can provide a kind of 'surrogate prudence' that can
provide the temporal extension that the child lacks. The parent is not only the
agent of the present child, but of the whole temporally extended person: in
much the same way as she is the advocate and protector of the child *vis-à-vis*
society, she must also be the advocate and protector of the child's future self
vis-à-vis the present child. This fact is the source of a kind of *prudential*
authority for parents: the child ought to obey the (competent) parent simply
because it is in her best interest to obey the directives of a person who is mani-
festing prudence on her behalf if she cannot do so herself.

However, this prudential authority is only one dimension of parental
authority. The problem of childhood lack of temporal extension and the role
of the parent in helping to overcome it also have important social dimensions
which go beyond the simple bilateral fiduciary relationship of parent to child,
and which help to explain the moral (as opposed to merely prudential)
authority of the parent. To see these social dimensions of the problem of
childhood lack of temporal extension, consider just how deeply the assumption of temporally extended agency is embedded in the moral community and
its practices.

The moral community—at least as it exists in contemporary Western liberal democratic societies (whose legitimacy I cannot undertake to examine here)—assumes a significant degree of temporal extension in the agency of its members. It seeks to provide a setting in which agents can devise and carry out plans and projects over time, and in which they can engage in cooperative enterprises in order to achieve goals that are of mutual benefit. The first of these presupposes that agents are beings who pursue projects and goals over extended periods of time, balancing the satisfaction of short-term preferences against commitments to longer term projects. The second rests on the assumption that an agent can see the future benefits of present cooperation as accruing to *herself*.

In addition, the moral community typically assumes that individuals are capable of managing their resources over time; economic systems and social institutions provide resources to persons but leave them relatively free to manage them so as to satisfy their present and future interests and pursue their long- and short-term projects. Moral, legal, and political practices assume that the mere passage of time neither changes one person into a new person nor dissolves the rights, responsibilities, and obligations of the earlier self. In practice as well as in theory, the moral community, at least as it exists in contemporary Western liberal democracies, assumes that members are temporally extended agents.[7]

This fact poses a significant barrier to the child's full participation in the moral community as an equal member. The practices and theoretical presuppositions of the moral community (at least as it is instantiated in contemporary liberal societies) require a kind of temporal extension that the child is typically not in a position to display. This requirement, I suggest, is an important source of parental authority. The parent's role as a substitute for the temporal extension that the child lacks is necessary because the moral community requires its members to display temporally extended agency. The child cannot do this on her own, so she must have the parent's help if she is going to be integrated into the moral community. This particular kind of parental help involves the parent taking up an authoritative position over the present self of the child. For the temporally extended agent is one who recognizes that the interests of her future self have some authority *vis-à-vis* the interests of the present moment, and it is this authority that the parent must assume in the child who lacks temporal extension. The parent, in effect, helps the child achieve temporal extension by exercising authority *vis-à-vis* the child's present self in the name of the future self. If a temporally extended agent is one who grants authority to both present and future interests, the child can gain temporal extension when the parent exercises authority in the name of the child's future self.

The parent, then, acts as an interface or bridge between the child and the moral community by providing a kind of surrogate for the authority of the future self of the child. Perhaps the most common way that the parent does this is through surrogate decision-making for the child. We saw that membership in the moral community presumes the ability of members to make decisions (including resource-allocation decisions) that balance the interests of the future self against the desires of the present moment. Because a temporarily extended agent can recognize both sets of interests as her own, she is in a position to do this kind of balancing. But until the child can make a choice about whether to sacrifice her own future—seeing it clearly as her *own* future—the parent's surrogate decisions must reflect the whole temporally extended person's interests in a way that the child's temporally bound decisions cannot.

A second way that the parent performs this interfacing function is by acting as a guarantor of the child's commitments to other members of the moral community. Typically she does this by taking moral and legal responsibility for fulfilling the commitment if the child should fail to do so. In this way, she allows the other party to the commitment to have some assurance that the child will be required by the parent to recognize that her commitments generate ongoing obligations that do not evaporate with the passage of time. And in doing this, the parent enables the child to participate in the moral community even though she does not yet have the fully developed temporally extended agency which will eventually allow her to do this on her own.

In the long run, probably the most important way that the parent performs this interfacing function is by encouraging the development of the temporally extended agency necessary for the child to enter the moral community in her own right. To achieve this temporal extension, the child must develop the experience, motivational stability, and deliberative skills necessary to extend her own agency into the future. The parent has a vital role in aiding the child in his development. In part this means helping the child develop certain skills such as delay of gratification techniques and common-sense decision theory, and helping her understand the advantages of multi-purpose goods and the wisdom of keeping options open. It also requires the parent to help the child understand that many of the preferences and goals of childhood will be abandoned later on, and that those (as yet unknown) preferences, goals, and concerns of her future will be just as much her own as her present preferences.

As the child's own temporal extension becomes solidified, the parental function is less crucial and eventually unneeded. In the transitional period the exercise of parental authority is probably best if it shifts from a directive to a veto role. Rather than making decisions and allocating resources for the child, a good parent allows the older child to practise doing these things for herself, but retains the authority to veto any disastrously imprudent decisions made by the child. The choice of how to balance future versus present is ultimately a decision for the autonomous, temporally extended, individual. But until the child develops the temporal extension necessary to fully appreciate the fact that her future interests really are her own, *and* that they may be different from her present desires, she cannot make that choice for herself.

In providing a surrogate for prudence by representing the interests of the child's own future self, parents face a serious epistemic problem. They must protect and promote the interests of the future self of the child, but those interests are not yet fixed, and it is extremely difficult even for the parent to predict what they will be. How is the parent to care for the as yet mysterious future self of the present child that she knows and cares for now?

The situation parents face is structurally similar to the situation of the contractor in Rawls's Original Position: both must protect and promote the interests of someone whose particular goals, concerns, attachments, and values they do not know (Rawls 1971). As Rawls argues, the way to see what decisions you should make when acting on behalf of someone whose goals, concerns, attachments, and values are unknown to you is to ask what would be prudent if *you* were (temporarily) taken behind a veil of ignorance behind which you did not know the content of *your own* goals, concerns, attachments, and values. Thus we can speak of a '*parental* veil of ignorance' that hides the particulars of the future adult self whose interests the parent is to protect and promote. This parental veil of ignorance, then, is similar to the Rawlsian veil of ignorance, and should presumably have similar effects on decision-making.

Similar, but not identical: for there are some important ways in which the situation of the parent is unlike the situation of the Rawlsian contractors. First, while the Rawlsian veil persists throughout a relatively discrete (and in some sense merely virtual or hypothetical) decision, the parental veil is rele-vant to an ongoing, real-life decision-making process that lasts throughout childhood. In addition, the parental veil of ignorance is less complete than the Rawlsian veil of ignorance, and it gradually dissipates as the child develops. The parental veil of ignorance is less complete because the parent already knows much about the future adult simply because she knows the present child. Thus she typically knows the sex (though perhaps not the gender) and ethnic background of the future adult. She also knows that the future adult will have been raised by parents of a particular sort, that she will have grown up in an environment of a particular kind. In addition, the parental veil of ignorance gradually dissipates as the child approaches adulthood. As the child matures, much more of her future adult self will become discernible, though often vaguely and imperfectly. The closer the child gets to adulthood, and the more stable her identity becomes, the less the parental veil of ignorance obscures at least the first stages of the child's adult self. The parental veil of ignorance, then, is less like a veil of fixed opacity than like a window that is now fogged over, but which will gradually clear as the child approaches adult-hood.

However, it is important (both as a theoretical and as a practical matter) not to overestimate the extent of the information parents have about the future self of the child. While the parent does know the childhood that will become the history of the child's future adult self, but she must keep in mind that history is not destiny. Even though the future adult may have been the quiet, traditional Catholic girl that the parent is now raising, the adult still might turn out to be a gregarious lesbian Zen Buddhist. This caveat still applies—though perhaps a bit less strenuously—to older children for whom the veil of ignorance has begun to dissipate. The fact that a teenager has a passion and talent for auto mechanics or history or astronomy does not tell us that the future adult will for certain become a mechanic or historian or astronomer. She may instead become a business person who tinkers with her car for entertainment, or a philosophy professor who is addicted to the History Channel, or a plumber who runs a local astronomy club.

With these caveats in mind, let us return to the Rawlsian prescription for decision-making behind a veil of ignorance. Rawls argues (persuasively, in my view) that the sensible thing to do in a veil of ignorance situation is to keep as many options as open as possible and to store up what Rawls calls 'primary goods' that will be of use no matter what projects, values, and commitments one turns out to have.

Because this notion of a primary good is so useful in this context, it will be worthwhile to consider it a bit further. As Rawls explains it,

Primary goods ... are things which it is supposed that a rational man [sic!] wants whatever else he wants. Regardless of what an individual's rational plans are in detail, it is assumed that there are various things which he would prefer more of rather than less. With more of these goods men [sic] can generally be assured of greater success in carrying our their intentions and in advancing their ends, whatever these ends may be. The primary social goods, to give them in broad categories, are rights and liberties, opportunities and powers, income and wealth. (1971: 192)

Although I will borrow this concept of primary goods from Rawls, there are a couple of ways that it needs to be modified and developed to make it suitable as a guide for parental surrogate prudence. For one thing, Rawlsian justice theory focuses mainly on goods that can be provided by social institutions to persons who are *already* fully developed moral agents with a conception of the good and a sense of justice. But these two 'moral powers' are *themselves* goods that must be provided to persons *before* they become fully developed moral agents. Thus the two moral powers (and, I would add, temporal extension as well) belong in a category more basic than primary goods, for they are the very preconditions for membership in the community of moral agents. These 'pre-primary' goods are initially absent in children but are necessary for the child's integration into the moral community.

Second, I think we also need to add the idea of a 'secondary good' to Rawls's account. Let us call a *secondary good* one which does not harm anyone to whom it is provided, but which may not be useful to *everyone* to whom it is provided, though it will be useful to a wide variety of people with a wide variety of conceptions of the good, life-plans, and world-views. Thus diverse groups of people will find a given secondary good extremely useful, and those who do not will not have their position worsened by gaining access to it. Such a good is one that would be useful or valuable from the point of view of a wide enough variety of evaluative frameworks that providing access to it would be genuinely benevolent for many people. I am inclined to think that such things as some sort of continuity with biological ancestors, membership in a religious or intellectual tradition that has been passed down by one's ancestors, and ties to an ancestral homeland or social and ethnic heritage might all be goods of this sort: Some of us think these things matter very little, but a great many world-views and value systems count them as very important components of a good life.[8] Because this is so, genuinely benevolent surrogate decision-makers working behind a veil of ignorance should attempt—when possible—to secure these secondary goods for the principals in whose interests they act. However, the fact that they are secondary goods suggests that their provision is less morally imperative than the provision of the more basic primary and pre-primary goods. This is because it is nearly impossible to live a good life without a proper share of the primary goods, and impossible to be a member of the moral community without the pre-primary goods, but it is quite possible to live a good life without access to any given secondary good.

One final adjustment to the Rawlsian account of primary goods seems necessary when discussing children. Rawls does not include the most basic of goods—food, shelter, etc.—in his list of primary goods, though in some ways they fit his definition. Presumably the assumption is that fully developed moral agents in a moral community will be able to use the primary goods of income and wealth to provide these goods for themselves. For children, however, this is not the case—such goods must, for the most part, be provided to children in quantities that will ensure their flourishing. But since these goods are necessary for life itself, and because when children are concerned we cannot simply subsume them under the category of primary goods, for children they constitute the very most basic category of goods.

Putting all of this together, we arrive at the following hierarchy of kinds of goods relevant to children. At the top are the most basic goods necessary for life itself; then come pre-primary goods, which are necessary for full membership in the moral community; next come primary goods, which are useful for members of the moral community who have virtually any value system and any set of goals; next are secondary goods, which are harmful to none, and useful to persons with a great variety of value systems and goals; finally we have specialized goods which are useful for a relatively narrow set of purposes—they will be highly useful for persons with certain specific (and not particularly widely held) goals or values, and useless or nearly so to others.

In general, it is worse to lack an adequate supply of goods near the top of this hierarchy than to lack goods near the bottom of it. This means that the duty to provide children with goods near the top is more imperative, more urgent, than the duty to provide goods near the bottom. However, all of the goods are good, so to speak, and a good parent will attempt to provide goods of all categories. Thus the priority embodied in this hierarchy of goods is not lexical. The good parent should not maximize the quantity of a higher ranked good before providing any of a lower ranked good. Instead, the good parent will provide an appropriate balance among the various classes of goods, even if this sometimes means providing less than the maximum of a more primary good in order to provide an appropriate less primary good. Sometimes a child needs a bike more than she needs another hundred dollars in her college savings account (assuming, of course, that she is well-fed, has a roof over her head, is developing moral agency, etc.). Similarly, it is often worthwhile to give in to the child's whims, or engage in frivolous pleasures, rather than take the opportunity to teach yet another lesson about prudential planning, morality, or character.

The point, then, is not that higher ranked goods should always take precedence over lower ranked ones, but rather that the provision of an adequate supply of higher ranked goods is normally more urgent than the provision of lower ranked goods, and that therefore the duty to provide higher ranked goods should be given more weight than the duty to provide lower ranked goods in the parent's balancing decisions. However, in cases in which an adequate supply of the higher ranked goods is being provided, the parent is free to decide in favour of the provision of a lower ranked, more special purpose good. Primary and pre-primary goods are, in the case of children, largely forward-looking: they are primarily goods that are provided for the sake of the child's future self. While the parent does have an important duty to the child's future self, she also has duties to the present child. And sometimes what children need is attention, fun, and play for its own sake. Childhood is an important time, and providing a happy childhood is no less (but no more) important a part of the parental duty than helping to ensure a happy adulthood. Thus, the parent's duties to the present child are not to be neglected in favour of her duties to the child's future self; rather, they are to be balanced with them.

The appropriate balance here seems likely to change over time. The provision of primary goods is most important when the child's future interests are most difficult to discern. As the child grows, and the parental veil of ignorance begins to lift, it is appropriate for the parent to provide more special purpose goods (or to allow the adolescent to begin to trade some of the previously stored primary goods for them), especially when they serve goals and projects that seem to have become relatively stable features of the child's character. These trade-offs are difficult, of course. And, like so much about parenting, they are deeply dependent on context. It is very much a matter of finding an

Aristotelian mean, relative to the individual child and the situation at hand, between too much emphasis on the future and too much emphasis on the present.

The Sense of Moral Decency

So far, I have claimed that the parent–child relationship—and along with it parental authority—can be better understood when we see it as a kind of interface between the child and the moral community. This interface is necessary because children have not yet developed three components of moral agency necessary for full membership in the community of moral agents. Those components are temporal extension, a value system or conception of the good, and the sense of moral decency. I began by discussing temporal extension, and that discussion led, by way of a discussion of the parental veil of ignorance, to the conclusion that the three components of moral agency are pre-primary goods. We have yet to discuss the other two components of moral agency, and to that task I now turn.

Without offering a full account of the necessary and sufficient conditions for a thing's being a moral community, I think we can safely say that membership in any genuinely moral community requires and presupposes a willingness to give and accept moral considerations as reasons for action. The moral community requires that its members understand, value, and have at least some motivation to act upon, norms of moral decency. Parents play a crucial role in the development of this pre-primary good.

The details of how this happens depend on empirical facts about child psychology, many of which remain controversial and poorly understood. However, I think that we are fairly safe in telling the following very schematic story about its development.[9] Infants and very young children begin in an 'egocentric predicament.' Their concern is focused on their own immediate interests. From this initial stage of straightforward, naïve, and immediate egoism, the child progresses to a stage of more enlightened—though still quite direct—egoism. In this stage, punishment, reward, and the desire to please and imitate the parent operate to make morally decent behaviour pay off in a purely short-term, self-serving way.

Over time, the child typically progresses to a stage of enlightened indirect egoism. This stage is reached when moral norms are followed even when there is no direct, overt reward or punishment, and even when the child is not consciously intending to please the parent. Instead, the moral norms have now become directly motivating. The correct description of the transition to this second stage remains rather controversial. It may consist of internalizing parental norms through some sort of identification with the parent involving the substitution of the child's own self-praise and self-blame for that of the parent. It may consist of developing dispositions to avoid morally indecent behaviour because of their prudential value. Or it may consist of acquiring a deep-seated (and perhaps not always consciously articulated) conviction that morally indecent behaviour is typically imprudent, and that the costs of detecting exceptions to this general rule outweigh the benefits of capitalizing on them. In any case, by this point, the child has acquired a direct motivation to act on moral considerations.

Many people hold that there is a further step to what one might—somewhat tendentiously—call a morality of genuine altruism or pure duty, in which the person acts on moral considerations without any tacit, indirect, or unconscious self-serving motives at all. Whether such a disposition is necessary for genuine morality is a controversial issue that I will avoid here. Enlightened indirect egoism seems sufficient to support citizenship in the moral community, for it leaves one open to persuasion and reasoning based on moral considerations without the need for any 'external sanctions'. Those who have reached this stage of moral development find moral considerations directly motivating in and of themselves, without external threats or inducements. For most *practical* purposes, this is what matters.

If moral decency does not develop, then we are faced with a child who is a kind of 'moral psychopath'. Such a child poses a dilemma for society. On the one hand, he is not a fit member of the moral community, and our obligations to others favour excluding him because of the dangers he poses. Yet if the person is a moral psychopath because of things that happened—or failed to happen—before he developed sufficiently to be responsible for his own character, then excluding him from the moral community and its vital benefits seems patently unfair. He never had a chance, and to penalize him further seems to be punishing a victim for something over which he had no control.

But while there is an air of paradox about society punishing someone for having been raised a psychopath, there is nothing paradoxical about placing upon children the requirement—as a precondition for entrance into the moral community—to submit to the authority of a parent who is charged with the task of raising a morally decent child. Thus part of parental authority arises from a sort of 'entrance requirement' to develop morally decent character that the moral community imposes on prospective members. In order to avoid the paradoxes of punishing a person for the character that was imparted to her, or of placing moral obligations on someone who has not fully developed moral agency, we require children, as a precondition for entrance into the moral community, to obey parents who are in turn obligated to raise them to have a morally decent character. We make having a morally decent character a requirement for membership in the moral community, and we make parents both the main enforcers of that requirement and the main facilitators of the child's meeting it.

Now one might wonder whether the interest of society in producing morally decent children is opposed to the (initially selfish) interests of the child herself, and thus whether the parent's fiduciary duty towards the child conflicts with her duty to the moral community to instil a morally decent character in the child. After all, the child starts out as a kind of egoist, and moral decency does make at least some requirements that egoists will find burdensome. However, the fact that moral decency may be burdensome to someone who is already a committed egoist does not show that a commitment to egoism is the most beneficial one for the child to have. Personal ideals that espouse pure egoism or evil projects hinder (at least) a person's integration into the moral community. Given that a person is much better off within society than outside of it, parental steering of the development of the child's character in a morally decent direction is itself in the interest of the child. Whatever you think of Hobbes, he was surely right about at least one thing: the state of nature is a bad place, and certainly no place for children. Since the moral community requires moral decency, it is in the child's own interest to develop a morally decent character that will allow her to fit into that community.

Because children have not yet developed characters devoted to morally indecent values or goals, parents are in a position to guide the child's development in such a way that the moral decency that society requires does not clash with the child's value system, and so that the demands of moral decency are no more burdensome than necessary. If all goes well, the child will develop a sense of moral decency that she would not choose to be without, one that is deeply integrated into her own value system (compare Churchill 1998). Such a child will see moral decency as a precondition for her own happiness and flourishing.

Thus we can reconcile the duty of the parent both as advocate of the child to the moral community *and* as agent of the moral community who sees to it that the candidates for entrance into society are fit. The parent must, as a member of society, act as a sort of screening agent for the moral community to ensure that entrants into it are morally decent. Yet as an advocate of the child, she will also do everything in her power to see to it that her child passes the test, so to speak, and develops a morally decent character. Thus she functions like a good teacher, one who enforces high standards but does whatever she can to help her students meet those standards.

Family Values

We turn now to the third component of moral agency: the conception of the good or what I will call a value system. A value system, as I will understand it here, includes not only moral values, but also the person's personal ideals of the good life, and the fundamental concerns, commitments, attachments, and projects that make her life worth living. Value systems often rest on more or less well-articulated world-views—what Rawls (1993) calls 'comprehensive doctrines'—or fundamental political, religious, or philosophical convictions. Because value systems are often inextricably linked to world-views, much of what I have to say about value systems will also apply to the world-views on which they rest.

In order to progress from merely biological, impulse-driven, simple agency, and to develop genuinely human reflective moral agency, the child must develop a value system that encompasses more than just biological drives. Indeed, any coherent rational choice presupposes the existence of evaluative criteria to judge some option to be choice-worthy, and a person's value system is an important, perhaps indispensable, source of such criteria. An agent without any evaluative criteria would be a lost soul indeed, for she would lack an evaluative compass to give her life meaning and direction. Her decisions would largely be whim or impulse rather than reflections of an intelligent reflection on her future interests, fundamental concerns and goals, or moral norms.

Where is the child to get her value system? One is tempted to say that the person herself should formulate her own values and goals. But while our liberal society does make the individual the ultimate arbiter of her value system, a value system created out of thin air can only be arbitrary.[10] Non-arbitrary choices can *only* be made by presupposing some initial set of evaluative criteria. This is even true of choices to modify, adjust, or give up some of one's values or goals. One cannot be a choosing agent unless one has some values or goals on which to base one's choices; otherwise choice degenerates into mere impulse or arbitrary whim. Even the choice to modify or reject some part of one's own value system requires *some* values or goals to supply reasons on which to base that choice.

When we see that even the choice of whether to keep, reject, or modify one's values or goals already presupposes some values or goals—when we see that choice cannot be both self-generated and non-arbitrary 'all the way down'—there seems nothing intrinsically immoral or illiberal about giving the parent at least prima-facie permission to instil her own value system and the world-view on which it rests as an initial 'default' position. Since there is no getting around the need for *some* initial set of values, we might just as well let the parents instil theirs, at least within certain limits which I will discuss below.

Several additional considerations favour giving parents a limited permission to pass on their value systems and world-views to their children. First, the most practical and efficient way of ensuring that children develop value systems is to allow parents to instil their own value systems (and the world-views that support them). In a free pluralistic society it would be morally problematic—and probably wildly ineffective—to force parents to teach and advocate world-views and value systems to which they themselves do not subscribe. Also, many value systems and world-views prize continuity with the past, and so there is some prima-facie reason to facilitate passing them down through generations. Intergenerational continuity of world-views and value systems—the inheritance of 'traditions'—would seem to be a secondary good: It is important for many though perhaps not all reasonable outlooks. Finally, there is (what I would regard as a weak) prima-facie interest on the part of parents to perpetuate their own value systems and world-views by offering them to (though not imposing them on) the next generation.

All of these considerations make a strong case for the practice of allowing parents to pass on their value systems and world-views. However, they neither assume nor entail that parents have anything like property rights over children or free-standing unconditional rights to perpetuate their own beliefs and values into the next generation. In particular, this rationale for letting parents offer children their own beliefs and values does *not* apply to unreasonable, intolerant, and morally indecent value systems or world-views. Beliefs and values of *that* sort hinder one's participation in the moral community of a diverse, pluralistic society: from the point of view of the child's own interests and the interests of the moral community, such values and beliefs are pernicious. The parent's right to instil values and beliefs derives from her role as dual representative of the child and the moral community. Instilling intolerant, morally indecent, or otherwise pernicious values or beliefs serves *neither* the child nor the moral community. Instead, the child and the moral community are served when the parent provides the child with a provisional, morally decent value system which she can later, as an autonomous moral agent, keep, modify, or discard as she sees fit. Within these limits, parents are free to choose which value system and world-view to impart, but they have this permission only because a child must have *some* values and some world-view, and it is for several reasons best to permit parents to impart theirs. Nothing gives the parent any right to give the child a morally indecent value system or world-view.

Similarly, nothing gives the parent a right to make the child closed-minded with regard to other value systems or world-views, or to try to make her unable to reflect upon her own as she grows into a full-fledged moral agent. We may not be able (morally and practically) to force a closed-minded parent to raise an open-minded child, but conceding this does not force us to concede that the parent has a right to raise a closed-minded child. In particular, we need not—and I think should not—accord the parent a *right* to keep the child from moderating influences of other social institutions (such as public education) just because they will foster an open-mindedness that the parent frowns upon. The parent's limited permission to pass on her values and beliefs does not give her any right to deny the child access to the intellectual skills of critical thought and reflective reason that may assist her later on in evaluating, and perhaps deciding to change, those beliefs and values.

In the end, we cannot keep our hands completely off the development of the child's value system and world-view; we cannot give the child a completely open future by making her present free of any values or any metaphysical or religious doctrines. To do so would prevent the child from progressing from a special agent to a fully developed, temporally extended moral agent with a value system and sense of moral decency. Yet none of this requires us to allow parents to programme the child blindly to follow a dogmatic, closed-minded, or evil way of life. For if we assume that a child really is a person—even if, for the moment, she is a special agent—then we must empower the child herself to decide how to live. While parents can best do this by offering their child an initial world-view and value system, parents must not try to force the child to keep them forever. For to do so is to usurp the child's right to self-determination. It is to deprive her of the full benefits of membership in the moral community, a membership that it is the parent's duty to help her secure.

Conclusion

So we can now see why the parent–child relationship is a very unusual kind of fiduciary relationship, and why it gives the parent a kind of authority not seen in other fiduciary relationships. Parental authority arises from the fact that the parent is not only the agent of the child, but also the agent of the moral community. While some of the parent's commands no doubt derive a kind of 'prudential authority' directly from the child's own interests, the parent's *moral authority* derives from her status as an agent of the moral community, as the instrument through which the 'entrance requirements' for membership in the moral community operate.[11] Because of the child's special kind of agency, she is not yet ready to fulfil these requirements, and the parent–child relationship reflects this fact. The special agency of the child requires something similar to but more profound than the traditional fiduciary relationship; in that relationship the parent must represent not only the child who exists today, but the largely unknown future adult whom that child will become, and the moral community which she must join if she is to thrive and flourish.

In a sense, then, we can see the parent as having 'contracted' tacitly or hypothetically with society to undertake this particular function with regard to one or more particular children. In return, we can see society as investing its moral authority to insist on the terms of membership, and thus to impose requirements on those who would enter it, primarily in the parent. Thus the source of parent's moral authority is the moral authority of the community of moral agents to set the requirements for membership in that community, much (though not all) of which is delegated to the parent. In return, the parent acquires the enabling rights to limited discretion and limited freedom from outside interference in carrying out this function.

So the parent must balance two roles. As an agent of the moral community, the parent must enforce its demands that members fulfil the requirements of moral agency. As an advocate of the child, the parent must also do everything in her power to see to it that her child meets those requirements. Yet the role the parent plays on behalf of the moral community is a role that is in the vital interest of the child as well as the community. Keeping in mind that the term 'agent' has two difference senses (one denoting an purposeful actor and the other denoting a party to the fiduciary relationship), we can see that parents and children are both very special agents.[12]

Notes

1. I reject radical child liberationism of this sort for (not especially novel) reasons discussed in Brennan and Noggle 1997.
2. For some thoughts on reconciling children's different set of rights with their equal status as persons, see Brennan and Noggle 1997. I would add to that discussion the claim that certain rights protect the exercise of a kind of moral agency that children have not yet fully developed, and that this fact also helps us to see why giving equal consideration to children is compatible with treating them somewhat differently from adults.
3. While I think that these three psychological features are necessary for moral agency, I do not claim that they are sufficient. Presumably a full account of moral agency would also include (among other things, perhaps) some account of moral responsibility. Stating and defending such an account would take me too far afield for the present project. However, I think that one could probably extend the same story I will tell about these three components of moral agency to moral responsibility, at least on any plausible view about what it is, how it develops, and why most adults have it but very young children do not.
4. A person's core values and fundamental concerns are not always explicit or transparent, even to the person to whom they belong: often one can only find out what they are by a lengthy process of self-discovery, introspection, and perhaps psychotherapy.
5. The philosophical psychology sketched here is developed in more detail in Noggle 1999*a* and 1999*b*.
6. By 'not merely biological' I simply mean not produced directly by biological drives or instincts, without the mediation of human social or cognitive processes.
7. While I cannot argue the point here, I suspect that most if not all feasible human social structures that would count as instantiations of a moral community will also require agents to be temporally extended. So while I am concentrating here on contemporary Western liberal democratic societies, I suspect that my remarks here would apply to many if not most other viable kinds of society as well. Of course making good this suspicion would require defending a set of necessary and sufficient conditions for something's being a moral community, a task which goes far beyond the scope of this chapter.
8. Thinking of relationships with biological kin as a secondary good might be a promising way to give *some* weight to biology in custody disputes without having to posit some sort of absolute right to a relationship with biological kin, and without having to postulate anything like parental ownership of children.

9. The account I give here is based largely on the work of Jean Piaget, Lawrence Kohlberg, and their followers. I discuss that work further and in reference to John Rawls, in Brennan and Noggle 1998.
10. For defences of this claim e.g. Kymlicka 1990: 449–78; Strawson 1986: 48–50.
11. I regard this as only a partial account of parental authority; I suspect that some of the parent's authority derives from the parent's property rights—to her house, for example—and autonomy rights to pursue projects in addition to child-rearing, as well as from a sort of compensation for undertaking the job of child-rearing in the first place: In return for undertaking the job of raising the child, we might speculate that the parent receives some rights to make certain (reasonable) rules for her own convenience and domestic tranquillity.
12. I thank David Archard, Samantha Brennan, and Colin Macleod for very generous and detailed comments on this chapter. Earlier versions of the chapter were presented at a conference entitled 'Paying Attention to Children' held at the University of Western Ontario in March 2000, at the 2001 annual conference of the Association for Practical and Professional Ethics, and to an audience at Virginia Tech. I am very grateful to members of all three audiences for very helpful comments.

7

Autonomy, Child-Rearing, and Good Lives

Eamonn Callan

I

People need to be autonomous if they are to have good lives. That at least is what some liberal philosophers say. Important claims about education and child-rearing follow from this. Children can be reared or schooled in ways that gravely impair the realization of autonomy. Once they suffer that impairment, then given that autonomy is necessary to their good, we must infer that their rights have been infringed, or at least that a basic interest of theirs has been invaded. But why believe that autonomy is so important? I want to assess one particular and attractive answer to this question, which for convenience I call 'the instrumental argument'. The leading ideas of the argument are these: autonomy enables us to choose intrinsically good lives; autonomy confers that ability without creating bias against any particular ways of life that might have intrinsic value.[1]

Much in the instrumental argument is right. In fact I have nothing to say against the claim that autonomy enables us (or at least helps us greatly) to live good lives. My disagreement is with the claim that the cultivation of autonomy does not bias our choices against ways of life that give little scope for the exercise and development of autonomy. That being so, no argument for the centrality of autonomy to good lives can succeed unless certain assumptions are granted about the superior intrinsic value of autonomous over alternative ways of life, at least other things being equal. This flaw in the instrumental argument is not trivial. It casts a distorting light on the nature of autonomy, on how its value should be understood, and on what kind of upbringing might help children to live autonomous lives when they become adults. In particular, the argument occludes the internal connection between autonomy and character, and it emphasizes the value of autonomous revision to conceptions of the good without registering the symmetrical value of autonomous adherence. That in turn has tended to motivate a one-sided suspicion of relatively insular, tradition-bound styles of child-rearing and an overly sanguine view of the degree to which the 'diversity' of typical Western democracies favours children's interests in achieving autonomy.

My critique of the instrumental argument opens the way to an amended conception of autonomy, its value, and the upbringing suited to its realization. Part of the attraction of the amended conception is that it might capture an ideal congenial to many people who reject autonomy as it is represented in the instrumental argument, including many who might do so in the name of religious tradition. But the amended conception still requires that we consider the value of lives that might be increasingly difficult to sustain in societies where autonomy flourished widely. I claim that whatever value they have cannot plausibly be said to outweigh the value of autonomy. Unfortunately, the conception I endorse turns out to be more rather than less distant from the strongest cultural currents in contemporary liberal societies than standard liberal notions of autonomy.

A caveat should be entered here. The liberal case for state action intended to promote the development of autonomy among children does not depend decisively on any argument designed to show that autonomy enables them to live good lives. If autonomy were unnecessary to our good, it might still be necessary to the personal virtue of justice under conditions of diversity; its cultivation might also pose no serious risk of making lives bad (Callan 2000: 42–69). These considerations likely suffice to justify autonomy promotion by the liberal state in many circumstances. What they fail to show, however, is whether being raised in a way that thwarts the development of autonomy harms children, regardless of its larger civic consequences. That possibility is what I want to consider.

II

Here is my informal account of the instrumental argument:

1. We want to live good lives. But we disagree about which lives count as good. On two important points, however, virtually all of us will agree. First, we can be mistaken about the goodness of our own and others' lives. The seemingly good life may not be really so. To deny this would be to imply that one could never rightly disagree with another about the goodness of particular lives. Very few of us could accept this conclusion. If we cannot accept it, we must be ready to say that the seeming goodness and the goodness of a life are distinguishable. Second, people might live according to correct beliefs about their good at one point in their lives, and then, when circumstances change, fail to revise their ideas in ways that new conditions would warrant. *The capacity rationally to initiate revision to one's conception of the good is necessary if we are to cope with the fallibility of our ethical understanding and the need to adjust our ends to changing circumstances.*
2. Since mistakes about the good might even corrupt the deepest ethical convictions or loves, the sovereignty of rational criticism over these must

hold as well. Nothing here entails that ridiculous metaphysical fiction: Michael Sandel's (1982) 'unencumbered self'. But it does mean that the self is only *revocably* encumbered, through and through, by attachments one should renounce once rational criticism suggests that one should. *The capacity rationally to revise a conception of the good includes the capacity to assess identity-conferring ethical beliefs and values and, when appropriate, to change belief and conduct accordingly.*

3. Asserting the sovereignty of rational criticism in the ongoing construction and reconstruction of someone's idea of the good says nothing by itself about whose criticism should carry authority. Why should the best critic not be one of the countless alternatives to the particular individual whose life it is? Occasionally the best critic might be someone else. (Thus the instrumental argument could establish that autonomy is necessary to the good only in a loose sense.[2]) But in the great majority of cases this will not be true. It will not be true because *a normative requirement of good lives, on any plausible account of such lives, gives us warrant to assign each one of us a strongly privileged epistemic perspective in determining whether our lives are going well or badly.*

Nothing can add intrinsic value to our lives unless we can appreciate it ourselves as intrinsically good. The piety that might enrich a life must be experienced from within as a heartfelt love of God rather than fearful compliance with priestly authority. Real friendship, the erotic love worth having, and the career that is truly fulfilling and not merely outwardly successful, all require that I can appreciate these as good from my own, experientially grounded perspective. This is sometimes called the 'endorsement' criterion of living well, though perhaps 'endorsement' implies a level of self-consciousness not strictly necessary required by the criterion in question. The fact that I appreciate the poem I read is what makes my life go better, other things being equal; whether I pass some judgement on the experience that counts as endorsing its value is not the same thing.

An appealing way of interpreting the requirement of appreciation is to see it as implicit in the idea that, because people are different in their personalities, native predisposition, etc.—their individual natures—establishing a suitable congruence between these and the life they will lead is necessary. Not everyone is cut out to be a monk, a parent, or a philosopher. Someone might be able to interpret philosophical texts well, construct substantial philosophical arguments of her own, and still fail to appreciate what she is doing (Darwall 1996). Try as she might, her philosophical efforts continue to feel pointless. The natural inference to make would be that philosophy is not suited to her. Her individual nature is incongruent with the life of a philosopher, and hence to choose that life is to waste *her* life. Self-deception or mere lack of self-knowledge might deny one the lucidity of the authentic, first person singular view-point on the congruence between the externally described life and the appreciative engagement of the one whose life it is. Yet ceding the authority to others to say what we do or do not appreciate is dangerous, to say the least. The things we truly care about might often be opaque to us. But the supposition that what we care about would in general be more transparent to (benevolent?) others is far less than credible. This is not to say one cannot readily relinquish autonomy when one finds its continued exercise unsuited to one's nature. To suggest otherwise would be introduce the very bias into autonomous choice that it is supposed to avoid.

At any rate, making judgements about the life one will lead on the basis of individual experience and through the exercise of learned capacities for critical self-reflection seems in general the only prudent course. *Therefore, individuals must construct, implement, and when necessary revise their conceptions of the good on the basis of their own experience and reasoning.*

These considerations give us a distinctive conception and defence of autonomy as an element of good lives. Autonomy is the capacity critically to assess and revise one's own conception of the good. I assume 'capacity' here refers to a repertoire of skills or abilities realized through learning over an extended period of time. Autonomy so conceived is claimed to have a compelling instrumental value in achieving and maintaining good lives: it enables us to escape many mistakes and miseries we could otherwise avoid only by brute luck. And the fact that the value claimed for autonomy is purely instrumental would be a great justificatory asset, given that the benefits autonomy confers appear to favour no particular view of what is intrinsically valuable in human life. By favouring no such view, the instrumental case for autonomy avoids 'perfectionism'—namely, the view that some ways of life are intrinsically better than others.

So we have good news for everyone. As long as they are instrumentally rational and know how autonomy would benefit them, the inhabitants of Amish colonies or religious studies departments, devotees of Romantic spontaneity or cautious followers of 'life-plans' will all cherish autonomy equally. For in learning to be autonomous the will is not inclined in any particular direction: one might as easily choose autonomously in deciding for a life of servitude as one could in opting for rootless independence.

Strictly speaking, the evasion of perfectionism is illusory. As Tom Hurka (1994) has shown, the instrumental argument does presuppose perfectionist ideas. The claim that there is a truth about the individual good that human beings fallibly seek to grasp is the very bedrock of the argument, which is to say its adherents assume that some lives are indeed intrinsically better than others (see 1 above). Yet the perfectionism Hurka reveals is minimal because it says nothing about the ends to which we should direct our lives; it only singles out what is said to be a necessary means for each of us to figure that out for himself. I claim that the perfectionism inherent in the ideal of autonomy cuts deeper than this and is incompatible with the instrumental argument.

III

Suppose for the moment that the instrumental benefits of autonomy are just as great as exponents of the instrumental argument say. They must still agree that the realization of those benefits very often depends on the exercise of autonomy in settings inhospitable to its exercise.

For example, children in the world as we know it grow up in an environment where powerful influences pull them away from autonomy, on any reasonable conception of what autonomy might be. I have in mind a popular culture that projects an image of well-being as ceaseless and thoughtless consumption; peer groups in which belonging depends on an unreasoned contempt for those who do not belong; the pressures of particular religious or ethnic traditions in which seriously to question what one is taught during childhood or adolescence immediately raises the spectre of love's withdrawal or at least provokes the disappointment and anxiety of those whose love one craves, and so on. Possessing a capacity for autonomy in circumstances such as these is not enough to secure its instrumental benefits because the power of the emotions and desires those social pressures repugnant to autonomy will evoke cannot be opposed by a motivationally inert capacity. What is needed rather is a certain character such that the pressures pitted against autonomy can be effectively resisted.

Notice that some of our pre-reflective intuitions about autonomy are very often about such resistance and the character it discloses. Our ordinary paragons of autonomy are people who cleave with poise and fortitude to their own considered view of good and evil, right and wrong, under almost overwhelming pressure to abandon it. They enact self-rule when most of us would surrender to the rule of others. And they evince the emotional susceptibilities we would expect of those for whom autonomy is a reflexively valued constituent of identity. We expect them to assert their autonomy when they believe they should, to feel a certain pride when they do so under difficult circumstances, and to succumb to shame when they fail through weakness of will. When our expectations in these respects are defeated, we have grounds to infer that they were not autonomous (or not so autonomous) after all, irrespective of evidence that they had the capacity to do otherwise. But if autonomy is an amalgam of capacity, desire, and emotional susceptibility, it is a constituent of character. The cultivation of character is not the same as helping someone to develop a capacity whose acquisition leaves the learner's ends unaffected.

My argument here depends on the functional correspondence between autonomy and other facets of character—in particular, virtues—whose value consists in enabling us to live as we should under conditions of countervailing desire and emotion. I do not appeal to any philosophically developed conception of character or virtue in using these concepts. My assumption is merely that skills and habits are internal to character only when they are part of a psychological ensemble of settled motivation, interpretive and perceptual propensities, and emotional responsiveness of the kind we identify through such words as compassionate, patient, and the like.

The instrumental argument collapses once we acknowledge that autonomy is a virtue (or putative virtue). The possibility that an autonomous person might choose a life of servility, for example, is now much more puzzling than it would seem if we believed that autonomy were merely a capacity rather than a part of character. On the capacity model, the choice would be intelligible in just the way that never using a tool one owns is intelligible. Possessing a tool does not predispose one to use it or not, and according to the instrumental argument, being autonomous is having a capacity one could as easily never use as regularly exercise. But autonomously choosing to be servile is as odd as compassionately choosing to be cruel or courageously opting for cowardice. To be sure, an autonomous person choosing a life of servility is still a possibility, but in so choosing one acts *against* the grain of character. People who have learnt to be autonomous find themselves endowed with a character that renders the autonomous self and the end of appropriately asserting autonomy scarcely distinguishable.

This is where a strong perfectionism becomes necessary if we are coherently to claim that autonomy is central to good lives and the upbringing on which they will in part depend. We must agree to the following: whatever intrinsic value inheres in lives that an autonomous person would be predisposed because of her autonomous character to reject must be less than the intrinsic value of autonomy itself and (or) the lives it inclines us to accept. If this were false, we could have no grounds to say that an education for autonomy is better for the child who receives it than the best illiberal alternatives, all things considered. Notice that the necessity of perfectionist comparison does not entail that the defenders of autonomy assign intrinsic value to autonomy itself. They might say that the value of autonomy lies entirely in the intrinsic value of the lives it enables and inclines us to accept. But the question still arises whether the value of those lives must be greater than the value of the lives autonomy inclines us to reject.

IV

An interesting attempt to circumvent the strong perfectionist question might be developed along the following lines. Not all virtues are alike. The internal diversity of the category would seem to open the possibility that autonomy might belong in a family of virtues that does not bend the will toward some ends rather than others. In that event, strong perfectionism could be evaded, and the only revision necessary to the instrumental argument would be the substitution of 'virtue' for 'capacity'. I am doubtful that any such family of virtues could exist. But regardless of that, the virtues to which autonomy is most obviously akin are not 'end-neutral', so to speak.

Some virtues directly entail the pursuit of particular ends (for example, compassion); others characterize agents and their lives adverbially in that a great many utterly different, even mutually repugnant, lives might be lived in the manner determined by the virtue. A serial killer might evince extraordinary patience in stalking his prey. And the man who devotes his life to caring for Alzheimer's patients might also demonstrate an extraordinary patience. Intuitively, autonomy does seem less like compassion than patience. But consider now the parallels between autonomy and patience more closely.

To be patient is to see the world in particular ways that would be hard or impossible for someone who lacked patience; it is to be resistant, even impervious to emotions of rage or despair that would defeat others in their pursuit of particular ends; it is to be especially mindful of the distinctive fulfillments that patience can give us, and, of course, it is to be inclined to behave in ways that are habitual for patient people (Callan 1993). Patience becomes second nature when it is successfully cultivated and, among other things, this means it will colour the attractiveness of possible ends and inform perceptions of their salience or marginality as options in deliberation. The allure of final ends must differ for the patient and the impatient to the extent that what the latter could only do (if at all) against the pull of second nature, the former can accomplish with little or no sense of burden. Furthermore, goods or supposed goods whose pursuit only lightly limits the indulgence of impatience will exert a weaker attraction for those who understand and can pursue the goods beyond impatience without acting against the grain of character. Other things being equal, impatience (and a little self-knowledge) must make child-rearing or teaching less than attractive roles. And other things again being equal, the patient individual is less inclined to be captivated by a life that revolved around New York singles' bars and a tumultuous career on the floor of its Stock Exchange than she might be otherwise be.

Parallel claims can be made about autonomy, even though the virtues differ in another important respect (see n. 10 below). Autonomy requires the moulding of desire and perception—not just behavioural patterns—so that ways of life alien to autonomy are interpreted in an autonomy-biased direction. The risks of surrendering the capacity critically to reflect on received beliefs about the good and the right will be salient to the autonomous chooser; and the charms of a life in which the burdens of reflective choice are relieved cannot be compelling for someone whose character is such that those burdens can already be carried without great strain or anxiety.

Another, more speculative point is worth some attention. The pedagogy of character formation is such that encouraging children to enjoy the exercise of the virtues we wish to inculcate is perhaps a natural, even an inevitable task. Thus we urge young children to take pride and pleasure in their proto-patience or their foreshadowings of real autonomy, regardless of the small mishaps and frustrations their actions might cause. Mishaps and frustrations must not be allowed to sap motivation that would sustain their efforts to become virtuous. Exhortations about the long-term benefits of patience, say, would very likely mean nothing to a child whose patient waiting for something has only resulted in tearful disappointment. I suspect that sensible parents or teachers who wish to instil patience will respond with emotional comfort and high praise for the patience that the child evinced. But then it seems as if patience is presented to the child as a constituent of an admirable life, not merely an instrumental trait whose good consequences alone should make us value it.

The same point would seem to apply, mutatis mutandis, to the cultivation of autonomy. The child who stands up against petty cruelties among her friends may incur the loss of friends. We naturally respond in praising her moral independence as admirable in itself, something to be cherished in the image of the human being she should want to be. But if instilling this attitude is close to a necessary task in the cultivation of autonomy, then a purely instrumental attitude to the value of autonomy in one's own autonomous character must be at best a rare psychological phenomenon, and so too must be the lack of any disinclination to choose ends at variance with the ongoing exercise of autonomy.

Richard Arneson and Ian Shapiro in their defence of the instrumental argument seem to concede that autonomy will indeed bend the will towards some ends rather than others (Arneson and Shapiro 1996: 365–411). They still think that state-enforced autonomy promotion can be justified on grounds that do not themselves presuppose strong perfectionist assumptions of any kind. These grounds are disclosed through a thought experiment that requires a guardian to choose between a 'secular worldly' (and autonomy-promoting) and a 'religious traditionalist' (and autonomy-inhibiting) style of child-rearing for a particular child. The religious tradition they have in mind is the Amish, though the generality of the label under which they subsume that case suggests, very unfortunately, that religious tradition is pervasively autonomy-inhibiting.[3] I return to that point later. My immediate interest is in two constraints built into the thought experiment:

No assumption is made about the relative value of the two options, but it is assumed that individuals differ in their traits so that for some individuals the secular way of life is better, and for some, the traditionalist way is better ... [It] is assumed that choosing after well-informed critical deliberation, or autonomously, increases the probability that an individual will choose a way of life, secular or traditionalists, that is better for her. (Arneson and Shapiro 1996: 401–2).

With the addition of some other assumptions that need not detain us, the guardian must opt for the worldly, autonomy-promoting education, or so say Arneson and Shapiro. But the relation of the first to the second sentence I have quoted is puzzling. It could not in general be true that people would be more likely to choose the better life were they to choose autonomously unless it were also true that *most* (not merely some) people were suited to the autonomous life. This would not be so if autonomy were only a capacity because a mere capacity would not pull one towards any particular ends. But autonomy is internal to the character of the agent, and therefore, young adults who have learnt to choose autonomously will to that extent be inclined to reject autonomy-inhibiting lives, even when they might be more suited to their (first) nature.[4] (In that case, the lives their cultivated second nature inclines them to choose would be in conflict with what they would otherwise be naturally disposed to choose. Given conflict of sufficient intensity, the claim that autonomous lives are badly suited to their nature becomes plausible.) So long as the guardian knows only that some are suited to heteronomy and some to autonomy, she *cannot* assume that choosing a way of life autonomously increases the likelihood of choosing well. By the same token, she cannot be compelled to infer that the secular, autonomy-promoting education is best for the child.

To avoid this impasse, Areneson and Shapiro might amend the first sentence so that the guardian assumes people are in general more suited to the autonomous life. But that assumption patently could not be squared with the claim that the thought experiment is unbiased in favour of autonomous ways of life. As I have already shown, in learning to become autonomous we acquire no neutral instrumentality but a character primed to resist the attractions of heteronomous lives. So Arneson and Shapiro come to grief on the following dilemma: either the guardian does not know the child is more likely than not to be suited to an autonomous life, in which case the guardian's decision is arbitrary; or the guardian does know, in which case the experiment is viciously circular because it assumes from the beginning the value of what it purports to justify.

So we are back to the conclusion reached at the end of section III. Whatever intrinsic goods we realize or are inclined to embrace by virtue of the accession of autonomy must be weighed against the intrinsic value of whatever ends its accession bends the will to reject. The instrumental argument purports to tell us what autonomy is and what is good about it without entangling us in messy disputes about the comparative intrinsic value of the lives that could be led among the Amish and the lives possible among the cosmopolitan denizens of Silicon Valley. But the argument must fail because autonomy belongs to character, and therefore, its justification must involve perfectionist comparative judgements of just this kind.

The comparative judgement that would favour autonomy cannot rest on any compelling argument unless it could be demonstrated that nothing of distinctive value is possible in lives without autonomy. I do not understand how this could be demonstrated. But much can be said that clarifies that choice for us and, when that is said, I believe any ethical appeal lives without autonomy might have will be greatly diminished.

Suppose the best conception of autonomy turned out to exclude no or very few lives that we would reflectively consider as good. This would be possible if we could show this: alluring lives many might regard as inconsistent with autonomy are not in fact inconsistent; and putatively good lives autonomy does in fact preclude have significantly diminished appeal on close scrutiny. So far as a conception of autonomy satisfied this criterion of reflective endorsement, it would be ethically inclusive. An ethically inclusive conception of autonomy would make very plausible the comparative perfectionist judgement that the justification of autonomy requires. An inclusive conception in this sense might be at odds with the lives that very many of us actually live, as a matter of social fact. Thus a normatively inclusive ideal is not necessarily socially inclusive.

I shall try to make persuasive the claim that autonomy is ethically, though unfortunately not socially, inclusive. But before this, more needs to be said about the nature of autonomy.

V

According to the argument in (1), the value of autonomy resides in the ability appropriately to revise one's conception of the good. 'Appropriately' is not a dispensable adverb here. That is so because a capacity for so-called autonomous revision could be good only so far as it helped us to enact appropriate revision.[5] The badness of bad choices is not mitigated whenever they are done after critical reflection. Yet if possessing an autonomous character enables and inclines one to make appropriate revision, it must also enable and incline one to resist the pull towards inappropriate revision. Autonomous revision and adherence are twin facets of the one virtue, and neither is inherently more laudable than the other. We need to think more about how these exercises of autonomy are related. I want to approach the relation through an example. My example is developed from Nicholas Wolterstorff's autobiographical essay (1993). Wolterstorff is a renowned philosopher and theologian at Yale University.

Induction into 'a public tradition of the Christian church'—the Dutch Reformed Church—was the defining experience of Wolterstorff's life. Before he could even understand what occurred at religious services, the austere beauty of the church and its rituals had affected him indelibly. And as understanding developed, the repetition of liturgy and Scripture 'sank their roots so deep into consciousness that nothing thereafter, short of senility, could remove them':

> My induction into the tradition, through words and silences, ritual and architecture, implanted in me an interpretation of reality—a fundamental hermeneutic. Nobody offered 'evidences' for the truth of the Christian Gospel; nobody offered 'proofs' for the inspiration of the Scriptures; nobody suggested that Christianity was the best explanation for one thing or another . . . The scheme of sin, salvation, and gratitude was set before us, the details were explained, and we were exhorted to live this truth. (Wolterstorff 1993: 263)

Yet Wolterstorff's childhood was not a time of intellectual quiescence or social deference. He recalls the friendly but disputatious family gatherings after Sunday services, when everything from theology to Hubert Humphrey's politics might become a topic of controversy, and anyone able to participate, regardless of age or gender, was welcome to join in. Within the received boundaries of the tradition, the intellect could move freely, unhampered by any social hierarchy, and for Wolterstorff at least, the boundaries were experienced as no constraint (Wolterstorff 1993: 265–6).

At Calvin College, his intellectual development continued to unfold within those boundaries. Here all the disparate cultural products of Western civilization were available for scrutiny. Nothing was off limits. Yet scrutiny was invited within the overarching frame of the Christian hermeneutic that had been implanted during childhood: 'The challenge constantly placed before us was to struggle to understand this massive inheritance in "Christian perspective"' (Wolterstorff 1993: 265). Now surely this could not be as safe an intellectual exercise as Sunday morning arguments about Hubert Humphrey. Much in that 'massive inheritance' of Western culture is intended to subvert the Christian perspective. And Wolterstorff recalls (fondly) students who came to the college already alienated from the Reformed tradition, and happy to find in Nietzsche an arsenal with which to besiege it in the classroom.

Wolterstorff left Calvin College not merely with a more intellectually well-armoured version of the hermeneutic he brought to it, along with some happy memories of a few Nietzschean apostates. He had also begun an apprenticeship in philosophy, and in a few glancing sentences, he suggests that he knew engagement with the philosophical tradition had to be more or other than a straightforward application of his faith. To participate in the philosophical tradition is to shape it in some measure, and that effort would bear the imprint of the self that was formed prior to participation. Yet to participate was also to allow the tradition to shape you, in ways that might discomfit the self as it was before philosophy (Wolterstorff 1993: 268–70).

I want to develop this story a bit further. But since the facts do not sufficiently fit my purposes, I take leave of the real Wolterstorff and invent Wolterstorff II. Wolterstorff II had a life exactly like Wolterstorff until they both left Calvin College. As he embarks on graduate training at Harvard, Wolterstorff II eagerly begins to study philosophy in an environment where his faith is not taken for granted. Gradually he comes to the painful realization that as a philosopher he cannot meet the challenge posed at Calvin College. Some of the arguments against theism and Christianity that he encounters seem overwhelmingly powerful, and he is too intellectually scrupulous to pretend that this does not matter. Inside philosophy, the Christian hermeneutic seems to yield and crumble, only to be built anew, and then to disintegrate again in a cycle of anxious belief and doubt.

Yet, despite his intellectual travails, Wolterstorff II finds that he cannot bring himself to assent to the sceptical conclusions that his studies often seem to thrust upon him. For when he sets aside his troubling engagement with philosophy, he finds that his world is just as it had always been. When he tries to prays, doubt dissolves and the same intense feeling of being in contact with the God of Christianity overcomes him; the solace of reading Scripture is just as it was from the time he began to read with real understanding; and religious ritual has the same sacramental quality he dimly felt as a small child in church. The worries of the would-be Christian philosopher then seem small and foolish to someone for whom the world cannot but be experienced save through an encompassing Christian hermeneutic. His anxious oscillation between philosophical doubt and religious engagement begins to fade, as doubt comes to seem increasingly irrelevant to the life he should lead. Wolterstorff II decides to give up philosophy and become an accountant.

The story I have told is obviously compatible with Wolterstoff II being heteronomous in adhering to his faith. The interesting question is whether the only plausible inference we could make is that he acted heteronomously, given the facts of the case as I have described them. I want to examine some considerations that might be adduced to convict him of heteronomy—I call them 'the case for the prosecution'. They do not merely condemn Wolterstorff II. They also suggest a familiar mode of child-rearing that avoids the great hazards to autonomy that Wolterstorff II's upbringing would seem to create. I claim that the case for the prosecution, and the educational prescriptions derived from it, express an excessive preoccupation with protecting the conditions for autonomous revision to the good that obscures the equal importance of autonomous adherence.

VI

Here is the case for the prosecution. Wolterstorff II's inability to accept conclusions to which his philosophical studies drew him showed that he was unable to revise his conception of the good when compelling reasons warranted revision. The self proved to be irrevocably moulded by the Christian hermeneutic that was so forcefully instilled from early childhood (see (2)). Indeed, nothing else could be rationally expected, given that his intellectual development was so narrowly contained by religious orthodoxy. Supposed truths by which children and adolescents are 'exhorted to live' without any appeal to evidence, argument, or serious reflection on alternative views are a barren ground for the growth of autonomy. For if these 'truths' define a taken-for-granted perspective within which young adults are instructed to interpret all else, the perspective effectively becomes a hermeneutic cage. Someone whose intellect can to a degree break free of confinement—for example, Wolterstorff II at Harvard—is liable to find that his intellect has merely become a loose cog in a machine that runs without it. Wolterstorff II does not rule his own life. His tradition runs it for him, and that condition was virtually guaranteed by his upbringing.

Furthermore, Wolterstorff II's cautionary tale suggests some sensible ideas about the kind of upbringing that would protect children from his fate. Suppose we place styles of child-rearing on a continuum from the most insular to the most open. The most insular would shield children from just about any experience that might pose a challenge to the way of life they share with their parents. In the most open, a coherent matrix for the formation of the self disappears entirely in a Babel of disparate influences and counter-influences. The prosecution admits that an upbringing free of all credal or cultural bias is impossible. It also agrees that close proximity to the open pole of the continuum imperils the emergence of a coherent, much less an autonomous self. Yet it still insists that an education with good prospects of realizing autonomy must be far more open to different conceptions of the good than the one Wolterstorff II experienced. Thus even if children are initiated into the religion of their parents, insistent didacticism must be avoided at all times. Parents should inform children about alternative religious (and irreligious) perspectives as their understanding grows enough to absorb the information; they should encourage curiosity about these alternatives, welcome questions, even doubts that cut to the core of their own faith; they should place their children frequently in social settings where they must cooperate and find friendships with children of a different faith or none at all, and so on. By such means they would teach their children that religious commitment is a matter they must decide for themselves as adults, without blinkers fixed by an education that made it psychologically impossible or at best very painful to remove them. They would freely abandon the faith of their parents once they came to regard it as intellectually untenable. Their selves would be revocably encumbered, all the way down, just as (2) requires.

This is all much too quick. First, why assume that in abandoning philosophical doubt for the Christian hermeneutic that had always sustained him, Wolterstorff II failed to enact rational revision to his conception of the good? Why is it unreasonable to suppose that his choice was an instance of rational *adherence* to his conception of the good? In a perfectly familiar sense of 'acting for a reason', the fulfilment and reassurance that religious practice continued to give him despite his philosophical crisis constituted a reason to keep the faith. The prosecution might be quick to say that it was not a good enough reason, and therefore (2) still requires us to condemn Wolterstorff as a heretic to autonomy. But if it could not count as a good enough reason that must be so because good reasons are deemed to be 'public' in some strong sense, so that the reasons of philosophy count, whereas reasons found in individual experiences of prayer or worship do not. But this is an exceedingly odd line to take in the context of the autonomy argument. For the objection stipulates an interpretation of (2) that would appear to be inconsistent with (3) by declaring the particularities of the 'inside' or appreciative aspects of the good life to be irrelevant to rational revision or adherence.

More importantly, the strongly public view of reasoning about the good is deeply counterintuitive anyhow, regardless of its incongruity in the autonomy argument. If I found persuasive some philosophical argument for the existence of the God to whom worship is due, but every effort at prayer made me feel like an idiot talking to himself, would autonomy necessitate that I continue those efforts indefinitely so long as I can find nothing amiss in the argument? No. Only a fool would exalt his powers of ratiocination so thoroughly over the content of personal experience to persist in 'worship' that cannot be experienced as such. The distinction between reasons that are in some strong sense public and those that are not may well be critical for a liberal conception of public reason.[6] But whatever the truth of that, the distinction cannot do double duty by marking out a notion of practical reason that rightly applies both when we deliberate autonomously about our own good and when we reason together about the common good.

The relevant contrast here between the public and the personally experiential is not a contrast between reasons we register as alien, impersonal threats to our identity and reasons that comfortably reside within an identity to which we cling as best we can against the external threat. If that were the case—and one could certainly imagine yet another Wolterstorff about whom it would be the case—then the reasons of philosophy do not really count as reasons at all in deliberation about the individual's beliefs and values. They would only be temptations to be resisted for the preservation of an identity hostile to any truth they might disclose. Then it would become implausible to think of him as genuinely engaged in his own reasoning about the true and the good because reason is warped in ways that shield fundamental aspects of identity from its claims.

But nothing in the facts of the case compels us to understand Wolterstorff II in this way. On the contrary, he is depicted as someone who directly confronts the reasons of philosophy as considerations that rightly belong inside the field of critical self-reflection. They are 'his own' reasons as much as the reasons of his uniquely personal experience are; they are 'public' only in the sense that the reasons of philosophy are accessible to our common reason independently of experiences whose bearing on truth cannot properly be universalized. The thesis that reasons of the second kind must always trump reasons of the first kind is not entailed by the thesis that people should think for themselves and rule their own lives.

Another facet of the prosecution's case is less easily dismissed. Wolterstorff II is candid about the enormous formative power of non-rational influences in shaping his religious identity. (For example, I take it that the repetition of a liturgy during childhood does not count as giving anyone a reason to do or believe anything, irrespective of how capacious the concept of non-public reason should be.) Precisely because such powerful non-rational influences were exerted in establishing the Christian hermeneutic, a legitimate concern is that what Wolterstorff II claims to be the deep and authentic personal fulfil-ment his faith gives him might really be something entirely other than that. Perhaps his 'faith' is nothing more than the upshot of causal processes that operate at the back of deliberation, driven by fears of authority, or anxieties about exclusion from a safe world where he need not think or feel for himself. He consciously regards himself—and presents himself to others—as bravely confronting the arguments of the philosophers and then reflectively endors-ing deeper values at the centre of his identity. The truth is that he has not escaped his childhood.[7]

As a moral criticism of the way Wolterstorff II was reared, this interpreta-tion of the case should worry us even if we had some way of knowing that the interpretation was strictly false and that Wolterstorff II had in fact chosen autonomously. For the reasonable worry would persist that the kind of upbringing he underwent creates unacceptably high *risks* of precipitating the species of heteronomy just described. So the argument has shifted now to more general ground. The case against Wolterstorff II in particular may fall short of the mark. But the case against the style of child-rearing his story exemplifies can still be pressed hard by virtue of the alleged hazards to auton-omy that it typically poses. The grounds for worrying about these derive from (2) and (3). And I do not think they can be dismissed as the parochial concern of Western Romantics who fret about an authenticity to which others are sensibly indifferent. The idea of a good to be achieved, in part at least, through a process of inner development and discipline that is exposed to psychologi-cal and cultural pressures that the self may not consciously register is, I would think, common ground between the Protestant Christian and the secular Romantic. And I would suspect (though I do not know) that it might have application in other cultural contexts as well.

To continue to embrace a conception of the good merely because one has internalized norms that were imposed by authority during childhood is to be rendered the servile instrument of the will of others. Protestant Christianity began in the rejection of servility on matters of faith. Yet some historians have noted that the child-rearing it has sometimes sponsored blurs the distinction between supreme parental authority and the supreme authority of God (Greven 1977; Sangster 1963). I am no theologian. Yet that sounds suspiciously like blasphemy to me.

Many of us care nothing about such things. But the rejection of servility is inseparable from recognizing ourselves as right-holders whose moral worth equals that of any other (Callan 1997: 152–7). People who are servile cannot sustain that self-recognition. They live their lives as the instrument of another's will, either because they see themselves as naturally subordinate to the authoritative other or because their upbringing has disabled them from seriously entertaining any choice repugnant to the other's will. In the second case, an illusory sense of his standing as the bearer of equal rights may take hold, but this merely disguises the true character of a life that is still the instrument of another.

The need to protect children from the vice of servility gives the alternative, more open mode of child-rearing proposed by the prosecution much of its appeal. The alternative forgoes any forceful didacticism, opens the mind to a sympathetic understanding of rival conceptions of the good as early as possible; and though the growth of a bias-free perspective cannot be expected even then, we would have far weaker grounds to worry that the choices of the adult would be marred by an inability rationally to revise an ascribed conception of the good. In fact, there would be no ascribed conception of the good, strictly speaking.

The advantages of the open child-rearing are perhaps especially striking when we note how unusual Wolterstorff II's story might be as an example of relatively insular, tradition-bound upbringing. The openness to argument among kin that Wolterstorff recalls from childhood and adolescence, as well as the egalitarian relations among all those who argued, is not uniformly evident, for example, throughout other theistic, including Christian traditions. The rote learning of the widely popular Accelerated Christian Education (ACE) schools, with their relentless insistence on incorrigible 'right answers' to all questions, is a great distance from the cherished place of intellect and understanding at least in the later phases of Wolterstorff's upbringing (Rose 1988). And I doubt that Nietzschean critics of Christianity are quite so welcome at all other Christian institutions of higher learning as they evidently were in philosophy seminars at Calvin College.

All this looks plausible to me. But if it were true, it would seem to me one-sidedly true. First, if the kind of upbringing Wolterstorff II exemplifies creates risks that individuals will be unable autonomously to revise their conceptions of the good, the open alternative recommended by the prosecution would seem to incur risks that individuals will be unable rationally to adhere to them. Coming adequately to appreciate many things that make our lives good requires a certain steady resistance to distraction and a constancy that do not come easily as we grow to maturity. Lives devoted to the perfection of some artistic or intellectual talent, say, would generally fit this pattern, and so too do lives in which erotic love is disciplined by marital fidelity. Being unable or disinclined to adhere to the good we seek in the face of distraction or episodic doubt and temptation may damage our lives as much as an inability or disin-clination to revise one's conception when that is called for. A reasonable claim is that coming to understand a rich and complex conception of the good, and learning autonomously to cleave to it, is much harder when a child's forma-tive environment does little to block a nomadic drift from one gleaming possi-bility to another. And arresting that drift may often involve the exertion of non-rational influences of the sort that loom so large in Wolterstorff's child-hood—shielding children from experiences one believes would confuse or corrupt them, engaging them in activities whose presuppositions they do not yet grasp, instilling beliefs whose grounds remain for some time unexamined.

The style of upbringing that Wolterstorff II's life exemplifies poses risks to the development of autonomy. By the same token, it seems to provide strong insurance against risks to a cluster of dispositions needed to ensure autonomous adherence to conceptions of the good that greater openness would at some point endanger. I very much doubt that empirical investigation could ever tell us much about when that point will be reached exactly or just how great the hazards to autonomy are in cases like Wolterstorff's.[8] But I think that this much can be said with a fair degree of assurance. Whatever makes it plausible to imagine Wolterstorff II autonomously choosing to keep the faith is surely tied to a narrative that reveals a gradual opening of the mind preced-ing the choice: the young adolescent learns that the earthly authority of the elder members of his extended family does not make their views less subject to error than his own; the college student begins to study authors whose bril-liant arguments are aimed at destroying his faith, and so on. The case I presented patently would not be the same if the choice of faith or philosophy were not placed within that narrative context. That being so, I very much doubt that any credible case can be made for the autonomy-conducive char-acter of forms of child-rearing that fail to encourage a parallel opening of the mind. And if autonomy is a good for all, then the opening of mind that Wolterstorff delineates cannot be the privilege of those with unusual scholarly aptitudes; it must also find a place in the education of those whose formal education ends with high school. The sheer internal variety of the categories 'religious upbringing' and 'religious schooling' make it pretty certain that much that is comfortably located within each category has a place for the opening of mind that autonomy necessitates; it also makes it equally certain that much that is located there is repugnant to autonomy.

But now another problem comes into view. If a necessary part of the development of autonomy is an opening of the mind that makes possible critical revision to given conceptions of the good, as well as critically informed adherence, then we might ask to *what* does the mind open when all goes as it should. A commonly assumed answer among many liberals seems to be that we need not bother much with the question. Once we liberate our children's lives by exposing them to the diversity around them and encouraging them to think for themselves, then all will be well. That would make sense only if the diversity that abounded around them really were an edifying ethical pluralism. But is it?

What exposure to diversity really amounts to is very often something like this. We instil a consumer hermeneutic that offers a ready interpretation of anything that comes its way, from religions to art to forms of family life and sexual expression. (Another familiar phenomenon is parents and teachers cast as rueful spectators to this demoralizing process, unable or unwilling effectively to counteract the seductive power of consumer culture.) In any event, the social world that engulfs the child insistently says that objects of consumption alone are fit objects of desire, or at least the only key to all that is desirable. That message is conveyed through the ubiquitous manipulation of the advertising industry and mass entertainment, whose persuasive strategies are designed to short-circuit independent thought in order to elicit the desire to consume what will never be needed and was never before wanted.

The ease with which just about anything can be 'read' according to the code of consumption creates an appearance of diversity that disguises the levelling uniformity beneath. The mercurial lives so often led in these circumstances might tempt one to infer that here we have the best possible conditions for autonomous revision to conceptions of the good. But even this is false since the consumer hermeneutic makes more or less unimaginable the value of lives that track ends other than consumption. Faithful adherence to any alternative conception would seem to be in dangerously short supply. And one might wonder if conceptions of the good, as opposed to mere objects of desire, have much real purchase here at all. In any event, the lives of those who consume become the instruments of those who profit from consumption in a way that bears a striking resemblance to the fate that befalls the servile instruments of some fundamentalist religious and ethnic traditions.

My local newspaper, *The San Jose Mercury*, recently published an article written by a young woman who had just that summer been married in an ancient Roman Catholic chapel in Florence. The woman was not a Catholic, nor was her husband. None the less, she had wished dearly to be married in such a church, and though initially rebuffed by the Catholic authorities, she had persisted. As luck would have it, her husband discovered that he had been baptized as a Catholic. (For some unexplained reason he had been ignorant of that fact.) This enabled her finally to secure Church approval for a Catholic wedding. The day of her wedding was perfection itself: a quaint ceremony, amidst sumptuous Renaissance architecture, followed by a traditional Italian feast for American friends and family. The weather was also great. Nowhere in the article was the religious significance of the ceremony so much as mentioned.

My response to that article was something close to horror. That is not because I have much regard for the Catholic Church in which I grew up. What appalled me was the woman's utter blindness to the human significance of *not* being Roman Catholic. How could anyone be so cavalier about conducting her wedding through a ritual that expressed beliefs of the highest importance in human life to which she gave little or no thought?

My questions express an archaic earnestness that would be merely embarrassing or funny for those who live within the consumer hermeneutic. There a wedding ceremony is an expression of individual style rather than conviction and those who think otherwise simply fail to get the point. One chooses between one ceremony and another as one chooses between honeymoon destinations or wedding dresses. The distinction between the good and the merely pleasing or seemingly good life largely dissolves (compare (1)). Servility must indeed be contrasted with autonomy, but so too must polymorphous nihilism.[9] When liberal philosophers talk about the need to expose children to ethical diversity we seem to envisage something extremely high-minded, in the spirit of Isaiah Berlin's pluralism perhaps. But we should worry that what children actually *get* when the wide world beyond the family opens up to them is far more light-minded and homogeneous than that.

In his fine and disturbing book, *Cold New World*, William Finnegan has vividly depicted the aimless lives of adolescents in downwardly mobile American families (Finnegan 1998). He sees them trapped between the lure of consumerism and thoughtless solidarities spawned by disparate forms of fundamentalism—the Nation of Islam, Nazi skinhead groups, warring gangs. Finnegan rightly emphasizes the role of poverty and negligible educational and economic opportunities in creating the plight of his subjects. Nevertheless, affluence by itself could hardly enable these adolescents to live meaningful, self-directed lives. Money would certainly put an end to misery. It would also give them the consumer goods they crave, but not necessarily anything else. And because some fundamentalist groups are much more wholesome than others, Finnegan's subjects might well be better off there—and no further away from autonomy—than as affluent consumers and nothing more.

VII

Becoming autonomous is as much learning autonomously to adhere to a conception of the good as it is learning autonomously to revise it. Therefore, we must be equally mindful of possible threats to autonomous development that impinge on both facets of its growth. In the light of what I have argued so far, the development of autonomy begins to look like finding a mean between contrary vices, with servility threatening it on one side and the disintegration of all ethical perspective on the other. I have shown that autonomy can be evinced as fully in steadfast adherence to received tradition as in bold revision to ethical beliefs that carry one away from received tradition. That being so, learning to be autonomous cannot by itself favour the disruption of ethical tradition over its continuity across generations. Furthermore, the reasoning that motivates autonomous adherence or revision quite properly draws on particularities of experience and feeling that do not belong within the ambit of impersonal reason. These particularities will in turn reflect to varying degrees the imprint of rituals and teachings absorbed during the formative years of childhood, and the imprint of tradition will include influences that are strictly non-rational. I hope these points do something to assuage the concern that autonomy, once it is recognized as a strongly perfectionist ideal of character, could only be widely cultivated at the cost of other important, intrinsically valuable ways of life in which the continuity of tradition figures prominently. To the extent that the concern has been assuaged, the thesis that autonomy is ethically inclusive has been made more plausible.

What seriously alluring conceptions of the good are lost or eroded in a world where many more people are autonomous or more fully autonomous than they are now? Of course, many do seem to want lives of servility or polymorphous nihilism, and want them for their children too. Autonomy is not socially inclusive. Yet the world as we know it is congenial enough to what such people care about, and if an education for autonomy might do a little to suggest alternative ways of thinking about human well-being, then I would think that is a very good thing. If I am wrong about that, it must be because far more can be said in favour of servility or ethical nihilism than I can possibly imagine.

Finally, the argument I have traced suggests that schools that are genuinely open to ethical diversity might be much more difficult to create in current circumstances than their adherents have recently imagined.[10] For example, consider Arneson and Shapiro's very upbeat account of the 'typical American high school', an institution they believe to be signally well equipped to prepare children for their civic responsibilities in a pluralistic democracy:

To this [civic educational] end, a high school education is not a panacea, but it does provide some skills and knowledge needed to be a competent democratic deliberator. One might add that the experience of attending a typical contemporary high school—

be it public or parochial—introduces the youth to people of different backgrounds, of different creeds, beliefs, ethnicity, and social class than her own. The experience of informal negotiating with one's classmates and adjustment to differences among them is itself a helpful preparation for the responsibilities of democratic citizenship (Arneson and Shapiro 1996: 337)

I am interested for the moment only in the image of the admirably diverse high school evoked in this passage. Whether that school is indeed typical or civically uplifting are matters I set aside.

Suppose we add some extra detail compatible (at first blush) with Arneson and Shapiro's sketch. Let us imagine that the many creeds to which students claim to subscribe in this school have an almost uniformly feeble hold on their lives. They are Methodist or Muslim, say, only because they are coaxed or compelled by their parents to attend a church or a mosque, and the thought of giving much reflection to any other religious faith is simply too tiresome to bother with. Ethnicity is on bold display in hairstyles, clothing, the fluctuating boundaries of peer groups, and in proclamations of group pride. But at their most serious, these phenomena seem to be part of collective, symbolic opposition to racism rather than a deep engagement with ancestral traditions. At a very common and more frivolous level, they are markers of instant and perhaps fleeting belonging in an institution where belonging nowhere is sometimes quite dangerous and always painful. And differences of social class are conspicuous too in disparities between those who take the academically rigorous classes and those who do not, as well as in the bitter envy and resentment of the poor as they confront the condescension of the rich. And enveloping all this teeming diversity is a common consumer hermeneutic so deeply rooted that ideas beyond its boundaries are almost unimaginable.

Shapiro and Arneson would no doubt be appalled by my elaborated version of their 'typical', diverse high school. That is not what they could have in mind on any charitable interpretation of the passage I quoted. Yet what I have depicted might often be what some parents *see* when they look at a particular American high school. To be appalled by that spectacle is not necessarily to favour a traditional religious upbringing nor is it necessarily to be any respecter of autonomy. Still, one can certainly imagine religiously devout parents who believe their faith could only have meaning in their children's lives if it were autonomously embraced being justifiably insistent in refusing to send their children to any such school.

Within recent liberal political philosophy the resurgence of interest in questions about civic education and the proper limits of parents' and the state's authority to educate has produced much valuable work about the frailties of arguments old and new for wide parental authority in education. A bright thread running through almost all that liberals have said on the subject is insistence on the need for exposure to diversity in children's and adolescents' lives in order to bolster their developing autonomy. I believe that is true.

But the liberal argument for common schools must fall short in the absence of greater clarity about how an edifying diversity could be made available in common schools despite the autonomy-destroying pressures of popular culture. Were that clarity available, we might find that we liberals have much more in common with many who cherish faith and tradition than we ever thought we had.

Notes

I had great difficulty writing this chapter and seriously considered abandoning it on more than one occasion. Dave Archard and Colin Macleod gave me extremely helpful criticism (and encouragement) that dissuaded me from giving up when the chapter was not very far from completion. Randy Curren was my gracious host when I read an earlier version to a friendly, gently sceptical, and extremely helpful audience at the University of Rochester. I also owe much gratitude to people who discussed the essay with me at length or gave me written comments. Thanks to Harry Brighouse, Randy Curren, Debra Satz, Jim Johnson, Rob Kunzman, Jon Levinsohn, Ira Lit, Ken Strike, Rob Reich, Rich Ryan, Rami Wernik, and Nicholas Wolterstorff.

1. See Kymlicka 1989: 34–5, 59–64; 1990: 200–4; 1995: 81–2; Arneson and Shapiro 1996: 365–41; Macleod 1997: 117–140. A closely similar argument, albeit with some concessions to perfectionism, is to be found in Brighouse 2000: 67–73.
2. It is prospectively necessary, so to speak. I mean that if one looks to the future of any particular child or adolescent, and assumes the continuity of some very general social conditions that currently obtain, it is hard to imagine her faring well without autonomy, even if rare good fortune might enable some to live without it. This is the sense in which we might say that the acquisition of literacy is necessary to our good.
3. Arguments among political, legal, and educational theorists about parents' and children's rights are almost always marred by the exchange of stereotype and counter-stereotype. Arneson and Shariro's assumption that the radical curtailment of autonomy among the Amish might be representative of 'religious tradition' is akin to Shelley Burtt's defence of the Amish on the basis of the 'long and distinguished traditions of religious scholarship to reflect critically on one's own (perhaps unquestioned) religious commitments' (Burtt 1996: 416). Yet the Amish have contributed nothing to those traditions of critical reflection and would be loath to do so. Christianity has embodied the tension between philosophy and faith from before the birth of St Augustine, but the Amish are about as far from the critical currents within Christianity as one could possibly get. To criticize or defend religious tradition on the basis of such coarse-grained stereotypes helps no one and illuminates nothing.
4. To object to the assumption that people are in general more suited by nature to autonomous lives is not to imply that they are not. One might simply find the idea of a life 'suited to one's nature' too obscure to give it one's assent.
5. One might say that the 'appropriate' choice autonomy requires is only such in the *very* wide sense applicable to the patient psychopath and the patient altruist when they choose well by the standard of patience. But if we are considering how

autonomy is conceived and valorized in the liberal tradition, I cannot think of any argument of consequence that does not assume or explicitly acknowledge the need for a sense of justice that constrains the realm of choice within which autonomy tracks the good. If anyone's linguistic intuitions suggest that autonomy is properly ascribed without regard to moral criteria, I shall happily accommodate them. Wherever I say 'autonomy' they are free to substitute 'autonomy constrained by a sense of justice'.

6. The literature on the political distinction between public and non-public reason and the role of religious faith as it bears on the distinction is vast. Some examples are Audi and Wolterstorff 1995; Perry 1991; Gutmann and Thompson 1990. Much of the recent literature is at least in part a response to John Rawls's turn to political liberalism (e.g. Rawls 1993, 1985).

7. David Archard has pressed the importance of another possibility. The kind of upbringing that Wolterstorff experienced might create no insuperable obstacle to the development of autonomy. But it could still block autonomous choice by making the emotional costs of choosing against the values of one's upbringing prohibitively high. Thus the prosecution might argue that the costs of forfeiting or at best greatly straining relations with kin and community will likely thwart the exercise of autonomy in such circumstances. I am not entirely sure what to make of this. I do not know, for example, that the child who announces to devout parents in the Reformed tradition that he intends to abandon the faith will in general be less vulnerable to a hostile or contemptuous response than one who tells atheistic, academic parents that he is abandoning philosophy for the Reformed tradition. Parents (and others) with strong beliefs about which lives are good or bad will be not be pleased when someone they love chooses a life they strongly believe to be bad. Whether the displeasure is more likely to motivate hostility, ostracism, or something equally unpleasant in the case of people with traditional religious beliefs I just do not know, and I am not sure anyone else knows either.

8. What I have said about conditions needed for growth in the ability autonomously to adhere to a conception of the good has involved some empirical speculation. I doubt that philosophy can have anything to say with assurance about such matters; I also doubt that developmental or social psychology will help us much either because the difference between 'autonomy', in the sense that matters here, and its antonyms will commonly depend on subtle differences between self-ignorance and self-knowledge (see 3) regarding which robust empirical generalization will likely be elusive. The fact that autonomous adherence also involves an 'appropriate' exercise of practical reason further compounds the difficulties of scientific investigation. For it means that investigation would require some defensible empirical proxy for appropriateness. And finally, a reasonable surmise is that what helps or hinders the development of autonomy in the relevant sense is sensitive to many factors within and across cultures which questions about the comparative advantages and disadvantages of insularity or openness do not illuminate. No doubt the behavioural sciences will continue to reveal much about the growth of 'personal autonomy', in other important senses of that richly ambiguous word, but the concept of autonomy under consideration here may well prove to be much more empirically intractable.

9. Jim Johnson has urged me to see not two but one antonym here. The servile adherent to a religious tradition departs from autonomy in just the way my so-called polymorphous nihilist does. Each is merely an instrument to the will of others. I see the force of this. My only hesitation is that servility seems not to disable one from making ethical judgements, at least in some thin sense, though these judgements are not one's 'own' in the pregnant sense that the language of self-rule and autonomy evokes.

10. I am one of the adherents. But for reasons indicated here I find it harder to imagine what the practice would look like in contemporary circumstances than I used to do.

8

Children, Multiculturalism, and Education

David Archard

Brian Barry has rightly drawn attention to the confusion which can arise from using the term 'multiculturalism' both to describe the fact of cultural diversity and to characterize a programme, a set of normative recommendations, that is a response to this fact (2001: 22). Someone who acknowledges the existence of the fact need not be committed to the politics of 'recognition' or 'difference' that some have commended as required of 'multiculturalism' in the latter sense. Yet even the fact of multiculturalism that arguably presents a problem for the modern liberal democratic polity should not be simply taken as the present existence of a number of well-defined but diverse cultures. It is not diversity as such but a persisting diversity that is problematic. In turn this persistence should not be thought of as a simple natural given. For cultural groups have to be reproduced. Their reproduction is a function of many factors—political, economic, cultural, social, and legal—some of which are the results of deliberate human action, others of which are not. Crucially, reproduction is effected across generations. For a cultural group to preserve itself is just for the next generation to share the essential defining of the imme- diately preceding generation. For a cultural group to endure is for the children of the present members of that group to become the future members of the group. I grant that a cultural group could reproduce itself if children other than its own came to share its values and way of life. But it is most probable that it should be by means of its own children that a group endures, and it is in respect of its own children that a group and its members can most obvi- ously make claims to see that way of life transmitted.

For that reason it is understandable that education should be central to multiculturalism both as a fact of persisting diversity and as a politics of recognition of that diversity. For, most obviously, those who belong to a particular group and who wish to see the group continue to flourish will want their children to make up the group of the future. At the very least they will want to be assured that any public education does not subvert or vitiate their own attempts, as parents and members of the group, to pass on to their own children those characteristics which presently define their group. As a result there are the familiar demands for separate schools or for the exclusion from a national curriculum of certain materials. Much discussed examples are provided by the American cases of *Wisconsin v. Yoder* [1972] and *Mozert v. Hawkins County Public School* [1985]. In the first the Old Amish Order sought exemption from the requirement that their children should attend public school to the statutorily required age so that they might prepare them for life within their own community. In the second case a group of fundamentalist Christian parents sued the Tennessee school board to prevent their children from being exposed to reading material whose content they considered violated their own deeply held religious convictions. In both cases parents objected to a public education inasmuch as it annulled or undercut their own efforts to pass on to their children that which constituted them as a group.

At this point it is worth pausing to consider terminology. The dramatis personae of multiculturalism are variously described as 'groups', 'communities', 'cultures', 'identities', and 'minorities'. It is important not to obscure the different forms that diversity can take. For instance Will Kymlicka draws attention to the distinction between 'polyethnicity' and 'multinationality' (1995). However, since I want to discuss general issues, I will largely elide or ignore these distinctions. I am concerned principally with the inculcation by parents of their children in the values, ways of life, practices, and beliefs that may be said to be definitive of the group to which the parents belong. Talk of values may not be especially relevant to the transmission across generations of some shared identities but such talk does allow for a clearer focus upon the central issues of interest to social and political philosophy.

What is striking, and relevant to this volume, is that debate over multiculturalism has principally if not exclusively been conducted as a debate over what adult citizens can make claims to and from the state. Do cultural groups have rights? If they do, do they do so only as a means, indirectly, of protecting the rights of individuals to associate with one another, to make life choices, and to have their identity recognized? If groups have rights that do not, in this fashion, reduce to the rights of their individual members, how shall we balance these two sets of rights one against another? In all of this discussion the rights or interests of children have not been extensively considered.

What follows is an attempt to become clearer about the balance that needs to be struck between the interests individuals or groups have in reproducing their identity and the interests children have in acquiring or in not acquiring an identity. I shall first say something about the interests of groups and their adult members, then I shall discuss two indirect arguments that advance the interests of children in autonomy, and then finally I shall say something about the interests of the children.

Let me suggest that there are three very different kinds of strategy to show that it is legitimate for a cultural group to reproduce itself by transmitting to children the defining values of the group. The first strategy is one that claims that the cultural group has a right to reproduce itself and to do so through the transmission of a shared way of life to the next generation. I shall call this the group strategy. The second strategy consists in appealing directly to the claims that parents may make in respect of their children. If parents are entitled to mould children in a certain image of their own choosing and if the image should be that of the parents' cultural identity, then the children must and most probably will acquire that identity. This strategy proceeds by means of a key claim about parenting and I will call it the parenting strategy. The final strategy is indirect. It appeals to the value of familial life. It does not directly insist upon the rightfulness of parents moulding children to their own way of life. Rather it esteems the shared life of the family. The foreseeable consequence of such a sharing of one's life is a sharing of key values. Yet that effect is not directly aimed at; nor is it claimed that the effect is justified in its own right. Rather it is an inevitable and permissible outcome of what is rightly valued, namely a shared family life. I shall call this the familial strategy.

In order to focus on the interests of the child I shall assume that, independently of its implications for children, a group's way of life does not give the policy-maker reasons to discount its claim to be reproduced. This might be the case if the practice of its way of life violated the basic rights of some of its members or of those who are not members. I shall further assume that there are no pressing general reasons why there should not be cultural groups, that is, I shall assume that the fact of cultural diversity is not, in itself, an obviously bad thing. In short there are good reasons for there to be a variety of cultural groups and no reasons, other than those having to do with children, why there should not be those particular groups that do exist.

Let me take the group strategy first. In his *Multiculturalism and 'The Politics of Recognition'* Charles Taylor invokes the example of the French Canadian demand for 'la survivance' (survival) of their identity. This is the demand for that identity literally to live beyond the present generation: 'Policies aimed at survival actively seek to *create* members of the community, for instance, in their assuring that future generations continue to identify as French-speakers. There is no way that these policies could be seen as just providing a facility to already existing people' (1992: 58–9; see also 40 n. 16).

Those who are to be the future French Canadians do not yet exist; they have to be made. Taylor concludes that if the policies that aim at 'la survivance' are to be justified this cannot be in terms of the interests of present members; they do not serve 'already existing people'. That leaves two sets of interests: those of the group as a group, and those of the future members of the group. The context for Taylor's invocation of 'la survivance' makes it clear, I think, that he intends the group as a group to have a claim to survive. Even if he believes that individuals, both present and future, do have an interest in their group existing, his invocation of the demand for 'survivance' is intended to canvass the interest of the group as such in its own continued existence.

Of course, existing individuals do straightforwardly have desires for what shall happen after their death—that their families will be adequately cared for, their inheritance properly dispersed, their intellectual legacy respected, their life work carried on. Most directly and relevantly it is obviously true that if I have lived my life by a certain set of values I would not wish to see these values disappear. I should be disappointed if no one after me should take these values seriously and try to live by them. Further if I have striven to realize these values, to give practical effect to them, I would wish to see what I have created endure.

It would be a mistake to see such desires as simply being my wish for immortality, my wanting that my name and whatever bears it should live forever. If I want those things I value to endure it is not merely or not even because *I* value them; it is because I *value* them. The religious believer does not want his religion to outlive his own death because it is *his* religion and because the endurance of the religion gives *him* immortality. He wants his religion to command allegiance from those who will come after him because it is the true faith and because those who share his belief will thereby know what is true.

Consider, then, that a cultural group consists of individuals who share those values and ways of living which serve to define their membership of that group. We may grant that each individual would wish to see those values live on, and to do so precisely in the form of the group and its practices which they currently endorse. Does this not give individuals an interest in seeing their group survive? It does and—to repeat—not simply for the reason that it is *their* group. Rather it is a group whose identity they happen to value and which, insofar as they value it, they would like to see live on after them.

On this account those who make it up make the claim to 'la survivance' of the group. If Taylor does intend the group to have a warranted claim, as a group, to survive then this can only be because he believes the group has an irreducible value. This claim is not mysterious but it does at least need further exposition and defence. This does not need to be essayed here. For whether it is the group which claims an interest in survival, or the individuals making up the group who do, the fact is that such a claim must be weighed against the interests of the children whose future attachments and identities are the sole guarantee of the group's survival. And it seems clear that it would be wrong for children to be so used.

First, it is evidently wrong to treat children merely as means to the fulfilment of parental wishes. It is wrong to use another solely as an instrument for one's own ends, even if one's ends are and can only be realized after one's demise. Second, the child arguably has an independent interest in how it is raised. Or, rather, the future adult has an interest in how she will have been raised as a child. Perhaps the child is not able to make a claim to be treated as an end in the same way as an adult is. After all, the child lacks the capacities for moral agency which qualify adult human beings. Even if this is the case, it remains true that children will become—in the normal course of events—adults who can make warranted claims against those who have brought them up. Children have, as Joel Feinberg argues, 'rights-in-trust' which are, strictly speaking, possessed by their adult selves (1980). Perhaps then a child has a right to an 'open future', a right not to have its life choices closed off. Creating a future member of one's cultural group may just amount to denying the child any other alternative as an adult but to be a member of that group. The nature and scope of this right of a child to an 'open future' will be considered further at a later point.

Now the parents might respond as follows. A child has an undoubted interest in acquiring the right values. In educating the child to acquire the values of the parents they are teaching the child what they, the parents, value not because these are their values but because they are the right values. This response echoes the earlier concession that individuals want to see their values survive not because they are theirs but because they are the correct ones. The counterclaim is now one that turns on what it is that the child has an interest in becoming, not on what the parents have an interest in seeing happen after their own death.

However the response to this claim is simple. Parents are no better placed than any other individuals to know what are the correct values by which their children should live. Or rather they are not better placed simply in virtue of being the child's parents. A parent may be better placed to know what their child wants or needs. But they are not better placed to know what is true or correct. There is a further point that broaches the crucial question of the value of autonomy to be discussed later. This is that the future adult will want to live the life that is informed by the right values, and not just the life that is informed by those values which she has come to believe are the right ones. She would not want to lead what is in fact the wrong life, however strong her beliefs that it is the right one might be. Her assurance that her values are correct cannot come simply from the fact that these values were passed onto her by her parents. She must also be assured that those values by which she lives have the right pedigree. Arguably this requires that she has been able critically and rationally to examine these values and has not found them wanting. This will not guarantee that her values are the right ones. But in the absence of any such autonomous scrutiny she can have no assurance that they are. The upshot is that she would not want merely to inherit a set of values from her parents. She would wish also to be equipped with the ability for her own part to review, and to confirm or to repudiate her inherited ideals.

The group strategy to show that it is legitimate for a cultural group to reproduce itself by transmitting to children the defining values of the group fails. It does so because it is wrong for the group or its members to use their children merely as the means by which their values live after them. It is wrong for the group or its members to believe that they can know what are the correct values by which their children should live. Moreover children themselves would wish to become capable, as adults, of evaluating those ideals they might have acquired from their parents.

The second strategy appeals directly to the claim a parent can make as a parent about what shall happen to her children. Being a parent, it is urged, gives an individual a special status with respect to the child. Thus a parent may determine what food her child shall eat, what television programmes she shall watch, what time she should go to bed, and so on. Her right to do so derives from the fact that she is the child's parent. Now if there is such a parental right then it is reasonable to think that it would extend to the determination of what a child should value and the way of life it would favour. In this manner the adult member of a cultural group has a right, as a parent, to pass on to her children the defining values of the group.

Of course the exercise of any such general right is constrained by a requirement that the parent shall not do anything seriously harmful to her child. More strongly, and positively, one might stipulate a minimum level of care from the parent to which the child is entitled. Such a requirement functions as an internal limitation on the scope of any right of parental choice. Thus a parent may not give her child poisonous food, nor allow her child to watch inappropriate material on the television, nor deny her child sleep to the detriment of her health. It is a familiar principle of child welfare and care policy that parents may bring up their children as they see fit so long as they do not do so in a way which occasions serious harm to the children. Or again, put more strongly, they may rear their children as they choose so long as their treatment meets a certain threshold of acceptable care. Whether or not bringing up a child to be a member of the parent's cultural group crosses that threshold is what is under consideration.

More immediately we need to ask what is the source of this putative right of parental control and education. Since it is a right to make choices for another it is, in the first instance, a right whose possession assumes the inability of the other to make choices for herself. Such an assumption would be challenged by those who deny that children are incapable of making their own choices (Cohen 1980). But let me grant an assumption that is in fact generally made. The parental right has two quite different possible grounds. The first is a duty to care for the child and this duty is primary. That is, the right to rear the child derives from the duty to do so. This is the content of the 'priority' thesis that maintains that the duty of care for the child is prior to, and gives a warrant to, as well as specifying the scope of, the right of parental authority (Blustein 1982). Such a ground for the parental right is to be found in some account of the *child's* as opposed to the parent's interests, a subject to which I will return. The other possible ground for a right of parental control and authority is to be found in an account of what it is to be the parent of a child.

Here I can think of two influential views. On the first, the parent has absolute dominion over his own child and does so because the child is his property. Thomas Hobbes, for instance, believed that parents may 'alienate' their own children, 'may pawn them for hostages, kill them for rebellion, or sacrifice them for peace' (1994: 23, 8). John Locke did not believe that children are the property of their parents. However, he did have a theory of legitimate property acquisition in terms of the 'mixing' of one's own labour with that to which title is thereby gained (1988: II, ch. V). This theory has an obvious extension to the case of the parent who can be said to labour to bring a child into existence. It does not help matters that the reasons Locke gives for denying this extension of his own theory are so unconvincing (Nozick 1974: 287–9). It is perhaps understandable then that the idea of parental proprietorship, the parent as owning her child, casts a long shadow over our thinking about parental rights.

Yet clearly we should not think of the parent as a child's proprietor even if we cannot help thinking along these lines. Children are not objects to be owned. They are human beings even if they are not yet fully adult human agents. Children are not to be alienated, destroyed, rented, sold, and exclusively used according to the will of their parental owner—which is precisely what the parental proprietarian thesis entails.

A more persuasive but distinct thesis claims that children are not so much the property of as an *extension* of their parents. Here are two concise statements of this view. Charles Fried writes that 'the right to form one's child's values, one's child's life plans and the right to lavish attention on the child are extensions of the basic right not to be interfered with in doing these things for oneself' (1978: 152). Robert Nozick writes, 'Having children and raising them gives one's life substance. . . . The children themselves form part of one's substance. Without remaining or serving your purposes, they yet are organs of you. . . . Children form part of a wider identity you have' (1989: 28).

The extension thesis does not view the child as literally an extension of the parent even if Nozick's language ('part of one's substance', 'organs of you') suggests as much. Rather the child is an extension of the parent in the sense that what the parent chooses to do with her life involves not just choosing for herself but also for her child. Choosing for the child is merely an extension of the parent's choices for herself. The parent's right of self-determination extends to rights over the child and it does so because the child is part of the parent's 'wider identity', 'gives substance' to the parent's life.

It is worth pausing to note the following. The pronouns 'you' and 'one' can denote singular or plural subjects. Their use by Nozick and Fried obscures this distinction. Yet it is an important one. For it would be a mistake to assume that the two parents of a child share the same life-plans, values, purposes, and projects. They may do and according to a certain ideal of marriage they should do so. But to the extent that they do not children do not form part of a single, wider identity nor do they represent an extension of a single set of life-plans.

I do not doubt that some such view as Nozck's and Fried's does ground a general common-sense belief that a parent may choose for her own child. Nor should it be denied that having and rearing a child can amplify and give shape to an individual's sense of herself, to the extent indeed of forming the whole of one's sense of what gives one's life purpose and meaning. A parent can sincerely feel that the fact of being a parent serves to define not just what she is, but what she is wholly, essentially, or to the exclusion of nearly everything else in her life. This may be granted but the question is why this fact should ground a right to choose for whatever it is that gives one's life substance. Consider all of the following which, plausibly, could be said to give substance to a person's life, form part of her wider identity: a significant long-standing friendship, employment within an institution, support for a sports team, membership of a cultural group. Can it be said that in these cases the individual's right of self-determination extends to rights of choice over the other? If the claim retains plausibility in the case of the child I suspect it can only be because the proprietarian thesis gives illicit support to the unadorned extension thesis.

For instance, Edgar Page argues that parenthood has a special value in itself and that what gives it value is the fulfilment of a desire to mould the child (Page 1984). Interestingly, he is explicit that the ultimate source of this desire, and its value, is to be found in a quasi-proprietarian interpretation of parental rights. Hence parental rights belong properly and in the first instance to those who 'generate' or produce their own children. But if children *are* owned by their parents then the importance or value of the parents' desire to mould what is theirs is, strictly speaking, beside the point. I am free to shape what is mine to shape, and do not need to justify the importance of this freedom. If, on the other hand, the exercise of parental rights over children satisfies centrally important desires, it is imperative to know why such desires *should* be satisfied. Is it simply because what a parent wants, and should be free, to do for herself naturally extends to what she wants to do for her offspring?

I have examined and found wanting the group and parental strategies for defending the legitimacy of a cultural group reproducing itself by transmitting to children the defining values of the group. The final, familial, strategy appeals to the value of familial life. The strategy is indirect for it does not directly insist upon the right of parents to mould a child to their own way of life. It argues as follows. Individuals have a right to found a family, and indeed such a right is recognized in most charters of human rights. The right is one to join with another adult and to share the duties of rearing children who may or may not be biologically related to those who exercise the right. The family thus founded is a small social group that will engage in a range of characteristic activities, many of which are related to the discharge of the duties of care for the children. Normally these activities take place in private, that is they are unsupervised and unregulated by other agencies or groups.

What is characteristic of family life—and what commends it to its supporters—is that it is both shared and marked by conditions of intimacy. By intimacy I intend closeness—a family is a small group sharing many activities in private and often intensely—and affective openness—a family is a group whose members, normally, unconditionally love and trust one another. Families ordinarily live together, sharing a residence, and this fact both makes possible and reinforces these characteristic features of intimacy and commonality. The probable outcome of a family sharing its life in this manner is a sharing of key values. This is especially so in the case of the children who are likely to adopt the way of life into which their parents introduce them. Such an adoption is facilitated positively by the strong feelings children will likely have for their parents. Negatively it is propitiated by the lack of any other context in which they could experience an alternative way of life and that could have anything like the same formative impact.

At its simplest imagine that a father regularly takes his son to see a local sports team play. Such trips are one of the important activities father and son share. Inasmuch as the father visibly supports the team it is hard to see how the son would not come to share this passion, feeling for the team's successes and vicissitudes as his father does. This is, it should be noted, not simply a case of a parent choosing for his son, of the son's life merely being an 'extension' of the father. It is a genuine case of sharing. Imagine, again and more pertinently, that a family practises a particular religion, regularly worshipping together, and marking many significant family events—those, for instance, concerning the births, deaths, and marriages of the extended family and family friends—within the context of that shared religious practice. Again it is hard to see how the children of the family would not come to share the religious outlook of their parents.

Where the parents are members of a broader cultural group the effects of the shared life are further amplified. For a family is nested within such a community in significant ways. There are communal practices and activities in which the family can participate as a family. The children are recognized as the young members of the group. The shared life of the family is echoed in that of many other families within the community. All of this is such that the children of one family share with those of other families the values of their own household even if they do not so in the same conditions of intimacy and privacy.

I want to clarify the difference between the extension version of the parental strategy and the familial strategy. Grant that adults have a right to the free exercise of their religion. Adults attend church (or mosque or synagogue) and, as parents, they take their children. According to the extension thesis, the right of the parents to take their children to church is no more than an extension of their own right to attend. The right to form the child's religious beliefs and values is just an extension of the parent's right to live his or her life by those values. According to the familial strategy, by contrast, part of what it is to be a family is to share activities, including religious observance and practice. If there is a right to be claimed here it is the right of a family to live together and to participate in common activities. If religious beliefs and values are transmitted to the child it is in consequence of sharing this common life; it is not claimed that the parents have a direct right to transmit them.

Now let me make two comments about the familial strategy. The first is that it can acknowledge the deep significance and value parenting has for an adult, the fact that 'raising a child engages our deepest values and yearnings' and that it would be a mistake to think of parents as 'no more than instruments of their children's good' (Callan 1997: 144–5). It can do this without committing the opposite error of thinking that children are no more than instruments of their parents' good.

The second comment about the familial strategy is that the effect of a shared familial life—the sharing of a way of life and a set of values—is not directly aimed at. Or at least it does not need to be. A religious zealot might have children for no other reason than to mould his children into his own beliefs and thereby increase the number of the faithful or ensure the continued existence of the religion. But such a case is not standard. Nor does the familial strategy argue that the sharing of familial values is justified in its own right. Rather such a sharing is a highly probable outcome of what should be seen as a good, or even as a right, namely the sharing of a family life.

It has been assumed that, independently of its impact upon children, the group's way of life does not violate the rights of its adult members or of non-members. The core values of the group are not, as values, ones the child has reason not to acquire. Thus the familial strategy does provide the individuals within a cultural group, as members of families, with good pro tanto reasons for seeing their children acquire the values of the group.

However this strategy is limited. It shows only that the parents do nothing wrong in sharing a life with their children and that there may be nothing wrong with the outcome of that shared life being a sharing of values. It does not show that the parents have a right to insist that the child be educated outside the family in just those values that the family shares. For remember that the familial strategy does not seek directly to justify the sharing of familial values. Rather it says, indirectly, that such a sharing is a likely result of what is justified, the shared family life. But can a parent legitimately complain if those values by which she lives, and by extension, by which her family lives, are in some way challenged or subverted in the course of her child's education? The complaint is not that the school does not teach her values; it is that the school teaches something other than these values, something that undermines her values.

This complaint could arise in two ways. If the school directly teaches that the shared familial values are mistaken then the complaint would be well grounded. It has been granted that the values by which each group lives do not give the policy-maker reason to see the group not reproduce itself. Nor then do they give the public schools reason to teach that these values are erroneous. If the complaint is that the school teaches the children generally to think about values in such a way as makes it possible that they will reject those values it has learnt from its family then the complaint may not be warranted. For the complaint would just be that the child should not acquire the capacity to think critically about values and to revise its own values if it so chooses.

Parents may complain that the 'mere exposure' of their child to alternative views—even when these views are not endorsed by the school nor are the values of their own group treated in a hostile fashion—is discriminatory or violates their rights (say to free exercise of religion). Some support this complaint (Dent 1988). But there does seem to be a way to distinguish, and a point in doing so, between the pejorative characterization within the school of a group's way of life and making children of that group aware of other ways of life. After all, children cannot avoid growing up in a general culture that publicizes and advertises a diversity of lifestyles. Children may bear the costs, sometimes painful, of being exposed to the differences between their own familial values and those of others in their society. But these costs are the unavoidable price of tolerating difference, and of seeing that difference is tolerated.

I have argued that the 'group' and 'parental' strategies, which seek to show that it is legitimate for a group to reproduce itself by transmitting to children the defining values of the group, fail. The 'familial' strategy is persuasive but of limited scope and effectiveness. I want now to turn to what claims can be made by the child or on the child's behalf. First let me say something briefly about parental rights. If the child can make warranted claims, or claims can be made on the child's behalf, to be brought up in certain ways, it follows that the child's parents are under an obligation to bring up their child as claimed. According to the 'priority' thesis, mentioned earlier, the rights of a parent derive from and are formed by this obligation. Some, however, deny that, properly speaking, any such rights are grounded in parental obligations. There are simply obligations and no parental rights (Montague 2000). But even if there are parental rights that do derive from a logically prior duty to bring up the child in an appropriate fashion it should be clear that these are severely circumscribed rights. Parents do not have the discretion in their exercise of any such rights that they would have if their rights over their children derived from ownership of the children or if they were merely 'extensions' of their own rights of self-determination.

When it comes to what it is that a child can claim many writers point to a conflict between the induction of a child into a way of life and the child's interest in having an 'open future'. This is a child's interest in being brought up so as to be able, as an adult, to make her own life choices. There are two arguments whose conclusion is that the child does have a right to autonomy or an open future, neither of which rests directly on a claim about what the child herself is entitled to. The first is in the person of the state and appeals to the civic ends of education. The second seeks to forge a link between what are universally recognized, and claimed, as political rights or liberties and the child's disputed right to autonomy.

The claim that children ought to be taught to be autonomous might be defended indirectly in the following manner. A liberal state must be reproduced and this requires that it ensure its future citizens at least have the minimal capacities necessary to function as participating citizens. In this context one could quote various relevant American Supreme Court judgments. In the case of *Wisconsin v. Yoder* (1972: 29) the Court concluded that the state had a legitimate interest in preparing 'citizens to participate effectively and intelligently in our open political system', to be 'self-reliant and self-sufficient participants in society'. In *Pierce v. Society of Sisters* (1925: 1077) the Court spoke of the need to teach 'certain skills plainly essential to good citizenship'. In *Prince v. Commonwealth of Massachusetts* (1944: 653) the Court spoke of the dependence of a democratic society 'upon the healthy, well-rounded growth of young people into full maturity as citizens, with all that implies'.

The key question is how to understand the 'all' that *is* implied. Much of course depends on what are taken to be the essential characteristics of a 'good' citizen. The fuller and richer these characteristics are taken to be then the fuller and more determinate must be the education of young people. Amy Gutman for instance, believes that a 'democratic society should educate all educable children to be capable of participating in collectively shaping their society' (1989: 77). For her that capacity is essentially one of autonomy, of being able rationally to understand and appraise different ways of living. John Rawls, for his part, thinks that within a liberal state the education of children should 'prepare them to be fully co-operating members of society and enable them to be self-supporting; it should also encourage the political virtues so that they want to honor the fair terms of social co-operation in their relations with the rest of society' (1993: 199). That would suggest that in addition to being independent ('self-supporting') citizens must have acquired a sense of justice.

It is not my concern to evaluate any particular claim as to which political virtues should be inculcated. There are many other competing arguments as to what is required (Macedo 1995; Brighouse 1998; Galston 1991*b*). The point, rather, is that an indirect argument for educating children to be autonomous could be made which appealed not to the interest of a child in becoming autonomous but to that of the state in having autonomous adult citizens.

The second argument that seeks to demonstrate that children should be reared to be autonomous appeals to the alleged contradiction between assert-ing a liberty right and denying autonomy. Imagine then a group that thinks of its defining values as not freely chosen but as handed down by tradition or as having some indisputable source in a text or authoritative personal pronouncements. The members of this group do not believe that it is for them to choose whether or not they endorse these values. In some sense it is rather that these values have chosen them. The group members do not in conse-quence think that it is appropriate that their own children should acquire a capacity of choice. It is appropriate only for them to acquire the values in question.

A liberal critic might argue against such a view in the following manner (LaFollette 1989). The parents assert the right to live by their values. This is a liberty right. They cannot consistently assert this right for themselves and deny it to their own children—if not as children then at least as the eventual adults these children will become. But if the parents simply make the children accept the values by which they as parents live then they are thereby denying their children the freedom to choose their own values for themselves. They are denying to their children the liberty right they claim for themselves.

Such an argument does not succeed for the following reason. What the parents assert is a right to the unobstructed practice of their values. They do not claim a right to the free or autonomous choice of these values. They do not claim this because, as imagined, they do not think of their values as ones that are freely chosen. The group esteems liberty not autonomy. It is not thus inconsistent of them to demand that their children have no choice over which values they acquire. For the parents do not think of these values as autonomously chosen. However they would want their children, once adults, to be as free as they, as parents, now are to live by these values.

Here is another version of the argument from the liberties of group members to their children's rights to autonomy. It maintains that 'in a demo-cratic society that honors freedom of expression, state policy towards the education of children ought to be consistent with the underlying principles that support freedom of expression' (Arneson and Shapiro 1996: 397). But, so the authors of the argument assert, this claim is warranted only if a right of free speech can be supported on the basis of a 'democratic faith' that such a guarantee ensures citizens make more considered choices under the 'welter of considerations' generated by free speech (Arneson and Shapiro 1996: 398). However, whilst it may be 'quixotic' simply and bluntly to assert the right in question, it is not unreasonable to assert other grounds for the right than the fostering of autonomy—such as the evils of censorship, the proper limits of government, the social utility of diversity, and so on. Thus, a group may consistently hold that its views are not freely, that is autonomously, chosen and assert the right publicly and freely, that is unconstrained by law or state policies, to proclaim them.

This second argument for an education in autonomy is then unpersuasive. However the first indirect argument—from the civic ends of education—may support a better version of the liberal response to the parents within the imagined group which esteems liberty but not autonomy. Such parents want their child not to choose their own values but at least to be free, as adults, to live by those that are passed on to them by their parents. The better response is to argue that the freedom of all—including these parents and the adults their children will become—is only firmly guaranteed by having a sustainable good liberal order that, in turn, requires that its future members be taught the basic prerequisites of citizenship (Macedo 1995: 485–6). These, according to the first argument, require an education in autonomy.

The indirect argument for educating the child to be autonomous does not depend on its being in the *child's* interest to become autonomous. It is rather that the state has an interest in its future citizens being possessed of the appropriate civic capacities. Indeed the indirect argument provides the liberal with a response to the charge that in educating children to be autonomous he is illicitly presuming the value of the autonomous life. Rawls distinguishes his own 'political liberalism' from the 'comprehensive liberalism' of Kant and Mill. The latter would design education so as 'to foster the values of autonomy and individuality as ideals to govern much if not all of life' (1995: 199).

Political liberalism, by contrast, does not presume the ideal of the autonomous life and thus would not aim to educate such an ideal. Yet the political liberal would educate children to be independent and self-supporting members of society, to understand and to be motivated to honour the terms of the political conception of justice. In consequence, a politically liberal education would mean 'in effect, though not in intention' educating them in a comprehensive liberal conception, that is, to be autonomous (Rawls 1993: 199–200). Amy Gutmann has termed this the 'spill-over effect' whereby an education in autonomy is the by-product of an education in the skills of democratic citizenship (1995: 571), and other writers have also noted its significance (Coleman 1998: 748).

However, independently of the state's 'indirect' interest in teaching autonomy, does the child herself have an interest in becoming autonomous, in having an 'open future'? In what remains of this chapter I will be concerned not so much to answer this question as to pose and to try to answer another. If a child does have such an interest is it such as to outweigh any claim the parents of a group have to inculcate that group's way of life in their children? I shall take it then that children do have an interest in having an 'open future'. I shall, moreover, assert without further argument that such an interest derives instrumentally from the value to an adult who seeks to lead the right life of being able rationally and critically to appraise the values by which she lives. It is also true that, if political participation is a good, either intrinsically or instrumentally, then each future citizen has an interest in acquiring the ability to participate. That, it has been suggested in discussion of the indirect argument, presupposes a certain level of autonomy.

It should be noted at the outset that autonomy is not an all-or-nothing capacity. It can be possessed and exercised to varying degrees. The degree of autonomy required effectively to participate politically, and to be a basically competent citizen, need not be the same as that required efficiently to review one's values and way of life. The acknowledgement that autonomy comes in degrees also raises the question of how open a child's future should be. Arneson and Shapiro interpret education for an 'open future' as requiring individuals to acquire 'to the greatest possible extent' the capacity to choose between 'the widest possible variety of ways of life' (1996: 388). They correctly point out several objections to such a 'maximising' interpretation. It may not be possible to quantify in a determinate fashion the number of options open to a future adult. Furthermore some fulfilling life choices are only available at the expense of denying the child a number of otherwise possible choices. For instance, a child intensively trained to realize his considerable innate musical abilities may be unable to pursue careers that would have been open to him in the absence of such a dedicated education. We might add the following criticisms. Requiring that a child be brought up to be able eventually to choose between as many options as possible may impose unreasonable burdens on parents. It also seems implausible to think that a child suffers if she is denied one or even several possible insignificant further options beyond some threshold number of choices. Is it really harmful to a child that she does not learn to play *all* of the orchestral instruments and is thereby denied the opportunity to pursue a solo career in those she does not?

Feinberg—to whom we owe the canonical statement of the child's putative 'right to an open future'—does sometimes talk only of the harms of closing off significant life choices. However he does also on occasion employ the language of maximization. '[Education] should send [the child] out into the adult world with as many open opportunities as possible, thus maximising his chances for self-fulfilment' (1980: 135; see also p. 151). It seems more plausible to offer a satisficing interpretation of a child's open future. She should have *enough* autonomy to be able to make reasonable life choices. The preconditions of autonomy are both internal (a capacity to think for oneself, to acquire and appreciate relevant information, and a volitional ability to act independently) and external (the provision of a range of feasible and valuable options). In respect of both conditions it is perfectly possible to have a good sense of what counts as adequate autonomy, even if there is no clear bright line marking the point of sufficiency.

The first point to make about a child's interest in an 'open future' is then that a child need acquire only *so much* autonomy not *as much as possible* autonomy. Second, becoming autonomous enough is consistent with also acquiring a set of values. It would, for instance, be a caricature of the liberal position to represent it as requiring that a child be taught nothing but choice. According to this caricature a stereotypical liberal parent is one who is anxious not to transmit any values or way of life to her children lest this preempt the child's own eventual choices. An upbringing that does not foreclose future options is not one that does, or could, consist only of teaching choice. This is because choices must be made from somewhere. Choices are made within the context of and with respect to a set of already acquired values. A self that had no values could not be said to choose. How could it choose and what would there be for it to choose?

One strand of the communitarian critique of liberalism does suggest that the liberal understanding of the self is one of an empty shell devoid of desires, values, or purposes. An ideal of a self prior to its ends is seen as recommending a self without any ends. But, as liberals respond, this is a misunderstanding. The liberal commends the capacity of the person rationally to revise her ends and, in consequence, prizes the freedom to act on any revised understanding of her ends.

[F]ree persons conceive of themselves as beings who can revise and alter their final ends and who give first priority to preserving their liberty in these matters. Hence, they not only have final ends that they are in principle free to pursue or to reject, but their original allegiance and continued devotion to these ends are to be formed and affirmed under conditions that are free. (Rawls 1974: 641)

The communitarian critique confuses two distinct claims: that a self can, at any one moment, revise all of its ends and thus lack any; and that a self can, at any one moment, revise any one of its ends. The liberal does not affirm the first claim. He does affirm that there is no end that cannot, in principle, be revised or rejected. 'What is central to the liberal view is ... that we understand our selves to be prior to our ends, *in the sense that no end or goal is exempt from possible re-examination*' (Kymlicka 1989: 52). So it is entirely consistent with liberal principles that an upbringing should transmit to the child a set of values and a way of life so long as the child can, as an adult, reflect upon these values and elect to revise, abandon, or endorse them for herself.

A third point follows from the two points made thus far—that a child need acquire only so much autonomy and that this is consistent with the acquisition of values. This is that it may be mistaken to think of religious schooling as self-evidently inimical to a child's open future. The danger is of representing the choice of educations in extreme and stereotypical terms. Arneson and Shapiro do this, admittedly for the sake of argumentative simplicity, when they contrast a 'religious traditionalist' and 'a secular worldly' way of life, along with their corresponding educational programmes of, respectively, 'withdrawal' from the world and preparation for different ways of life (1996: 401–2). It may be true of some forms of religious education that they prepare a child only for withdrawal from all ways of life save the religiously approved one. But it is also true that many religious traditions encourage criticism, rational deliberation, and independence of mind (Burtt 1996: 416–7).

Fourth, an essential precondition of being autonomous to any degree is that one exhibits a certain measure of psychological and physical health. Independence requires steadfastness of character, strength of resolve, and the physical wherewithal to execute choices. Being brought up within a stable family home, enjoying the unconditional and enduring love of one's parent or parents is, as a plausible general rule, a necessary condition of growing up fit and strong in body and mind. Strong and healthy characters do come out of dysfunctional families, just as happy families can produce unhappy children, but these are exceptions. Importantly, the ideal upbringing amounts to a child sharing its life with parents under conditions of affective commitment which, as the familial strategy made clear, means coming to share values.

Fifth, membership may be a good. Kymlicka famously thinks it is a primary social good (Kymlicka 1989: 16), whilst Raz and Margalit eloquently describe its value by saying of membership of a group that it supplies its members with 'an anchor for their self-identification and the safety of effortless secure belonging' (Raz and Margalit 1995: 86). If membership is a good then its enjoyment may involve some trade-off with autonomy. That is, a child can come to lead a life that encompasses the good of membership only at the expense of some loss of its autonomy. Such a loss need not be so great as to deny the future adult what has been referred to as sufficient to live a life that is chosen and not servile nor 'withdrawn' from the world. Moreover, the life lived is, on balance, a valuable one. Whilst providing a child with a firm and secure sense of her identity may not allow her to enjoy a maximally 'open future', this latter may be guaranteed only at the cost of a degree of rootlessness, a feeling of having no steady or fixed sense of who one is.

Much more needs to be said than can be said here. It needs to be shown that membership is a good. At most what can be said is that the acquisition of a way of life *may* be in the interests of the child. Moreover, what has also been argued is that conceding that children do have an interest in an 'open future', if construed in terms of a sufficient rather than maximal degree of autonomy, can be consistent with the transmission to children of a way of life. The state's distinct interest in having autonomous citizens gives a further reason— beyond what is in the child's own interests—for an instruction, even if indirectly, in the autonomous life.

Where does that leave the 'problem' of multiculturalism? It has been argued that neither the group nor the parents, as members of a group, have a right directly to transmit their defining way of life to the next generation. There is a right of parents to share their familial life with their children and the exercise of that right may be such that children grow up to share the values of the group. However inasmuch as children do have a right to a sufficiently open future they lay claim to become adults autonomous enough to leave the group if they choose. This suggests that—at least in so far as we are considering what follows from the interests of children—the choice is not a simple and exclusive one between a liberal secular education and the reproduction of cultural diversity. Rather it is a choice between different kinds of multiculturalism, both as a fact and as a political programme.

Note

I am grateful to Colin Macleod for a number of very helpful suggestions and criticisms of an earlier draft of this chapter.

9

Answering Susan: Liberalism, Civic Education, and the Status of Younger Persons

Joe Coleman

The voices of younger persons are absent from debates about liberal civic education. Liberals debate which virtues to promote, the best means to achieve these, whether or not doing this unjustly violates the wishes of parents, and whether or not inculcating liberal values is consistent with liberal legitimacy. But liberals do not debate the idea that a given approach to civic education might infringe too much on the liberty of children themselves. Liberals do not worry that younger persons—particularly adolescents—might view some forms of liberal civic education as too paternalistic because liberals assume that younger persons are different from older persons in a fundamental and morally relevant way. How do liberals know this?

Imagine the following scenario. It is early September. Political theorists have gathered, as they do every year, to debate and explore their ideas. This year they have decided to work on what liberalism requires in the way of civic education. The debate covers an impressive array of topics including such notions as deliberative skills, liberal virtues, ethical servility, the 'Great Sphere', autonomy-facilitating education, and the like (see e.g. Brighouse 1998, 2000; Callan 1997; Galston 1991b; Gutmann 1987; Levinson 1999; Macedo 2000; Rawls 1993: 199–200; Tomasi 2001a, 2001b). Reflecting current research on the character-shaping effects of school culture and institutions, participants variously advocate such reforms as democratic classrooms, school uniforms to help instil discipline, student-centred pedagogies, stronger codes of conduct for schools. Others question whether or not liberal civic education is consistent with liberal legitimacy. Each participant musters an impressive case for her or his position. Because of the variety of values called upon, agreement seems unlikely. But all seem mutually satisfied with the quality of their debate.

Then, from the audience, a child addresses the panel. Her name is Susan. Susan is 15. She is in high school, the tenth grade to be exact. She is too young to drive a car. She is not old enough to drop out of school. Susan says the following.

I have been listening to you, and I am worried. You all seem to agree on one point. When it comes to younger persons, civic education is authoritative and mandatory, whatever form it should happen to take. This is in direct contrast to the gentle and voluntary approach you advocate for the civic education of older persons (e.g. Macedo 1996, 2000; also see Gutmann 1987; ch. 9). When civic education is applied to people like me, it is understood as something that older persons do *to* younger persons. Your debate reflects a single-minded concern with the kind of human being that I will be in the future and does not consider who I am now. No one here questions whether or not the worry about good citizens—however you understand the term—always justifies limiting my ability to act on my choices, preferences, or interests through these kinds of programmes. Just because we think we need good citizens does not mean that we can do whatever we want to produce them.

Let me be clear. At least with respect to civic education, I am a free and equal person just like you. Like you, I want to make my own decisions about the kind of human being that I am and will become. But the ways you want to pursue my civic education will unfairly prevent me from making these decisions. You want to treat me in a way you would not treat an older person. So, suppose I object to one of your proposals because it limits my choices in a way that would not be acceptable if I were older? What if I say I don't want to wear a school uniform? What if I say I don't want to attend a democratic classroom?'

How are liberals able to respond to Susan? On what grounds would they be able to legitimately answer her objections? Liberals might respond by explaining that there are public purposes that are so important that they justify limiting a person's freedom. Call this the response from public purposes. They might say, 'Having good citizens is necessary in order to secure the liberal democratic state. Without a sufficient level of political virtues present within society, the political autonomy that is secured by citizenship would not be available at all.' But the response from public purposes misses Susan's point. She is not objecting to the reasons liberals have for thinking that some form of civic education is desirable or to the kinds of virtues and knowledge liberals think ought to be the subject of civic education. She did not say, 'I don't want to learn the basis of equal respect.' Susan's point is deeper. To see why, let us return to the conference and consider Susan's response to this justification.

Susan might reply,

Even if I agreed with you that we need good citizens, that argument still fails to explain why you have picked *me* to be the subject of these specific civic education programmes. For example, why is it all right for you to require me to wear a school uniform while it is not proper for you to do the same with my parents? Just think how bizarre your debates would sound to normal citizens in a liberal democratic society if you were talking about requiring adults to wear uniforms in order to help teach them good citizenship.

Liberals might try a second response by arguing that Susan's parents were required to undergo civic education. They completed their schooling and that is why we do not subject them to further requirements. Susan is not being treated differently than her parents. Call this the response from equal treatment. But the response from equal treatment simply repeats the problem. Liberals do not specify how we justified subjecting Susan's parents to whatever form of civic education they might have experienced. To see this, consider the following example.

Suppose we lived in a society very much like our own except for one fact: the older generation in this society never experienced any formal programme of civic education. Now suppose this older generation decides to impose some form of civic education on the younger generation. Would liberals feel the need to say that for this to be fair the whole society must be subject to these programmes? I do not think so. Liberals would instead say older persons do not need this civic education in the same way younger persons do.

Liberals might support this view that older persons do not need civic education in the same way younger persons do by claiming that older persons display civic virtue and younger persons do not. Call this the response from civic virtue. But the response from civic virtue is both insufficient and unsatisfying. This response is insufficient because it relies upon a dubious empirical assumption. In our own world, voter turnout rates continue to decline, elected officials are frequently embroiled in scandal, and people try to duck jury duty almost as if it were a competitive sport. Moreover, many studies show that younger people today are increasingly engaged in voluntary service to their communities (Younis and Yates 1997: ch. 1; Wuthnow 1997). Thus, it is more likely that many older persons do not display sufficient civic virtue and many younger persons do. Moreover, this tack depends on there being a generational difference between older and younger persons. If differences between younger and older persons in this imaginary society merely reflected a life-cycle effect, then there would be no reason for liberals to think civic education was necessary since the older persons who did not receive civic education in this example turned out to be good citizens.

Claiming that older persons having sufficient civic virtue is the only reason liberals have for not imposing civic education upon them would be unsatisfying because it dramatically conflicts with the kinds of legitimate authority theorists usually associate with liberalism. Liberals may believe it is permissible to promote civic virtue in adults. But they also tend to believe that older persons are sufficiently mature that forcing them to go back to high school for civic education would be an invasive and unreasonable way to go about promoting those virtues.

Notice, however, that this is precisely the point Susan wants to make with regard to herself. Civic education may be reasonable, but not all forms of it are. The reasonableness of the civic education proposals suggested for Susan seem all the more suspect to her to the extent that they are not suggested for older persons.

Liberals might try again by noting a problem with the above example. What if the older people in that imaginary society grew up under an authoritarian regime and had no knowledge of liberal principles, institutions, and ideals? Liberals would only be troubled by requiring civic education for older persons if those persons lived in a liberal society and were therefore likely to understand how that society operated. This suggests that Susan's lack of civic knowledge can be a legitimate reason for treating her differently from older persons. Call this the response from civic knowledge.

But Susan has a ready reply:

Your argument sounds like you're comparing me to an immigrant. Once deemed eligible to apply for naturalization, the main qualification an immigrant needs for citizenship in the United States is civic knowledge. But you are not even treating me in the way you would treat an immigrant. Immigrants are not forced to undergo civic education. It is up to them and they are allowed to do it on their own. And if they choose to do so it amounts to little more than studying for a test and not breaking the law.

And even if you have an answer to that, I have a related complaint. I have been reading some of these civic report cards being produced by the Department of Education in the United States. I am appalled at the findings. *Older persons* seem to know very little about their government. According to the 1996 National Household Education Survey for example, 30 per cent of Americans over the age of 18 did not know what office Al Gore held; 44 per cent did not know whether Congress, the President, or the Supreme Court determines if a law is constitutional; 36 per cent did not know which party had a majority in the House of Representatives; 67 per cent did not know what proportion of votes Congress needs to override a presidential veto; 49 per cent did not know which party was more conservative at the national level; 54 per cent did not even know what the first ten amendments to the Constitution were called (Nolin and Chapman 1997: 5–6). And if Americans knew absolutely nothing about politics, they could still be expected to answer many of the NHES survey questions correctly somewhere between 33 to 50 per cent of the time, depending upon whether there were two or three possible answers. If any persons need civic education, surely they are those Americans who do not know these simple facts about their political system and who have the right to vote!

Liberals can concede all of the above points and fall back on their deepest and most secure response: Susan is a child and children lack the capacity to be citizens. Not all beings are capable of citizenship. Armadillos are not. Maybe Susan is not. This difference in capacities is how older persons are different from younger persons and this difference is morally relevant to questions about civic education. Call this the response from citizenship capacities. Susan's lack of the capacities of citizenship is why it is acceptable to treat her differently than her parents. Susan is not an equal. She is a kid; her parents are adults.

Hearing the response from citizenship capacities, Susan asks one last question: 'How do you know I'm a kid?' We are finally at the heart of Susan's challenge. Bracketing concerns about public purposes, equal treatment, civic virtue, and civic knowledge allows the importance of citizenship capacities to emerge more clearly. Even if we can answer questions about what virtues to promote or why having good citizens is important, we still need to answer Susan's question about why we apply these answers to younger persons differently from the way we apply them to older persons. What is the difference between older persons and younger persons when it comes to questions about civic education? How do liberals know whether someone is a child?

Citizenship and the Moral Powers

Citizenship is the standard liberals can try to use to show Susan that she is in fact a kid and that her parents are adults. To be an adult means to be capable of citizenship. To be a child means to be incapable. This understanding of citizenship is conceptually prior to questions about political borders and political virtues, both of which are usually associated with the idea of the citizen (see Kymlicka and Norman 1994). Before we can ask either, 'Should we let those people over there into our political community?' or 'What does it mean to be a good citizen?' we have to know if the beings we have in mind are actually capable of citizenship in the first place. It makes no sense to ask 'Should French dogs receive the same recognition as US citizens do from the US government?' or 'What traits make a cat a good citizen?' To ask if someone is capable of being a citizen means to ask if they are the kind of being that can take on and be owed certain kinds of moral obligations, specifically those associated with political autonomy.

The above considerations are of course distinct from whether or not a being is owed moral obligations such as access to basic human rights and the right to a guardian (see e.g. Rawls 1971: 209, 504–12). These moral obligations hinge on whether the being in question is potentially capable of citizenship. As a human being, Susan is potentially capable of citizenship in a way that cats, dogs, and armadillos are not. And so, when I say that individuals may not be capable of citizenship, I mean that they are not capable of independently exercising the liberty that citizenship confers. If liberals can show that Susan does not *adequately* possess the capacity to be a citizen in this sense, they will have sufficiently answered her objections. So what, specifically, does it mean to be able to be a citizen from a liberal perspective?

The simplest answer is that to be able to be a citizen means to possess what John Rawls calls the two moral powers—the sense of justice and a capacity for a conception of the good—and the powers of reason (1971: 12, 504–12). Citizens need the powers of reason to make judgements and inferences about the right and the good. The sense of justice means a citizen is a being that can understand, use, and respect rights and duties in a principled way. This entails a capacity for reciprocity and autonomy. To have the capacity for reciprocity means a person recognizes value pluralism and/or what Rawls refers to as the burdens of judgement. These in turn entail the ability to make and evaluate political claims in a way that is independent from one's particular vision of the good life. Finally, concerning the second moral power Rawls writes, 'The capacity for a conception of the good is the capacity to form, to revise, and to rationally pursue a conception of one's rational advantage or good' (1993: 19).

Of these three capacities, the second moral power requires some discussion. There are a variety of ways in which I might form and revise my conception of the good. I might unreflectively receive my conception from my community's religious traditions or I might engage in critical self-reflection to ascertain whether or not such a conception truly has value for me as an individual. Whereas the latter of these two approaches requires complex capacities, the former approach does not. Given that the way in which persons come to hold a conception of the good can itself be a part of that good, can liberals say anything about this capacity?

Liberals are divided on this question. On the one hand, political liberals are motivated by a desire to respect reasonable conceptions of the good, including those that value unreflectively adopting traditions. Holding such a conception of the good is what characterizes those individuals whom Charles Larmore (1996: ch. 6) refers to as reasonable Romantics. Thus, if political liberals use the second moral power as a capacity standard, that standard could not be particularly rigorous. The more rigorous political liberals make this ideal, the more likely they are to exclude persons who hold reasonable conceptions of the good life from citizenship. On the other hand, comprehensive liberals in the vein of John Stuart Mill might deny that political liberalism can or ought to succeed in accommodating all reasonable comprehensive conceptions. Theorists such as Amy Gutmann and Eamonn Callan at times seem to argue that the capacity for a conception of the good has a substantive content that undermines some reasonable comprehensive conceptions. This substantive content might even involve promoting an appreciation of the burdens of judgement and the value of autonomy as components of the good life (Callan 1988, 1997: ch. 2; Gutmann 1995; Levinson 1999: 14–22). Call this standard the strong capacity for a conception of the good.

What does a strong capacity for a conception of the good actually entail? Comprehensive liberals might claim that this capacity entails the development of moral autonomy. To be able to form, revise, and pursue a conception of the good means to be able to reflect critically upon different visions of the good. It means a citizen is able to distance herself from her traditions and values in order to consider the possibility of adopting new ones.

Upon closer examination, however, a strong capacity for a conception of the good adds little substantive content to the liberal citizenship-capacity standard. The main difference between comprehensive and political liberals is not found in their specific definition of autonomy. The autonomy found in

Rawls's sense of justice is the same as comprehensive liberal understandings of the capacities needed for moral autonomy. Both entail an ability to distance oneself from one's personal attachments in order to approximate an impartial perspective. Political and comprehensive liberals are distinguished simply by their views on to which areas of life autonomy ought to be applied. Political liberals hope to restrict autonomy to political matters; comprehensive liberals want it to shape people's views about life more generally. The difference between political and comprehensive liberalisms is one of scope.[1] At best, the strong capacity for a conception of the good requires that liberals look for evidence that Susan is critically reflecting on her view of the good or that she has done so in the past.

For political liberals there is another way to use this moral power as a citizenship standard. Having a capacity for a conception of the good might mean having a set identity, regardless of that identity's content. Citizens have their own lives to live. As such, liberals might try to claim that actually having a stable identity or a more or less settled life-plan are elements of their citizenship-capacity standards (see e.g. Purdy 1992). The idea behind this standard is, if a person does not have a stable identity, then they can have no interests related to that identity that they have a claim to act upon autonomously. For example, no one is worried about the injustice of parents forcing a 3 year old to go to church against her wishes. The toddler has no claim to free expression rights because we can be sure that, since she does not have a stable, long-term vision of the good life, she does not have anything to express yet.[2]

But this approach is too strong for political liberals. Rawls defines the capacity for a conception of the good as the ability to form, *revise*, and rationally pursue a vision of what makes life meaningful. Having this capacity involves being free to change one's mind. What grounds could political liberals have for claiming that having a stable identity is more valuable than being in a state where one is pursuing a stable identity, or vice versa for that matter? These are precisely the kinds of judgements political liberals are trying to avoid. People who do not have a stable life-plan do not necessarily lack the capacity for one. Rather, they have yet to find a life-plan that appeals to them. Only if a person did not have this capacity to look for a stable life-plan could political liberals claim that person failed to meet this citizenship standard.

These then are the standards liberals can call upon if they want to justify the claim that younger persons are not owed obligations in the same way as these are owed to older persons. If they can show that Susan does not possess the powers of reason, the sense of justice, or the capacity for a life of her own, they will have answered her objections. I now turn to the field of developmental psychology to see if Susan does in fact fail to meet the citizenship-capacity standards of either or both political and comprehensive liberals.

Developmental Psychology and Flunking the Citizenship Test

The capacities of citizenship have obvious analogues in the field of developmental psychology. The powers of reason are the subject of cognitive developmental psychology, itself heavily influenced by the research of Jean Piaget. The sense of justice is the focus of moral developmental psychology, particularly the works of Lawrence Kohlberg. The capacity for a conception of the good can be discerned in studies of identity formation stemming from the research of Erik Erikson and James Marcia.

Concerning the powers of reason, Piaget's work casts a large shadow over the field of developmental, cognitive psychology, despite subsequent research that suggests that reason is a more complex phenomenon than Piaget recognized.[3] Prior to the age of 9 or 10, human beings are still developing those forms of reasoning that allow humans to make logical inferences about the world and otherwise act as rational agents in some rudimentary sense. Very young children do not, for example, understand the principle of conservation of mass. Nor do they understand that age and height are two different phenomena. Such beings do not have the cognitive skills needed to act on their moral powers.

By age 9 or 10, children develop what Piaget called concrete operations. A being that possesses concrete operations can reason in logical, systematic ways about the world. As David Moshman (1999: 11) puts it, 'She or he understands the logic of classes, relationships, and numbers, and routinely makes proper inferences on the basis of coherent conceptual frameworks.' The concrete-operational thinker, however, has difficulty reasoning beyond the world she is presented with. The kinds of cognitive abilities she has developed are not abstracted from their concrete manifestations. Concrete operations merely use the logic apparent within reality without suggesting that reality might be fundamentally different.

Formal operations represent that level of cognitive reasoning where individuals can go beyond reality to consider other possibilities. It is at this point that truly abstract reasoning develops. Formal-operational thought involves deducing conclusions from previously given premises independent of how those premises and conclusions correspond to reality. And so there is awareness that logic and truth are not always the same. To possess formal-operational thinking also means to be able to 'reason at a purely symbolic level about hypotheses rather than facts,' and that relationships can be expressed in terms of symbolic propositions (Danner 1989, 55). Ultimately, formal operations allow thinkers to go beyond concrete reality in order to grapple with relationships involving possibilities and probabilities not suggested by that reality (Danner 1989: 55–6; Kohlberg 1976; Kohlberg and Gilligan 1979: 76–8; Lapsley 1996: 60–2).

Despite earlier estimates to the contrary, recent research suggests that the majority of human beings do not fully develop formal operations. And even when people do develop formal operations, their use tends to be limited to specific domains. For example, a physicist might display formal operations in her work, but fail to do so when it comes to other areas of her life such as thinking about ethical dilemmas. Finally, studies show that within-group variation in this ability among adolescents and among adults is significantly greater than variation in average ability between these two groups. When it comes to formal operations, it is very difficult to clearly distinguish between adolescents and adults as gross populations (Danner 1989: 58; Dulit 1979: 35; Kohlberg and Gilligan 1979: 79; Lapsley 1996: 60–2; Moshman 1999: 40).

These facts suggest a strange sort of moral equality between Susan and older persons. They are equally unable to meet this particular citizenship-capacity standard. While Susan fails to demonstrate formal operations, she does not do so in a way that differentiates her from most older persons.

What about the first moral power? Kohlberg sees moral development as progressing through three main stages, roughly corresponding to Rawls's three moralities (1971: 453–79). The stages are: the preconventional, the conventional, and the postconventional. Preconventional forms of moral reasoning entail no real understanding of rules. Individuals see laws and moral injunctions as external motivations imposed upon them by others. Conventional moral reasoning means that individuals come to support laws because they are the laws of the community or nation with which those individuals identify. Finally, postconventional moral thought means that 'acceptance of society's rules is founded upon the individual's own capacity to construct and comprehend the general principles from which the rules derive' (Rosen 1980: 72). Postconventional moral thought reflects the development of autonomous, moral reasoning where individuals are able to step back and critically evaluate values and principles (Kohlberg 1969; 1976: 35–5; Kohlberg and Gilligan 1979: 80; Lapsley 1996: chs. 3–4; Rosen 1980: 70–80).[4] Postconventional moral reasoning therefore corresponds to Rawls's use of the sense of justice.

Who is capable of postconventional moral reasoning? Current research shows that few people ever fully develop postconventional moral reasoning. The main moral developmental transition that characterizes the life course of human beings is the shift from preconventional to conventional forms of moral reasoning. This shift usually occurs approximately by the age of 13 for the majority of individuals (Colby *et al.* 1983; Power *et al.* 1989: 29–30; Kohlberg and Gilligan 1979: 80–3; Lapsley 1996: 78; Moshman 1999: 48–9; Rosen 1980: 71–2).[5] As with formal operations, human beings in general do not seem to develop their sense of justice. Susan again shares in a strange sort of equality with older persons. They are equally unlikely to have a sense of justice.

What about the second moral power? Does Susan have a life of her own?

Reflecting the influence of Erikson and Marcia, psychological research on identity focuses on describing four identity states: identity-diffused, identity-foreclosed, identity-moratorium or crisis, and identity-achieved. Identity-diffused individuals are those who are not actively concerned with identity. They have no strong commitments nor are they looking for any. Identity-fore-closed individuals are those who have unreflectively internalized identities given to them by their parents and/or other socializing agents. Identity-mora-torium or crisis means the individual has no strong commitments but is actively looking for them. Finally, identity-achieved individuals are those who have passed through a state of moratorium and have committed to a particu-lar identity (Marcia 1980: 1993*a*; Moshman 1999: ch. 8).

The identity-achievement state is particularly well suited for evaluating whether Susan demonstrates the strong capacity for a conception of the good in that it tracks the idea of moral autonomy. Who reaches identity-achieve-ment? While there is little longitudinal data on this point, there are compelling reasons to believe that many individuals never reach this state. Erikson (1968: 245) speculated that reaching an identity-achieved state required the posses-sion of formal operations (also see Marcia 1980: 164–5; Marcia 1993*b*: 29; Moshman 1999: 90–1). Without formal operations, individuals would not be able to engage in the critical self-reflection characteristic of the identity-mora-torium state that leads to identity-achievement. But as was shown above, formal operations are an uncommon achievement. Because of these facts, liberals have some reason to suspect that both Susan and her parents are likely to fail to meet the strong capacity for a conception of the good standard.

Of course, none of the above should be surprising. Identity-foreclosed states correspond to many of Larmore's reasonable Romantics. These are the individuals who believe that unreflectively receiving identity is itself an important part of the good life. Given the tenacity of this view in Western culture, it would be surprising if a significant number of adults did not display identity-foreclosure. This suggests another reason for comprehensive liberals to suspect that many individuals do not possess the strong capacity for a conception of the good.[6]

There is a lower standard available to political liberals. For these liberals the capacity to have a life of one's own need not be characterized by a particular identity or even a particular way of thinking about one's identity. Instead, to have this capacity an individual must simply have the ability to recognize that she is an agent in the world that can have her own values, ends, and beliefs about what makes life worth living. Does Susan meet this minimal threshold?

Marcia (1980: 160) argues 'What is important about identity in adolescence, particularly late adolescence, is that this is the first time physical development, cognitive skills, and social expectations coincide to enable young persons to sort through and synthesize their childhood identifications in order to construct a viable pathway toward their adulthood.' Despite including social expectations in his definition, Marcia describes adolescence as that period of development when individuals have finally developed the capacity to have an identity. The common claim among psychologists that the main developmental task of adolescence is the development of an identity makes no sense unless adolescents already have the capacity to perform this task. Adolescence is that period in life when individuals recognize that they have or can have commitments in the world that make life meaningful. This contrasts with the sorts of imitation and role-taking experiences that characterize pre-adolescent development (Josselson 1980; Marcia 1980: 159–60; 1993a: 3; Moshman 1999: ch. 8; Waterman 1993; Wigfield *et al.* 1996: 151).

Psychological research data show that the main developmental task of adolescence is the development of an identity. But this task is not the development of a capacity for an identity. Youth are actively trying to develop life-plans in a way consistent with what it means to have the second moral power for political liberals. Both Susan and her parents meet this standard. However, neither Susan nor her parents are guaranteed to have the achieved identity status that corresponds to the autonomous self required by the strong capacity for a conception of the good. This in turn suggests a divergence between comprehensive and political liberal views when it comes to determining who is capable of citizenship.

Yet, for both political and comprehensive liberals most if not all humans fail to have a capacity for the sense of justice. In the best-case scenario it appears humans in general are only partially able to meet the standards upon which liberal, political respect rests. What is a liberal to do?

The Status of Childhood and Radical Liberal Guardianship

The path liberals followed in order to answer Susan has led them a strange place. Our common-sense intuition that the age of minority ends at age 18 appears to be wrong. The status of childhood extends to more individuals than previously recognized. Liberals treat someone as an adult when that person is owed respect. Liberals display respect for someone when they allow that person to make her own decisions about the nature of the good life (see e.g. Dworkin 1985: ch. 8). But if most people do not possess the capacities of citizenship what claim to respect can they possibly have? What can liberals do if their ideal conception of the person fails to match up with real human beings? Liberals might respond to this conclusion in one of three ways. They could (1) try to find a way to challenge the citizenship-capacity standards I have laid out, (2) face up to the fact that many real humans are ill suited for citizenship and adulthood, or (3) reconsider the relationship between liberal respect and the capacities of citizenship.

First, liberals unnerved by the above might attempt to challenge the citizenship-capacity standards I have set out in this chapter. They might attempt to disprove the findings of developmental psychology and present an alternative theory of how people develop the capacities of citizenship. The most promising targets for both political and comprehensive liberals would be their common 'enemy': Kohlberg and related research projects. Liberals might instead try to develop social learning, socio-cultural, or psychoanalytical based theories of citizenship. But such an attempt is unlikely to give them what they want. Much of the debate within this field of psychology focuses on such issues as whether or not stages are necessarily sequential and non-reversible, determining the causal mechanisms that lead to the acquisition of moral capacities, the relationship between moral reasoning and actual behaviour, the role of moral emotions and virtues, or whether or not moral reasoning is structured by domains (Damon 1988; Lapsley 1996: chs. 5–12). But in making my argument I have made no claims that hinge on these kinds of issues. I have used Kohlberg's work and psychological research in general only to generate a descriptive portrait of human beings. There is little if any research that challenges the longitudinal picture that Kohlberg's work presents. Further, Kohlberg's findings have been replicated numerous times and enjoy considerable robustness (Lapsley 1996: 81–2). Demonstrating that different causal mechanisms produce the capacities of citizenship or that different capacities apply to other moral domains would not impact on my argument.

But there is an even larger challenge that liberals face if they seek a different theory of the development of citizenship capacities. There is a fundamental compatibility between Kohlberg's theory and liberal views about human beings. Kohlberg's view is inherently anti-authoritarian. Humans develop as moral beings not through a system of rewards and punishments, the blind mimicking of others, or the irrational sublimation of pleasure impulses. Humans grow in significant part through engagement with moral conflict (Lapsley 1996: 86–90; Power *et al.* 1989). Moral reasoning develops through the exercise of moral reason. Humans are neither coerced nor moulded into becoming capable of citizenship. To the extent that liberals seek more authoritarian theories of the development of citizenship capacities, they may find they have significantly to adjust their broader political theory to accommodate that authoritarianism. Because political theory is rooted in its assumptions about the nature of human beings, challenging these assumptions can have far-reaching consequences that liberals need to address. The worry here is that this accommodation will render liberalism unrecognizable.

Rawls provides a specific example of this worry in *A Theory of Justice* (1971: 453–79). In this work, he draws on Kohlberg and Piaget to answer worries about the stability of a just constitutional regime. He wants to know how people will freely come to develop a sense of justice under a liberal state. The worry is that the liberal state will not be legitimate if people do not freely give their assent to it, and that the sense of justice is tied up with this free assent.

Any theory of moral development that claims that humans can only be moulded into beings capable of citizenship seems incapable of explaining why we ought to consider such development as consistent with liberalism. If we have to make people into certain kinds of humans, and if the sense of justice plays a role in legitimating the state, how could that state ever be said to enjoy liberal legitimacy?

These are, I think, formidable challenges that liberals must overcome if they wish to reject the findings of developmental moral psychology. Proceeding in the above fashion threatens the legitimacy of liberal states. Liberals would have to engage in serious reconstruction of their theories if they chose this path.

The second option available to liberals would be simply to accept that most humans are still children. They could embrace a radical liberal guardianship and begin to apply their citizenship standards in earnest. When a being does not have the capacity to act on her citizenship justice requires that she be given a guardian to make choices for her. For this reason, liberals could say, 'Susan, you are absolutely correct. You have our apologies. Please inform your parents that the school bus will stop to pick them up tomorrow at 7.00 a.m.' There is no longer a reason for pursuing civic educational ends in a gentle way when it comes to older persons. It seems theorists such as Stephen Macedo (2000: ch. 9; 1996) are *too* liberal when they advocate the gentle promotion of liberal virtues in older persons. As persons in need of guardians, Susan's parents have no claim to make their own choices.

Of course, a liberal might object that even if radical liberal guardianship is theoretically justified, worries about oppression of those capable of citizenship might warrant acting as if most people were suited for citizenship. Specifically, liberals might worry that radical liberal guardianship would require us to develop citizenship-capacity tests that would be arbitrary or abused when it came time for officials to determine who was capable of citizenship. The United States, to take but one example, has a long history of oppression stemming from the abuse of such tests. And so, while they might agree in principle, real-world concerns about violating the political autonomy of some citizens could lead liberals to reject radical liberal guardianship.

This objection fails in two ways. First, it fails to recognize that guardianship is an obligation, not a benefit. Being a guardian is not like winning the lottery. It is not a windfall one can use to one's advantage or set aside when one feels like it. It is a moral duty. Failing to act paternalistically for a child is as unjust as acting paternalistically for an adult. Each such person is owed justice, but it is owed to her or him in different ways. Justice requires that liberals allow the adult to act on her own. Justice requires that liberals do not allow the child the same freedom (see e.g. Rawls 1971: 209, 504–12).

Second, the above objection does not recognize that it too relies upon arbitrary standards. This objection fails to explain how we ought to decide whether or not a person can be allowed to act on their citizenship. Unless liberals want to abandon the project of differentiating between older persons and the very young, they need to explain how such a distinction could be made in a way that was not morally arbitrary. But how liberals might do this is extremely unclear given that so few people develop the capacities of citizenship. Thus, while their worries about the abuse of citizenship-capacity tests are well founded, liberals can offer no morally superior alternative.

Note also that if liberals choose to embrace radical liberal guardianship there is no reason for that guardianship to stop with civic education. If most people do not qualify for citizenship, why should liberals let them vote, give them standing in court without a guardian, or hold them accountable for contracts that they enter into? All of the benefits as well as obligations of citizenship would be subject to liberal paternalism.

Yet, it would be a strange liberalism that advocated far-reaching, paternalistic policies in this way. Liberalism is a doctrine committed to securing liberty for the vast majority of human beings. Before liberals embrace radical liberal guardianship they ought to reconsider how political respect is linked to the capacities of citizenship. This is the third option open to liberals. For liberals, respect is owed to others because they have their own lives to live. There is a fundamental value in people living their own lives from the inside, even if such persons are not capable of justice. Liberals not anxious to reconfigure fundamentally the liberal project would do well to focus on the moral weight of the capacity for a conception of the good. Technically, both Susan and her parents may enjoy the status of childhood due to their lack of a sense of justice. But it is unclear whether this means that liberals should treat them like children. If the second moral power is what liberals truly care about, then Susan and her parents still have claims to liberal respect simply as beings with the ability to live their own lives.[7]

But notice what this third option entails. The autonomy claims of both Susan and her parents would apply in the same way to various proposals for civic education. Liberal civic education must be conducted in a way that respects the political autonomy of citizens who have their own lives to live. Susan has a legitimate claim to be treated the same as her parents when it comes to this issue. The response from citizenship capacities has failed.

Citizenship, Political Autonomy, and Civic Education

Having come all this way, liberals need a new answer for Susan. Her questions have revealed that it is no longer possible to maintain the old terms of liberal debates about civic education. Liberals need to rethink fundamentally what it means to pursue civic education for younger persons. I want to suggest this new answer and thereby defend the project of liberal civic education.

Contrast two broad approaches to civic education: those that are authority-oriented and those that are participation-oriented. Both are about making schools more like communities. In recent education theory and political socialization literature the role of institutions and whole-school experiences are increasingly recognized as having significant civic educational and character-shaping effects. Authority-oriented approaches to civic education are those that prioritize the role of older persons in defining the nature of schools-as-communities. Such approaches view civics students as being the recipients of civic education. Teachers and officials act upon students in order that they might be shaped and moulded into good and capable citizens. Civic education is something done *to* students. Liberal theorists interested in this approach have advocated increasing discipline and student work responsibility, such as is found in Japanese schools, mandatory public-speaking courses (Galston 2000), school uniforms, giving more authority to adults so they might have a strong hand in creating a school ethos and be able to engage in 'moral leadership', and generally making public schools more like parochial schools (Macedo 1996, 2000). Other examples of this approach include calls for virtue-based character education, and some proposals for mandatory community service. Overall, this approach seeks to make public institutions such as schools into communities where there is an expectation that there will be a sense of shared purpose, a stronger sense of authority, and more discipline (Bennet 1992: 56–60; Kilpatrick 1992; Ryan and Bohlin 1999; Wynne 1986; Wynne and Ryan 1993).

In contrast, participation-oriented approaches to civic education view students as something like equals, and therefore understand schools-as-communities as being democratic in nature. Educators pursue civic education *with* students. These approaches operate by giving substantive responsibility to students for making decisions about their education and their school. Examples of these approaches include democratizing the governance of schools and classrooms, relying on student-centred pedagogies, and offering programmes that create opportunities for student expression and engagement both within school and with organizations and problems outside of school. Some service learning programmes also reflect this approach (Battistoni 1985; Burstyn 1996; Coleman 1998; Mosher *et al.* 1994).

There are at least five ways in which liberals can judge these varying approaches to civic education to determine if they are consistent with the demands of liberal respect. These approaches can be compared against one another with regard to how much political autonomy they provide students; they can be compared to liberal views about what are appropriate approaches to the civic education of older persons; they can be viewed in light of concerns about liberal legitimacy; they can be evaluated based upon questions about whether civic education can be mandatory; and they can be considered with regard to the civic education of persons younger than Susan.

First, comparatively it is clear which of these approaches provides more political autonomy to students. Participation-based approaches by definition provide more opportunities for students to make decisions that will impact not only on their education, but also on their ability to live their own lives. Some reformers and theorists attempt to justify these approaches based upon evidence that shows they are more effective at civic education than authority-based approaches. But efficacy is no longer an overriding consideration. The appropriate standard for evaluating either approach is whether or not it is consistent with the respect that is owed fellow citizens by virtue of the fact that they have their own lives to live. Liberals now have a significant moral reason to prefer participation-based to authority-based approaches.

Second, civic education is a duty citizens owe other citizens, regardless of their age. Even if we have reasons to prefer political autonomy in general, sometimes liberty needs to be limited in order to secure overriding public purposes. Susan accepted this possibility in her initial comments. And so, perhaps authority-based approaches are warranted because of a need for good citizens and the belief that these approaches are more effective at creating citizens. Maybe proponents of participation-based approaches are unduly optimistic about the benefits of their favoured mode of civic education. This scenario is possible. But if this scenario were true, similar forms of civic education would have to be instituted for older persons as well. A compulsory year of national service, for example, would be required of everyone, with exceptions going only to those suffering from severely limiting physical and medical conditions. Having a career would not count as a reason to be exempted from service as this is simply to say one has a life of one's own to live, a claim open to all citizens. A compulsory system of uniforms if deemed necessary for the civic education of younger persons would also apply to all older persons. Public institutions generally could be given more authority to set codes of behaviour and exercise 'moral leadership.'

Of course this is all very Orwellian, or at least Rousseauian. Indeed, given the kinds of abuse that seem likely in such an extensive system of civic education, liberals ought to be uncomfortable with this approach. A civic educational regime raises the spectre of rights violation as opposed to simply their limitation. That there are participation-oriented approaches available to liberals makes it reasonable for theorists to resist authority-based approaches to civic education. Indeed, I suspect it is for these kinds of reasons that civic education for older persons in America looks the way it does. Such civic education is a function of public libraries, newspapers, public media, and participation in local democratic institutions, public forums, and celebrations. These approaches to civic education are all participation-oriented. That these are the kinds of institutions upon which liberals typically rely for the civic education of older persons suggests liberals have some faith in the efficacy of participation-based approaches. But again, since older persons and younger persons share the same moral status with respect to the demands of civic education, the institutions through which civic education is pursued must be comparable.

Third, liberal theorists are increasingly concerned with the legitimacy of liberal states. Harry Brighouse (1998, 2000) has recently expressed a concern that liberal civic education cannot promote the uncritical acceptance of liberal ideals and virtues without undermining the ability of students to consent freely to a liberal state. John Tomasi (2001*a*) argues that concerns about neutrality and the unintended individualizing effects of liberal institutions raise worries about whether or not people will actually consent to the liberal state, particular those individuals who value unreflective attachments and non-autonomy based visions of the good life. But participation-based approaches to civic education minimize these kinds of concerns. By being participatory, students are agents of their own socialization. They are not merely subjects being shaped and moulded into citizens. Rather, they are being exposed to material, experiences, and roles they can then evaluate and explore on their own. And it is not open to parents to claim a right to limit the exposure of their adolescents to these kinds of experiences. Such claims are made on the grounds that exposure undermines parents' attempts to pass along their vision of the good life to their children. But if adolescents are the same as older persons with regard to their capacity to have a life of their own, then this kind of claim does not make sense. Such a claim would have just as much or little validity if parents made it over their neighbours. At best, this sort of objection must be based on the complaints of the students themselves.[8]

Fourth, Susan might raise one last objection. Even if liberal civic education were pursued through participation-oriented approaches, Susan's civic education would still be mandatory in a way that it is not for adults. Indeed, liberals increasingly argue that schooling should be mandatory precisely because of the need to pursue civic education. That argument is no longer open to liberals. Civic education cannot be mandatory only for Susan and still be consistent with liberal respect.

Despite this conclusion, there are still two ways in which it might be legitimate for liberals to use schooling as a vehicle for civic education. First, they might simply lower the age of compulsory schooling to something like 13 or 14. This age seems to be when younger persons begin to exercise their capacity to have lives of their own. By making schools voluntary, the civic education that occurs within schools would then accurately reflect the civic education of older persons.

Second, liberals might back away from the claim that the reason for making schooling compulsory rests on worries about good citizenship. There are other reasons for schools to be mandatory. For example, even if the civic knowledge of younger persons does not differentiate their situation from that of most adults, it may very well be the case that Susan does not know enough about other areas of her life to be totally autonomous. Recent studies show that while ambitious, most younger persons are ill informed about how to translate their educational and career goals into a plan of action (Schneider and Stevenson 1999; also see Csikszentmihalyi and Schneider 2000). How to obtain necessary job training and/or higher education is a body of knowledge that individuals need to possess in order to be considered self-determining. Liberals have a duty to ensure that younger persons—even young adults such as Susan—acquire this knowledge. Maybe this knowledge is so important that it justifies making education mandatory through secondary schooling.

Thus, it would not be the case that civic education was being made mandatory even though schooling was. Of course, liberals would be justified in worrying that this second solution merely represented a disingenuous loophole, allowing unequal treatment of younger persons when such treatment is neither desirable nor necessary. But this would only be a serious worry if the sort of supposedly voluntary civic education that occurred within schools itself conflicted with students' liberty. But as this is precisely the sort of conflict that participation-oriented approaches to civic education avoid, liberals now have another reason to prefer these to authority-oriented approaches.

Finally, what about the civic education of persons younger than Susan? Those likely to not have a capacity for a conception of the good do not have the same moral claims to equal treatment when it comes to civic education that Susan does. The liberals' initial response to Susan is appropriate for this group of persons. Such persons are entirely in a state of guardianship because they fail to demonstrate all of the relevant capacities of citizenship.

But notice what has changed. The civic education of Susan's cohort ought to be participatory. But because these sorts of programmes tend to pervade the institutions of schools, they are likely to result in radically different high schools. Democratizing the governance of schools and classrooms, for example, is a demanding and new experience for many teachers and students. If schools become participatory places where students gain significant opportunities for political autonomy and, therefore, responsibility, primary schooling must prepare children for these demands.

And so, while younger children themselves cannot make claims to have their civic education mirror that of Susan and her parents, the guardians of those children have a moral duty to prepare their charges for the participatory nature of life within secondary schools. While there may be no injustice involved in liberals requiring pre-adolescents to wear school uniforms as a means of civic education, only requiring school uniforms would mean that liberals were failing to live up to their duties towards children. Questions about the age-appropriateness of the specifics of various participatory approaches to civic education are of course relevant when it comes to these children. But these concerns must not be allowed to obscure the duty parents and educators have to ensure that their charges are able to participate in institutions that they will necessarily become a part of later on in life.[9]

On all five evaluations then, liberals have significant reasons to prefer participation-based approaches to civic education. And this is the case even when it comes to pre-adolescents, although it is so for substantively different moral reasons. To use Susan's two examples, while school uniforms represent approaches to civic education that do not sufficiently attend to the respect that is Susan's due as a person with a capacity to have a life of her own, democratizing classrooms entails no disrespect and still meets the same civic educational needs. Democratic classrooms allow Susan to express herself while being comparable to the sorts of civic experiences to which older persons are subject. Mandatory uniforms do neither.

The justification I am proposing for participation-based approach to civic education substantively changes the terms of liberal civic education debates. It is not uncommon for liberals to advocate participation-based approaches to civic education. But when they do so, liberals justify participation-based civic education based on merely instrumental reasons. They think that participation-based approaches are more effective than authority-based approaches. But in answering Susan, liberals must now recognize that instrumental considerations are secondary. Susan has a moral claim to participation-based approaches independent of the efficacy of such approaches. Liberal respect demands participation-based civic education. Democratizing classrooms is not a good idea; it is a just one.

Liberals must recognize that they have not always treated Susan with the respect that is her due as a fellow citizen. But at the same time they can continue to encourage good citizenship when it comes to citizens such as Susan. Liberals are right to insist children need civic education. They were simply wrong to assume that the status of childhood is always limited to persons below the age of 18 and that possessing the status of childhood necessarily means being treated like a child.

Notes

For their suggestions, comments, and support, many thanks to David Archard and Colin Macleod, Jason Barnosky, Harry Brighouse, Eamonn Callan, Susan Coleman, Holly Emidy-Coleman, Carl Kaestle, Bryan McGraw, Jim Morone, Joel Osterich, Nancy Rosenblum, Art Stein, John Tomasi, and Emily Weinstein.

1. Rawls does consider the possibility that the need to educate children for justice will lead to a social world where individuals freely adopt moral autonomy as a comprehensive ideal (1993: 199–200). But he never suggests either that moral autonomy be considered a qualification for autonomous citizenship or that civic education can legitimately entail the intentional cultivation of such moral autonomy as a comprehensive ideal.
2. Elsewhere, Joel Feinberg (1980) uses this same example. To be clear, this example

is not meant to speak to controversies concerning ethical subservience and the permissibility of the illiberal indoctrination of children into some belief systems. Imagine then that the church in this example is of a suitably liberal nature.

3. Examples of other forms of rationality include what David Moshman refers to as informal, nonformal, and metacognitive rationality (Moshman 1999: chs. 3–4; also see Greeno and Collins 1996).

4. While research on moral reasoning divides each stage into two substages, the differences they are meant to represent are quite fine and not useful for this discussion.

5. It might be objected that relying upon Kohlberg introduces a gender bias into my argument, given the findings in Carol Gilligan's *In a Different Voice* (1982). But subsequent research has found that there is no statistically significant relationship between gender and Kohlberg's stages of moral reasoning. Women are as (in)capable as men when it comes to moral reasoning, although they do tend to slightly prefer the ethics of care to the ethics of justice (see Lapsley 1996: 140–3; Moshman 1999: 53–4 for surveys of these findings).

6. To be clear on this point, there is a difference between, say, a Christian fundamentalist who reflectively endorses her faith and one who has simply never evaluated her beliefs in a critical light. The former is an example of identity-achievement, the latter foreclosure. Despite this difference, however, the latter is a reasonable Romantic. The former may be a reasonable Romantic as well, or she may be some other species. Perhaps it would be more accurate to call her a reasonable Millian Romantic.

7. This solution is by no means certain. Liberals still need to do the work to show that there is nothing morally worrying about providing autonomy to persons not yet fully capable of citizenship. This seems to me to be a particularly pressing concern for comprehensive liberals. Further, the remainder of this chapter does not address how these findings apply to the authority associated with other youth institutions, particularly education more generally conceived. Just because there are no morally relevant differences between younger and older persons when it comes to civic education does not mean that this is always the case. Both of these are problems I develop in my Ph.D. dissertation (Coleman, 2002).

8. I pursue this possibility in the context of debates about school choice in Coleman (forthcoming).

9. None of this is meant to deny that there might be other moral reasons supporting participation-oriented approaches to civic education for persons younger than Susan. For example, one might wonder whether or not younger children might in fact be capable of, for example, certain cognitive skills necessary for participatory schools at ages earlier than research has lead us to believe. What if children only appear to be incapable because we treat them as if they were incapable? If this were true, then a critic might claim that older persons have a moral obligation to provide participatory schools to children younger than Susan for reasons substantively similar to those that warrant such schools for Susan. While not necessarily opposed to such an extension of my argument, there are two significant problems with this claim. First, the limits of cognitive development and the effects of intentional efforts to stimulate cognitive growth are controversial. At best, we might have a weak obligation to explore this possibility. Second, and more important,

Susan's claim to be treated similarly to older persons does not rely solely on her possessing rationality. Susan's claim is strong precisely because we have reason to believe that she has a capacity for a life of her own. Even if we could determine how to promote this capacity at an earlier age, how a liberal state could do this sort of promotion without becoming entangled with neutrality issues would require serious consideration. Political liberals would seem bound to avoid this sort of encouragement. Comprehensive liberals, if they could sort out who, if anyone, was capable of citizenship, would probably have an easier time with this issue.

III

Children, Families, and Justice

10

Silver Spoons and Golden Genes: Talent Differentials and Distributive Justice

Hillel Steiner

To set the context for the argument I want to advance, it may be helpful to say a few general words about both distributive justice and talents. Distributive justice is concerned with judgements about who should get what and who should give what. But it is not concerned with all such judgements. Rather, only those gettings and givings that are thought to be justifiably enforcible fall within its domain. And while this may cover quite a lot of morally desirable interpersonal transfers, most persons would regard it as not exhausting them. Your giving someone a hand with his heavy shopping-bags is unquestionably a morally good thing to do. But in the absence of some sorts of special circumstance, we would tend to regard your failure to do so as an unkindness rather than an injustice.

Theories of distributive justice are accounts of the reasons we can plausibly and coherently offer for these getting and giving judgements. And the subject of this chapter—talent differentials and distributive justice—is motivated by the common view that at least some of what people should get or give should have at least some connection to what they do. Now what they do obviously depends, in part, on what they can do: on what their talents or abilities are. And what their abilities are in turn partly depends upon what was previously done to or for them when they were children. Hence the focus of this chapter is on how our thinking about distributive justice can be brought to bear on problems surrounding the formation of children's abilities.

Children have always posed a big problem for political philosophy in general and theories of justice in particular. Just *when*—at what age—a person's minority ends, will presumably remain a perennial subject of legal and political debate.[1] But we can all agree that persons below some age or other are definitely minors. As minors, they are assumed to lack enforcible duties and thus to be incapable of giving binding consent. They do not *do* social contracts, actual or hypothetical. And they are not the ones who are liable to legal action for whatever harm their behaviour may cause to others.

Whether they are therefore better understood as lacking rights altogether or, alternatively, as having rights which various sets of adults exercise on their behalf, is a matter of complex and long-standing philosophical dispute and one which I hope to side-step here.[2] That is, I hope to resist the very considerable pressure which a topic like the present one inevitably exerts for adopting a position on this undeniably important issue.

A major source of that pressure is the tendency of our moral thinking to operate within a conceptual framework which, following Kant, exhaustively divides the contents of the world into two categories: *persons* and *things*.[3] Things—rocks, plants, machines, arguably members of other species—are items which we can permissibly treat merely as means to our own ends. But persons are not. Persons are, in some elusive sense, ends in themselves. They— at least *adult* persons—are repositories of agency and, as such, are the generators of whatever is morally good or bad. And their being so is something that must be taken into account when we interact with them in the course of pursuing our own ends. Just exactly what this 'taking into account' amounts to is another matter of deep controversy. But it is fairly common ground amongst the controversialists that a broad description of it includes the idea that, in pursuing those ends, we must not violate others' just rights, either through direct force or, more indirectly, through exploitation. Regardless of how worthy our ends may be—and even when they strongly include concern for the well-being of others—we are not allowed paternalistically to impose these upon them. Persons must be treated as what Kant called 'their own masters' or, in a more recent phrase, as 'self-owners'.[4] Practices like slavery and the Nazi eugenic programmes are only the most dramatic examples of not treating persons as self-owners.

Indeed I would argue that, unfamiliar as this notion of self-ownership is (outside the confines of political philosophy), it is this right that seems to supply the underlying justification—and, especially, the *demarcation*—of such more familiar human rights as those against murder, assault, rape, arbitrary arrest and detention, interference with free speech, free contract and free association, and so forth. Why does my right of free speech *not* give me a protected liberty to shout in your ear? Why is interference with an act of rape *not* a violation of the rapist's right of free association? Why is consensual medical surgery *not* a form of assault, whereas forcible prevention of a sane person's suicide *is*? Questions like these each have their own particular answers, of course. But as soon as we press on those answers and ask why the human rights they invoke do or do not count as reasons for allowing the actions involved, we are invariably led to something like each person's self-ownership as the common underlying right that both sustains and specifies them. For it is this right that is needed to reconcile and render mutually consistent the various liberties and protections afforded by those traditional human rights: rights which would otherwise encumber us with numerous incompatible demands or conflicts of duty.[5] And an important implication of persons being self-owners is that, in the absence of any wrongdoing, they must not be subjected to any involuntary servitude. So their abilities and, for that matter, their body-parts must not be *conscripted* into the service of others.

Now this obviously places serious constraints on the range of permissible forms of redistribution that can be undertaken to overcome differentially distributed well-being. Vitally aware of glaring interpersonal inequalities, both within and between societies, we are naturally—and, I think, rightly— drawn to the view that their reduction is morally imperative. We think it is desperately wrong that some people lead hungry, homeless, and disease- ridden lives, while others enjoy an abundance of consumer goods and services. But the requirement that we respect persons' self-ownership imposes substantial restrictions on how we may go about putting this right. It tells us that, although all *voluntary* forms of such redistribution are entirely permis- sible, the same is not true with regard to many forms of enforced redistribu- tion. We *can* and *must* compel those who harm others to pay them compensating damages. But we cannot permissibly compel those who are well endowed with talents or abilities to transfer goods or services, produced by those abilities, to those who are badly off. Not only is direct conscription of their abilities prohibited, but so too is the taxation of the *fruits* of those abili- ties.[6]

The core of the argument, connecting an exclusive entitlement to one's abilities to an exclusive entitlement to the *products* of one's abilities, is not all that hard to construct. If you devote time and effort to developing some profi- ciency in mathematics or a robust cardio-vascular system, you are better placed to win certain card games or to go mountain-climbing. It seems implausible—and certainly contrary to self-ownership—that benefits you secure from exercising those abilities should be morally liable to taxation. And so the same implausibility seems to attach itself to the taxation of monetary income streams that flow your way because, instead of deploying those abili- ties in card-playing or mountain-climbing, you choose to exercise them as a professional accountant or athlete. *Exchanging* the products of our abilities with one another, rather than consuming them ourselves, does not seem to increase their *moral* liability to taxation—at least, not in any obvious way. Self- owners are each responsible for their own choices and cannot justly compel one another to undo the distributive consequences of those choices. So if this argument is correct, there is not much permissible inequality-reduction to be had along these lines. Differential holdings of *artefacts*, the things we unequally produce in exercising our unequal abilities, do not legitimately occasion enforcible redistribution.

A more promising approach begins by directing our attention to the fact that those unequal abilities cannot be developed from *nothing*. Self-owning adults who develop them must construct them on some already-present foundational ability which was laid down prior to that construction and prior to their becoming adults. Speaking very broadly, we can say that the factors entering into the production of this foundation are of two types: initial genetic endowment and an enormous variety of post-conception inputs which most obviously include gestational, nutritional, medical, and educational factors. The quality of these two types of production factor vary considerably from one minor to another, as do the levels of ability—or disability—that are produced from them. And those ability-level rankings generate valuations of the factors jointly involved in producing abilities: the initial genetic endowments and the diverse post-conception inputs. Here, I suppose, we loosely tend to follow the economist's way of thinking about production functions, and we say that one genetic endowment is more enabling—*more golden*—than another if the cost of the post-conception inputs needed to produce a given ability level with it is *less* than what would be needed with the other endowment. Correspondingly, one set of post-conception inputs is a *more silver* set of spoons than another if, in combination with any given genetic endowment, it produces a higher ability level than the other. So the lives of identical twins have often served as a testing site for the quality of different kinds of spoon.

Now, the question we want to address is one which asks how a conception of justice, that takes the Kantian ends-means injunction seriously can allow— let alone require—us to reduce interpersonal differentials in ability level. Can we justly employ legal measures to constrain these inequalities? We have seen that justice prohibits us from enforcibly reducing differentials in *well-being*. Can it take the opposite view with regard to inequalities of *ability*? I think the answer is 'yes'. But I also think that *how* it can do so is significantly altered by central aspects of what has come to be called 'the genetic revolution'. So let us begin this part of our exploration by persisting a bit longer with our *pre*-revolutionary understanding of what is involved here.

One thing that seems clear is that, under both our pre- and our post-revolutionary understandings, the items we are calling post-conception inputs— spoons—all look like counting as *artefacts*. And you do not need to have undergone pregnancy or to have raised children to understand why. Virtually everything that goes into the production of *us*, following conception, is something supplied by our parents or by people elected or employed for that purpose. They are the ones who supply us with our pre-natal environment, our medical care, our schooling, our music lessons, football kits, and all the rest of it. It is they who largely determine the enabling quality of these inputs. And increasingly these days, where that quality is deemed to have fallen short of some acceptable standard, it is they who may be held legally responsible for those shortfalls. Thus legal actions have already been brought or proposed, not only against parents or guardians for smoking or drug-taking during pregnancy, for child abuse, and for failing to curb truancy and aggression, but also against schools for educating badly.[7]

Now whatever we may think about the merits of such litigation—personally, I think it is to be welcomed—what it more generally signifies are three points of great relevance to this discussion. First, it supports or presupposes the view that post-conception inputs are indeed artefacts: they and their resultant impacts on minors' ability levels are the products of particular persons' efforts and negligence. Second, it is *those producers*—rather than the public in general—who are liable for damage inflicted by their products. And third, the product standards to which those producers are held, though certainly not sufficient to ensure that each minor receives an *equal* amount of these inputs, are none the less meant to ensure that each receives some *minimum* amount of them. That is, these standards have the effect of constraining differentials in the *silverness* of the spoons delivered to different minors. It is the existence of such standards that gives at least sense, if not always veracity, to any complaint along the lines that 'You [i.e. some relevantly placed adult] wrongly deprived me of the higher ability level I would have had on my arrival at the threshold of adulthood'.

A highly significant aspect of our *pre*-revolutionary understanding is that this same complaint is precisely *not* one which can be made in respect of lower ability levels which are attributable to poor initial genetic endowments. I cannot say to my parents 'You wrongly deprived me of the higher ability level I would have had on my arrival at the threshold of adulthood, because you knowingly conceived me from gametes or germ-cells carrying genetic information which severely constrains my mathematical or cardio-vascular capability.' Why can I not say this to them? Well of course, for one thing, they *did not* know that. And for another, it may not be *true*. But that is not the point. Nor, strictly, are these reasons why I *cannot* say it to them, but only why I *should not*.

No, the reason why, pre-revolutionarily speaking, I cannot say this to them has ultimately to do with our underlying conception of *personal identity*, with what underpins our idea of who we each are, and why we are not some other person. And that reasoning goes in two steps, as follows. First, it is an accepted feature of my personal identity that if my parents, instead of using *that* pair of their germ-cells to conceive a child, had used *another* pair—another sperm and/or another egg—then that child would not have been *me*. No matter how closely that child might have resembled me, it would have been someone else. Indeed, the different pair of cells they used four years later *did* produce someone else: namely, my brother. Let us call this the *precursor condition* of personal identity: to be me, I *had* to have been conceived from that particular pair of precursor cells. And second, if—to be me—I had to have been conceived from those particular cells, then, to be me, I *had* to have the particular initial genetic endowment I did have. There was no way my parents could have conceived *me* without thereby creating a zygote with that endowment. Let us call this the *genetic condition* of personal identity. *I* had to be a person with, say, a severely genetically constrained mathematical or cardio-vascular capability. The presence of that genetic disability in me is not the doing of my parents—it is not an artefact—but rather simply a piece of bad luck dealt to me by *nature*. Indeed, it is not strictly dealt *to* me, in the way that an impoverishing poker hand or a crippling lightning bolt is dealt *to* me. Rather it is actually a *constitutive* aspect *of* me: part of who I am, in a way that the effect of being hit by lightning or bad poker hands—or even, for that matter, irradiation as a foetus—would *not* be part of who I am but, instead, something that happens to an already constituted me.

So, however disabling my initial genetic endowment may be, there is no point in my contemplating bringing a charge of what's sometimes called 'wrongful life' against my parents: one alleging that they have harmed me because I would have been better off conceived genetically differently. It is true that wrongful life charges have indeed been brought in some instances of severely genetically disabled children. But even in the few such cases that have not simply been dismissed, the plaintiffs—the persons considered to have been wronged—are invariably the parents themselves, and the defendants are various persons who allegedly failed to provide the standard of pre-conception genetic counselling expected of them. And any damages awarded have been based on parental suffering rather than the remedial costs of the disability borne by the child. The child's genetic disability is not deemed to be anyone's fault: it is not a *tort* committed against the child.[8] Rather it is an essential component of that child's identity and is entirely a *natural* precipitate.

Now in the otherwise highly diverse range of justice theories associated with the Kantian ends–means injunction, whereby persons are their own masters, one premiss that is shared by all of them—though often only implicitly—is that something's being a natural object gives it a significantly different moral status from that of artefacts. The Kantian twofold division of the world's contents—into persons and things—further requires a subdivision of the 'things' category into artefacts and natural objects. Differential holdings of artefacts do *not*, as we have already seen, warrant enforcible egalitarian redistribution, for this would violate self-ownership. But differential holdings of natural objects *do* warrant such redistribution. Unequal possession of what we can comprehensively call 'natural resources' occasion a justly enforcible duty in those who have more valuable ones proportionally to compensate those who have less valuable ones.

Where does this duty come from? How is it justified? Well, some have argued that it is based on something like John Locke's seventeenth-century theological premiss: that God gave the earth to humanity in common, rather than only to divinely anointed monarchs.[9] Alternatively, that duty can be derived from some more secular set of principles. In either case, the thought is simply that no one has any stronger prior moral claim than anyone else to

the exclusive use of those things which are not artefacts. No one is more entitled than anyone else to these resources, which are the products of no one's
labour or effort. And consequently, everyone owes everyone else an equal
share of the value of whatever such natural things he or she claims exclusively.[10] (Perhaps I should add, parenthetically, that I have so far found no
compelling reason for thinking that this reference to 'everyone' can be
anything other than *global* in scope: it applies to everyone, everywhere. In
which case, the *per capita* equalization mandated by that distributive requirement would be an *international* one—possibly in the form of each person's
equal entitlement to what is currently called an *unconditional basic income*.)[11]

The concept of 'natural resources' itself, of course, covers quite a lot of
territory—literally! At its most compendious, it includes all geographical sites
as well as the spatial locations above and below them: that is, it includes all
portions of the earth's surface, all subterranean natural resources, and things
like air-space, the ozone layer, the electromagnetic spectrum, and so forth.
Natural resources also comprehend those elements of the biosphere that are
not the products of human labour including, as the Darwinian story implies,
vast amounts of encoded genetic information. Most of these natural resources
are used by us in the course of our various activities. And many of them are
bought, sold, and rented with great frequency. Accordingly, they clearly have
an assessable value. And justice requires that value to be distributed equally.

So, telescoping a rather extended chain of reasoning,[12] we arrive at the
conclusion that, *ceteris paribus*, the egalitarian proviso on natural resource
distribution requires that those who produce children with golden genetic
endowments—those who appropriate more valuable genetic information
with which they conceive a child—owe net transfer payments to those who do
not. And those who do not are thereby supplied with the wherewithal to invest
in remedial spoons which are sufficiently silver to raise the lower ability levels
that would otherwise result from their children's poor genetic endowments.
For since the concerns of justice do not extend to the advancement of any
particular conception of the good life, what they aim at securing is a distribution of ability *levels* rather than any particular ability *per se* (such as the ability to play chess).

Since ability and disability levels are identified and measured relative to
some social mean, and since the valuations of genes and spoons are determined on that basis, we might reasonably expect that, under such a redistributive arrangement, these compensation flows would considerably reduce
differentials between children's ability levels at the threshold of adulthood,
when the further development and deployment of their abilities must become
matters of their own choice.[13] Arguably, those *current* public policies which
make special educational and medical provision for disabled children represent some highly imperfect approximation to at least the expenditure (though
not the taxation) aspects of this sort of redistributive arrangement. Perhaps

such policies even signify some very fragmentary recognition of the more general idea that the costs of those adversities which are due to *nature*—rather than to the activities of particular persons—should be borne by all of us and not just by those whom they befall.

That, it seems to me, is how justice addresses the problem of talent differentials under our *pre*-revolutionary understanding. So how does our *post*-revolutionary understanding mess this story up? Probably in lots of ways. But I want to focus on what I take to be the central one.

The core of what it does, I think, lies in its impact on what I previously labelled as the *genetic condition* of personal identity. You will recall that this condition stated that since, to be me, I had to have been conceived from the particular precursor cells I was conceived from, then—to be me—I had to have the particular initial genetic endowment I did have. My genetically constrained mathematical or cardio-vascular ability is an essential constituent of my identity. So I cannot intelligibly complain that I would have been better off had I been conceived *without* it, and that I was therefore harmed by being conceived *with* it.

Now, the radical move that our post-revolutionary understanding makes is precisely to sustain, rather than deny, the intelligibility of that kind of complaint. It does this by breaking what we pre-revolutionarily believed to be the *necessary link* between the precursor condition of personal identity and that genetic condition, which it simply *discards*. It tells us that although, to be me, I certainly and necessarily did have to be conceived from those particular cells, there was *no* necessity about them carrying the particular genetic information they did carry. They would still have been the same cells—*their* identity would have been unchanged—even if, prior to my conception, the components of that mathematically or cardio-vascularly disabling information had been snipped out of them and replaced with something less disabling. It becomes no longer true that, to be the person I am, I had to have that genetic disability. So, without falling foul of the precursor condition of personal identity, I *can* reproach my parents for harming me.[14] Or rather, such reproaches will increasingly be able to be made as our knowledge of the human genome advances and, with it, our capacity to manipulate its information loads.

What the genetic revolution does is to give a massive shove to the always moving frontier between nurture and nature. It puts events and objects which we have long treated as natural firmly into the domain of choice. Our distinction between genes and spoons gets drained of the moral relevance I previously attributed to it—genes become the moral equivalents of spoons—and our initial genetic endowments get reclassified as *artefacts*.

All of which brings us to a very worrying question. For we now have to ask whether this post-revolutionary development does not seriously threaten our capacity to reduce children's ability-level differentials, while still remaining within the parameters of what justice permits. Recall that a substantial portion of that capacity rested on our pre-revolutionary assumption that initial genetic endowments are natural objects. But if it is now, or about to be, the case that they are artefacts, can their unequal distribution still warrant compensating redistribution? After all, unequal holdings of *artefacts* do not, in themselves, permissibly occasion enforcible transfers from those who have more of them to those who have less.

I think the answer to that question can be 'yes'. Yes, we *can* justly require such compensating redistribution on our post-revolutionary understanding. But the direction or form of that redistribution must be different. For the genetic revolution, in forcing us to discard the genetic condition of personal identity, shifts responsibility from nature to particular persons. What were, pre-revolutionarily, natural adversities now become torts. If genes are spoons, then the same sort of product quality standards that currently apply to the *post*-conception inputs entering into the production of children's ability levels, can equally apply to the *pre*-conception ones. Since, post-revolutionarily, we *can* say that some conceptions harm the persons thereby conceived, we are able to make sense of the notion of 'wrongful life' and to vest persons with rights against it. Just as they can sue schools for poor education, so too can they be empowered to sue for having been endowed with disabling genes. And presumably the damages awardable in such cases would bear some close relation to the cost of the remedial spoons needed to offset that genetic shortfall: remedial spoons which might well come to include various forms of *somatic cell* gene therapy.[15]

I will not pause here to explore the sorts of incentive structure that such a right might predictably bring to bear on people's procreative choices. Perhaps these are obvious enough. And as far as I can see, they all seem to press in the right direction. What may be worth some brief mention, not least because it continues to attract a good deal of anxiety about the genetic revolution, is the issue of *cloning*. Should considerations of distributive justice cause us to worry about the prospect of human cloning?

I cannot really see why. None of the arguments advanced here has been particularly concerned with the *kinds of precursor cell* we use to conceive persons. The same liability rules apply, so to speak, regardless of whether we do that exercise by combining two whole germ-cells or, instead, by combining an enucleated germ-cell—an egg—and a somatic cell with induced totipotency and supplied by either the same donor or a different one. *Any* technique for conceiving persons seems, as far as justice goes, to be as permissible as any other. The standard worry about cloning is the production of interpersonal uniformities and the consequent loss of various dimensions of diversity. But if there *are* morally relevant differences—between those uniformities which are genetically induced and those which are induced, say, by a national educational curriculum—they are not differences which concern justice.[16] It would be difficult, to say the least, to sustain a claim that the existence of *identical twins* represents some sort of *injustice*. What post-revolutionary justice *does* need us to worry about is any conception that imposes genetic disadvantages on the person thereby conceived. And there is no particular reason to suppose that cloning would do this either more or less than any other conception technique, ancient or modern.

Let me close this chapter, then, on a slightly upbeat note about human rights. In the recent Hollywood comedy, *Mars Attacks!*, there's a moment when that arch-portrayer of boisterously cynical characters, Danny de Vito, remarks: 'If you wanna conquer the world, you're gonna need lawyers—right?' What de Vito is telling us here, I take it, is that the *transaction costs* of such ambitious imperial projects have increased substantially since the days of Alexander the Great and Attila the Hun. And I do not think it is oversanguine to suppose that a major factor in that increase has been the fact that it is no longer quite as easy as it once was simply to roll your elephants or your tanks or your secret police over other people's human rights. That set of constraints on oppressive projects has, especially in recent years, become very much more real and far less negligible than it used to be.

What that set of rights is meant to protect us against are various forms of harm and disablement at the hands of others. So, to conclude, it does not seem utterly far-fetched to imagine that—before too much longer—a right against *genetic* disablement might come to be seen as a proper member of that set.

Notes

This wonderful phrase used in the title, 'silver spoons and golden genes', is *not* one of my own devising: I owe it to Thomas Nagel who used it in his H. L. A. Hart Memorial Lecture (Oxford, 1996) entitled 'Justice and Nature'. An earlier version of the present essay was given as one of the 1998 Oxford Amnesty Lectures published in Burley (1999).

1. See the report in the *Independent* (4 Mar. 1997), entitled 'Labour redefines the age of innocence': 'Children between 10 and 13 should be deemed "capable of evil", Jack Straw, the shadow Home Secretary declared yesterday . . . as he urged the scrapping of the presumption against [their] criminal responsibility'.
2. I do, however, address this issue in Steiner (1994: 245–6), and in Steiner (1998: 259–62), where I argue that minors do *not* have rights.
3. A good indication of the aforesaid pressure is that, in his rather spare jurisprudential classification of basic types of right—as either property or contract—Kant (1996: 98–100) found it necessary to devise a third category, 'Rights to Persons Akin to Rights to Things', to cover parental rights with regard to minors.
4. Cf. Kant (1996: 63). Moral duties, for Kant, fall into a fourfold classification: (*a*) perfect duties to oneself, (*b*) imperfect duties to oneself, (*c*) perfect duties to others, and (*d*) imperfect duties to others. Of these, only duties of the third type are the concern of justice and correlatively entail rights (such as self-ownership);

cf. Kant (1965: pp. xiv–xv). A thorough explication of the concept of *self-ownership* is to be found in Cohen (1995: 209–28); see also Vallentyne (2000: 2–5), and Steiner (1994: 231–48).

5. On the significance of, and conditions for, rights not being mutually inconsistent, see Steiner (1994: 55–108, 224–8), and Steiner (1998: 262–74).

6. That is, a moral code embracing the right of self-ownership as a requirement of justice *can* regard a general egalitarian redistribution of wealth as commendable, and even obligatory. What it *cannot* endorse is the achievement of such a redistribution by enforced measures.

7. Cf. the *Independent* (9 Dec. 1997), 'Blair puts parents in firing line over school attendance': 'Parents could be fined £1000 if they fail to make sure that their children are attending school, the Government warned yesterday'. Also the *Independent* (2 Dec. 1996), 'Pupils sue schools for bad education'; a lawyer for the pupils argued that 'If you have a car where the brakes fail there are victims; similarly, if you have a school which fails its pupils, there are victims'. The case followed one in which an out-of-court settlement resulted in a '20-year-old [accepting] £30,000 damages after claiming compensation for bullying at school ... Both cases have been made possible because of government policy which requires inspectors to say when schools are failing.'

8. Cf. Heyd (1992: 26–38): 'Tort is universally defined as some sort of *worsening* in the condition of a person (damages being an attempt to compensate for exactly that difference between the person's condition before the harm was done and that following it). But in [the case of genetic defects], the only condition that can be the subject of such a comparison and a point of reference for the assessment of appropriate compensation is nonexistence ... The inclination to avoid comparisons in wrongful life cases is not only motivated by the fact that nonexistence is not a state that can be given a value, but also because it is not a state that can be *attributed* to a subject. It is hardly a 'state' at all' (29–30).

9. Locke (1988: ch. 5, §25).

10. In Steiner (1994: 224–36), I argue that this duty and the duty to respect others' self-ownership are both directly implied by each person's having a foundational right to equal freedom.

11. Though perhaps an *unconditional basic initial endowment*, or *capital stake*—being less paternalistic—would be a more Kantian or liberal instantiation of this entitlement. An excellent account of the justice-based case for unconditional basic income is offered in Van Parijs (1995).

12. See Steiner (1994: 243–9).

13. Indeed, since the likely impact of an egalitarian redistribution of *all* natural resource values—on a *global* scale—would be considerably to reduce interpersonal inequalities of wealth generally, we might expect children's ability-level differentials to be still further reduced. For it is reasonable to suppose that the effect of this redistribution on opportunity costs, including those of producing a given level of ability in their children, would be downward for many more (largely poorer) persons than those (largely wealthier) for whom it would be upward. Having command over more silver production factors to combine with their children's genetic endowments, more people would have to sacrifice less to raise children who were healthier, more skilled, and better informed. In Steiner

(1994: 249–58, 273), I argue that the full value of dead persons' estates is also justly subject to such egalitarian redistribution. Still further reduction in global wealth inequalities might be expected from measures to secure restitution for past injustices, including the injustice of having withheld these redistributive entitlements.

14. Since, on this reading, my genetic characteristics are neither conjunctively nor disjunctively constitutive of my identity, perhaps what we have here is a fairly natural (sic) approximation to the otherwise elusive notion of the Kantian *noumenal self*.

15. Currently prominent among the justice theories associated with the Kantian ends–means injunction are several that take *equality of opportunity* as their central distributive principle. John Roemer has usefully explicated this conception of equality as follows: 'At a philosophical level, many people associate egalitarianism, and the policies of the welfare state in particular, with a view that society will indemnify citizens against all major harms, relieving them of the personal responsibility to make their lives go right. I shall not defend this kind of unqualified egalitarianism, which does not hold individuals responsible for their choices. Equality of opportunity, in contrast, is a view that society (the government) must level the playing field, but that after that, individuals should suffer or enjoy the consequences of their own choices. The question becomes: Exactly what is required to level the playing field? . . . Let us say that a person's actions or behaviour are determined by two kinds of cause: *circumstances* beyond her control, and *autonomous choices* within her control . . . A particular action a person takes, and its associated consequences, are caused by a highly complex combination of circumstances and autonomous choices. I say that equality of opportunity has been achieved among a group of people if society indemnifies persons in the group against that part of consequences they suffer due to circumstances and brute luck, but does not indemnify them against that part of consequences due to autonomous choice. Thus the purpose of an equal-opportunity policy is to equalize outcomes in so far as they are the consequences of causes beyond a person's control, but to allow differential outcomes in so far as they result from autonomous choice' (Roemer 1995*b*: 2–5, and, more generally, 1998). Such equal opportunity theories, however, sometimes display an incomplete application of the personal responsibility requirement, in so far as they assimilate—as due to 'circumstance'—those adverse consequences which persons incur at the hands of *others,* to those which are imputable to brute luck or what I here refer to as *nature*. In so doing, they are wrongly led to infer that compensatory liability for the former, as well as the latter, lies with society rather than the particular individuals responsible for those adversities; cf. Steiner (1997).

16. And there are good reasons to believe that Kantian—or, more generally, *liberal*—conceptions of justice cannot allow the enforcibility of moral values other than justice.

11

Equality and the Duties of Procreators
Peter Vallentyne

Introduction

What special duties do procreators have with respect to their offspring? Roughly speaking, I shall argue that (1) the only special duty that procreators owe their offspring is that of ensuring that their life prospects are non-negative (worth living), and (2) the only special duty that procreators owe others is that of ensuring that they are not disadvantaged by the procreators' offspring (*a*) violating their rights or (*b*) adversely affecting their equality rights and duties.

As we shall see, some of my claims are significantly at odds with common sense. I have been led to these views by an attempt to reconcile reflectively plausible moral principles with considered moral judgements in particular cases. Thinking about the moral status of children requires thinking about other non-autonomous beings with moral standing (non-human animals), and consistency here requires, I believe, some radical revision in how we think about children (as well as animals). Although I hope to provide enough justification to make my claims respectable, I have no illusions that my arguments will convince most readers. The prevailing judgements being challenged are extremely strong, and my arguments admittedly are not. So the most I can hope to accomplish here is to spell out and motivate a radical alternative to the received view.

Background

I shall assume—controversially—that with respect to *adult-to-adult relations* some form of moderate liberal egalitarianism is correct. More specifically, I shall assume that adults (agents) are protected by certain kinds of general rights of non-interference (for example, negative rights of bodily integrity or self-ownership rights[1]), and that, subject to the constraints imposed by these rights, agents have some kind of limited general duty to others to promote the equality of life prospects (opportunities for a good life) to the extent that this is compatible with the (Pareto) efficient promotion of people's life prospects. Although this duty is based both on efficiency and on equality (and is thus not subject to the levelling down objection), for brevity I shall refer to it as the equality duty. Furthermore, there is, I shall assume, no general duty to assist other adults except as required by the general duty to promote equality—although, of course, there can be various *special* duties to assist (based on specific past acts, such as wrongdoings, commitments, etc.). Finally, I shall assume that agents who violate these rights have a duty to compensate their victims to the extent that they are *responsible* in some specified sense for the wrongful harms. The specification of the relevant conception of responsibility (for example, for all causal effects or for only those that were reasonably foreseeable) has an enormous impact on the exact implications of the view I defend, but it would take me too far astray to attempt here to defend a particular conception thereof. For simplicity, I shall leave the qualifications about responsibility implicit, and when addressing specific cases I shall assume that the relevant responsibility conditions are met. These are, of course, controversial assumptions, but it is beyond the scope of this chapter to defend them here. Instead, I will address how children fit into this picture.

General Duties to Children

Although my main focus is on the special duties of procreators, I need first to discuss briefly what duties agents in general have to children. Because I shall argue in the next section that the special procreative duties to offspring are fairly minimal, it is important to note that this is in the context of very strong general duties owed to children (and others generally).

Childhood in the sense of non-adulthood can be understood in chronological terms (for example, less than eighteen years since birth), physical terms (for example, physical capacities that normally only chronological children have), or mental terms (for example, mental capacities that normally only chronological children have). I assume that for moral purposes it is *mental* childhood that matters, and that such childhood should be understood as *non-agenthood*, that is the non-possession of a robust capacity for reflection upon, and modification of, beliefs, desires, and intentions. Hence, I shall include non-agent chronological adults (for example, seriously mentally retarded adults) in the category of children.

Children, I claim, have, like adults, certain rights of non-interference and certain rights to have their life prospects improved by others when the demands of equality so require. I thus reject the view that only autonomous agents can have rights. According to this latter view—the *choice-protection* view of rights—the sole purpose of rights is the protection of autonomous choices. Since non-agents do not have the capacity for autonomous choices, they do not, it is claimed, have any rights, and thus others owe them no duties. Agents may have, on this view, duties to other agents *with respect to* non-agents, but there are no *duties owed to* non-agents.

This view simply does not make adequate sense of the duties that we have with respect to children (and other sentient animals). We have duties *to*— and not merely with respect to—infants and these are grounded in some kind of constraint protecting their interests. These duties are not impersonal duties (owed to no one), since children are owed compensation when these duties are violated. Nor are these duties owed to other agents, since they cannot be extinguished by all agents releasing each other from this duty. This view fails therefore to capture the sense in which the duty is indeed owed to the offspring. Furthermore, the fact that children cannot waive these duties, or even enforce them (for example, use coercion to prevent infringement or to extract compensation), is quite irrelevant. The duties of others can be appropriately sensitive to the *interests* of children (for example, the use of physical force against them is forbidden unless it is in their interest), and other agents can enforce the duties on behalf of the children.[2]

I agree that the choice-protection view captures the main sorts of rights that autonomous agents have.[3] I see no good reason, however, to assume that there can only be one kind of right. Both conceptions of rights are coherent. The only question is which kind is relevant for a given kind of being. I claim that autonomous agents have (mainly) choice-protecting rights, and non-autonomous sentient beings have interest-protecting rights. Of course, as autonomy develops, the interest-protecting duties owed to children are gradually supplanted by choice-protecting duties owed to agents, but I shall not address the important issue of how and when this happens.[4]

Children, then, have some rights. But what rights do they have? We are, recall, assuming that agents have certain rights of bodily integrity (against non-consensual contact with the body) and certain equality rights. Children, I claim, have both as well—although understood in interest-protecting terms.

Consider first the interest-protecting right of bodily integrity. It is exactly like the adult right of bodily integrity except that *non-harm* to the holder (as opposed to consent) is required to justify contact. Giving an effective and needed vaccine to a 4 year old against her will does not violate her rights of non-interference, whereas it would normally violate those of an adult in that situation. Giving a pointless or needlessly dangerous injection to a 4 year old, on the other hand, does violate her rights of non-interference. The relevant conception of harm here is the long-term setback of interests. Thus, the mere presence of a short-term harm (the pain of the injection) is weighed against long-term benefits. Agents are permitted to impose short-term bodily harms on the child—as long as this imposes no net long-term disadvantage.[5]

Children, then, have certain general rights of non-interference. They also have, I claim, the same equality-based assistance rights that adults have. Agents have, we are assuming, some kind of limited duty to promote equality of opportunity for a good life. Children are included in the class of beneficiaries of this duty. Furthermore, there is no reason in principle to give children any special status within the class of beneficiaries. Of course, as a matter of fact, children typically occupy a privileged position with respect to equality. For they are especially vulnerable to suffering significant disadvantages through no fault of their own. Because of this vulnerability and because they typically have much longer potential life span compared with most adults, providing resources to children will typically provide a much larger and longer lasting benefit than the same provision to an adult. Hence, typically equality will be more efficiently promoted by devoting resources in very large part to needy children. This is, however, only a general tendency. Sometimes equality is better promoted by helping some opportunity-disadvantaged adults rather than by helping an opportunity-disadvantaged child (for example, one for whom not much can be done). In addition, equality requires opportunity-disadvantaged adults before helping opportunity-advantaged children. In principle, however, children have the same equality rights as adults.

The crucial point for what follows is that there are typically fairly strong equality-based duties that all agents have to help children. The duties of procreators must thus be understood in this context. I shall first discuss the special duties the procreators owe *their offspring* and then I shall discuss the special duties that procreators owe *others*.

Special Duties of Procreative Parents to their Offspring

What special duties do parents owe their offspring? We need here to distinguish between procreative and biological parents. *Procreative parents* are the people who bear ultimate responsibility in some appropriate sense for bringing the child into existence. In the normal case, the procreative parents are also the *biological parents*—the providers of sperm and egg—but this need not be so. Individuals who perform *in vitro* fertilization in fertility clinics, surrogate gestational mothers, and prospective guardian parents who arrange for these services to be provided, may be procreative parents. Determining exactly what kinds of actions generate procreative parenthood is a tricky matter, and I shall not attempt to offer an account here. The core case is the old-fashioned one where two people voluntarily have sex in full knowledge of the possibilities of conception taking place.

Biological parenthood does not generate any special duties with respect to their offspring. People who are raped and then forced to bear a child or who are cloned against their will do not have any special duties with respect to the offspring. It is rather those who voluntarily bring the offspring into existence who have, if any one does, such special duties.[6] Procreative parenthood, that is, does generate special duties to the offspring. Although I shall focus on the procreation of human beings, the issues are, I believe, basically the same for the procreation of any kind of being with moral standing—for example, sentient animals that one creates through breeding or in the laboratory.

The only special procreative duties owed to one's offspring, I shall argue, are (1) the duty not to engage in procreative activity if there is 'an unacceptable risk' that an offspring will be produced with negative initial life prospects, (2) the duty, if one engages in procreative activity, to 'live up to the basic expectations', as they are at the time of the activity, for ensuring that the risk of offspring having negative initial life prospects is acceptable, and (3) the duty to compensate any offspring to the extent that their initial life prospects are negative.

The most central idea here is that of initial life prospects. The life prospects at given time, for a given individual, consist of the various possible futures that individual may have, each having a certain objective probability, given the prevailing social and natural circumstances.[7] These probabilities reflect, for example, how the procreator and others are likely to behave towards the child (such as who will raise the child). Each of the possible futures yields a certain quality of life for the being. I leave open how the quality of lives is assessed, but I assume that a life has zero value for a person where it is equally valuable for that person as non-existence. Negative values are worse than non-existence.[8] The value of these life prospects (the various possible futures) can, we shall assume, be evaluated, for example, based on their expected value.

Life prospects can be evaluated at different times. The above duties appeal to the *initial* life prospects of an individual, where these are, I now stipulate, to be understood as those at the time that the individual acquires *moral standing*. Although I believe that humans acquire moral standing at sentience, I shall not here take a stance on that issue.[9] The important point is that the initial life prospects are assessed relative to the time at which moral standing is acquired—and not (necessarily) relative to the time at which the organism comes into existence (at conception). Thus, for example, creating a human organism that would suffer terribly if she acquired moral standing (for example, at sentience), does not generate negative initial life prospects if it is certain that she will die prior to acquiring moral standing.

The first duty listed above is that of not engaging in procreative activity, if the risk of producing an offspring with negative life prospect is 'unacceptable'. I here offer no substantive account of the notion of an acceptable risk except to stipulate that 100 per cent risk is unacceptable and 0 per cent is acceptable. The problem here is quite general and not specific to procreation. If producing a given outcome (for example, certain death by shooting) is wrong, what is the status of actions that impose a risk that you *might* produce that outcome (for example, shooting at firing range)? I do not have a general view on this, and so I am just going to leave it open.[10] Obviously, a lot hangs on it.

The rough idea of the second duty above—the duty to 'live up to the basic expectations' if one does engage in procreative activity—is this. If the procreator made some commitments concerning the child's life prospects, then he/she must honour them. In addition, if the conditions justifying the procreative activity (that the risk of negative initial life prospects were acceptable) were met in part because it was probable that the agent would perform certain actions (for example, look after the child), then the agent has a duty to perform as many of those actions as necessary to ensure that agent does his part to meet the justificatory conditions. If the initial expectations only barely satisfied the justificatory conditions (acceptable risk of negative initial life prospects), then the basic expectations include almost all the initial expectations. If, however, the initial expectations significantly exceeded the justificatory conditions, then the procreator need only live up to enough of them so that the conditions would still have been met had they been based on the assumption that only these later actions would be performed. This is a fuzzy notion, and I will not attempt here to fill it in.

The third duty above—the duty to compensate any offspring to the extent that their initial life prospects are negative—requires those who impose a risk of negative life prospects (whether or not the risk is acceptable) to compensate their offspring for the negativity. Those who impose no risk of negative life prospects (probably an empty case in real life) have no duty to compensate their offspring for the quality of their lives (except, of course, to the extent they later wrong them).

The above claims are admittedly vague and require refinement. Rather than fine-tuning the claims, however, I will attempt to defend their general spirit. For simplicity, my defence will lump the above duties together under the heading 'the duty to ensure non-negative life prospects', which is the core idea.

The proposed view takes a minimal view of special procreative duties to offspring. It is therefore worth being clear about what I am not claiming. First, I am not denying that it is morally desirable for procreators to help their offspring. Of course it is, and it typically makes sense for members of society to provide incentives for them to do so. Second, I am not denying that procreators typically have significant duties to help their offspring. Procreators may make binding commitments to each other or to others to help their offspring, and, if so, they have a duty to live up to their commitments. Furthermore, all agents have a duty to promote equality and, given that children are typically needy and procreators are typically in a position to benefit them significantly, procreators will typically have a duty to their offspring to help them in various ways. This duty, however, flows from an agent-neutral duty to promote equality and not in virtue of being their procreators. Third, I am not here claiming that there are no other procreative duties. I am only claiming that there are no other procreative duties *owed to the offspring.* Below I shall consider what duties are owed to others with respect to procreation. Finally, I am not assuming—indeed, I reject the view—that procreators have a right to raise their offspring even if someone else would do a better job.[11]

The core claim is that the only special duty that procreators owe their offspring (as opposed to their general equality duties owed to them) is that of ensuring non-negative life prospects in the appropriate sense. Those who reject this view are likely to do so on the grounds that the recognized procreative duties are too weak. That is, most people will agree that having non-negative life prospects is necessary for permissible procreation, but most will deny that nothing more is owed to the procreated being. First, however, let us consider some objections that claim that the duties are too strong.

It might be claimed that agents are permitted to procreate no matter what the consequences for the offspring. One might hold this view, for example, on the grounds that there is a fundamental right to procreate. It is quite implausible, however, to hold that one is permitted to procreate no matter what the consequences for others. If there is a fundamental right to procreate, it, like all other rights, is constrained by the condition that one not violate the rights of, or directly and significantly harm, others.[12]

One might then claim that beings who do not currently exist have no rights, and so however the right to procreate is restricted, it is not restricted by duties owed to the offspring who are not currently alive. This objection does not question the duty to compensate existing offspring with negative initial life prospects. It only challenges the claim that a duty is *owed to potential offspring* not to engage in procreative activity—no matter how great the risk that they will have negative life prospects. For at the time of the activity, the potential offspring do not exist. This raises the well-known problem about how to make sense of our duties, if any, to beings who do not yet exist.[13] There are several ways of trying to deal with this problem. One is to concede that there is no duty to refrain from engaging in activity that is likely to harm them later, but hold none the less that agents are liable for such harm if it comes about. Another is to hold that there is an *impersonal* duty to refrain from such activity. Another—the view that I would defend—is to hold that all duties are personal, and that empirically possible people have a kind of secondary moral standing that includes the right not to be created with negative life prospects. Defending this view, however, would take us too far astray. Hence, for simplicity, I shall focus on the claim that the sole special procreative duty is the duty—perhaps an impersonal one—not to create beings with negative initial life prospects. I shall not attempt to defend my claim that this duty is owed to the potential offspring. Even the weaker claim faces serious objections.

Even if one grants that we have a duty not to procreate under certain conditions, some will still question whether the duty is as strong as proposed. One might hold more weakly, for example, that we have the duty not to procreate only when the offspring will have negative life prospects *and the negative benefits are not offset by benefits to others*. On this view, it might be permissible to procreate where the benefit to others—for example, the parents or other members of society—is sufficiently great. Utilitarians and unconstrained consequentialist egalitarians, for example, would take this view. The problem with this view is that it fails to recognize the moral separateness of persons (beings with moral standing). At least in the extreme cases where it involves a life not worth living, it is not permissible, except perhaps when necessary to avoid catastrophes, to make one person bear costs for the benefit of others. In more Kantian terms: it is impermissible to treat someone's very existence as a mere means of providing benefits to others.

The proposed view, I conclude, is plausible with respect to the duties that it recognizes. It also holds, however, that there are no further special procreative duties. Let us now consider objections to this claim.

The proposed view sets a fairly low life prospects standard that procreators must meet (mere non-negativity). There are many ways of setting a higher standard. One generic approach is to set an *absolute* standard, which is a standard that is not sensitive to the parental, social, or other circumstances. The proposed standard of non-negative life prospects is an example of an absolute standard, but higher absolute standards could be set by requiring (1) that all basic needs (nutrition, warmth, etc.) be met, or (2) that the life prospects be 'adequate' or 'decent', where this requires more than mere positivity (a level significantly above the zero level).[14] A second generic approach imposes conditions that are *comparative* in the sense that they are sensitive to the life prospects of others. It might be required, for example, that procreators ensure that their child have the best or at least average life prospects compared with their cohorts. A third generic approach imposes conditions that are *procreator-sensitive* in the sense that they are sensitive to what the procreators are capable of providing. It might be required that procreators provide the best life opportunities that they can (without violating the rights of others) for their child, or perhaps the best that they can without significant (or major) sacrifice.[15] Moreover, hybrid views are possible, such as an absolute or comparative approaches modified by the procreator-relative rider 'to the extent possible without significant sacrifice by the procreators'.

Pure procreator-relative (e.g., doing the best they can) and pure comparative approaches (e.g., ensuring at least average life prospects) on their own are too weak in that they do not require that the life prospects be non-negative. For, if the external circumstances are sufficiently dire (e.g., if essential resources are extremely scarce), or if the personal endowment of the offspring is sufficiently poor (e.g., unalterable severe pain), then even if the procreators do the best they can, and even if the child has the best life prospects of anyone (where everyone's prospects are negative), the child may still not have a life worth living. Let us therefore assume that the non-negative life prospects condition is accepted as a necessary condition, and that the only issue is whether additional conditions are plausible.

Absolute conditions that require more than non-negative life prospects (e.g., meeting basic needs) and comparative conditions (e.g., ensuring at least average life prospects) are too strong, if they are not qualified by some kind of procreator-relative condition on when it is permissible to procreate. For in situations in which it is possible to procreate with positive life prospects, but not possible to satisfy the additional absolute or comparative conditions, it is quite implausible to say that agents have an obligation to the prospective child not to let him/her acquire moral standing. For in this case the flawed existence is better for the child than no existence at all. So to be plausible, any additional condition on permissible procreation needs to have a qualification such as 'to the extent possible' or perhaps 'to the extent possible without significant sacrifice'.

So the core objections to the proposed view are that procreative parents also have a duty to their offspring to ensure, to the extent possible (perhaps: without significant sacrifice) (1) that all the child's basic needs are met, (2) that the child has adequate life prospects, (3) that the child has at least average life prospects, or (4) that the child has the best achievable life prospects.

From an egalitarian position, however, there is a generic problem with procreative duties beyond the provision of non-negative life prospects. For, as noted above, unless they are made procreator-relative (for example, to the extent possible for the procreator), it would follow that individuals have a duty to their offspring not to create them when the best they can do is provide the child with positive but substandard life prospects. This, however, is not plausible, given that positive prospects are, by definition, better than no life at all. Some sort of procreator-relative qualification is therefore needed—such as: to the extent possible, or to the extent possible without significant sacrifice, for the procreators. But if some such qualification is introduced, then there is a different problem. For with the procreator-relative qualification, the effective value of the rights of offspring against their procreators is higher the more advantaged their procreators are. From an egalitarian viewpoint, however, this is suspect. Why should children in advantaged families have effectively more valuable (although formally equal) rights than children in disadvantaged families? The most striking problem arises if procreators have a duty to provide the *best* life prospects they can for their offspring, but the same problem arises (although to a lesser extent) on the other views (for example, if procreators have a duty to ensure adequate life prospects to the extent they can without significant sacrifice). Thus, egalitarians cannot accept a procreator-relative qualification, and without such a qualification, any duty more onerous than ensuring non-negative life prospects is implausible. Hence, from an egalitarian perspective—which I am assuming here—the duty to ensure non-negative life prospects is the only procreative duty owed to offspring.

Now, strictly speaking, this argument is too quick. For there is nothing troubling from an egalitarian perspective with some children having more valuable rights *against their procreators* compared with others—as long as the *total* packages of rights they have (against any individual) are equally valuable. So, for example, there is nothing troubling in principle with rich children having more valuable rights against their procreators, as long this difference in value is offset by having less valuable rights against others (for example, less valuable equality rights against others). So, if perfect equality will be achieved if everyone discharges their duties, then there need be no problem with some children having more valuable rights against their procreators.

The problem, however, is that perfect equality of opportunity may not be achievable and that, even if it is, the duties to promote equality may be limited and thus full compliance may not ensure that equality is achieved. In these cases, there is indeed something troubling about advantaged children having more valuable rights against their procreators. So, from an egalitarian perspective, there is a generic problem with imposing procreative duties to offspring beyond those of non-negative prospects. Instead, egalitarians should simply hold that the only procreative duty to offspring is that of ensuring that the offspring have non-negative life prospects. All agents have the further agent-neutral duty of promoting equality of life prospects.

There is one other reason why some may think that the proposed special procreative duties to offspring are too weak. Why is it only at the time of procreation that the life prospects must be non-negative? Why not through-out the child's life, or at least up to the acquisition of adulthood (autonomy)? After all, even if the prospects are initially non-negative, things can go poorly later and life prospects can turn negative. One problem with requiring non-negative life prospects at each point in the life of offspring is that it holds procreators accountable for the self-regarding autonomous choices of their offspring once they are adults, and there is no reason in principle to hold parents so accountable. Procreators are not accountable for the mess that adult offspring make of their lives—although they are typically at least partially responsible for their disposition to do so, as reflected in their initial life prospects. Perhaps, then, procreators are accountable for ensuring posi-tive life prospects at each point *up to adulthood*. The problem with this, however, is that it holds procreators accountable for the actions of others and for acts of nature during that period. Parents do indeed have a duty to live up to their commitments and to the basic expectations for promoting the offspring's life prospects, but this does not require that life prospects be non-negative up to adulthood. If procreators do everything they are reasonably expected to do, and the offspring is unpredictably struck by lightning—thereby giving the offspring negative life prospects—parents have no special procreative duty to ensure that life prospects become positive again (except to the extent this is part of their basic expectations). Of course, procreators, as well as others, have equality duties and this may indeed require them to help those struck by misfortune. It is not, however, a special procreative duty.

So far, we have considered procreative duties to the offspring. Let us now consider what duties to *others* procreation imposes.

Special Duties of Procreative Parents to Others

The only special procreative duties owed to others, I shall argue, concern (*a*) the possibility that one's offspring will violate the rights of others, and (*b*) the possibility that one's offspring will have initial life prospects that are sufficiently low (for example, below average) that others will suffer either increased equality demands (to help the offspring) or reduced equality entitlements (because the offspring displace them in equality entitlements). In both cases there are three relevant duties: (1) the duty not to engage in procreative activity if there is 'an unacceptable risk' of such possibility, (2) the duty, if one engages in procreative activity, to 'live up to the basic expectations', as they are at the time of the activity, for ensuring that there is no 'unacceptable risk' of such possibility, (3) the duty to provide compensation to those who are disadvantaged by the realization of such possibility—to the extent that one's procreative and later activities contributed to such realization.[16]

The crude idea is simple: one has a duty to ensure that others are not disadvantaged in certain ways by the presence of one's offspring. More specifically, there are two relevant kinds of disadvantage: rights violations and disadvantage in equality rights or duties. The latter kind of disadvantage can arise in either of two ways when the offspring is below average in initial life prospects. If the equality demands on each agent are *limited* in the amount of self-sacrifice that they require, then, if the offspring is sufficiently disadvantaged in initial life prospects, some individuals will cease to be entitled to help (because the offspring has a stronger claim to the help). If, on the other hand, the equality demands on each agent are *not limited* in the amount of self-sacrifice, then the second kind of equality disadvantage that can arise is that agents will have to make greater sacrifices to help the offspring in addition to helping the others.

If one procreates and one's offspring disadvantages others by violating their rights or by adversely affecting their equality rights and duties, then one has a duty to provide some compensation to the victims.[17] The level of compensation owed, however, depends on how much one contributed to the risk of disadvantage. If, for example, one has an offspring that is virtually certain to violate rights of others (a highly hypothetical case, of course), then one would be liable for virtually all the wrongful harm one's offspring imposes. If, on the other hand, one has an offspring that is virtually certain to violate no rights (also a highly hypothetical case), then one would be liable for virtually none of the wrongful harm she imposes. Exactly how contribution is to be measured for these purposes is a tricky business, and I will not attempt to defend an account here. None the less, the general idea should be clear enough.

It might seem strange to hold procreators accountable for the rights violations of their offspring when they are adults. Some authors have argued that parents should be liable for damages imposed by their *minor* offspring,[18] but few, if any, have argued that the liability holds for adult offspring. Why should procreators be accountable for the choices that their offspring make as autonomous agents? In response to this concern, one could modify the proposed duty so that it holds only as a backup duty. If the offspring can be made to compensate their victims fully, then the procreators would not be liable. If, however, the offspring cannot be made to fully compensate their victims (for example, if the offspring have died, disappeared, or simply do not have adequate resources), then the procreators would be liable for up to some amount based on their contribution to the risk of the rights violation. There is a fair amount of plausibility to this view, but I am inclined to believe that it is less plausible than the proposed view. For, arguably, if adult offspring are predisposed to violate the rights of others, and this is due to genetic or environmental factors that the procreator contributed, it makes more sense to hold the procreator directly liable for the damages. This, of course, raises deep issues about free will and compatibilism, and hence I shall not attempt to defend this aspect of the proposed view. The core idea is that procreators are somehow accountable for some of the wrongful harms that their offspring inflict on others.

My claim, then, is that concern for rights violations by one's offspring and for equality disadvantages imposed by their presence are the sole bases for procreative duties owed to others. This view will be challenged as being too strong. I cannot, however, think of any minimally plausible reason to think that the view is too weak. It is not plausible, for example, to hold that procreation is impermissible, or that procreators are liable, merely because their offspring are not sufficiently likely to be virtuous or beneficial to others. Hence, we can consider only objections that the proposed view imposes too many obligations on procreators.

Why, one might ask, are procreators accountable for the impact of their procreation on people's rights and duties of equality? The advantages that equality rights bring and the disadvantages that equality duties bring vary depending on the circumstances, and there is no reason to suppose, one might argue, that people have a right not to have the value of these rights and duties affected by the actions of others.

Clearly, the procreated child has the same equality rights as others, and so the costs of compensating her for any equality disadvantages (at least if severe enough) should be borne either by the procreators or by others (and not by her). The question is whether it must be borne by the procreators. A plausible conception of the rights and duties of equality will, I claim, answer affirmatively. For, without such a duty, individuals would be free (under certain conditions) to procreate massive numbers of offspring (perhaps millions through cloning) who have lives barely worth living and significantly below average in life prospects. Given that such offspring have equality rights, this would lead to the impoverishment of all (since equality would require transferring resources to these poorly off individuals). Given the gross implausibility of the view that agents are permitted to do this, it seems clear that agents have a duty to cover the equality costs of their procreative activities.[19]

A second objection to the proposed view is that, although agents may have obligations not to procreate when the offspring are sufficiently likely to violate the rights of others, procreators bear no liability to provide any compensation to their victims. In this crude form, the objection is implausible. For at least in cases where the offspring are highly likely to engage in horrible rights violations (and the procreators know this), the procreators have an obligation to others not to procreate. Moreover, when one knowingly violates a duty to others, one is liable for providing compensation. At least in this case, liability for compensation is plausible, given that one wronged the individuals by procreating. A more sophisticated version of this objection grants that in cases of wrongful procreation procreators are liable for compensation, but it holds that individuals are not so liable when the act of procreation was permissible. Let us consider this objection more carefully.

Why should those who permissibly procreate be liable for compensating their offspring's victims? The answer is that, in procreating, one imposes a risk on others that their rights will be violated. Imposing this risk may be permissible (and not violate a right of theirs) if the risk is acceptable (sufficiently low), but the permissibility thereof does not entail that one has no liability.[20] Indeed, it is quite plausible—both in general and in the specific case of procreation—that those who impose risks of rights violations on others (even if permissibly) are liable for compensating them (if relevant responsibility conditions are met).

A third objection to the proposed view is that it imposes undue hardship on poor people, since they will have greater difficulty ensuring that the acceptability of the risk that their offspring will disadvantage others by rights violations or by impact on equality rights and duties. Not only do poor people have less money, their children also typically have lower life prospects and hence require more money to cover their equality costs. The problem is further exacerbated if children in poor families are more likely to engage in rights violations. To reply to this objection, we need to distinguish two cases. One is where the parents had at least average initial life prospects but as a result of their choices (bad choices, choosing leisure over wealth, unlucky gambles, etc.) ended up poor. Here the reply is that they will indeed be disadvantaged by the above accountability standards, but the disadvantage is the result of their own choices. Poor people are disadvantaged in all kinds of ways, but if those disadvantages are due to their own choices from an equal starting position, then there is nothing wrong with them suffering that disadvantage. The disadvantage of accountability for one's offspring is simply a special case. The second case is where the parents had less than average life prospects. Here, accountability for one's offspring exacerbates the disadvantage of the parents. In this case, the reply is that this disadvantage is taken into account in assessing the initial life prospects of the poor parents, and they will be entitled to some (perhaps very significant) equality-promotion benefits in virtue of this disadvantage. In principle, at least, such parents will suffer no net disadvantage.

Conclusion

The proposed view of special procreative duties agrees with common sense in that it holds it holds that agents have a duty not to procreate when the offspring's life prospects are negative. The rest of the view, however, is controversial. First, it holds (essentially) that there are no other special procreative duties owed to the offspring. There is no special procreative duty in this regard, for example, to ensure that one's offspring have life prospects that are as high as reasonably possible. Much of the counterintuitiveness of this position disappears, however, in the context of an egalitarian theory that holds that people have significant duties to promote people's life prospects by promoting the equality thereof. The duty to help one's offspring, on this view, is simply a special case of one's duty to help others. The second way that the proposed view departs from common sense is that it holds that procreators have duties to others to compensate them for disadvantages imposed by the existence of the offspring (from rights violations and from negative impact on equality rights and duties).

Throughout I have focused on rights and duties without any reference to whether they are enforceable—that is, to whether the use of force is permissible to ensure that the rights are respected or the duties fulfilled. I would argue that each of the rights involved (and all the duties on the proposed view are correlative to rights) are in principle enforceable. If this is right, then the state (and others) may in principle legitimately enforce these rights. It's worth noting, however, two qualifications. First, just as it is not permissible to enforce a choice-protecting right when the right-holder does not consent to the enforcement, it is also, I would argue, not permissible to enforce interest-protecting rights when the enforcement is not in the holder's interest. So, there may be some cases where the enforcement of children's rights is not permissible (e.g., preventing a parent from beating a child where the result of such prevention would be worse for the child). Second, that a right is permissibly enforceable does not entail that it is obligatory to enforce it. The duty to promote equality will impose some duties to enforce rights, but, where trade-offs must be made in promoting equality, it will sometimes allow some rights violations not to be enforced.

Obviously, extending the proposed view to a theory of legitimate state (and individual) enforcement is the topic for another paper. Enough has been said, I hope, to make the position worthy of further development and examination.[21]

Notes

1. For discussion of why some kind of rights of non-interference, and self-ownership rights in particular, are needed, see Vallentyne (1998, 2000, 2001).
2. For discussions of the issues between choice-protecting and interesting-protecting conceptions of rights, see Sumner (1987), Steiner (1994), Kramer *et al.* (1998), and Brennan (2002). For scepticism about whether all duties (and imperfect duties in particular) owed to children can be captured by rights, see O'Neill (1989).
3. I probably reject a pure choice-protecting theory of rights for agents. For I endorse soft-paternalism, which allows infringements of rights so as to ensure that the agent is making an informed choice. I believe that justifying soft-paternalism probably requires invoking some interest-protecting considerations even in the case of agents. For simplicity, however, I ignore this point in what follows.
4. The crucial point is that, once one becomes sufficiently autonomous for certain kinds of decisions, then one's consent is required to waive the right rather than mere non-harm. Although the capacity for well-being is still present, its moral significance is overridden by the capacity for autonomous choice when the latter is present.
5. I assume throughout that the interest-protecting rights of children protect their interests *directly* in the sense that whether a right is infringed by a particular action is determined by the impact of that action on the holder's well-being. Rights so understood are not infringed when no harm is done to the holder. Indirect interest-protecting rights, by contrast, ground the content of rights in the instrumental benefits to the holder of *having* those rights, and such rights may be infringed even if the holder is not harmed. A full defence of the proposed view would thus require a defence of the direct view against indirect views.
6. If there is a duty to share certain medical information (e.g. about vulnerability to various diseases) with those with whom we are closely genetically related, then biological parents have this duty with respect to their offspring. My claim should be understood as holding that biological *parenthood* imposes no special duties with respect to offspring that are not also imposed by on all those with comparable or greater genetic similarity (e.g. siblings).
7. Throughout I assume the existence of objective probabilities. If there are no such things, then a more sophisticated account is needed in terms of epistemically warranted subjective probabilities.
8. Many deny that one can make judgements about whether a life is better or worse

than no life at all. See e.g. Heyd (1992: ch. 4). I shall not here attempt to defend this assumption, but see Roberts (1998: ch. 1) and Buchanan *et al.* (2000: ch. 6).

9. Because I hold that empirically possible beings can have a kind of secondary moral standing (that gives them a right not to be brought into existence with negative initial life prospects), I should, strictly speaking appeal here to *primary* moral standing, where this is understood as the kind of moral standing that only existing beings can have. For simplicity, however, I ignore this point.

10. For discussion of whether risks of primary rights violation are rights violations, see Thomson (1990: 242–8) and Nozick (1974: 73–8).

11. I would defend the view that (roughly) the right to raise a given child can be validly claimed by anyone for whom possession of the right is in the child's best long-term interest. See Vallentyne (2003).

12. For further discussion of how the right to procreate cannot be unconditional, see Archard (1993: ch. 8).

13. For discussion of the person-affecting restriction in the context of possible future people, see e.g. Parfit (1984: part IV; 1986), Woodward (1986), Heyd (1992), McMahan (1998), Roberts (1998). (The Roberts work is an especially promising way of satisfying the person-affecting restriction.)

14. If basic needs are sufficiently expansive and the criterion of adequacy for life prospects is sufficiently weak, a person could have adequate life prospects while having unmet needs. None the less, on typical understandings the adequacy requirement entails the basic needs requirement. Lomasky (1987: 174) appeals to basic needs ('adequate to prepare the child to live as an independent project-pursuer'). Mill (1859) appeals to both basic needs ('food for its body, [and] instruction and training for its mind', p. 128) and adequate life prospects ('the ordinary chances of a desirable existence', p. 132). Shiffrin (1999) appeals to the absence of harms, where harms can be present even if life prospects are positive. Purdy (1996) appeals to both basic needs ('normal health', p. 46) and adequate life prospects ('minimally satisfying life', p. 45). Steinbock and McClamrock (1999: 195) appeal to 'decent chance of a good life'.

15. Ruddick's (1980: 130; 1999: 247) Life Prospects Principle requires something like the best life prospects achievable without significant parental sacrifice.

16. As with the discussion of procreative duties to offspring, I appeal to the general notion of an 'acceptable risk' of primary rights violation and to the notion of basic expectations for ensuring that no unacceptable risks are imposed. See the brief discussion of these notions in the previous section.

17. As in the previous section, I leave open here whether conditions of fault are also required for accountability.

18. See e.g. Rakowski (1991: 247).

19. For further defense of the special procreative duty not to disadvantage others in their equality rights and duties, see Rakowski (1991: 152–4) and Casal and Williams (1995). Casal and Williams also argue (correctly) against the view that, where children are a public good, everyone has a duty to contribute towards the costs of raising them. This view is defended in George (1987).

20. For discussion of the difference between property rules (which prohibit the activity) and liability rules (which permit it, but then hold the agent liable for damage), see Calabresi and Melmed (1972).

21. For their insightful comments, I thank David Archard, Samantha Brennan, Paula Casal, Roger Crisp, Tony Ellis, Brad Hooker, Matthew Kramer, Colin MacLeod, Andy Mason, Trenton Merricks, Gene Mills, Eric Rakowski, Hillel Steiner, and Andrew Williams.

12

Liberal Equality and the Affective Family

Colin M. Macleod

The aim of this chapter is to investigate a significant tension between two attractive ideals embraced by many contemporary liberal theorists. On the one hand, there is the ideal of a loving family. Despite occasional misgivings, liberals celebrate the value and importance of the association of individuals into distinct family units whose adult and child members are bound together by mutual affection, concern, and loyalty. The family is treated as an institution that merits protection and promotion. On the other hand, there is the ideal of liberal equality. This ideal offers a distinctive interpretation of the basic equal moral standing of individuals according to which individuals should be equally indemnified against morally arbitrary sources of disadvantage that can seriously impair their overall life prospects. However, the ideal of liberal equality also treats competent adults as capable of assuming responsibility for the direction and character of their lives. As a consequence, liberals hold that some differences in the success individuals enjoy in their lives, including the benefits and opportunities they are able to acquire through their choices, are not unjust. The ideal of liberal equality is attractive partly because of its incorporation of a principle of individual responsibility within egalitarian distributive norms. However, the fact that the ideal of liberal equality tolerates choice-based inequalities creates a problem for liberals given their endorsement of the family. Parents typically care more about their own children than other children. Those parents who have prospered (for example, through their diligent pursuit of economic activities) often seek to express their partiality by conferring benefits on their children. But the operation of such of parental partiality can result in inequalities between children of different families that the ideal of liberal equality should condemn as unjust.[1]

The chapter is organized in the following way. First, I provide a fuller account of the affective family. I identify various reasons for affirming its value and its claim to remain a specially protected social institution. Second, I sketch the main contours of the ideal liberal equality and consider how the ideal should interpreted with children in view. Liberal egalitarians have not adequately addressed the place children occupy within a theory of justice. I argue that children should be given direct recognition as full, equal, and distinct subjects from the point of view of liberal equality. Recognition of this status for children generates a problem in reconciling liberal justice and the affective family. Third, I describe and defend an institutional strategy for harmonizing liberal justice and the family. Although liberal equality permits some social and economic inequalities to obtain between adults, children's access to resources and opportunities should not be significantly determined by parental entitlement to resources. A reasonable harmony between the potentially conflicting resource entitlements of children and parents can be achieved through a strategy that combines public provision of basic resources directly to children with modest constraints on the ways which parents can legitimately confer special advantages on children.

The Affective Family

The family as a social institution has a chequered past. It is widely assumed to be an extremely valuable social institution and there is understandable anxiety about forces in contemporary culture that threaten to fracture the family. Yet it is also true that horrific injustices, particularly to children, have occurred within the special sphere of human relations traditionally delineated by the family. The social reproduction of troubling attitudes and political commitments (such as misogyny or racism) can also occur within the family. Given its sometimes sad historical record, it is understandable that there have been occasional calls for the elimination of the family. While I acknowledge the need to challenge many problematic aspects of traditional family practices and structures, an attractive model of affective association that nurtures its members is often displayed in the family. In its best form, the family is certainly worth preserving. Part of my aim is to provide qualified vindication of the potential value of the family as a central social institution for the rearing of children.

One difficulty that immediately arises in assessing the value of the family concerns specification of its defining features. Family structures are historically and culturally diverse and this can render hazardous generalizations about the value of the family. Some ways of characterizing the family—such as having a nuclear structure in which a male head of the household exercises dominion and authority over his wife and children conceived as his property—hardly merit celebration. Moreover, such narrow construals of the family arbitrarily exclude other forms of human relationships that merit recognition as families. So as to avoid constructions of the family that are either unduly narrow or that have problematic assumptions about its value built into them, I offer the following loose construal of what I call the affective family. The affective family is a social group comprised by one or more adults and one or more children who are linked together by a special history (for example, as biological kin or adoption) and by sentiments of mutual affection. Some of the adults in such a group have a socially and legally recognized status as parents or guardians that confers upon them a special measure of authority over and responsibility for the children in the group. Members of the family typically display special concern for the welfare of each other that is not usually displayed, at least in a consistent and ongoing fashion, to persons outside the family. It is in this way that familial relationships are characterized by partiality. I do not assume that the terms 'parents' or 'guardians' refer exclusively or even primarily to the biological mother and father of a child. Nor do I assume that parents or guardians must be married or heterosexual. This account implies that adults involved in a close, ongoing affective relationships do not, strictly speaking, constitute a distinct family unless they have children. This is not to say that they do not belong to a family.

It is frequently assumed that families can only flourish and generate value, both for their members and for society in general, if the family is treated as a special protected sphere of interaction in which its practices and activities are not subject to significant intrusion or regulation by either state authorities or members of the community. Meddling in, or even significant monitoring of, the day-to-day life of the family is thought to jeopardize the intimate relations at the heart of the family (Shoeman 1980). This is one reason why the family is appropriately viewed as constituting a kind of private sphere that is specially insulated from outsiders, especially public authorities. There are, of course, circumstances (such as physical abuse and neglect of children) in which public authorities may legitimately intervene, without invitation, in the family. However, the justificatory threshold for intervention is usually held to be fairly high. It is sometimes held that direct intervention in the family is only warranted if public authorities have evidence of a clear and present danger that is posed to the health and welfare of children. Whether the threshold is really so high can be disputed but that the family constitutes some specially protected sphere seems plausible.

One way to determine the degree to which it is appropriate to treat the family as a specially protected sphere is to identify the goods that can be realized by the family. We need to determine not only what benefits can be secured through the family but also the extent to which provision of these goods is dependent on maintenance of the family as a protected sphere. There are various potential beneficiaries of the affective family that can be distinguished: (*a*) children (*b*) adult family members (*c*) particular cultural or national communities, and (*d*) members of the broader political society. However, I shall focus primarily on the value of the family for children and adult family members. Very briefly, here are seven ways in which the family is a source of value. This is not meant as an exhaustive list. Also the distinction between different dimensions of value does not imply that there is no overlap between some of the values.

Familial Intimacy

Members of the affective family have close, loving relationships characterized by both mutual concern and participation in shared activities and projects. Since the scope of our possible affection for and connection to others is limited we cannot stand in this sort of relationship intimacy to all persons. Such relationships, in a way parallel to the value of friendship, seem to have inherent worth.

Positive Identity Formation

Families can provide individuals, especially children, with a tangible sense of identity. Children come to have a sense of self partly by locating themselves in a distinct family history and ongoing participation in the practices identified as valuable by the family. In a closely related way, the family also plays an important role in supplying a context of choice from which individuals can deliberate about the merits of different conceptions of the good (Kymlicka 1995: 82–5; Macleod 1997).

Maintenance of Culture and Diversity

Families can play an important role in the maintenance and social reproduction of distinctive and valuable cultures and their traditions. Children often come to embrace and seek to perpetuate the cultural heritage and language that is supplied to them by their parents. The family thereby serves as a vehicle for the preservation of cultural traditions, many of which can have value in their own right. In this context, parents have a reason to value children because children can play a role in implementation of parental conceptions of the good.

Basic Resource Provision

Families are strongly motivated to ensure that their members have adequate food, shelter, clothing, and education. Families acquire and distribute these benefits to their members. Families thus promote basic elements of human welfare.

Developmental Benefits

In addition to providing basic resources, families can play an important role in nurturing and developing crucial cognitive, emotional, and moral capacities of children. The family is often depicted as especially important to the development of a sense of justice (Rawls 1971: 462–79).

Specific Need Identification

The closeness of the relationships between family members allows for efficient recognition and response to the particular needs of particular individuals.

Reciprocity of Care

The mutual affection and concern between parents and children is important in the first instance because parents can be expected to provide needed care to vulnerable and dependent children. As parents and children age, however, the direction of the care-giving relationship changes and children can play an important role in securing the interests of their parents.

If we focus on the goods that can secured through the family for children and adult family members, we can draw some distinctions concerning the significance of partiality to successful provision of these goods. First, many goods— for example, familial intimacy, distinct identify formation, and the maintenance of distinct cultural heritage—are strongly partiality-dependent in the sense that partiality is an important, and perhaps even necessary condition, for realization of the good. These goods cannot be fully realized for parents and children in the absence of partiality. Indeed, in the case of familial intimacy partiality is an inherent aspect of the good. Second, some goods can be adequately realized in the absence of partiality but partiality can enhance their value. This is true for instance of the provision of some educational opportunities. Schools can provide specialized instruction and teach skills but a child's enthusiasm for learning and her mastery of certain skills can be enhanced by the special support and encouragement she receives from her family. Third, the value of some goods is largely partiality-independent. Goods such as basic food, shelter, and clothing can be adequately supplied to persons (and children in particular) without reliance on relationships of partiality. Moreover, the provision of such goods through relationships of partiality does not significantly enhance their value. This is not to deny that there is not value in providing such goods via relationships of partiality. It may, for instance, be an important expression of parents' love for their children that parents cook special food or buy special clothes for their children. However, in these cases partiality does not augment the basic nutritional value of the food or the protective value of clothing. Rather the provision of special food and clothing is a way of realizing goods of intimacy.

The fact that many of the goods provided by the affective family are strongly partiality-dependent helps to explain why the family can merit its status as a specially protected sphere of interaction. In order to realize such goods, we must secure conditions conducive to the establishment and maintenance of (healthy) affective ties between persons. It seems plausible to suppose that one such condition is social recognition of a special sphere of interaction. Affective relationships to particular others are most likely to develop and flourish in conditions in which individuals are assured that they can display their special concern for one another and exhibit their intimate feelings and vulnerabilities without fear of public scrutiny or censure. It is partly through recognition of and sympathetic identification with the specific needs, desires, and characteristics of particular others that we develop special attachments to others. By limiting the kind of access that outsiders have to the family realm, we enable both parents and children to establish these special kinds of intimate understanding and connections. The specially protected sphere of the family must not only be insulated from outside interference but it must also be recognized as a sphere in which family members enjoy the prerogative of devoting special attention and care to each. To degree that the goods realized through the affective family cannot be realized by other forms of child-rearing such as communal collectivism, the family will enjoy a strong claim to protection and promotion. A different source of support for protection of the family is provided by considerations of individual liberty. Although there is some controversy as to whether adults have an unqualified right to found a family (Harris 1989), there is a strong presumption that the scope of protected individual liberty gives adults the prerogative to form special relationships (for example, marriage) and to bear and raise children of their own. Abolishing the affective family would entail a loss of valuable liberty for adults and would be problematic on this basis alone. The liberty claims here are defeasible. The prerogative to found a family can be denied or constrained if parents, prospective or actual, pose a threat to the well-being of their children. This does not make them insignificant. For instance, even if collective rearing of children could supply the same range of goods to children as the affective family, the latter form of child-rearing could be justified as superior, overall, by appeal to the importance of parental liberty.

I hope to have established main two points through the foregoing remarks. First, the substantial benefits that the institution of the affective family can confer on children, parents and the broader community give us good reason to value the affective family highly and to recognize the legitimacy of according it status as a protected sphere of interaction. By taking this position, I do not wish to diminish the harmful potential of the family.[2] The point is not to turn a blind eye to oppression or injustice in the family but rather to address such problems in a way that displays adequate recognition of the value of the affective family. We have good reason to resist any wholesale dismantling of the family. Second, the value of the affective family is importantly dependent on permitting and, indeed, encouraging partiality. We should not lament the phenomenon of familial partiality *per se*. However, we should also acknowledge that there are ways of expressing partiality that can generate injustice. We must now consider how familial partiality can give rise to injustice and whether problematic effects of partiality can be addressed without compromising the family.

Liberal Equality

I wish to explore these issues from the vantage of a liberal egalitarian conception of justice. It is, of course, a matter of heated controversy as to how precisely the ideal of liberal equality should be understood or even whether justice is appropriately conceived in egalitarian terms. However, for the purposes of this discussion, I will simply adopt and not expressly defend the following broadly Dworkinian conception of liberal equality (Dworkin 2000). The animating nerve of this conception is an abstract principle of equality or impartiality according to which everyone's life matters and matters equally. 'No government is legitimate that does not show equal concern for the fate of all those citizens over whom it claims dominion and from whom it claims allegiance' (Dworkin 2000: 1). This principle of equal concern gives rise to a complex theory of distributive justice according to which a distinction can be drawn between different kinds of inequality. Inequalities in the life prospects of individuals that are traceable to the influence of arbitrary factors of social or natural contingency are unjust. Certain factors such a person's race, sex, class background, or natural endowment should not serve as significant determinants of a person's overall life prospects. An ideally just society aims at securing a distribution of transferable resources that eliminates, in so far as is feasible, inequalities that can arise from such factors. However, not all differences in the resource holdings of individuals are traceable to the influence of such morally arbitrary factors. Liberal egalitarians recognize that a just distribution should also display sensitivity to the choices responsible citizens make about how to lead their lives. It is not a violation of egalitarian principles if there are differences (even over a lifetime) in the resources (for example, income and other goods) to which individuals have access, providing such differences appropriately track choices.

The theory of liberal equality thus has two dimensions. First, individuals should not face significant disadvantages in the resources and opportunities to which they have access in virtue of factors that lie outside the sphere of responsibility. Broadly speaking, the problematic factors are those forms of brute bad luck that cannot be insured against by individuals on fair terms. Second, inequalities in the resources and opportunities to which individuals have access are just in so far as such inequalities are traceable to the choices made by responsible individuals from a fair initial position. Since the distribution of resources generated in any real world setting will reflect a complex interplay of luck, endowment, and choice, devising a feasible strategy for tracking these different dimensions of justice is extremely complex.

In my view, liberal egalitarians have not yet devised a fully satisfactory theory about how these dimensions of justice are to be interpreted or how a suitable balance can be achieved through feasible institutional arrangements (Macleod 1998). However, whatever its precise form, we can anticipate two probable implications of such a theory. First, there is the expectation of what I shall call *significant differential entitlement*. On the reasonable assumption that responsible individuals will respond differently to the opportunities for economic advancement they face, there will be some significant differences in the economic benefits that accrue to individuals in light of their choices. Some degree of significant economic inequality that obtains between responsible adults as a result of different choices is not unjust. (I would stress that the degree of defensible economic inequality is certainly much less than the degree of inequality that currently exists both within and across nations.) Second, there is the expectation of what I shall call *wide discretionary control of private resources*. This is the idea that individuals should enjoy wide latitude in determining the uses to which they put the private resources to which they are justly entitled. In particular, individuals should be free from significant constraints to devote their fair share of privately held resources to the development and implementation of the legitimate projects and life-plans they value.

Much like the partiality expressed in the family, these commitments seem unproblematic when viewed in isolation. However, once the ambit of liberal equality is extended so as to speak directly to the claims of children, as I shall now argue it should be, the tension between ideals liberal equality and the affective family becomes apparent.

Treating Children as Equals

A problematic feature of most liberal theories of justice is that they adopt an unduly narrow conception of the scope of distributive norms. To a large degree, work in this area by liberal theorists has focused on the identification of principles of distribution that provide a basis for regulating the entitlements to resources that can be claimed by independent responsible adults. The entitlements to resources that can be directly claimed by children have been given insufficient attention.[3] Indeed, liberal theory has tended to treat the claims of children to resources as mediated by the seemingly prior parental entitlements. Adults are conceived as the principal bearers of justice-based entitlements to resources and, with some qualified exceptions (most notably entitlement to basic education), children's entitlements to resources are assumed to be subsidiary to that of their parents. This mediated form of consideration of children's claims is, however, inconsistent with the animating principle of equal consideration endorsed by liberals. Though their interests are importantly different in many respects from adults, children are distinct beings with distinct interests. The close relationship between parents and children and dependency of children on adults do not establish an identity of their interests such that equal consideration of parental interests derivatively ensures equal consideration of children's interests. Similarly, the fact that children initially lack and only gradual develop the prerequisites of responsible agency should not disqualify them from receiving equal and unmediated consideration of their interests. The important point is simply that children are distinct members of the moral community with distinct interests who are, from an egalitarian perspective, appropriately viewed as a 'self-originating sources of valid moral claims' (Rawls 1980: 543) with an equal moral status. Though important resources are often delivered to children from parents, children's entitlement to many resources ought to be viewed as independent of this relationship.

The complexion of liberal equality is complicated by viewing children's entitlement to resources as unmediated by parental entitlements. The difficulty is that against the background of the affective family, children's entitlements to resources can, in effect, come into conflict with the entitlements of adults. Whereas the form of resource distribution that is endorsed by liberal equality in the case of adults is one that permits significant differential entitlement, liberal equality favours a stricter form of resource equality for children. Children initially lack and only gradually develop the capacities for responsible autonomy that make the idea of a choice-sensitive distributive norm so attractive in the case of adults. So the entitlement-generating considerations of individual responsibility that can be invoked to justify inter-adult inequalities cannot be invoked to justify inter-child inequality. Since choice cannot be used to differentiate children's claims to resources and since justice aims at the elimination of arbitrary disadvantage, liberal equality should condemn as unjust to children significant disparities in the resources and opportunities to which different children have access over the course of their childhood. Children's entitlement to resources should not and cannot be choice-differentiated. For the purpose of identification, I will label this implication of ideal of liberal equality as the criterion of strict equality for children.

It is important not to be misled by this label. The implications for the distribution of resources to children can be more complicated than the label might initially suggest. In particular, the criterion of strict equality should not be understood as entailing that there can be no differentiation between the bundles of resources to which different children have access. The key is that differentiation should be aimed at fairly mitigating significant forms of arbitrary disadvantage. A crucial issue that arises in the context of interpreting equality for children concerns the significance of differential genetic endowment. Perhaps the most important natural assets children receive from their (biological) parents are their genetic traits. Differences in a person's natural endowment can affect how well their life goes both as a child and as an adult. Some differences in genetic inheritance, especially those that give rise to serious disabilities, can generate problematic inequalities. It is not a violation of strict equality to provide supplemental resources to disabled children where this supplementation is designed to alleviate disability-imposed burdens. The precise form and extent of disability compensation is a complex matter that I cannot address here. I assume that disabled children have special entitlements to resources that are aimed at securing levels of basic well-being and functioning that are reasonably commensurate with the levels of well-being and functioning typically possible for children without disabilities. The provision of these resources to disabled children should be socially guaranteed and access to relevant goods should not be influenced by the economic standing of parents. It is less clear whether other kinds of differences in genetic inheritance between children, such as differences in natural talents, add further complexity to interpretation of the criterion of strict equality for children. There is an important difference between lacking a talent and suffering a disability. Whereas lacking a given talent does not, in itself, present a general impediment to leading a good life (either as a child or an adult), suffering (an uncompensated) disability pervasively hinders the leading a good life (Macleod 1998: 110–13). I do not think the liberal egalitarian concern to eliminate the ill effects of arbitrary differences in the circumstances of persons implies that children are entitled to compensation merely on the grounds that they lack certain, potentially valuable, natural talents that other children have. Children who are not endowed with special mathematical skills are not entitled to compensation merely because some other children have such skills. Differences in natural talents can acquire greater significance when possession of certain talents generates an advantage over others in acquiring the benefits of social cooperation. The fact that economic advantages can accrue to those with special talents poses an important problem for the theory of liberal equality. However, since children, qua children, are generally not able use their talents to secure economic advantages over other children, the problem of how to extinguish the impact of natural talents on the distribution of resources is primarily a matter that concerns fair treatment of responsible adults. Of course, it seems appropriate, at least to some degree, to make the provision of educational resources sensitive to differences in the natural talents of children. It is reasonable to devote resources to nurturing and developing special talents of particular children and it is reasonable to devote extra educational resources to children who require remedial assistance in developing basic skills.

The fact that children lack the capacities for responsible self-direction has another implication that merits brief comment. The strict equality for children criterion provides an insufficient account of the justice-based entitlements of children because it does not specify the particular kinds of resources to which children have an equal claim. In the case of adults, this is not a deep worry because, for the most part, we assume that adults can determine for themselves what particular kinds of resources it makes sense for them to acquire given their own plans and projects. However, because children lack developed capacities for responsible choice, it makes little sense to assign them authority to determine the resources they need. Instead we must identify on behalf of children the specific kinds of resources that will permit them both to flourish as children and to develop into responsible adults. We do not extend equal consideration to children simply by assigning each child with an equal share of income to spend as she pleases. (This is one reason why Dworkin's use of a hypothetical auction of resources to define equality of resources is problematic. Dworkin's model (2000: 65–71) presupposes that participants in the auction are competent and responsible in a way that children are not (Macleod 1998: 221).) Rather we should aim at securing children with an equal share of the particular resources that speak to their particular interests as children. The criterion of strict equality for children is primarily concerned with regulating the distribution of these children-focused resources.

I do not propose to offer an exhaustive catalogue of the relevant children-focused resources or an account of how they are appropriately identified. Broadly speaking, the relevant resources are those that contribute to the healthy development of children's cognitive, psychological, physical, and moral capacities as well as those that contribute to the well-being and happiness children enjoy as children. Some of the most important children-focused resources are: (1) education; (2) health care; (3) nutritious food; (4) safe and comfortable shelter; (5) a loving and supportive family; (6) opportunities for play. (There is some parallel here with Rawls's doctrine of primary goods.) Before proceeding, I want to draw attention to a feature of these resources that is sometimes ignored in discussions of just treatment of children. It is often pointed out that the sort of access that children have to these resources can have a significant impact on the opportunities and benefits that they will be in a position to enjoy and pursue as adults. So one familiar reason for ensuring that all children are furnished with decent primary and secondary schooling is that access to such resources is necessary for the possibility of meaningful equality of opportunity as adults. This perspective puts emphasis on a prospective dimension of justice—the significance of a child's current treatment is primarily assessed in terms of its bearing on the child's future success or well-being as an adult. An unfortunate feature of this focus on prospective justice is that it obscures the independent significance of the bearing that children's access to resources can have on their current welfare and their enjoyment of opportunities for children. For instance, the recreational and leisure opportunities to which a child has access can affect the quality of her childhood even though they may have no bearing on her future success or opportunities. Although a necessary part of childhood involves preparation for entry into the adult world, childhood should not be viewed as merely as a transitory phase. We should also be concerned to ensure that children have good lives as children and that they are fairly treated as children, not merely as prospective adults. The focus of egalitarian concern should be on the fair provision of child-specific resources that have a bearing on both current and future well-being. This means that we have justice-based reasons to be concerned with significant differences in the resources to which children

currently have access, even if it is true that current inequality does not significantly diminish future opportunities or well-being. It is partly for this reason
that I think discussions of the family that focus on the possible impediments
the family can place in the way of realizing genuine equality of opportunity
(Fishkin 1983; Lipson and Vallentyne 1989) offer an incomplete analysis of
just treatment of children. Extending the principle of equal consideration to
children requires more than ensuring that the treatment of children does not
unfairly impair the opportunities they will have as adults.

Let me now bring together the various strands of my discussion and
explain the tension they reveal between liberal equality and the affective
family. I have suggested that liberal egalitarians have reason to adopt the
following commitments:

(1) a choice-sensitive account of distributive justice that implies the legitimacy of significant differential entitlement and discretionary control of
resources;
(2) strict equality for children as the criterion for the distribution of children-
focused resources.

These dimensions of liberal equality do not necessarily conflict but when
conjoined to the ideal of the affective family a tension is evident. Parents in
affective families will be sometimes strongly motivated to pursue opportunities for achieving economic advantage. The advantages that accrue to them in
virtue of their choices are not unjust. But the partiality that the affective
family both encourages and harnesses means that parents will, in the absent
of constraints, be inclined to exercise their discretionary control over
resources to confer advantages on their children that are not enjoyed by other
children. The exercise of discretionary control will lead to violations of strict
equality. Of course, the degree to which departures from strict equality that
can be expected to arise in this way are troubling will vary with the substantive impact that such violations have on the lives of children. But I shall adopt
the possibly pessimistic assumption that this process, left unchecked, is likely
to give rise to significant differences in the current and prospective welfare
and opportunities enjoyed by children.

Note that there are two different kinds of problematic inequality that can
be distinguished in this context. First, there are inequalities in the transferable
resources that are made available through the affective family. Some children
will enjoy access to better health, educational, and recreational resources as
well as better (safer, more pleasant) neighbourhoods than others. Second,
there are less tangible but no less significant inequalities in the sort of parental
attention, affection, support, and encouragement children receive from their
parents. Both these sorts of inequality matter and both can be affected by the
way in which social institutions and policies respond to the family. In the
former case, objectionable inequalities can be addressed, in principle through

direct redistribution of transferable resources. In the latter case, inequalities cannot be directly addressed—love and attention cannot be redistributed. However, efforts can be made at least to foster some of conditions conducive to the development of loving relations between parents and children—for example, via programmes of parent education and family planning, by designing flexible work policies so as to reduce needless stress on parents.

Achieving a Reasonable Harmony

The tension I have described can be represented as a conflict between the resource entitlements of responsible adults and the independent resource entitlements of children. Adults have an entitlement both to acquire resources through the choices they make and to exercise discretionary control over such resources. Children are entitled to an equal share of basic children-focused resources. These entitlements conflict when parents exercise discretionary control in ways that upset strict equality for children. A solution to this conflict that preserves the family will involve some ranking of the relative importance of these conflicting entitlements. I think there are good reasons to give priority to protection of children's entitlements over the potentially competing claims of adults.

First, meeting children's claims to just treatment seems to enjoy a general priority over meeting the comparable claims of adults. Let me try to motivate this claim through an example. There is a sense in which children and adults have a similar interest in avoiding suffering severe pain that can give rise to a comparably strong entitlement to access to pain medication. Yet where circumstances force a choice between providing pain-relieving medication to a child and providing medication to adult suffering the same pain, we seem to have reason to give priority to recognition of the child's claim. I suspect that this general priority is grounded in various related factors. Children are vulnerable and dependent in many ways on adults for protection of their most basic interests. Because they cannot effectively represent and secure their own interests we naturally attach moral urgency to ensuring they receive fair treatment. The fact that children are developmentally fragile also seems significant. Children often seem to suffer more and are less able to recover from the ill effects of unjust treatment. So even when their moral claims seem comparable, caution suggests favouring the claims of children. More generally, children's status as innocents who can be assigned no responsibility for their plight or for ameliorating unjust treatment they face supports a general priority of children's claims. There seems to be an important difference in the relative urgency of the particular competing entitlements in this case. In sum, moral ties go to children.

Second, and perhaps more importantly, in the case at hand, the competing entitlements do not seem equally strong. Consider, to begin with, the normative importance of the adult-based claims. The normative importance of differential entitlement and discretionary control seems to be grounded primarily in the equal interest adults have in pursuit and implementation of valued life-plans. To pursue most worthwhile projects, a person needs access to a certain threshold of resources in order to engage in the project at all. Yet we can often enhance the value we derive from pursuit of a worthwhile project by devoting more resources to it. For instance, a person with a modest income may develop an interest in wine and may, given her interest, choose to pursue demanding but lucrative employment in order to have more resources to devote to her expensive tastes for wine. Mere possession of the extra resources would not be valuable to her. She must also be able to devote those resources to pursuit of her project and expenditures must contribute to the realization of her valued projects. In some cases, access to and control over supplemental resources significantly enhances the successful pursuit and implementation of projects. In other cases, the addition of resources above the threshold does not significantly enhance pursuit of valuable projects. For instance, cultivating and maintaining a friendship is certainly valuable and probably requires some minimal resources. But the value and success of a friendship does not seem to be interestingly augmented by access to extra resources. Rich friends, even if they are generous with their wealth, are not better friends in virtue of their wealth. The value of differential entitlement and discretionary control is conditional on the projects adults wish to pursue. Since the value of many of such projects can be enhanced by additional resources, differential entitlement and discretionary can contribute to the control individuals have over their lives (for example, which projects they elect to pursue) and their success in implementing them. But differential entitlement and discretionary control have limited value for other projects. In these cases, the loss or limitation of differential entitlement or discretionary control does not impede the pursuit of valuable projects and it does not constitute an assault on the equal moral standing of adults.

Now consider the normative significance, from an egalitarian point of view, of children's entitlement to an equal share of basic children-focused resources. To the degree that this standard is violated, the fundamental equal moral standing of children is challenged. Some children will enjoy benefits and gain advantages over others that are denied to others simply in virtue of factors, such as the wealth of parents, which are clearly morally arbitrary. The moral gravity of the challenge to equal status will, of course, depend on the character and extent of the disadvantages that children face. Children who are denied equal access to substantial health and educational benefits are more seriously disadvantaged than children whose recreational opportunities are unfairly constrained. None the less, strictly speaking, the basic egalitarian impulse to extinguish the influence of brute bad luck on life prospects is offended by all undeserved and arbitrary inequalities that affect the quality of life enjoyed by children. The fact that unfairly disadvantaged children are also vulnerable, dependent, and developmentally fragile only compounds the injustice of such treatment. On the basis of these considerations, I conclude that priority should be given to equality for children over the potentially conflicting requirements of choice-sensitivity for adults.

There are two responses to the tension between liberal equality and the family that I will mention only to set aside. The first is wholesale abolition of the affective family and establishment of some form of collective rearing of children. This does not appear to be a feasible or attractive response, especially if the affective family is as valuable as I have suggested. There are also concerns that collectivism diminishes diversity and erodes individual liberty (Archard 1993: 135–7). The second response is to reject completely the idea of choice-sensitive theory of distributive justice (Carens 1985). This alternative is theoretically more appealing than the first. However, the underlying conception of individual responsibility and fairness invoked by contemporary liberals is attractive. And wholesale rejection of choice-sensitivity may be premature. The strategy I prefer involves modification of the way in which appropriate institutional recognition is given to the ways in which considerations of individual responsibility can affect entitlement to and control over resources. We can give priority to meeting the resource entitlements of children while still respecting the most important dimensions of the responsibility-grounded entitlements of adults.

The solution I propose draws upon Thomas Nagel's suggestion that we resolve conflicts between impartiality and partiality by structuring of institutions in a way that creates a feasible 'moral division of labour' (1991: 53). We rely primarily on public social and political institutions to achieve basic egalitarian distributive requirements but we design these institutions in such as way as to permit individuals ample opportunity to pursue their own valuable personal ends. In this way, partiality is permitted but the forms of its legitimate expression are regulated through institutional design. Public political institutions can function in two ways to ensure the achievement of egalitarian objectives. First, public institutions can provide access to important resources and opportunities. For instance, health and educational resources can be made available to individuals through a form of public provision that ensures that everyone has equal access to the resources they need. This means, in effect, that some portions of the resources generated by social cooperation are treated as public rather than privately held resources. Second, with respect to private resources, modest constraints on the discretionary control that individuals enjoy over such resources can be established. Thus certain types of exchanges that threaten the achievement of egalitarian objectives can be prohibited or blocked. For example, one way in which democratic political equality is achieved is through prohibitions on vote-buying and the creation of limits on private donations to political parties.

Public institutions can be shaped to achieve a reasonable harmony between liberal equality and the affective family in the following way. First, we identify the class of children-focused resources that: (*a*) can be publicly provided to children and (*b*) have the most direct and significant impact on the current and prospective well-being and opportunities of children. The most obvious candidates for inclusion in this class are quite familiar—quality education, health care, nutritious food, and adequate shelter. Second, these resources are made available to all children on a fair and equal basis. Third, for this class of special resources only constraints on the discretionary control over privately held resources should be established that prevent adults from using private resources in ways that violate the standard of equal public provision. This does not mean that parents cannot provide any supplementation of resources to their children but some forms of parental supplementation should be prohibited. For example, there should be restrictions on parental supplementation of basic health care and education. Rich parents should not be permitted to buy better health care or education for their children.

This combined strategy of public provision and discretionary control operates only with respect to the special class of basic, transferable resources. It is aimed at securing the most basic and important aspect of strict equality for children. Of course, there can be other forms of resource inequality between children that are objectionable. Inequalities in the distribution non-basic resources such as access to recreational and entertainment resources are not as urgent but they should not be ignored. Fairness in the distribution of non-basic resources should be achieved through policies of generous public provision that ensure that all children have reasonable access to a decent level of a wide spectrum of such resources. For example, the state should ensure that a wide variety of leisure and recreational opportunities are available to families through uniformly good community centres. Similarly, excellent public parks, both local and national, should be freely available to children and their families. In the case of these non-basic resources parents can legitimately exercise their discretionary control over resources to augment their children's share of non-basic resources.

The institutional arrangements just sketched shape the way in which the partiality of parents to their children can be expressed but they do not disrupt the kinds of partiality upon which some of the values of the affective family depend. The family remains a specially protected sphere of interaction that provides parents an opportunity to form special nurturing and affective relationships with their children. In this setting partiality can flourish—parents can lavish children with attention and love and include them in distinctive common projects. Indeed, within the parameters established by the background institutional structures, parents can, in the public realm, act as vigorous and highly partial advocates of their children's interests. Moreover, though the institutional structures constrain, to some degree, the discretionary

control parents have over their privately held resources, their claim to significant differential entitlement can be honoured. Choice-based inequalities
between adults are not eliminated and in the realm of non-basic resources
economically successful adults can share the benefits of their prosperity with
their children. More generally, the share of resources that adults can lay claim
to remains sensitive to considerations of individual responsibility. Adults who
voluntarily forgo opportunities for economic gain must accept, as just, a
smaller share of resources than others who elect to pursue those opportunities. However, the institutional structures protect the children against suffering significant arbitrary disadvantages because of the choices of their parents
for which the children cannot reasonably be held responsible.

The idea that there should some minimal public provision of basic and
even some non-basic resources to children is, I hope, not very controversial.
But my proposals go beyond minimal provision aimed at meeting basic needs
in two related ways. First, I contend that the relevant normative standard is a
more demanding criterion of strict equality. A social guarantee that children's
basic needs are met falls short of satisfying the demands of liberal equality.
Second, whereas a basic needs approach is compatible with granting parents
the prerogative to confer significant additional benefits on their children, I
contend that significant limitations on discretionary control can be established in order to achieve strict equality. This second dimension of my
approach may seem particular vulnerable to objection—at least two can be
anticipated.

First, constraints on supplementation might seem to jeopardize the
integrity of the affective family by blocking the realization of some important
partiality-dependent goods. After all, it is plausible to suppose that the possibility of sustained familial intimacy depends importantly on tangible demon-
strations of love and concern. Parental declarations of affection and routine
parental monitoring of children's basic well-being must be suitably comple-
mented by devoting significant parental time, energy, and resources to children. Thus it is understandable why practices of gift-giving involving the
transfer of resources often have a special place in families. It might be
suggested that limitations on significant resource supplementation from
parents to children fatally undermine an important practical condition of
familial intimacy. Intimacy is diminished and thus the bonds of the family
threatened by blocking significant intra-family resource transfers. I think
there is some truth in the suggestion that familial intimacy depends on some
kinds of intra-family resource transfers. But the objection misconstrues the
significance of resource transfers to intimacy. Their importance is primarily a
function of thoughtfulness displayed in a transfer rather than the contribution receipt of the resource *per se* makes to a person's welfare. My 5-year-old
son's gift of simple drawing of a flower is a valuable contribution to perpetu-
ating our intimate relationship but, viewed simply as scrap piece of paper

marked with crayon, it has no impact on my welfare. Similarly, the intimacy value of his gift is not increased if he instead gives me a lottery ticket that turns out to be a winner and the money increases my welfare. No doubt substantial parental supplementation of their children's basic resources can augment their children's welfare. But we should not conclude that such supplementation is an important contributing factor to familial intimacy. And we should not, therefore, view limitations on such supplementation as a threat to the integrity of the affective family. It is also instructive to view the matter from the perspective of the child. A child in a community that imposes limits on parental supplementation cannot interpret this a diminution of parental love. In this setting parents do not give fewer additional resources to their children because they love their children less but because such supplementation is prohibited by the state. Finally, it is important to remember that my argument only rules out supplementation of a sort that has a bearing on the achievement of equality in basic resources. Other forms of supplementation are available to parents and it is implausible to suppose that familial intimacy can only be augmented through donations of basic goods.

A second possible problem is that restrictions on parental supplementation constitute an objectionable type of levelling down in which the possibility of genuine gains for some children is held hostage to a maintenance of a less than fully satisfactory lower but uniform standard of benefit for others. It is true that the proposal aims at securing an expressly egalitarian distributive criterion that involves a kind of levelling. This seems true of any egalitarian distributive proposal. But I think the concern about levelling down is misplaced for two reasons. First, the restrictions on supplementation operate in concert with generous provision of basic resources so the levelling occurs at a high rather than low level. If the health and educational programmes to which children have access are of a uniformly high quality then there is less reason for parents to provide supplementation in the first place and hence less reason for them to be concerned about not being permitted to provide it. Second, it is worth asking who is wronged by restrictions on supplementation. The most obvious candidates for wronged parties are the children who are the potential beneficiaries of such supplementation. Are restrictions on supplementation unfair to potential beneficiaries? In considering this question, it is important to remember that the resources over which restrictions on supplementation can be placed are resources that can have a significant impact on children's current welfare as well as their future opportunities. This means that receipt of supplemental resources by privileged children can confer significant advantages on them over others. Children denied such a resource could reasonably complain that they are unfairly disadvantaged. But it seems implausible to suppose that, as the objection supposes, children are entitled to resources that give them unfair advantages over other children. Consequently, it hard to see how denying children resources to which they have no justice-based entitlement can be wrong. For these reasons, I think the force of the levelling down charge can be diluted.

No feasible egalitarianism can fully eliminate all arbitrary sources of inequality traceable to the family. The proposals I have made permit us to achieve a reasonable but imperfect harmony between liberal equality and the affective family. The ideal I have defended goes beyond the standard of equality of opportunity yet the strategies for the achievement of liberal equality I have advocated should be congenial to defenders of equality of opportunity. To be sure, the suggestions I have made constitute only a framework for addressing one aspect of ensuring justice for children. The precise substantive character of appropriate public provision and appropriate constraints on supplementation needs further examination. But I hope the interpretation of liberal equality developed here proves useful in guiding such an examination.[4]

Notes

1. The tension I explore is similar, in some respects, to the problem of the way in which realisation of equality of opportunity can be threatened by the institution of the family (see Rawls 1971: 74, 511; Fiskin 1983; Lipson and Vallentyne 1989). However, as I explain below, liberal equality is a more demanding standard of justice than equality of opportunity and this affects the character of the tension between equality and the family.
2. Nor do I wish to endorse the view that intervention in the life of a family is only warranted if there is evidence of a clear and present abuse threat to children in the family. There is room for considerable debate about the nature and extent on the authority parents may legitimately wield over the content of their children's religious, cultural, and moral education (Macleod 1997).
3. There are various ways of explaining the inattention to the claims of children in recent liberal theory. One likely source is uncritical acceptance of a version of the public/private distinction, which places children in a private realm of the family. Since liberal principles of political morality are often depicted as setting the fair terms of interaction for individuals in the public realm, direct consideration of the claims of children is obscured. Rawls's depiction of the contractors to the original position as 'heads households' has also, given the enormous importance and influence of Rawls's theory, contributed to the exclusion of children from appropriate consideration (Brennan and Noggle 1997). The libertarian idea that that children have no or diminished moral status and can therefore be treated as parental property has probably also had some lingering influence in liberal thought even though the basic conception of moral standing it depends on is repudiated by contemporary liberals.
4. I would like to thank David Archard and Peter Vallentyne for helpful comments and suggestions. A draft of this chapter was presented to the Children's Rights and Family Justice: Paying Attention to Children conference at the University Western Ontario, 3–5 Mar. 2000. I am grateful to the participants at the conference for their discussion of it.

13

What Children Really Need: Towards a Critical Theory of Family Structure

Shelley Burtt

Every child, no matter where in the world she was born, no matter what her race, ethnicity, religion, or socio-economic status, has at least two parents—the man and woman whose genetic material combined to create this new human being. The relationship a child can expect to have with these adults has differed over time and between cultures, but most children at most points in history have grown up in the same household as both their biological parents. For children in the advanced industrial societies of North America and Europe, this expectation has now shifted dramatically and most likely irreversibly, nowhere more tellingly than in the United States. Over half of all American children born in the 1990s will live in a single-parent family at some point in their lives; in 2000, 26 per cent of families with children were headed by a single parent (Hernandez 1993: 71; Dupree and Primus 2001: 8).

If this change brought with it equally dramatic increases in positive social outcomes for children, we could regard the transformation with equanimity. But as family structures have become more fluid and diverse, there has been no comparable improvement in child well-being. In the United States, for example, over half of the children living in mother-only families (82 per cent of all single-parent families) are poor, compared to only 12 per cent of children living in families with an adult male (Rodgers 1996: 11–13).

Recognizing the close correlation of poverty rates to family structure and concerned with the number of children in single-parent families at risk for deviant behaviour and low achievement, scholars and politicians across the political spectrum have concluded that what children need to better their outcomes is a return to the 'traditional' family in which a man and a woman united by marriage, but divided by traditional gender roles, raise their biological offspring together. Cheerleading for the unique virtues of this family form has both a nice version in which 'stable intact [two-parent] families' are valorized for making 'a vital contribution to the nurturing of future citizens' (Elshtain *et al.* 1993) and a nasty version in which unmarried teen mothers on welfare are scapegoated as cause and symptom of the nation's moral and financial crises. (The latter was especially in evidence prior to the 1996 over-haul of the American welfare system; see, e.g. Murray 1993; Wilson 1993; Whitehead 1993.)

If we take seriously the evidence marshalled in favour of two-parent fami-lies, there is little point in countering either the nice or nasty version of this debate with a claim that family structure does not matter; the fact is that chil-dren do better in precisely the sort of family structure the family values lobby advocates. On the other hand, acknowledging the many advantages of grow-ing up in a traditional two-parent family does not require one to believe that all families ought to conform to this model. I argue in this chapter that, what-ever the benefits of 'stable intact' two-parent families, making sure there are more of them should not form the centrepiece of a nation's family policy. In fact, to make the encouragement of any particular family structure the goal of domestic public policy is a mistake. To do so compromises the two proper ends of state involvement in family life: increasing the number of children whose developmental needs are well met and promoting just relations between family members (as the state already does between citizens). (While these aims are not uncontroversial, they cannot be defended here at any length. For a defence of the first proposition, see Burtt 1994; for the second, see Okin 1989.)

The first part of the chapter provides a critical review of the case for promot-ing the two-parent family. I argue in this section that establishing a strong corre-lation between traditional nuclear family structure and good social outcomes for children does not necessarily establish the political virtue of this family form. What is needed to advance discussion is a critical theory of family struc-ture. The second part provides that critical theory in embryo. In the final part, I suggest ways in which application of this critical theory might change the terms of the current debate. This chapter is primarily concerned to address the decade-long American debate about proper family structure begun in the early 1990s and thus draws its examples primarily from the American context. However, to the extent that similar issues concerning child well-being and the shape of family policy face other nations, as is certainly the case in Great Britain and, to a lesser extent, in the non-Scandinavian states of Western Europe, both my critique of new familism[1] and the critical theory of family structure outlined here have more general application.

Problems with the New Familism

Those who urge political and social support for the two-parent nuclear family—the 'new familists'—argue that certain family structures are better suited to raising good children and turning out good citizens than others. Thus Elshtain (1994) announces, 'We *know*, because the evidence is in, that some familial arrangements are better than others.' As a general observation about the conditions for children's well-being across time and cultures, this claim is certainly correct. Of course, Elshtain is primarily concerned with normally functioning children in the contemporary United States. Here, too, social science research bears out her claim. McLanahan and Sandefur, for example, use a number of longitudinal studies to look at three major indicators of future well-being for children (educational attainment, labour force attachment, and early family formation). They conclude:

Children who grow up in a household with only one biological parent are worse off, on average, than children who grow up in a household with both of their biological parents, regardless of the parents' race or educational background, regardless of whether the parents are married when the child is born, and regardless of whether the resident parent remarries. (1994: 1)

While one may disagree with McLanahan and Sandefur about the causes of this differential in well-being, there is little point in disputing that, on the whole and given America's current family policies, to be raised in the United States by both one's biological parents as part of a traditional family unit produces better outcomes than to grow up in a step-family, as a child of divorce, or as a bastard. The question is what political difference this should make.

For new familists, the answer is simple. Acknowledging the advantages attached to living with both one's biological parents leads to the conclusion that there is 'One Best Model' of family life:

the characteristics of an ideal social environment for child-rearing consist of an enduring, two-biological-parent family that engages regularly in activities together, has many of its own routines, traditions, and stories, and provides a great deal of contact between adults and children. The children have frequent interaction with relatives, with neighbors in a supportive neighborhood, and with their parents' world of work, coupled with no pervasive worry that their parents will break up. (Council on Families in America 1994)

In this ideal family, the parents are heterosexual, married, and not previously divorced; the children are the biological issue of both parents; and the household is financially self-sufficient (most probably because the father but not the mother works full-time outside the home). Although new familists differ in their tolerance for alternative family forms, they are united in the claim that the available historical, sociological, and psychological evidence overwhelmingly establishes that the two-parent family (as defined above) is best for kids—and because good for kids, good for the country.[2]

On one level the argument of the new familists is absolutely correct. The economic, social, and political institutions of our society all privilege this form of raising children (and arranging male–female relations) over others. Given our current family law and social policies and taking into account persistent social, economic, and legal inequality between men and women, it should surprise no one that children in never-divorced two-parent families are on the whole better off than children growing up in other sorts of social or familial settings. (This is particularly true if these two parents can both afford and choose to embrace a traditional gendered division of labour.) What is problematic about the new familists' position is the political significance they attach to this finding. Concluding from their evidence that 'two-parent families are better able to discharge their child-raising duties', many of these scholars argue that a rational social policy will encourage this functional family structure and discourage others. But are they correct?

In the next several pages, I will make the case that we cannot and should not move seamlessly from a finding that two-parent families currently produce good social outcomes for children to the conclusion that the more families conforming to this model the better. I do not argue that the sort of family children are raised in does not matter, because the evidence over-whelmingly establishes that it does. Rather I will argue that the new familists' 'One Best Model' family policy fails on other grounds.

I begin with three claims about good family policy which I hope appear sensible since I do not undertake to defend them here. A desirable family policy must advance, rather than subvert, just social relations. It must respond to, rather than nostalgically deny, structural transformations of the economy and social life. And it must not take as 'natural' or given elements of social life which are the products of social and political choice. It is based on these criteria that the new familists' effort to link their social science findings to their social policy falls short.

The first problem with the One Best Model approach to matters of family structure involves the critical question of gender justice. My description of the new familist position deliberately reproduces the ambiguity of this literature when it comes to the appropriate division of labour between husband and wife within this most desirable family form. Clearly, the good two-parent family has at least one parent employed outside the home, earning enough money to provide for the family's needs. But is this One Best Model of family structure flexible enough to accommodate two parents working full-time outside the home? In another words, would the new familists endorse a household in which financial responsibility for children is shared by both parents? Praise for the 'traditional' nuclear family obviously excludes such households, because this family form is defined by its gendered division of labour. The female partner cares for household, kin, husband, and children, while the male partner provides the income necessary to finance these tasks, normally through employment outside the home. And indeed the most conservative promoters of 'family values' make clear their commitment to this ideology of separate spheres (e.g. Kristol 1994; see also Blankenhorn 1995, Popenoe 1996, and the writings of Gary Bauer of the Family Research Council; these commentators are all savvy enough to recognize that this family form is 'traditional' only if we choose America in the 1950s as our historical baseline).

But not all new familists favour this overt embrace of the 'traditional' nuclear family. The Council on Families in America, for example, is at pains to explain that 'because of the importance of female equality and the changing conditions of modern society, that previous model of life-long, separate-sphere gender roles within marriage is no longer desirable or possible on a society-wide scale' (1994: 2). Their platform praises a generic two-parent family 'based on a lasting, monogamous marriage', suggesting indifference or equanimity regarding the nature and extent of a mother's workforce participation. Yet it is hard to make sense of the claim that the two-parent family is so much better than the single-parent family without imputing to it a traditional division of labour.

Consider one of the major strikes against the single-parent family: the extraordinary challenge of combining the roles of financial provider and full-time care-giver. But how does getting married solve the problem of providing high-quality loving childcare if both parents are still full-time workers? The impact of poor quality daycare on a child's social and cognitive development is the same whether he is placed there by two parents on their way to low-wage jobs or by his mother only. A child who returns home after school to an empty apartment because both parents are at work is just as disadvantaged by the situation as a child home alone because her only parent is not there. These examples suggest that more is at stake in the current debate about family structure than the right number of adults in the home. Also on the table, although not always acknowledged directly, is a question about what these adults should be doing. (Note that the Council on Families' platform rejects only 'life-long' separate-sphere gender roles.)

One does not need to be a new familist to recognize that returning to full-time work when a baby is three weeks old is bad for both mother and infant or to appreciate that young teens do better when at least one parent is available for them after school. But to acknowledge the benefits of parental care for children does not in itself establish the best way to secure that care. Some new familists argue that children should not be sacrificed on the altar of women's equality and that the price of female domestic internment for five to ten years while one's children mature is not too much to pay for healthy, happy offspring. If these choices were the only ones available to communities at the beginning of the twenty-first century, I might agree. But family policies already in place in Scandinavian countries, and to a lesser extent in other European nations (lengthy paid maternal leave, for example), demonstrate that it is possible to satisfy children's need for 'continuous individual' care while still accommodating the interest most adults have in ongoing, gainful employment outside the home.

One possible way to meet children's developmental needs for parental care, love, and attention is to limit labour-market participation to one parent only, assigning the other exclusive responsibility for child care-giving. But much of what a 'male breadwinner–female care-giver' family offers a child could also be supplied by 'dual-provider' families if these families' choices were supported by generous maternal and parental leave policies, reliable, high-quality daycare, and school hours adapted to the workdays of employed adults. (Details of these practical policy proposals can be found in, among others, Leach 1994; Hewlett and West 1998; Brazelton and Greenspan 2000.) Co-housing or community living arrangements in which domestic labour becomes a social rather than a private task could also alleviate the exhausting 'second shift' of domestic labour which working mothers (single or married) must undertake evenings and weekends (Hochschild 1989; on the benefits of co-housing to single and working families, see Alexander 1994: 352–5). Family policies supportive of these options would allow male and female child-rearing partners to participate more equally in the worlds of both work and family without shortchanging the needs of their children. New familists who wish, in contrast, specifically to affirm the value of a traditional, gendered division of labour between husband and wife must address directly the justice of allowing married men but not their spouses to enjoy the economic independence and sense of personal accomplishment provided by participation in the labour market.

A second related problem with the familist position is its demographic exclusivity. In my introduction, I asserted that a rational family policy must respond to, rather than nostalgically deny, structural transformations of the economy and social life. In assessing the desirability and feasibility of the new familist policy proposals, it is important to understand the myriad family forms excluded or devalued in the new familists' family romance. Remember that just getting two adults into the same house with a child is not enough to secure his well-being in the strong version of this account. Children need these adults to be their direct genetic kin (step-parents do not count), of different sexes (gay families do not count) and married to each other (long-term partnerships are out as well). These criteria exclude most of the American households currently charged with the responsibility of raising children, ranking as second best a long list of family forms including two-parent families with adopted children, 'blended' families combining biological offspring with step-children, and families in which the parents are same-sex partners. Also excluded, of course, are all lone-parent families, whether created by divorce, death, estrangement, or abandonment. In short, the new familist literature promotes as normative a model of family life to which a majority of American families fail to conform. Such demographic exclusivity raises the question of whether the new familists' preferred policy alternatives adequately confront the reality of American children's family experience in this new millennium.

One possible response to the growing plurality of family forms is to declare a national crisis ('the current disintegration of the well-functioning, two-parent family is a central cause of rising individual and social pathology: delinquency and crime . . . drug and alcohol abuse, suicide, depression, eating disorders, and the growing number of children in poverty': Council of Families in America 1994: 2), the solution to which involves restoring the nuclear family to the prominence it enjoyed in the 1950s. A few statistics will suggest the enormity of this task. At the end of the 1950s, 88 per cent of all children lived in two-parent households, 70 per cent with their biological parents. In 1990, that number had dropped to 72 per cent and 50 per cent respectively (Coontz 1997: 37). These numbers appear to have held steady through 2000, although the most recent census did not separate out blended families from other married couple households, thus making exact comparison impossible (Dupree and Primus 2001).

For minority children, the figures are even more dramatic. In the thirteen years from 1980 to 1993, the number of Hispanic children living in two-parent homes dropped from 75 to 64 per cent, although this figure increased somewhat in the 2000 census. And while two-thirds of black children lived in two-parent households in 1960, just under 40 per cent did so forty years later. Since these households include remarried parents as well as, in some instances, unmarried couples, the percentage of Hispanic and African-American children whose homes conform to the One Best Model of family life is even lower. Perhaps most disturbing of all, an astonishing 9.7 per cent of African-American children had no residential contact with either of their biological parents (Rodgers 1996: 6; Dupree and Primus 2001: 13). No one disputes the significance of these statistics or the challenges they pose to children's well-being. But little is gained by treating the growing plurality of family forms as a pathology which a responsible government must contain by favouring one family structure over others. To do so confuses long-term demographic change, to which any responsible social policy must adapt and respond, with short-term social crisis.

Most sociologists of the family describe a profound transformation of Western family structure over the course of the last two centuries—a transformation linked to so many features of social modernity that it would be extraordinarily difficult to undo (Goode 1970; Shorter 1975). This large-scale transition concerns new familists less than three developments concentrated in the years since 1960 and described in, among others, Glendon (1989) and Coontz (1997): a relaxation of the divorce laws, increased acceptability of out-of-wedlock pregnancies, and the return of 'co-provider' families in which men and women share breadwinning responsibilities. Taken together, these trends account not only for most of the decline of the 'traditional' nuclear family, but also for an extraordinary shift in the degree to which children can expect their biological parents to be present in their home. In 1960, the percentage of American children under 18 who lived through the divorce of their parents was less than 1 per cent; by 1990, almost half did. In 1960, just under 20 per cent of American children under 6 had mothers in the labour force; by 1990, the number had increased to almost two-thirds (Rodgers 1996: 10). No imaginable social policy can counter demographic shifts of this magnitude, however well the earlier era served children.

Of course, the simple fact that history has moved on does not guarantee that the needs of children have been correspondingly transformed. It is at least an empirical possibility that children do best in communities where marriage almost always precedes childbearing and where divorce is as rare as maternal employment outside the home. If so, the best way to raise children may be in a family structure the social preconditions for which have disappeared and we will have to acknowledge a profound disjunction between the needs of children and the forms of family life made possible by the social and economic developments of the late twentieth century. But before we commit ourselves to the idea that breathing life into a dying family form is the only way to make children better off, we should be absolutely certain that the relevant variable in children's outcomes is the family structure itself and not, for example, public policies which comparatively advantage certain family structures over others.

This the new familists do not do. Rather, they cast the challenge faced by today's families as one of adult citizens behaving badly (failing to conform to a desirable social norm that we know advantages children), the solution to which lies in changing such self-indulgent behaviour, not in updating our social and economic policies to better serve a new spectrum of family forms. Popenoe, for example, urges those concerned for America's children to spearhead 'a new social movement whose purpose is the promotion of families and family values'. The goal: 'to reinvigorate the cultural ideals of "family," "parents", and "children" within the changed circumstances of our time' (Popenoe 1990: 48). Such initiatives, he argues, ought specifically to replace the 'development of extensive governmental programs offering monetary support and social services for families, especially for the new "nonnuclear" families' (1990: 47).

I have already suggested that the causes for the revolution in family structure are too profound to respond in any dramatic way to such calls for cultural renewal. As dearly as we may wish the vast majority of children to grow up in traditional two-parent families, the fact remains that the covenant marriage and fatherhood movements (visit e.g. www.marriagemovement.org or www.fatherhood.org) promise no more than small gains, even if the decline in nuclear family formation has been halted. Shapiro (2001) reports as 'heartening news' the fact 'that the number of black children living in two-parent families increased from 34.8% to 38.9%' in the five-year period from 1995 to 2000. While new familists may cheer this positive trend, it seems more relevant to ask what is being done to meet the needs of the other 60 per cent whose families do not conform to the One Best Model of family life.

A further question concerns the source of the forces that will ground the cultural renewal on which the new familists pin their hopes. Every child advocate dreams of some sort of cultural transformation in American attitudes towards the next generation, if only to pry a bit more money out of the federal government for its needs. Leach (1994: 6) makes the telling point that 'during the eighties ... less than 5 percent of the federal budget [was spent] on programs supporting families with children, compared with 24 percent spent on people over sixty-five years old'. But how are we to promote new more family-friendly policies in workplaces and communities while simultaneously sending the message that only certain sorts of families are desirable? Should we offer children's allowances or parental leave only to married or never-divorced mothers? And who can we count on to support such a divisive initiative? Surely not the majority of American families who fail to live up to the new familists' ideal. A society that wants its members to re-embrace parenting as the emotional centre of adult life needs to reach out to all parents who, partnered or not, genuinely want the best for their children.

I turn now to the third and last difficulty with the new familists' effort to make advocacy of the One Best Model of family life the touchstone of American family policy. I suggested earlier that a defensible family policy must not take as 'natural' or given elements of social life which are the products of social and political choice. To do so would distort the processes of policy formation by treating as beyond the policy-makers' reach (because natural) certain things which could actually be changed because they were the product of social or political choice.

Suggesting that the most we can do for our children is increase the number of them living with both their biological parents constitutes not just a nostalgic denial of real demographic change but a misrepresentation of the structural obstacles to children's well-being. What is particularly troubling about the new familist position is its failure to acknowledge that at least one reason why two-parent families do a better job of raising children than their alternatives is because an array of social and governmental choices made over the last century have, taken together, created a society in which only nuclear families characterized by the traditional division of labour can command sufficient resources to provide adequately for their children. Purely from the point of view of children's needs, the repeal of such discriminatory arrangements would certainly do as much for children's well-being as maximizing the number of children raised within traditional nuclear families. To respond that such maximization is imperative because children in single-parent families do so much worse misses the point. They fare more poorly now at least in part because the legislative and social policy deck is stacked against them.

Put another way: defenders of family values like to explain the superior outcomes of children in two-parent families not in terms of the structural advantages enjoyed by the traditional nuclear family but as a consequence of (and evidence for) the intrinsic superiority of this family form as a social institution for raising children. An entirely understandable exasperation with this line of argument leads Young (1994) to speak of 'making single mother-hood normal'. If we *expected* children to spend at least part of their childhood living with only one parent (as is the case now for almost 95 per cent of African-American children), we would spend more time thinking about how to make such family structures work (Popenoe 1996: 22). The attribution of moral normality to single parenting (to match its statistical normality) could also change social outcomes for children by shifting attention to other, more salient sources of success and failure than 'abnormal' family structure. McLanahan and Sandefur (1994) conclude, for example, that more children do better in two-parent homes (with both biological parents) than in any other family structure. But they emphasize that the main reason for this outcome is that other family forms are so closely associated with loss of income and residential mobility. It is these two factors which really harm children. Social policies which directly addressed these problems (such as a 'guaranteed minimum child support benefit') would increase positive outcomes for children of never-married, divorced, and remarried parents—without changing the structure of the families in which they were raised.

We can see the force of this point through an analogy to the treatment of children with mental disabilities. Until quite recently, the developmental problems of children with mild mental retardation were ascribed almost entirely to their physiological pathologies. The poor outcomes of such children were ascribed to their 'abnormal' biological structure just as the challenges faced by children of single-parent families are attributed to their 'abnormal' family structure. Children with developmental disorders are no longer written off in this fashion. Aggressive early intervention and thorough-going family support systems have transformed our expectations regarding the performance of children with a wide range of disabilities. We now know that the challenges these children faced were significantly exacerbated by the cultural assumptions, laws, and social practices which denied them the financial resources and social supports which could have helped them reach their full potential, resources that were considered either inappropriate or useless to provide them because of their deviance from the desirable social norm of full mental capacity. As this analogy suggests, we cannot know if family structure really makes a difference for children until families with different structures are treated equally. Because we have not yet reached this point, we have grounds for questioning if family structure is the most or only relevant variable in securing good social outcomes for children.

A family policy truly suited to the needs of the twenty-first century would resist the temptation to treat the overwhelming comparative advantages enjoyed by a particular, historically structured version of the two-parent family as evidence of its normative superiority. It would also avoid dividing households with children into 'good families' (those conforming to this historically privileged norm) and 'bad families' (those that do not). Finally, it would question both the justice and rationality of an effort to advance children's well-being grounded in greater and greater conformity to a One Best Model of family life. Rather, its aim would be to equip diverse family forms to serve the needs of children, their long-term care-givers, and the polity as a whole. Stated another way, the goal would be to increase the number of family structures within which the developmental needs of children could be met and met well.

Towards a Critical Theory of Family Structure

But can we really expect diverse family forms to serve the needs of children? To answer this question we need a critical theory of family structure. The aim of such a theory would be to specify more completely the connection between family structure and child well-being by matching an account of children's developmental needs to the family forms capable of supplying them. Such a theory would begin with the premiss that, in order to flourish, children require environments which contain the resources necessary to meet their developmental needs. To determine whether a variety of family structures can be relied upon to provide such an environment (or whether only the traditional nuclear family will do), one first needs an account of what these needs are and how they might be supplied. With this account in place, one could specify the different roles adults must play in children's lives in order to ensure these needs are met. This exercise would then allow us to assess different family forms in terms of their ability to supply (within or without the household) the adults capable of filling the different social roles required to meet children's needs.

This critical theory takes seriously the claim of new familists that certain family structures perform family functions better than others. But it seeks to specify the connection between family structure and family function more completely than in the current literature. For example, in a society without paid parental leave policies, without housing allowances for single parents, without universal child health insurance, and without adequate funding for daycare and after-school programmes (a society much like the United States today), there would probably be only one family form able reliably to meet children's developmental needs: two-parent families in which one parent worked and the other provided full-time childcare. But this fact does not mean that the traditional nuclear family is everywhere and at all times the only family structure capable of helping children flourish. A critical theory of family structure offers a way of thinking about what a family is and does that could lay the groundwork for a more constructive comparison of the relative advantages and deficiencies of possible family forms.

This effort to unpack the connection between family structure and family function begins with a definition of the family. Of course, how we define what will count legally and socially as a family is both a matter of political debate and the subject of volumes of sociological research. A generation ago it was not uncommon to define a family as 'a social arrangement based on marriage and the marriage contract, including the recognition of the rights and duties of parenthood, common residence for husband, wife and children, and recip-rocal economic obligations between husband and wife' (Ball 1974: 28). This account manages to build in, as normative features of family life, not only marriage but the traditional gendered division of labour ('reciprocal economic obligations'). More recent writing emphasizes three aspects of modern families which distinguish them from other social institutions: (1) they are individuals' main if not exclusive source of emotional intimacy; (2) they are the primary providers of care to children; and (3) they are unusually well insulated from the claims of both market and state (e.g. Thorne 1992). Since the beginning of the twentieth century, the primary function of the family defined in either of these ways has been child-rearing. Child-rearing itself I understand as a practice intended to give children the capacity, when mature, to participate meaningfully and successfully in the various spheres of adult life: cultural, economic, social, personal, and political. To parent a child well is in part to ensure that the child leaves home ready to function respon-sibly and successfully not only as an independent, productive member of soci-ety but also as a loving spouse, parent, friend, and neighbour. The new familists believe that only one sort of family structure is capable of consis-tently producing such outcomes. A critical theory of family structure can help establish whether or not this claim is true.

I approach the task of elaborating a critical theory of family structure as described above, by asking what children need to do well and then by attempt-ing to clarify the functional adult roles that correspond to the provision of these goods. In their recent book, *The Irreducible Needs of Children*, a promi-nent pediatrician and a child psychiatrist identify six needs of the growing child, without which its development would be seriously compromised. These are the need for ongoing nurturing relationships, the need for physical protec-tion, safety, and regulation, the need for experiences tailored to individual differences, the need for developmentally appropriate experiences, the need

for limit-setting, structure, and expectations, and the need for stable, supportive communities and cultural continuity (Brazelton and Greenspan 2000). At
least two features of this list are worth noting. First, even a cursory overview
of these requirements suggests the degree to which parents are dependent on
the wider community to help create and sustain an environment in which
their children can flourish. The 'need for physical protection, safety, and regulation' is primarily a matter of public responsibility; provision of health care
and control of environmental hazards are the two goods Brazelton and
Greenspan emphasize. Likewise, the 'need for stable, supportive communities
and cultural continuity' underlines the extent to which children in any family
structure are dependent for their well-being on choices made by the wider
community in which they live. (To what extent the existence of these needs
places a claim on the nation's resources to satisfy them is a matter of some
debate that I cannot address here in any detail, although O'Neill (1994) makes
a helpful beginning.) Brazelton and Greenspan's list also brings home the
incredibly demanding nature of the individual parent's job, if the goal is not
simply that a child get by without too much misery, but that he have the
opportunity to develop to his full potential. How many parents can even
imagine spending half their infant's waking hours in its direct active stimula-
tion, or limiting their pre-schoolers' television viewing to two half-hour
programmes a day—two of these doctors' most prominent recommendations?

Urie Bronfenbrenner of Cornell University, another respected voice in the
field of child development, offers a similarly demanding account of what children need to develop well. His list begins with 'good health care and adequate
nutrition', while emphasizing the 'developmentally sensitive interaction'
necessary for the child 'to grow socially, psychologically, and cognitively'. Most
important for Bronfenbrenner is the presence of at least one adult completely
in love with a child and available to care for him on a continuous basis.
Children need to be cared for the majority of their waking hours by someone
who thinks them 'especially wonderful, especially precious'—ideally, by a
parent who loves them (1990: 29). Bronfenbrenner also believes that for the
primary care-taker relationship to function optimally, the child needs 'the
availability and involvement of another adult, a *third party* who assists,
encourages, spells off, gives status to, and expresses admiration and affection
for the person caring for and engaging in joint activity with the child' (1990:
33). A spouse would be the ideal adjunct, but not the only adult capable of
fulfilling this role.

The list concludes with two other requirements for the child's optimal
development. There must be effective communication and mutual accommodation between the home and the other 'principal settings in which children
and their parents live their lives: . . . child-care programs, the school, and the
parents' place of work' (1990: 36). Family-friendly workplace policies are

crucial if mothers or fathers are to discharge their child-rearing responsibilities effectively. Finally, successful child-rearing requires wide-ranging public support, both cultural and institutional, for the practices which best meet children's needs (1990: 37). Like Brazelton and Greenspan, Bronfenbrenner believes that all families require extensive support from the communities in which they live in order to function well.

As we seek to link these accounts of children's needs to the policy initiatives which will best serve America's children, it is worthwhile noting how far our commonly accepted child-rearing practices are from the standards these experts believe will nurture children's optimal development. Considering only the univocal insistence that every infant requires continuous, individual attention from a loving adult in ensuring her flourishing, it seems that virtually every childcare setting in America today, from schools and daycare to parental homes themselves, is structured in such a way as to compromise some aspect of a child's development. Meanwhile the most successful family policy in recent years has been the overhaul of AFDC in favour of a programme (Temporary Assistance to Needy Families) the explicit aim of which is to get mothers out of the home and into the labour market. It is possible to conclude that the new familist notion that the Western family at the beginning of the twenty-first century is in crisis may not be as far off the mark as I earlier implied. However, the extent to which this crisis is linked to a decline in a particular family structure which we ought now to undo remains unclear.

The fact that children's needs are extensive and largely unmet in today's society does not in itself justify a family policy designed to promote a One Best Model of family life. Building on the accounts given above, I suggest that the families best able to meet children's developmental needs are those able to supply (within or outside the family setting) adults who can fill separately or in combination the roles of lover (soulmate), physical care-giver, homemaker, financial provider, socializer, moral educator, teacher, and gender role model. This preliminary list is certainly open to refinement. But if accepted it would make possible a different sort of definition of a 'good' family—not one with two parents but one able to make available adults capable of performing each of these roles well. Before turning to consider how the debate over family structure might in consequence be remade, I discuss briefly the nature of each of the listed roles.

Lover (Soulmate)

For children to develop to their full potential, they need sustained attention from someone who loves them—not for the first three months of life, or the first three years, but for their entire childhood and adolescence. From the first days of the newborn through the difficult years of adolescence, love for the child provides the basis for the sorts of interactions with adults that children need to develop well. (In this context, recall the earlier cited statistic, that almost 10 per cent of black children and 5 per cent of Hispanic children in America live with neither of their biological parents.) Obviously children do not need a lover in the adult sense of the term, but there must be, in Bronfenbrenner's wonderful phrasing, 'one or more persons with whom the child develops a strong, mutual, irrational, emotional attachment' (1990: 29). Infants and toddlers need one person to lavish virtually full-time attention on them and them alone. (We can hardly imagine a mother of triplets coping with her babies by herself. Why then do states set infant daycare ratios at 1:3 or 1:4?) Pre-schoolers can manage three to six hours apart from their primary care-giver but we are not meeting their developmental needs when we place them in group care for the length of our workday. In order for school-age kids to develop optimally they need a parent at home at the end of the schoolday, time to relax with that adult, and the opportunity to seek his or her help (Brazelton and Greenspan 2000: ch. 1; Leach 1994: ch. 4).

Obviously a traditional nuclear family in which the mother opts out of paid employment offers one way of achieving these ideals. But this accommodation is not the only way in which a child's need for a besotted soulmate can be met. If the goal is to maximize parental time with young children, the option of instituting or increasing parental leave exists, as does the possibility of providing more flexible working hours for primary care-givers. Sweden, for example, provides eighteen months paid parental leave for each child and the option of working a six-hour workday until a child is 6. These benefits are attached to the birth of a child regardless of the parents' marital status (Leach 1994: 100–1).

Physical Care-Giver

Every child requires one or more adults to provide for her immediate physical needs, a task which is almost continuous in the first year of a child's life and which declines in importance as the child learns to provide for these needs independently or in partnership with the parent. This role can be assumed entirely by one individual or it can be apportioned between parents, parents and babysitters, extended family members, or parents and daycare centres.

There is another form of physical care-giving which cannot be the parent's responsibility alone. Children cannot thrive if the neighbourhoods in which they grow up are environmentally toxic or physically unsafe. The fact that married couples, because usually better off, can afford to raise their children in less dangerous neighbourhoods is hardly a ringing endorsement of the value of two-parent families in securing good outcomes for children. Surely new familists do not believe the physical quality of a child's environment should be dependent on the marital status of her parents. If not, we can go a long way to meeting children's physical needs by promoting policies for safer neighbourhoods regardless of the type of families inhabiting them.

Homemaker

The responsibility for keeping a house neat, clean, stocked with food and in good repair is often erroneously subsumed under the role of physical care-giver. But this is because the family form which is culturally normative in our society (but demographically in the minority) typically assigns both these roles to the stay-at-home spouse. Children need their home to be kept in good repair but there is nothing about this responsibility that requires a traditional nuclear family. In fact, research on the subject shows that domestic labour is more equitably divided in non-traditional family units (Goldscheider and Waite 1991; Coltrane 1996).

Financial Provider

The child, from the moment of his birth, requires, in addition to a lover and a physical care-giver, a financial provider. While there is good reason to expect the biological parents to contribute the majority of a child's financial requirements, it has been several hundred years since the financial responsibility of raising children fell on the parents alone. The state funding of public schools and universities is only one example of the way in which the role of financial provider is and has been shared consistently with the community at large. From the child's point of view, this financial provider need not reside in the household nor, indeed, be a family member. It may be politically unpopular to rely on income transfers from local, state, or national governments to play the role of financial provider for indigent children, but the political unpopularity of a policy alternative is not in itself proof of the intrinsic superiority of the One Best Model of family structure. Because married couples do best at providing children's financial needs without recourse to government coffers, states may have huge and valid incentives to lower both divorce rates and the percentage of unmarried teen pregnancies (Harden 2001). But this is because two-parent families are far cheaper for the government to support—not because they are in themselves better for children.

Socializer

Perhaps the most important work of childhood is socialization, a process which 'ensures the integration of the individual into society as a respected participant' (Damon 1988: 3). It is unclear the degree to which successful socialization hinges on the presence of two biological parents in the home, as socialization literature says little about this issue. However, as most adults who have stayed home to raise children full-time would probably attest, the more adult support a primary care-taker receives during the socialization process, the more successful it is. In fact, it is usual, and almost inevitable, for the role of socializer to be shared by all the significant adults in a child's life—neighbours, teachers, grandparents, etc.

Moral Educator

Related to the role of socializer is the role of moral educator, the individual or individuals who give the child the values by which he makes sense of his condition, experience, and responsibilities. Again, it is hard to see why an adequately supported single parent would do worse in this role than a married couple. The motivation to educate morally is not distributed differentially by family structure and, as with socialization, it may be accomplished through institutions other than the nuclear family. If we believe an adequate moral education is part of meeting children's developmental needs, we ought to put in place policies which provide all parents motivated to instruct, protect, and guide their children the precious gift of time to do so. (The heroic efforts of one single parent towards this end, without the benefit of such supportive policies, is documented in Boo 2001.)

Teacher

As their cognitive capacities mature, children come to need not only social-ization but teaching. Attendance at school ought to provide children with the social and intellectual skills as well as the technical knowledge to compete successfully in today's global economy as well as to discharge knowledgeably and responsibly a variety of civic duties. Most parents in the United States attempt to meet this developmental need by sending their children to public school. Unfortunately, many of these schools fail both parents and children.

Access to an adequate education ought not to depend on family structure. Yet because single-parent households are disproportionately poor, the chil-dren in them are disproportionately at risk of living in neighbourhoods in which the public schools are grossly inadequate. Direct attention to the improvement of failing schools seems as sensible a way of addressing this problem as seeking to increase the number of children who, because their parents are married, can afford to avoid schools of the lowest calibre.

Gender role model

I include this category really as a concession to the recent literature concerned with the effects of father absence. The importance of a gender role model is linked to the idea that children need to be provided with a sense of the sorts of adult lives open to (or, more constrictively, appropriate to) their sex. However, defined in this way, it is not a role that must be filled by a biological parent or an adult living in the child's household. If the teaching profession were not so sexually stratified, we might be less concerned about the avail-ability of gender role models for young boys in single-parent homes.

Aspects of this list are certainly open to debate. My aim is to invite reflection about what precisely children need from adults in order to flourish and what, if anything, about these needs requires the presence of two biological parents in the home. Thinking in these terms, we see that stable, intact two-parent families produce good social outcomes in children in part because they are extraordinarily well positioned to marshal the resources necessary to fill the social roles required to meet a child's developmental needs. But they do not represent the only sort of family that could do well at this task. If single mothers could count on the state to fulfil the role of financial provider—to mention the most obvious example—they would be free to assume all the roles now filled by the stay-at-home spouse in a two-parent family. Some may suggest that, even with such support, unmarried mothers will still struggle with the job of raising children. I say more about the implications of this possibility in the next section. This list of needs also makes clear that no family can provide by itself the variety of goods, resources, or caring adults required for a child to flourish. Every family is supported in its effort to raise the next generation of citizens by an array of state and community initiatives, covering all sorts of issues from education and law and order to health care. When we consider policy initiatives designed to support new family structures, we are thus talking about shifting or enhancing an already well-established parent–public partnership in the raising of children. With this account in place, I turn now to a consideration of how a critical theory of family structure developed along the lines I have just suggested might help inform the current debate over the relative political virtues of the one- and two-parent family.

Good Families, Bad Families

Not all families are the same when it comes to producing good social outcomes for children. But what can a critical theory of family structure tell us about why this is the case? Certainly, a focus on what children need clarifies the joint partnership between parents and polity which underlies good child-rearing arrangements. Parents are dependent on their communities not only to provide the schools their children need to learn, but to secure the safe environments and reliable health care without which their children cannot survive. Measured purely in these uncontroversial terms, we see that family policy in the United States already has a long way to go if it is adequately to discharge its responsibilities to American children. Attendance at safe, effective schools does not have to be dependent on the marital status of one's parents and access to basic health care does not have to depend on whether or not they have a job. The fact that family structure currently makes a difference in how children's educational and medical needs are met is evidence that our society tolerates such disparities, even if it does not actively choose to enforce them. The effort to provide financial security for one's family does not have to force parents into an unholy alliance with substandard daycare centres. The fact that even many married working parents must now make such compromises reflects how low a priority state and national governments place on distributing social resources in such a way as to ensure high-quality infant care or responsible maternal employment.

The first contribution, then, of a critical theory of family structure is to emphasize the degree to which all families, regardless of family form, would benefit from a government committed to more child-friendly social policies. Unfortunately, the latest census data reveals that married couples with children make up less than 25 per cent of all American households. Factoring in single-parent families still leaves the total of households with children under one-third. We cannot, then, make the case for a realignment of government priorities on numbers alone. Any argument for the entitlement of children to a greater share of the nation's resources (an argument which I do not have the space to develop here) would have to emphasize both children's special vulnerability and their unique status as social works-in-progress ('adults-to-be') as two factors making additional provision for them a matter of justice.

If we turn our attention directly to single-parent households, a critical theory of family structure helps to identify the factors that place children raised in such families at greater risk of poor social outcomes. For new familists, identifying the family structure is enough to explain its dysfunctionality: there is one parent where there should be two, a single mother where there should be a father as well. But a critical theory directs our attention away from the number of adults in a child's household (and their gender) towards the ability of those adults to meet the child's developmental needs. Considered from this perspective, there are at least two ways in which single-parent households are specially challenged. The first has to do with the sheer physical impossibility of combining at least two of the three principal roles children require from the adults in their lives: physical care-giver and financial provider. To leave the home to earn the money necessary to support oneself and one's child means that the responsibility for feeding and caring for the child as well as establishing an ongoing relationship of love and trust with it must be left to someone else—in many cases, a childcare provider paid the minimum wage and responsible for two or three other infants as well. For unmarried or divorced mothers to stay home to provide the love and physical care their children require is in almost all cases to forfeit the role of financial provider and condemn the family to greatly reduced standards of living if not actual poverty.

Folbre (2001) points out one interesting exception to this rule: widows. The US government currently pays bereaved spouses generously to stay home with their children. In 1997, the average amount widowed parents with two children could expect to receive from the government was over $18,000 a year (compared to an average welfare payment for the same-size family of $4,500). Nor is the programme so small as to be financially insignificant. In 1997, the welfare budget (for Temporary Assistance to Needy Families, the programme which replaced Aid to Families with Dependent Children) was approximately $33 billion (one-half contributed by the federal government, the other half by the states). The amount spent on survivor assistance was about $55 billion.

We see, then, that American family policy currently distinguishes between 'worthy' and 'unworthy' single-parent families, the former of which can count on the government to fulfil the role of financial provider, the latter of which cannot. There may be some plausibility to differentiating between adults who need help because of sheer bad luck and those whose straitened circumstances result from their own choices. However, it seems unduly harsh to apply the same distinction to the children of these adults. If we do not begrudge the child of an alcoholic father who died driving drunk the resources necessary to secure his well-being, why is similar support not forthcoming to the child whose father simply drove out of state and never returned? (Financial support for a single parent could and should include mandatory child support payments collected from the absentee father, another area in which US family policy has only recently made any substantial effort.)

Treating the role of financial provider as conceptually separate from that of husband or spouse, as a critical theory of family structure allows us to do, suggests that the fact of single parenting or father absence may be less of a problem than the conditions in which it occurs. One reason two-parent families do so much better now than single-parent families in providing for their children is that, given America's own family policies, a child needs a minimum of two adults in the household to meet its needs in the first years of its life— one to provide the care it requires and the other to provide the family's financial resources. A family policy centred on children's developmental needs could eliminate or reduce this disparity by guaranteeing through a variety of programmes a minimum income to households with children, regardless of their parents' marital status.

Any proposition of this sort raises the legitimate question of funding— not so much whether the federal government has the necessary resources but whether the political will exists to direct them towards improving child well-being. But to ask whether America is willing or able to fund a child support programme that would guarantee children in single-parent households financial resources roughly equal to children in two-parent households (so that living in such families brought no greater risk of poverty, say, than living with married parents) frames the question of what family structure is better for children somewhat differently than the new familists. Of course, if such financial parity were achieved, single-parent families might still face deficits of parental time, attention, and patience which two-parent families are largely spared. They would still find it more difficult to put in place the 'third party' adult Bronfenbrenner considers crucial to child's good development and the gender role models recommended by others. But it is only at this very distant point of fair financial support to all children regardless of their parents' relationship that we could legitimately begin to discuss the innate advantages of two-parent over single-parent families.

I indicated that there were at least two problems facing single-parent households that a critical theory of family structure illuminates. The first has to do with the difficulty of combining the roles of financial provider and primary care-giver, as already discussed. The second has to do with care-giving capacities themselves. If we go back to the list of children's needs and the adult roles which supply them, we see that solving the problem of finan-cial provider will not address every challenge facing the single-parent house-hold. Not everyone able to bear children commands the emotional, physical, or cognitive resources to care for them effectively. Chronic depression, substance abuse, and/or simply being a child oneself are among the more prominent causes of a parent being unable to fill the multiplicity of roles (soulmate, physical care-giver, socializer, moral educator, and/or homemaker) which provide a young child with the goods and resources he needs to thrive. When a stay-at-home parent has no spouse or partner with which to share the responsibility of a child's upbringing, the risk to the child's flourishing is great indeed. (Solomon 2001) notes that, 'according to one recent study, 42% of heads of household receiving Aid to Families with Dependent Children meet the criteria for clinical depression—more than three times the national aver-age'.) Although the new familist is reluctant to admit it, the problems faced by children in these households—and I am thinking primarily of homes headed by never-married teens living in neighborhoods with high concentrations of poverty—have little to do with family structure. (Among the studies of single mothers which provide vivid evidence of this claim are Franklin 1997; Holloway 1997; Musick 1993.)

This analysis suggests that new familists treat all single-parent families as suffering from the same social pathologies, when in fact there is a vast differ-ence between single-parent households in terms of how well they can access the plurality of resources required to provide the conditions for their child's well-being. A 25-year-old mother of two who is recently divorced and has some labour-market experience needs a housing allowance, good daycare, and child support while she finishes college—not a lecture on the virtues of covenant marriage. The case is very different for a 15-year-old special educa-tion student living with her grandmother in a violence-ridden housing project and struggling with a substance abuse problem. Even the most rabid new familist knows that finding this child a husband will not measurably improve the social outcomes of her infant.

We are now in a position to see that 'the case for the two-parent family' (Galston 1991*a*) does not do justice to the different sorts of resources that different sorts of families can command. The new familists' position needs and does not have an argument explaining why our family policies should concentrate on promoting a particular family structure (the indirect route to securing the goods necessary for children to thrive) rather than providing more directly—and to families of all sorts—the goods leading to good social outcomes for children. Without such an argument, the evidence regarding the superior outcomes of children growing up in stable intact two-parent families has little political significance.

It is in some ways more palatable to say that children do better with two parents than to say that only certain sorts of adults raise children well—and then only if they have the financial support necessary to support them in this demanding job. But a critical theory of family structure instructs us that the right way to frame the social problem we face is the second way not the first. Children cannot thrive without an extraordinarily close, loving relationship to one or more adults absolutely committed to their well-being and willing to spend the time with them to prove it. Even if every mother and father in America were up to this job (and in some ways, we all fall short), almost no aspect of America's current family policy supports this outcome. What children really need is not more two-parent families but adults who can find the political will to reverse this situation for every child, regardless of whether his parents are married or divorced, separated or together, in his life or absent from it.

Notes

Earlier versions of this chapter were presented at the Conference for the Study of Political Thought, April 1995 and at the Dartmouth Lawyers Association Speaker Series, May 1996. For comments on these and other drafts, I am grateful to Donald Besharov, John Gould, Lawrence Mead, James Murphy, Molly Shanley, Rogers Smith, Joan Tronto, Iris Marion Young, and the editors of this volume.

1. I borrow this term from Popenoe 1992*a*.
2. Besides the works already cited, good sources for the new familist position include Kamarck and Galston 1990; Blankenhorn *et al.* 1990, 1999; Galston 1991*a*; Popenoe 1992*b*, and 1996; Blankenhorn 1995. Writers on the family who challenge the conclusions of the new familists without ignoring the real threats to child well-being in contemporary America include Skolnick 1994; Young 1995; Stacey 1996; Coontz 1997; Hewlett and West 1998. For these authors, US family policy, not US family structure, is to blame for poor child outcomes. Proposed remedies range from better funding for schools and daycare to a scheme whereby working parents could fund up to three years leave from the labour market by borrowing against their social security entitlements (Hewlett and West 2000).

14

Family, Choice, and Distributive Justice

Véronique Munoz-Dardé

[T]here is nothing to be said for a world in which those who
choose leisure, though they could work, are rewarded with the
produce of the industrious.

(Dworkin 2000: 2)

And whereas many men, by accident unevitable, become unable to
maintain themselves by their labour; they ought not to be left to
the Charity of private persons ; but to be provided for, (as farforth
as the necessities of Nature require,) by the Lawes of the
Common-wealth. For as it is Uncharitablenesse in any man, to
neglect the impotent; so it is in the Soveraign of a Common-
wealth, to expose them to the hazard of such uncertain Charity.

But For such as have strong bodies, the case is otherwise: they
are to be forced to work ; and to avoyd the excuse of not finding
employment, there ought to be such Lawes, as may encourage all
maner of Arts; as Navigation, Agriculture, Fishing, and all manner
of Manifacture that requires labour.

(Hobbes, *Leviathan, ch. 30*)

Choice and Distributive Justice: Effects of the Family

Considerations relevant to problems of distributive justice are many, perhaps
countless, but they can roughly be classified into two categories. The first type
concerns the *moral status* of requests for resources emanating from each of the
persons between whom the distribution takes place. A first person works very
hard to provide for her own needs and makes claims on others strictly if and
when absolutely necessary, a second suffers from a severe handicap for which
she is in no way responsible, a third in perfectly good health unreasonably
spends everything he is given, takes absurd risks, and is constantly demanding
more. If this is all we know, many will consider that the first two, but not the
third, have a claim to a part of the distribution. This reaction obtains even if

we ignore both the amount of resources available and the total number of people claiming a part of it. The moral status of each case can be evaluated individually. The main consideration is the individual responsibility of each person with respect to her own situation.

The second type of consideration concerns *objective social elements* affecting the distribution such as the size of the available supplies with respect to demands, the difficulty or ease with which resources can be replaced, and the number of people between whom the distribution is to take place. This perspective concentrates not on the status of individual requests, but rather on considerations of reciprocity: John's part is meagre if Mary seizes most of the cake. This second perspective can also *by itself* generate judgements regarding the justice of the distribution. But these will be deduced from the effects on *others* of what each receives: in the absence of other information, we think that it would be unjust for Mary to grab such a huge part of the cake, because her greed has negative effects on how John is nourished.

Our first inclination is to hold that any adequate perspective on distributive justice must necessarily be composed of a combination of these two elements. It then becomes tempting to link directly these two types of consideration. Some theories start from the second perspective, stressing that to give to one person is to deprive another of her resources (and/or of the product of her work), and that it is therefore necessary to limit distribution strictly to people who deserve it. According to this conception, people who are responsible for their lack of resources, for example because of their laziness or their unreasonable acts, have forfeited their right to resources or compensation.[1]

The aim of my chapter will be to question this line of thought, and to reach some provisional conclusions in two domains: distribution of resources (or, in a different vocabulary, of primary goods) and fair equality of opportunity. I will proceed by contrasting two types of theory of distributive justice. A first type of theory envisages the distribution of goods through the distinction between choices and factors or circumstances which do not reflect the agent's choices: so people who are responsible for their lack of resources have forfeited their right to resources or compensation. A second type of theory accommodates the legitimate considerations of reciprocity which underpin the first conception from an equally responsibility-sensitive perspective. But this second perspective starts from establishing a division of responsibility between institutions and individuals according to which background conditions of justice have to be established prior to allowing individual choices to affect the distribution.

The particular question I will focus on throughout this chapter is to determine which of the two types of theories constitutes a better response to the legitimate claims of children (as future citizens). The motivation for asking this particular question is constituted by the profound effects which the family has on problems which figure at the very core of distributive justice, such as life chances, distribution of resources, and even the formation of options and choices we are held responsible for.

There are several reasons to focus on the effect of the family on principles of justice. The family is almost certainly the first institution which we become conscious of.[2] In varying forms, it is present throughout our life. The different type of resources which we receive in it (or of which we are deprived) in the first years of our existence powerfully influence the direction our life takes, and the opportunities from which we will benefit. Theorists of distributive justice are, however, inclined to avoid this discussion. Not that the family is never referred to. On the contrary, the immediacy of the family, the fact that it is almost a paradigmatic case of community within which questions of distributive justice arise, means that it is often used to point out relevant parameters of distribution. (Typically the perspective appealed to is that of parents dividing resources between their children.[3]) This wealth of references to the family is probably prompted by some similarities between the family and the political community (normally national).[4] Neither of these are voluntary associations. (We do not choose our initial belonging to either.) In both of them limited resources have to be shared, taking into account incompatible needs, often without an active consensus of all members with regard to shared ends or values (precisely because neither are, properly speaking, voluntary associations or communities of shared ends). Finally the distribution these institutions effect is in both cases fundamental, because the resources at issue cannot be easily obtained elsewhere (at least in a world which gives such fundamental prerogatives to the family and the national community for the distribution of resources). Just think of what we intuitively consider orphans and stateless people to be deprived of.

Yet the specificity of the family as one of the main institutions constitutes only one type of consideration. An equally important group of considerations concerns the *effects* of the family on principles of justice. For one thing, these effects are so profound that, by its mere existence, the family may severely impede the access of individuals to equal life chances. Moreover, this institution induces inequalities that are not beneficial to the badly off and that are not the effect of a choice for which they can be held responsible. And the extent to which children might be thought to lose out is not limited to the distribution of material burdens and benefits. It also affects the realization of their capacities, their moral development, their capacity to form and pursue their conception of the good, and hence not only their welfare, but also aspects directly related to their future enjoyment of equal liberties. It would therefore seem natural for justice theorists to inquire into this, especially if concerned either by the position of the worst off in society, or by the distinction between brute luck and choices for which we are responsible. At any rate, these observations suffice to show that the family raises problems which are at the very heart of the two perspectives on distributive justice previously delineated. The effects

the family *itself* has on problems of distributive justice will therefore constitute one of the main focuses of my discussion.

The next section will be devoted to some preliminary considerations on
merit, opportunities, and how they affect the way we envisage distribution of
resources. A third section will examine two classical solutions to distribution
of resources, and the respective role they give to individual responsibility. We
shall see that neither escapes theoretical difficulties. (These difficulties are
highlighted by effects of the existence of the family as one of the main social
institutions.)

In a fourth section, I will consider possible solutions to these difficulties.
My main proposal will consist in revising and completing the Rawlsian
conception of division of responsibilities between individuals and institutions
in light of the distinction introduced by Thomas Scanlon between attributive
and substantive responsibility. Even if this proposal is successful, a problem
will still remain—namely, the question of fair equality of opportunities. I shall
return to Rawls's remark that insistence on delivering equality of life chances
may entail abolishing the family. My conjecture (for in this chapter it will have
to stay at that) will be that the revised conception of division of responsibility
between individuals and institutions I want to defend can only be sustained
by forgoing the priority of the principle of fair equality of opportunities over
the difference principle.

Merit, Opportunities, and Distribution of Resources: Some Preliminary Considerations

Let us imagine two people: Ann, inclined to be a 'grasshopper', and Thomas,
of the 'ant' type. Ann loves nothing more than to exercise her limited talents
for singing. (Maybe she enjoys the sound of her own voice, even if she is not
always in tune; she may also value the interaction with others through singing
in a choir, or may view singing as an expression of her love for music.) Ann
devotes as much of her available time as possible to singing (rather than to
earning a salary). She sometimes looks for a job, but finds that she can only
get low-qualified and low-paid ones. (She does not have a degree.) She only
stays in employment for short periods of time and scarcely manages with her
meagre earnings. Thomas has studied long and hard; he devotes most of his
time to working; in his very few moments of leisure he spends extravagantly;
he can afford it, for he has been successful in his ambitious professional aspirations. So far we have only very few indications regarding the lifestyle,
resources, and respective opportunities of Ann and Thomas. From these bare
elements, it would be very difficult indeed to deduce a stable perspective on
their respective rights to essential goods. We are lacking at least one of the two
elements highlighted in my introduction, namely the nature of their respective merits and what I called the objective social elements which affect the

distribution. In the first order of considerations, we can for example ask to what extent striking differences in their inclinations are explained by their family and social circumstances and, if so, whether this is a good reason to adjust the distribution of resources and opportunities between them. In the second perspective, we will for example consider whether, when she falls pray of illness or unemployment, Ann is likely to demand resources from Thomas (say through taxation), and if so, whether this demand is fair.

Here again the two types of considerations can be evaluated separately. That is: we can envisage answering the second of these questions without having dealt with the first. Even if Ann's inclinations are explainable by factors beyond her control such as her social and family circumstances in childhood, the demands for resources she makes of Thomas are not automatically unanswerable. But we can also say that there is something unjust in a world which places Ann in a situation of *initial* inequality of resources and opportunities. That is: the injustice of her situation is apparent independently of questions regarding the source of possible compensations to Ann.[5]

Finally the need for a redistribution from one to the other can arise independently of the respective merits, inclinations, and initial opportunities of Ann and Thomas: if factors external to them, for example, a sudden unforeseeable scarcity of resources, places one of them (and not the other) in a situation of acute deprivation or need.

Individual Responsibility, Family, and Equality of Opportunities

We could reformulate what we have seen so far in terms of responsibilities. Two types of responsibilities are at play: the moral responsibility of each person regarding the direction that her life takes, and a social responsibility with respect to initial inequalities of resources and opportunities, as well as to subsequent adversities which befall others.

Different theories of justice disagree both as to the definition of these respective responsibilities, and to the form in which they should be attributed. What I want to do now is to analyse differences between theories which start from otherwise similar premises, namely that justice requires a fair distribution of resources and opportunities, and that this fair distribution must be established within the constraints imposed by principles of individual liberty and responsibility. We shall see that for each of these positions, the institution of the family poses particular problems. I shall begin by a brief summary of two contrasting conceptions of responsibilities and fair distribution, and will then specify the difficulties created for each of them by the existence of the family.

1. A first type of theory envisages the distribution of goods through the distinction between choices (with varying emphasis on whether they are fully

under the agent's control) and factors or circumstances which do not reflect the agent's choices.[6] The main idea seems to stem from a very straightforward conception of fairness. I can legitimately aspire to certain compensation for deficiencies such as physical handicaps and socio-economic circumstances which do not derive from my choices. But it would be unfair to expect resources and/or efforts from others, to expect others to 'pick up the tab' for me when my disadvantageous situation results from my choices. Therefore social responsibility (the shared responsibility of others) should only be directed to relieving afflictions which are beyond the reach of individual responsibility.

Notice that social responsibility thus conceived is *derived* from a notion of individual responsibility, a notion in which the fact of choice plays a central role. That is, there is no independent definition of social responsibility other than that it picks up whatever does *not* flow from individual choices for which people are held responsible.

2. By contrast, the second type of theory starts from the establishment of a conceptual division of responsibility between principles for background institutions and principles for individual and associations. Institutions are responsible for the distribution of certain goods and, *in this context of justice of institutions*, individuals are responsible for how well their lives go. The liberties of individuals, their rights, as well as their fair access to social positions which procure different powers and economic rewards, are established by social, legal, and economic institutions. It is then up to individuals to choose their ends and goals in life and to make use of rights, liberties, and fair opportunities defined by these main institutions. *If* these fair circumstances are in place, then individuals are responsible for their success in pursuing their ends, as well as their resulting well-being or happiness. (That is, they are responsible for not requiring further transfers from others.)

Here too, then, fairness and individual responsibility are central notions, but the structure of their effect is envisaged differently. In particular, the justice of the basic structure of society[7] is *prior* (conceptually) to individual choices made within it. Individual choices therefore do not condition entitlements. The guarantee of rights and liberties and the fair assurance of primary goods necessary to make use of these rights and liberties are insensitive to individual choices made within the framework of these entitlements. These entitlements do not have to be deserved: the twin notions of choice and desert are introduced from a subsequent and clearly distinct moral perspective.

Let us pause now to envisage how the existence of the institution of the family may introduce difficulties for both of the two perspectives just sketched. Let me briefly sketch some of these problems, taking each of these two theoretical conceptions in turn.

3. The first perspective on distributive justice puts choices made by indi-

viduals, choices they are responsible for, at the core of the distinction between personal and collective responsibility (meaning by 'collective' that which is borne by other members of the relevant community). The person who suffers from a disadvantage or misfortune which results from a conscious decision on her part, disadvantage or misfortune which she could have avoided by choosing appropriately, has forfeited her rights to resources in the context of distributive justice. This perspective is what Thomas Scanlon has termed the Forfeiture View.[8]

This perspective derives its plausibility from the apparent injustice which would result from the fact that those who work arduously and/or behave wisely should pay for people who choose to be lazy and/or unwise. Dworkin echoes this moral indignation well when he refers to governments constantly having to 'take from the ants and give to the grasshoppers'. And he adds the comment with which I headed this text: '[T]here is nothing to be said for a world in which those who choose leisure, though they could work, are rewarded with the produce of the industrious' (Dworkin, 2000: 2).

It may appear that the main problem with which the severe perspective on rights adopted by the Forfeiture View is confronted is in determining if and when choices are really such. (I shall return to this aspect below.) But a more acute and fundamental challenge comes from asking whether the *circumstances* in which actual choices take place are such that it is justified to adopt this drastic perspective (to consider, that is, that rights to assistance with regard to predicaments which derive from these choices have been forfeited).

I want to suggest that it is this very problem which underlies Rawls's much commented upon phrase in a *Theory of Justice*, to the effect that 'Even the willingness to make an effort, to try, and so to be deserving in the ordinary sense is itself dependent upon happy family and social circumstances' (Rawls, 1999a: 64). More precisely the suggestion is this. Rawls is stressing family circumstances for reasons which have already been explored: the family is one of the main institutions of society; its effects on our resources and opportunities are present from the very beginning of our lives and, to a great extent, frame social inequalities. In other words: the family is one of the fundamental elements of the *context* of fairness or injustice in which individual choices take place. This is not to deny that these choices are such, but rather to note that they may take place in circumstances which would make it unfair for people to have to bear their full cost. Hence my reading of an anticipated response to the Forfeiture View in Rawls's sentence.

Before I expand on this aspect, one must note that the perspective recommended by Rawls is not without difficulties, some of which arise precisely from his quoted remark on family circumstances. Let me explore some of these difficulties with which Rawls, and more generally the second perspective on distributive justice, might be confronted.

4. This second perspective proceeds differently: it does not start from individual choices, but establishes instead first principles of justice for the *joint* functioning of the main institutions of society. The idea is that these institutions must fit together to deliver fair circumstances for individual conduct. Primary legal, political, and economic institutions affect our whole life and even the course it takes. They also influence fundamentally the way we think about the justice of these institutions themselves (a point made long ago by Rousseau in the *Social Contract*). For these two reasons, principles which concern these institutions have to be established independently, and from a prior perspective.

Rawls's theory is obviously the *locus classicus* of this perspective. In the context of the present discussion, the familiar difficulty for this theory, and others inspired by it, can be put succinctly as follows. The first principle this theory affirms is the protection of basic liberties as background conditions for individuals to be able to decide upon their own ends and pursue them. It is also in order for these liberties not to remain merely 'formal' and to have operativeness that certain fundamental goods are to be guaranteed to each person. (These goods are conceived as all-purpose means to achieve a wide range of individual ends.) The idea that the corollary of the protection of liberties to form and advance individual ends is responsibility towards the choices these liberties allow us to make seems straightforward. And it is this very idea which seems inconsistent with stating that some social circumstances, singularly family circumstances, could make it legitimate not to insist that individuals bear the consequences of their own choices.[9]

More precisely, the stress put on family and social circumstances raises two types of problems, one moral, and the second more strictly situated within the context of distributive justice.

(a) First, even if our attitudes can plausibly be explained in great part by contextual and social elements among which family circumstances have a fundamental place, this does not exempt us from blame. For these attitudes are nevertheless attributable to us; we do not seem exempt from responsibility for them, at least in as far as we can evaluate them, and evaluate some of their consequences for others.

(b) But whether or not they can excuse us from blame, thoughts of the type exemplified by Rawls's phrase on the causal relation between family circumstances and attitude to effort seem to justify (or even recommend) a world in which some hard-working and prudent people 'pay' for the lazy and those who take unreasonable risks: the familiar story of ants and grasshoppers.

But to these familiar difficulties we must add another. For even if we could restore plausibility from the perspective of individual responsibility (a task I turn to in the next section), a more troublesome objection would remain. This objection is raised by Rawls himself, following on from his remark on family circumstances. The internal life and culture of the family exercises such a powerful influence, it motivates or fails to motivate us in such a comprehensive way (among other aspects to benefit from available educational resources) that our whole life prospects are affected by it. Moreover, these effects are so pervasive that the mere existence of the family means that equal chances cannot obtain. Rawls returns to this problem several times in a *Theory of Justice*, first to ask how far the notion of equality of opportunity can be carried, and finally to envisage towards the end of the book the abolition of the family as the only solution to deliver a principle of fair equality of life chances (1999a: 64, 265, 447–8).[10]

This last suggestion is hardly a temporary concession to eccentricity or revolutionary ideas. Rather, it is advanced for reasons of coherence. For fair equality of life chances is the second principle of justice, a principle which is prior to the difference principle. However, Rawls concedes that *even* in a well-ordered society the mere existence of the family may prevent delivery of a principle of equal chances between individuals (1999a: 265).

Have we reached a double impasse? The existence of the family seems to create fundamental difficulties (in terms of responsibility but also of equality of opportunities) for the two types of approaches to distributive justice distinguished at the outset. The following section will be devoted to scrutinizing more closely the problem of individual responsibility and suggest some way out of the impasse, before I return in a last section to the question of fair opportunity of life chances.

Abolition of the Family, or a Different Conception of Responsibility?

The Idea of Abolition of the Family and its Effects on Both Types of Theory

First, Rawls does little more than to raise the question of the tension between the existence of the family and the principle of equality of life chances. After asking whether the family should be abolished, he concedes that, taken by itself and given the primacy he awards it, the principle of equality of life chances inclines in this direction, but he dismisses the urgency of the problem in the theory of justice as a whole. His suggestion, for it is no more than this, is that the difference principle once applied would have the effect of reconciling citizens with natural inequalities *and* with unequal conditions of human life such as these which obtain from the very existence of the family (1999a: 448).

Clearly the thought behind Rawls's suggestion that we should reconcile

ourselves with some inequalities bears a strong affinity with Williams's illuminating analysis of tensions within the idea of equality. Williams's view is
that we may push too far the ideal of equality of opportunity. For if we try to
cure every natural and social source of inequality, we may end up regarding
individuals as 'pure subjects of predicates, everything else about them . . .
being regarded as a fortuitous and changeable characteristic'. Which in turn
would destroy a sense of common humanity necessary for equality of respect
(Williams, 1973: 246–7).

Williams is right to warn us against extremes of absurdity and incoherence
if we insist on a thoroughgoing application of the principle of equality of
opportunity. But abolishing the family and replacing it with a more equality-
friendly institution for the rearing of children may be compatible with
preserving better equality of respect. At any rate, even if we stop short of advocating the abolition of the family (no one would want to envisage it as a serious policy proposal, I think), we may want to consider the thought
experiment just for purposes of clarity. For this thought experiment allows us
to identify the value (if any) which is such that (i) in a just society it would be
prioritized over the principle of equality of life chances and (ii) can only be
protected by the existence of the family.

I have suggested elsewhere that a way to gain some clarity, and to vindicate
Rawls's rejection of the abolition of the family, is to imagine parties in the
original position comparing a society in which the family exists in some form,
and a society in which this institution would have been abolished in favour of
a generalized and well-run orphanage (a model of generalized care for children within institutions similar to boarding schools, with secured comfortable environment and well-qualified carers and teachers, able to devote
individualized attention to children, but not attached to them through
parental links). My claim is that, even in this idealized form, parties in the
original position would not choose the generalized and well-run orphanage.
For the complete abolition of the family would pose threats to equal liberty, a
value which is indeed lexically prior for Rawls to equality of opportunity. (The
thought is that, if generalized over many generations, the orphanage would
endanger conditions for pluralism and result in a denial of individuality.[11]) So
this solution is not available within a Rawlsian framework. The problem of the
difficulty of delivering a principle of equal life chances for individuals therefore remains.

2. Second, the suggestion of the abolition of the family is prompted by
tensions within Rawlsian theory. But theorists who lean towards the Forfeiture
View could also have reasons to find it attractive. If all individuals were in
similar initial circumstances apart from inequalities in natural talents and
handicaps, which it then becomes easier to identify and, where possible, to
compensate, then a practical objection to the Forfeiture View which seems
contained in Rawls's phrase about family circumstances and their impact even

on willingness to do well fails. For the objection *could be read* as merely saying that it is impossible to reckon the extent to which desert is really such (and not due to luck in the lottery which places you at birth in this or that family).[12]

The least that can be said is that the idea of a society where the family would be abolished for this reason (that is, in order to remove practical difficulties in telling how much of our good or bad fortune is due to happy or unhappy family circumstances, and thus to get closer to the ideal of compensation for bad brute luck, not choices we are responsible for) does not strike us as a utopia in a just society. One of the main thoughts behind this spontaneous rejection must be a resistance to the drive for exposing our natural inequalities. There are two ways of understanding this thought, which are brought out by the different lessons that could be inferred from it. The first possible deduction is that theorists who rely on Forfeiture View intuitions have the right conception of justice, but that they should refrain from adopting policies which would undermine the self-respect of some individuals.[13] The right move in response is to try and imagine institutions which operate with the right luck/choice distinction, but without revealing to each individual how exactly they score (a task largely situated outside the framework of philosophy). The second reaction is to refuse this consequence, and to consider that thus having to pull apart individuals' self-conceptions and the way they are envisaged by institutions responsible for distributive justice is indicative of a mistake in the conception of the person with which these theories operate. I am inclined to draw this last conclusion, and to think that a theory which is committed to giving equally to each individual their due should do so in terms of a coherent conception of the person: a conception which can be used throughout, and justified to each of the individuals concerned.

Such a conception should do so, though, without losing sight of the problem of individual responsibility. In the next section, I intend to explore the distinctions necessary for this task.

Responsibility: Several Necessary Distinctions

The problem of initial inequalities with respect to social and family circumstances in which individual choices are rooted and operate cannot be removed. We must therefore find a different theoretical solution. To this end, I now propose to return to the Rawlsian division between social and individual responsibility. In particular, I intend to assess whether adopting the distinction introduced by Thomas Scanlon between substantive and attributive responsibility would allow one to address the problem the Rawlsian conception faces.

I began this article by saying that many accounts of distributive justice link directly the moral status of claims on resources (in particular the question of whether the person in need of resources is responsible for her own predicament) with the social objective elements which affect the distribution of fundamental resources, such as the relative scarcity of goods and the effects on others of what each person appropriates for herself. To this perspective, I opposed the Rawlsian conception according to which each of us *separately* has a *social responsibility* with respect to the institution of fair circumstances for the life of each member in society, and an *individual moral responsibility* with respect to how we lead our life, and make choices. The two notions of Scanlonian responsibility allow us to develop and specify this idea further. To recall:

- The first form of responsibility defined by Scanlon is *responsibility as attributability*. To ask whether someone is responsible for an action in this sense is to ask whether it can be *attributed* to an agent. 'To say that a person is responsible, in this sense, for a given action is only to say that it is appropriate to take it as a basis of moral appraisal of that person. . . . When we ask whether a person is responsible [in this sense] for a given action, what we are asking is whether that person is properly subject to praise or blame for having acted in this way' (Scanlon 1998: 248 and 290).
- By contrast, to say that someone has a *substantive responsibility* serves to express substantive claims about what people are required (or not required) to do for each other. 'To say that a person is responsible [in this second sense] for a certain outcome is . . . to say that that person cannot complain of the burdens or obligations that result' (Scanlon 1998: 290).

One of the main aspects of this distinction, one which is crucial here, is that these two types of responsibility can be considered separately (because they have different moral roots, Scanlon points out).[14]

- I can be considered responsible in the first sense, criticized for my laziness or admired for my courage, without a penalty or reward being automatically linked to this notion of responsibility. The fact that the sanction incurred can be separated from the moral evaluation of my action or attitude in terms of praise or blame allows us to preserve the intuition according to which, even if my laziness or my carelessness can be traced back to my social circumstances (even if it would be unjustified for me to 'pay the full prize' of their consequences), I am nevertheless able to envisage their effect on myself and on to others. So I am, at least in this sense, responsible for them.
- But I can also be responsible in the second sense, and have substantial responsibility towards others, even if the need or deprivation can in no way be traced back to any of my acts or choices in terms of attributive responsibility. In the context of distributive justice, situations of scarcity of certain goods can by themselves create the obligation to give away part of my resources, even if I am not responsible in the attributive sense for the predicaments I am called upon to alleviate.
- Finally the conditions required to *absolve* me from responsibility in the first

sense (the conditions required to consider me free from blame) are different from the conditions required to discharge others from the responsibility of providing help, directly or through institutions of distributive justice.
In other words, I can be responsible in the first sense without the obligation
of others in society to provide help being automatically released.

We can now go back to the problems with which the Rawlsian conception
seemed to be faced in terms of individual responsibility. Scanlon's distinction
allows us to accept the thought behind Rawls's reference to family and social
circumstances (and the consequence in terms of substantial social responsibility), whilst preserving the idea according to which I am not 'absolved' from
responsibility (at least in the attributive sense) with respect to my choices and
actions. The apparent tension between the protection of liberties to form and
advance individual ends and the unconditional distribution of some fundamental goods (and of those only), irrespective of responsibility for the choices
we use these liberties to make, is therefore not one after all.[15]

The advantages of this perspective are evident. We can now treat as a
distinct problem the fact that circumstances which affect any human society:
the relative scarcity of fundamental goods, social interdependence, and our
limited understanding (more precisely, our incapacity to calculate all the
effects of our acts on others and ourselves, and the fact that we tend to see the
world from a necessarily restricted perspective) generate a substantive social
responsibility (in terms of distributive justice) from each person with respect
to other members of her society.

This account of the social responsibility of each person with respect to the
provision of fair social circumstances allows us to avoid pitfalls the Forfeiture
View confronts *because* of its linking choice and rights. Let me just mention
the most obvious:

• First, the strict application of a principle with respect to which rights
depend on choosing one thing rather than another defines a society in
which many would be deprived of rights they would have been said to have
'forfeited' through decisions whose consequences were impossible to esti-
mate due to the circumstances in which they were made. It does not seem
that we adopt such a harsh perspective even for criminal acts; it therefore is
at the very least problematic to apply it to decisions made by each of us in
everyday life, often without any 'fault' other than our incapacity to assess all
the consequences which will follow.[16]
• Second (and more importantly), if we consider choice the decisive element
then our attention is directed towards whether our choices really are such,
or rather result from causes external to us.[17] But, as Scanlon reminds us, to
take choices (or even some notion of 'authentic' choices) as the *test* for what
we should or should not pay the price of sometimes yields an unfair result.
For even if an outcome results from a decision taken by an agent who did

consciously pass up alternatives, and in this sense undeniably from a *choice*, the intention from which the choice results may have been formed in circumstances which made it overwhelmingly probable that it would be the *wrong* choice.[18]

Some may object that theories of distributive justice which put all the emphasis on the fact of choice may still have space to consider background conditions in which these choices are formed. That is, they do not have to take the extreme view that there is *no* role for these considerations.[19] But I would contend that, even with some allowance for background conditions, to concentrate primarily on the fact of choice for decisions of distributive justice is already to miss Scanlon's lesson. For it seems that, if we understand this lesson properly, then we would not want to start from the idea that 'people should pay the price of the life they have decided to lead' (Dworkin 2000: 74). Rather, we would proceed in the fashion I described earlier, and distinguish between two stages. We would *first* secure background conditions such that everybody's choices, especially the choice of what life to lead, are taken in fair circumstances and *then*, but then only, hold people responsible for these choices. (Notice that at this second stage there is still scope for moral considerations about the conditions in which particular choices are taken to serve as an excuse. But these considerations may not have an effect on *distributive* justice.)

In these ways, then, the dissociation of fair distribution of primary resources and moral responsibility for choices allows for a more coherent picture. All members of society, 'ants', 'grasshoppers', wise, or daredevils, are jointly responsible for establishing and maintaining fair background circumstances for decisions and choices made by each of them. In contrast with the perspective which derives social provision from responsibility for our choices along blame/praise lines, this substantive social responsibility of individuals is conceptually both independent of and prior to responsibility for our choices (attributive and substantive). *If* these background circumstances of fairness are in place, then each person is responsible for her share of resources and for the satisfaction she derives from them.[20]

Each of the members of society is therefore considered responsible for the effects of the social structure of society to which all belong *and* from which all benefit as a result of their mere belonging to it.[21] Each is also responsible for the selection of the abilities and interests s/he wants to develop, for planning for their pursuit, and for the evaluation and revision of his/her aims, tastes, and desires. But the definition and satisfaction of the first type of responsibility does not have to suffer from the problems that a deductive link with the latter introduces.

Let me note before I return by way of conclusion to the question of equality of life chances that it is only this aspect of the application to the Forfeiture

View of distributive justice which I wish to argue against here. For everything I have said is compatible with, more, *starts* from, the acceptance of another claim which seems closely related to the spirit in which the Forfeiture View might be used for principles of distributive justice, namely that '[t]he true measure of the social resources devoted to the life of one person is fixed by asking how important, in fact, that resource is for others' (Dworkin 2000: 70). My argument in this chapter is that (i) this claim is logically separable from the reference to the work of the industrious rewarding those who choose leisure (or to the wise financing the imprudent), and (ii) that there is much to be gained by keeping them conceptually separated.

Back to the Family and Equality of Life Chances

So far my argument seems to vindicate the coherence of a theory which preserves an individualistic perspective on responsibility, by drawing distinctions without which we face important theoretical difficulties. It would therefore seem that the second perspective on distributive justice defined at the outset, namely the broadly Rawlsian framework on which I based essential elements of my argument, wins. But I have left unsolved one of the problems facing this conception, namely that the first part of the second principle, fair equality of life chances, cannot be satisfied for as long as the existence of the family (in any form) is preserved.

This problem threatens the very heart of the theory. For the application of the second principle of justice is not merely impeded within this or that particular institution, but within the basic structure of society as a whole. Other aspects to do with justice within the family have received subsequent attention,[22] but not this fundamental aspect. Moreover, in his recent treatment of the role of the family within the basic structure, Rawls raises this problem in sharp form, only to dismiss it immediately:

[The requirement that a just society does not take away the central role to the family in the raising and caring for children] *limits all arrangements of the basic structure, including efforts to achieve equality of opportunity* . . . I cannot pursue these complexities here, but assume that as children we grow up in a small intimate group in which elders (normally parents) have a certain moral and social authority.' (1999b: 596; my emphasis).

The central role fulfilled by the family in a just society is to provide a context in which each person can develop her individual capacities, in particular her two moral powers: the capacity for a conception of the good and a capacity for a sense of justice (1999a: 405; 1999b: 596). Plausible or not, this amounts to no more than an instrumental justification of the family in the light of its role in developing (in a necessarily unequal manner between families) certain capacities necessary in a just society. But this is at the price of a verified injustice, namely that people's fair equality of opportunity to realize their potential cannot be delivered. And if we take into account that inequalities must be arranged so that they are to the greatest benefit of the least well-off, then the instrumental justification looks doubly problematic.[23]

To summarize the dilemma, a just society must contain the family in some form, but as long as the family exists no society (even one governed by the principles of justice) will allow individuals to realize their potential in conditions of fair equality of opportunity. The full treatment of this dilemma would entail another article. But we can reach a provisional conclusion on this aspect.

It seems plausible that no society will be able to deliver perfectly fair equality of opportunity. It is no less plausible that we would not wish to abolish entirely the family, and that we must limit ourselves to subjecting it to the same constraints as all other institutions and associations, namely the protection of rights and liberties of each member. However, if we start from these entirely reasonable premises, we cannot just continue to hold the priority of an undeliverable principle of fair equality of opportunity over the distribution of other primary goods. So the priority of the principle of fair equality of opportunity over the difference principle in Rawlsian theory must be relinquished.[24]

Notes

For helpful comments I am grateful to David Archard, Miriam Cohen-Christofidis, Cécile Fabre, Samuel Freeman, Sebastian Gardner, Axel Gosseries, Steven Gross, Mark Kalderon, Rahul Kumar, Colin Macleod, Mike Martin, Joseph Raz, Mike Otsuka, Thomas Ricketts, Philippe Van Parijs, and Jo Wolff, as well as audiences at the Colloquium of the Department of Philosophy at the University of Pennsylvania, the London School of Economics, the Anglo-French Research Group on Contractualism, the London Research Seminar in Ethics, the Department of Philosophy of the University of Geneva, and the Chaire Hoover d'Ethique économique et sociale at Louvain-la-neuve.

1. This line of reasoning is the common ground between several contemporary egalitarian authors who wish to accommodate Nozick's libertarian appeal to responsibility. It is this common terrain, and in particular the effects of voluntary choices, with which I am primarily concerned in this chapter.

2. This is also true for people who are deprived of any family bond. For our attitude to orphans is precisely to treat the absence of a family as one of their most salient characteristics, one which affects our perception of their whole persona.

3. Let me mention just two of the most obvious references. In an oft quoted example, Thomas Nagel chooses to present his perspective on the idea of equality through the dilemma faced by a family having to choose between two incompatible ways of life which would benefit alternatively one or other of their children, one healthy and the other handicapped (1979: 124). Ronald Dworkin, in the first of his two influential articles on equality (2000: 11–64, original article published

in 1981), illustrates the difference between equality of resources and a welfarist perspective with the example of a wealthy father drawing up his will to divide his fortune between his children who happen to have very different talents, handicaps, tastes, and ambitions (the first of them is blind, the second is a playboy with expensive tastes, a third is a prospective politician with expensive ambitions, a fourth a poet with humble needs, and the fifth a sculptor who loves to work in expensive material).

4. This parallel is not normally noted. Quite the reverse: the family is often used as the paradigmatic example of a community where political rules of justice may not apply or, indeed, be needed. In opposition to this organic view of the family, one example of a contemporary author drawing a parallel between families and political communities is Elizabeth Anscombe. In particular, Anscombe notes the initial involuntary belonging to both institutions, and the fact that the subjects of authority are at least initially willy-nilly under both parental and governmental authority (1981: 135).

5. I do not introduce here considerations concerning the prudence or rashness of Ann or Thomas. But parallel observations could be made for this second contrast.

6. See e.g. Dworkin's definition of consequential responsibility: 'When and how far is it right that individuals bear the disadvantages or misfortunes of their own situations themselves, and when is it right, on the contrary, that others—the other member of the community in which they live, for example—relieve them from or mitigate the consequences of these disadvantages? I used the choice/chance distinction in replying to these questions. In principle . . . individuals should be relieved of consequential responsibility for those unfortunate features of their situation that are bad brute luck, but not from those that should be seen as flowing from their own choices. If someone has been born blind or without talents others have, that is his bad luck, and, so far as this can be managed, a just society would compensate him for that bad luck. But if he has fewer resources than other people now because he spent more on luxuries earlier, or because he chose not to work, or to work at less remunerative jobs than others chose, then his situation is the result of choice not luck, and he is not entitled to any compensation that would make up his present shortfall' (2000: 287). The distinction between choice and luck is also at the centre of G. A. Cohen's (1989) egalitarian theory, but with important qualifications to do with whether choice is dictated by features of our personality which we do not choose, and with the unchosen structure of prices to pay to satisfy our tastes. Another major exponent of an egalitarian perspective which considers inequalities acceptable when they result from choices for which the individual concerned is responsible is John Roemer (see in particular Roemer 1995b). See n. 8 for qualifications regarding Dworkin's conception of responsibility and choice.

8. This, obviously, is Rawls's phrase. The division of responsibility between principles which guarantee background justice and principles for individuals here briefly outlined is stated in *A Theory of Justice*, but important precision and qualifications are introduced in subsequent articles. (See in particular Rawls 1999b: 241, 283, and 369—these articles were originally published in 1974, 1975, and 1982.) For a recent succinct statement of this division of responsibility, see Rawls 2000. Rawls writes (2001: 54): 'Since a public conception of justice needs clear,

simple, and intelligible rules, we rely on an institutional division of labor between principles required to preserve background justice and principles that apply directly to particular transactions between individuals and associations. Once this division of labor is set up, individuals and associations are then left free to advance their (permissible) ends within the framework of the basic structure, secure in the knowledge that elsewhere in the social system the regulations necessary to preserve background justice are in force.' This understanding of division of responsibilities is also endorsed by Thomas Scanlon (1998).

8. See Scanlon 1998: ch. 6, p. 258, for the definition of the Forfeiture View. I shall return to Scanlon's alternative perspective on responsibility in the next section. There may be no example of a 'pure' Forfeiture View theorist. The closest example is probably G. A. Cohen (who himself notes affinities between his view and the Forfeiture View: 1989: 953 n. 64). As for Dworkin, although he quotes approvingly Scanlon's conception of responsibility (2000: in particular n. 4, p. 489, and n. 9, p. 490), it is not clear that he can adopt it without revising substantially some of his claims in *Sovereign Virtue*. To put it succinctly, Dworkin's view seems to oscillate uncomfortably between at least two perspectives on responsibility. Some of the formulations in *Sovereign Virtue* seem a quite straightforward appeal to the Forfeiture View. (I quote some of these in this article, in which I concentrate on this aspect of his theory.) But Dworkin also says that he accepts Scanlon's case (to be discussed below) against the Forfeiture View. That is, he accepts that there is a *case* for making a distinction between blaming a person for a choice and making her bear the cost of that very choice. (See in particular Dworkin 2000: n. 9, p. 490.) As noted by Ripstein (1999: 291) and, in written exchange, by Mike Otsuka, Dworkin's view also bears some important similarities with Harry Frankfurt's discussion of free will. But apart from the difficulty of mapping Frankfurt's discussion on to issues of *distributive* justice (in which factors extraneous to blameworthiness have to be taken into account), it is not clear how this reading of Dworkin allows us to interpret his appeal to, at least, forfeiture-based intuitions, such as the passage quoted in n. 6 or the idea that those who 'choose leisure though they could work' have forfeited their right to social benefits. I cannot pursue these complexities here, and can only note the tension between different elements of Dworkin's theory.

9. Robert Nozick is the author who presses most forcefully the idea of an inconsistency in Rawls's theory along these lines. But egalitarians who lean towards the Forfeiture View, such as G. A. Cohen, accept the spirit of this criticism.

10. I have provided a more extensive analysis of Rawls's position on the family, in Munoz-Dardé (1998, 1999).

11. This may appear a straightforward enough conclusion. The contrast with other discussions of tension between family, equality, and autonomy (see in particular Fishkin 1983) is that it is not the autonomy of the family, but of each of the individuals within it which is the focus of attention. So it is not the equal liberty of parents (their sphere of autonomy to bring up their children as they see fit) but of each person raised within a generalized state-maintained institution which is envisaged.

The main effect of this more thoroughly individualistic perspective on the link between liberty and the institution of the family is that it allows one to insist on the importance of an individualization of rights within the family. To conceive of the family as just one among various associations of individuals also leads to suggesting the abolition of institutional family regulations incompatible with the neutrality of the state with respect to different individual conceptions of the good (such as the exclusive availability of marriage contracts to people of the opposite sex). For more details on the family as an association of individuals and the effects of this conception, see Munoz-Dardé (1999).

12. I say 'could be read' because I do not think that this is the correct reading. That is, even if there were non-intrusive ways of telling exactly for each person which part is natural and/or family circumstances, and which part is the result of choice, this conception of the person would not, I think, be Rawlsian. (In contrast with Rawls's conception, this conception of the person seems external. For in many cases individuals would not care to adopt it in the first person. I return to this question in the main text.)

13. Thus Anderson (1999) and Wolff (1998) both criticize recent egalitarian thought because it would result in policies which undermine equal respect of individuals. Anderson is also alive to the problem of submitting intimate relations to the constant scrutiny of institutions with a view to determining entitlements.

14. The difference between the two types of responsibility is based on the distinction between whether it is appropriate to express moral condemnation or praise, and whether it is appropriate to impose a social sanction or burden. So the relevant questions to ask in each case are different. (i) Moral appraisal (attributability: blame or praise) is based on the idea of self-governance; so what is relevant is whether self-governance is effective or faulty. 'On my view this part of morality is ... what I call a system of co-deliberation, and moral reasoning is an attempt to work out principles that each of us could be asked to employ as a basis for deliberation and accept as a basis of criticism' (1998: 268). (ii) Moral justification of burdens and benefits (substantive responsibility: what people are or not required to do for each other), on the other hand, is based on grounds (circumstances of choice) which make it the case that we can or cannot complain of burdens that we bear.

15. Some may protest that Rawls's different treatment of expensive tastes (i.e. his refusal to subsidize them, whether they are genuinely chosen or not) and of effort or desert reintroduces this tension. I believe that it does not. For in both cases, Rawls would agree that we are attributively responsible. But his account of what is substantively owed to others through the provision of primary goods stops short of giving *extra* funds to people who happen to have expensive tastes. He thinks that we are substantively responsible for ensuring that no one suffers a deficit in their fair share of primary goods (which are a public measure of generalized needs and all-purpose means, so distinct from preference or desire satisfaction). But in this context of background fairness (i.e. assuming that the principles of justice are fulfilled), and in the light of expectations regarding our share of primary goods, we have to take responsibility for controlling and adjusting our wants, aims and desires. (See Rawls 1999*b*, esp. ch. 17).

16. Dworkin partly avoids this draconian implication of the link between choices we are responsible for and rights through the introduction of a system of insurance, the effects of which might be very similar to a Rawlsian provision of primary goods. I am not concerned here with the political effects of each theory, but solely

with questioning this theoretical link between choice we are responsible for and provision of social rights. I therefore leave Dworkin's insurance scheme aside.

17. By 'external' some views may refer to some features of a person's body (e.g. example handicaps).

18. Scanlon gives the example of why we would reject a principle that bound a 14 year old to a long-term contract entered without adult guidance. What is special about the case of the 14 year old, he says, is not that they *cannot* choose wisely, but that they are so likely not to do so (Scanlon 1998: 262).

19. I owe the formulation of this objection to Andrew Williams.

20. See n. 15 for individual responsibility for adjusting tastes, aims, and ambitions in this context of the fairness of social institutions (cf. Rawls 1999*b*: 241, 284, and 369–70).

21. For this idea of our benefiting from our individual participation in the total sum of the realized assets of others in society, cf. Rawls, 1999*a*: 458–61, in particular n. 4.

22. I refer in particular to feminist criticisms with regard to justice in the family, such as those advanced by Susan Moller Okin. Rawls responds at length on this precise point in his article on 'The Idea of Public Reason Revisited' (1999*b*: 595–601; article published in 1997). In particular, he rebukes the misconception according to which principles of justice do not apply to the family. (The principles of justice do not regulate the internal life of any institution, but they protect the rights and liberties of its members.) He also stresses that the claim that in a just society citizens would grow up in small intimate groupings does not presuppose any form of family, and in particular does not exclude same-sex parenting (1999*b*: 586 n. 60).

23. I summarize here something I explored at more length elsewhere (see Munoz-Dardé 1998, 2000).

24. This modification is perhaps less fundamental than it may seem. For it accords with the fundamental aim of a theory which defines liberty and the social bases of self-respect as the two fundamental primary goods, all the other goods (including opportunities) being means to define, pursue, and revise our aims in life: '[T]he thin theory of the good which the parties are assumed to accept shows that they should try to secure their liberty and self-respect, and that, in order to advance their aims, whatever these are, they normally require more rather than less of the other primary goods.' (Rawls 1999*a*: 349). Rawls himself is uncertain about this question, precisely for the reasons I note. Thus in a discussion of the family as a basic institution, Rawls writes: 'Some think that the lexical priority of fair equality of opportunity over the difference principle is too strong, and that either a weaker priority or a weaker form of the opportunity principle would be better, and indeed more in accord with fundamental ideas of justice as fairness itself. At present I do not know what is best here and simply register my uncertainty. How to specify and weight the opportunity principle is a matter of great difficulty and some such alternative may well be better' (2001: 163 n. 44). For reasons which I cannot pursue here, I think that it is the *diversity* of opportunities which is fundamental, not the fact that perfect equality of opportunity between individuals should obtain.

Further Reading

On the topic of children in general the following are the principal philosophical monographs and collections:

Aiken, William, and LaFollette, Hugh (eds.), *Whose Child? Children's Rights, Parental Authority, and State Power* (Totowa, NJ: Rowman & Littlefield, 1980).

Alston, Philip, Parker, Stephen, and Seymour, John (eds.), *Children, Rights, and the Law* (Oxford: Oxford University Press, 1992).

Archard, David, *Children, Rights and Childhood* (London: Routledge, 1993).

Blustein, Jeffrey, *Parents and Children: The Ethics of the Family* (Oxford: Oxford University Press, 1982).

Meyers, Diana Tietkens, Kipnis, Kenneth, and Murphy, Jr., Cornelius F., *Kindred Matters: Rethinking the Philosophy of the Family* (Ithaca, NY, and London: Cornell University Press, 1993).

Narayan, Uma, and Bartkowiak, Julia J. (eds.), *Having and Raising Children: Unconventional Families, Hard Choices, and the Social Good* (University Park, PA: Pennsylvania State University Press, 1999).

O'Neill, Onora, and Ruddick, William (eds.), *Having Children: Philosophical and Legal Reflections on Parenthood* (Oxford: Oxford University Press, 1979).

Scarre, Geoffrey (ed.), *Children, Parents and Politics* (Cambridge: Cambridge University Press, 1989).

Turner, Susan M., and Matthews, Gareth B. (eds.), *The Philosopher's Child* (Rochester, NY: University of Rochester, 1998).

Wringe, Colin, *Children's Rights* (London: Routledge & Kegan Paul, 1981).

The chapters of this volume address four broadly defined topics. Below are given suggestions for further reading in each topic.

Education

Brighouse, Harry, 'Civic Education and Liberal Legitimacy', *Ethics*, 108 (1998): 719–745.

Burtt, Shelley, 'Religious Parents, Secular Schools: A Liberal Defence of an Illiberal Education', *Review of Politics*, 56 (1994): 51–70.

Callan, Eamonn, *Creating Citizens: Political Education and Liberal Democracy* (Oxford: Oxford University Press, 1997).

Gutmann, Amy, 'Civic Education and Social Diversity', *Ethics*, 105 (1995): 557–79.

—— *Democratic Education* (Princeton: Princeton University Press, 1987).

Macedo, Stephen, 'Community, Diversity, and Civic Education: Toward a Liberal Political Science of Group Life', *Social Philosophy and Policy* (1996): 240–68.

—— 'Liberal Civic Education and Religious Fundamentalism: The Case of God v. John Rawls?', *Ethics*, 105 (1995): 468–96.

Children's Rights

Cohen, Howard, *Equal Rights for Children* (Totowa, NJ: Littlefield, Adams & Co., 1980).

Feinberg, Joel, 'The Child's Right to an Open Future', in William Aiken and Hugh LaFollette (eds.), *Whose Child? Children's Rights, Parental Authority, and State Power* (Totowa, NJ: Rowman & Littlefield, 1980), 124–53.

Kleinig, John, 'Mill, Children, and Rights', *Educational Philosophy and Theory*, 8/1 (1976): 1–16.

Kramer, Matthew, Simmonds, Nigel, and Steiner, Hillel, *A Debate over Rights: Philosophical Enquiries* (Oxford: Oxford University Press, 1999).

MacCormick, Neil, 'Children's Rights: A Test-Case for Theories of Rights', *Archiv für Rechts und Sozialphilosophie*, 6/2 (1976): 305–17.

Purdy, Laura, *In their Best Interests? The Case Against Equal Rights for Children* (Ithaca, NY, and London: Cornell University Press, 1992).

O'Neill, Onora, 'Children's Rights and Children's Lives', *Ethics*, 98 (1988): 445–63.

Schrag, Francis, 'The Child in the Moral Order', *Philosophy*, 52 (1977): 167–77.

The Family and Justice

Cohen, Joshua, 'Okin on Justice, Gender, and Family', *Canadian Journal of Philosophy*, 22 (1992): 263–86.

Exdell, John, 'Feminism, Fundamentalism, and Liberal Legitimacy', *Canadian Journal of Philosophy*, 24 (1994): 441–64.

Fishkin, James, *Justice, Equal Opportunity and the Family* (New Haven, Conn.: Yale University Press, 1983).

Kymlicka, Will, 'Rethinking the Family', *Philosophy and Public Affairs*, 20 (1991): 77–97.

Okin, Susan Moller, *Justice, Gender, and the Family* (New York: Basic Books, 1989).

—— 'Political Liberalism, Justice, and Gender', *Ethics*, 105 (1994): 23–43.

Munoz-Dardé, Véronique, 'Is the Family to be Abolished then?', *Proceedings of the Aristotelian Society*, (1999): 37–56.

Vallentyne, Peter, 'Equal Opportunity and the Family', *Public Affairs Quarterly* (1989): 27–45.

Autonomy and Parental Authority

Archard, David, 'What's Blood Got to do with it? The Significance of Natural Parenthood', *Res Publica*, 1 (1995): 91–106.

Bigelow, John, Campbell, John, Dodds, Susan M., Pargetter, Robert, Prior, Elizabeth W., and Young, Robert, 'Parental Autonomy', *Journal of Applied Philosophy*, 5/2 (1988): 183–96.

Brennan, Samantha, and Noggle, Robert, 'The Moral Status of Children: Children's Rights, Parents' Rights, and Family Justice', *Social Theory and Practice*, 23 (1997): 1–26.

Hall, Barbara, 'The Origin of Parental Rights', *Public Affairs Quarterly*, 13/1 (Jan. 1999): 73–82.

Harris, John, 'The Right to Found a Family', in Geoffrey Scarre (ed.), *Children, Parents and Politics* (Cambridge: Cambridge University Press, 1989), 133–53.

Macleod, Colin M., 'Conceptions of Parental Autonomy', *Politics and Society*, 25/1 (March 1997): 117–40.

Montague, Phillip, 'The Myth of Parental Rights', *Social Theory and Practice*, 26/1 (Spring 2000): 47–68.

Page, Edgar, 'Parental Rights', *Journal of Applied Philosophy*, 1/2 (1984), 187–203.

Schoeman, Ferdinand, 'Rights of Children, Rights of Parents, and the Moral Basis of the Family', *Ethics*, 91 (1980): 6–19.

References

Alexander, S. (1994). *In Praise of Single Parents: Mothers and Fathers Embrace the Challenge* (Boston: Houghton Mifflin Co.).

Anderson, E. (1999). 'What is the Point of Equality?', *Ethics*, 109/2: 287–337.

Anscombe, E. (1981). 'On the Source of the Authority of the State', *Ethics, Religion and Politics* (Oxford: Blackwell).

Archard, D. (1993). *Children, Rights and Childhood* (London: Routledge).

Aries, P. (1962). *Centuries of Childhood: A Social History of Family Life*, trs. Robert Baldick (New York: Alfred Knopf).

Aristotle (1984). *Nicomachean Ethics*, tr. by W. D. Ross, revised by J. O. Urmson, in *The Complete Works of Aristotle*, ed. Jonathan Barnes, ii (Bollingen Series LXXI-2; Princeton: Princeton University Press).

Arneil, B. (1999). *Politics and Feminism* (Oxford: Blackwell).

—— (2000). 'The Politics of Human Rights', *National Journal of Constitutional Law*, 11/2: 212–35.

Arneson, R. J., and Shapiro, I. (1996). 'Democratic Autonomy and Religious Freedom', in I. Shapiro and R. Hardin (eds.), *Political Order* (Nomos XXXVIII; New York and London: New York University Press), 365–41.

Audi, R., and Wolterstorff, N. (1995). *Religion in the Public Square* (Lanham, Md.: Rowman & Littlefield).

Baier, A. (1987a). 'Hume, the Women's Moral Theorist?', in E. F. Kittay and D. T. Meyers (eds.), *Women and Moral Theory* (Savage, Md.: Rowman & Littlefield).

—— (1987b). 'The Need for More than Justice', *Canadian Journal of Philosophy*, suppl. vol. 13: 14–56.

Ball, D. (1974). 'The Family as a Sociological Problem', in Arlene and Jerome Skolnick (eds.), *Intimacy, Family, and Society* (Boston: Little, Brown).

Barry, B. (2001). *Culture and Equality: An Egalitarian Critique of Multiculturalism* (Cambridge: Polity).

Battistoni, R. (1985). *Public Schooling and the Education of Democratic Citizens* (Jackson, Miss.: University Press of Mississippi).

Becker, L. C. (1977). *Property Rights, Philosophic Foundations* (London: Routledge, Kegan & Paul).

Bennet, W. (1992). *The De-Valuing of America: The Fight for our Culture and our Children* (New York: Touchstone).

Berlin, I. (1969). *Four Essays on Liberty* (Oxford: Oxford University Press).

Blankenhorn, D. (1995). *Fatherless America* (New York: Basic Books).

—— Elshtain, J. B., and Bayne, S. (eds.) (1990). *Rebuilding the Nest: A New Commitment to the American Family* (Milwaukee: Family Service America).

—— Horn, W. F., and Pearlstein, M. B. (eds.) (1999). *The Fatherhood Movement: A Call to Action* (Lanham, Md.: Lexington Books).

Blustein, J. (1982). *Parents and Children: The Ethics of the Family* (Oxford: Oxford University Press).

Boo, K. (2001). 'After Welfare', *The New Yorker* (9 Apr.).

Braybrooke, D. (1987). *Meeting Needs* (Princeton: Princeton University Press).

Brazelton, T. B., and Greenspan, S. I. (2000). *The Irreducible Needs of Children: What Every Child Must Have to Grow, Learn, and Flourish* (Cambridge: Perseus Publishing).

Brennan, S. (1994). 'Paternalism and Rights', *Canadian Journal of Philosophy*, 24/3: 419–40.

—— (1995a). 'How is the Strength of a Right Determined?: Assessing the Harm View', *American Philosophical Quarterly*, 32/4: 383–92.

—— (1995b). 'Thresholds for Rights', *Southern Journal of Philosophy*, 33/2: 143–68.

—— and Noggle, R. (1997). 'The Moral Status of Children: Children's Rights, Parents' Rights, and Family Justice', *Social Theory and Practice*, 23/1: 1–26.

—— —— (1998). 'Rawls's Neglected Childhood: Reflections on the Original Position, Stability, and the Child's Sense of Justice', in G. Matthews and S. Turner (eds.), *The Philosopher's Child* (Rochester, NY: University of Rochester Press).

Brighouse, H. (1998). 'Civic Education and Liberal Legitimacy', *Ethics*, 108/4: 719–45.

—— (2000). *School Choice and Social Justice* (Oxford: Oxford University Press).

Bronfenbrenner, Urie (1990). 'Discovering What Families Do', in D. Blankenhorn, J. B. Elshtain, and S. Bayne (eds.), *Rebuilding the Nest: A New Commitment to the American Family* (Milwaukee: Family Service America).

Buchanan, A., Brock, D., Daniels, N., and Wikler, D. (2000). *From Chance to Choice: Genetics and Justice* (Cambridge: Cambridge University Press).

Burley, J. (ed.) (1999). *The Genetic Revolution and Human Rights* (Oxford: Oxford University Press).

Burstyn, J. (ed.) (1996). *Educating Tomorrow's Valuable Citizen* (Albany, NY: State University of New York Press).

Burtt, S. (1994). 'Reproductive Responsibilities: Rethinking the Fetal Rights Debate', *Policy Sciences*, 27: 179–96.

—— (1996). 'In Defense of *Yoder*: Parental Authority and the Public Schools', in I. Shapiro and R. Hardin (eds.), *Political Order* (Nomos XXXVIII; New York and London: New York University Press), 412–37.

Calabresi, C. and Melmed, A. D. (1972), 'Property Rules, Liability Rules, and Inalienability: One View of the Cathedral', *Harvard Law Review*, 85: 1089–1128.

Callan, E. (1988). *Autonomy and Schooling* (Kingston: McGill-Queen's University Press).

—— (1993). 'Patience and Courage', *Philosophy*, 68: 523–39.

—— (1997). *Creating Citizens: Political Education and Liberal Democracy* (Oxford: Oxford University Press).

Carens, J. (1985). 'Compensating Justice and Social Instructions', *Economics and Philosophy*, 1/1: 39–67.

Casal, P., and Williams, A. (1995). 'Rights, Equality, and Procreation', *Analyse and Kritik*, 17: 93–116.

Churchill, P. (1998). 'The Obligation of Parents to Raise their Children as Altruists', in L. Houlgate (ed.), *Family Ethics: Readings in the Moral Problems of Marriage and Family Life* (Belmont, Calif.: Wadsworth).

Clark, K. J. (ed.) (1993). *Philosophers Who Believe* (Downers Grove: Intervarsity Press).

Clement, G. (1996). *Care, Autonomy and Justice* (Boulder, Colo.: Westview Press).

Cohen, G. A. (1989). 'On the Currency of Egalitarian Justice', *Ethics*, 99: 906–44.

—— (1995). *Self-Ownership, Freedom and Equality* (Cambridge: Cambridge University Press).

Cohen, H. (1980). *Equal Rights for Children* (Totowa, NJ: Littlefield, Adams & Co.).

—— (1998). 'Children's Rights and Borrowed Capacities', in L. Houlgate (ed.), *Family Ethics: Readings in the Moral Problems of Marriage and Family Life* (Belmont, Calif.: Wadsworth).

Colby, A., Kohlberg, L., Gibbs, J., and Lieberman, M. (1983). 'A Longitudinal Study of Moral Development', *Monographs of the Society for Research in Child Development*, 200/48: 1–93.

Coleman, J. (1998). 'Civic Pedagogies and Liberal-Democratic Curricula', *Ethics*, 108/4: 746–61.

—— (2002). 'Answering Susan: Liberty and Authority in American School Reform', PhD., Brown University.

—— (forthcoming) 'School Choice, Diversity, and Having a Life of One's Own', *The School Field*.

Coltrane, Scott (1996). *Family Man: Fatherhood, Housework, and Gender Equity* (Oxford: Oxford University Press).

Coontz, Stephanie (1997). *The Way we Really are: Coming to Terms with America's Changing Families* (New York: Basic Books).

Council on Families in America (1994). 'Eight Propositions on Family and Child Well-Being', Working Paper 21. Mimeograph on file with Shelley Burtt.

Csikszentmihalyi, M., and Schneider, B. (2000). *Becoming Adult: How Teenagers Prepare for the World of Work* (New York: Basic Books).

Dagger, R. (1989). 'Rights', in Terence Ball, James Farr, and Russell Hanson (eds.), *Political Innovation and Conceptual Change* (Cambridge: Cambridge University Press), 292–308.

Damon, W. (1988). *The Moral Child: Nurturing Children's Natural Moral Growth* (New York: Free Press).

Danner, F. (1989). 'Cognitive Development in Adolescence', in J. Worell and F. Danner (eds.), *The Adolescent as Decision-Maker: Application to Development and Education* (San Diego, Calif.: Academic Press).

Darwall, S. (1996). 'Valuing Activity', *Social Philosophy and Policy*, 16/1: 176–96.

Dent, G. W. (1988). 'Religious Children, Secular Schools', *Southern California Law Review*, 61: 886–93.

Dulit, E. (1979). 'Adolescent Thinking a la Piaget: The Formal Stage', in R. Mosher (ed.), *Adolescents' Development and Education: A Janus Knot* (Berkeley, Calif.: McCutchan).

Dupree, Allen, and Primus, Wendell (2001). *Declining Share of Children Lived with Single Mothers in the Late 1990s* (Washington, DC: Center on Budget and Policy Priorities).

Dworkin, R. (1978). *Taking Rights Seriously* (London: Duckworth).

—— (1985). *A Matter of Principle* (Cambridge, Mass.: Harvard University Press).

—— (2000). *Sovereign Virtue: The Theory and Practice of Equality* (Cambridge, Mass.: Harvard University Press).

Eekelaar, J. (1986). 'The Emergence of Children's Rights', *Oxford Journal of Legal Studies*, 6/2: 161–82.

—— (1992). 'The Importance of Thinking that Children have Rights', in P. Alston, S. Parker, and J. Seymour (eds.), *Children, Rights and the Law* (Oxford: Oxford University Press), 221–35.

Eisenberg, A. (2001). 'Using Difference to Resolve Rights-Based Conflicts: A Reply to Joyce Green', *Canadian Journal of Political Science*, 34/1: 163–8.

—— Aird, E., Etzioni, A., Galston, W., Glendon, M. A., Minow, M., and Rossi, A. (1993). *A Communitarian Position Paper on the Family* (Washington, DC: The Communitarian Network).

—— (1994). 'Single Motherhood', *Dissent*, 41/2: 267–9.

Erikson, E. (1968). *Identity: Youth and Crisis* (New York: W. W. Norton & Co.).

Farson, R. (1974). *Birthrights* (London: Collier Macmillan).

Feinberg, J. (1970). 'The Nature and Value of Rights', *Journal of Value Inquiry*, 4: 243–57.

—— (1973). *Social Philosophy* (Englewood Cliffs, NJ: Prentice-Hall).

—— (1980). 'The Child's Right to an Open Future', in W. Aiken and H. LaFollette (eds.), *Whose Child? Children's Rights, Parental Authority, and State Power* (Totawa, NJ: Littlefield, Adams & Co.), 124–53.

Finnegan, W. (1998). *Cold New World: Growing up in a Harder Country* (New York: Random House).

Fishkin, J. (1983). *Justice, Equal Opportunity and the Family* (New Haven, Conn.: Yale University Press).

Folbre, N. (2001). 'Leave No Child Behind?', *American Prospect*, 12/1: 20–1.

Frankfurt, H. (1988). 'The Importance of What we Care about', in *The Importance of What we Care about* (Cambridge: Cambridge University Press).

Franklin, B., and Franklin, A. (1996). 'Growing Pains: The Developing Children's Rights Movement in the UK', in J. Pilcher and S. Wagg (eds.), *Thatcher's Children: Politics, Childhood and Society in the 1980s and 1990s* (London: Falmer Press), 94–113.

Franklin, D. L. (1997). *Ensuring Inequality: The Structural Transformation of the African-American Family.* (Oxford: Oxford University Press).

Freeman, M. (1983). *The Rights and Wrongs of Children* (London: Frances Pinter).

—— (1992a). 'Introduction', in M. Freeman and P Veerman (eds.), *The Ideologies of Children's Rights: International Studies in Human Rights*, xxiii (Dordrecht: Marinus Nijihoff), 3–6.

—— (1992b). 'Taking Children's Rights More Seriously', in P. Alston, S. Parker, and J. Seymour (eds.), *Children Rights and the Law* (Oxford: Oxford University Press), 52–71.

Fried, C. (1978). *Right and Wrong* (Cambridge, Mass.: Harvard University Press).

Galston, W. (1991a). 'A Liberal-Democratic Case for the Two-Parent Family', *The Responsive Community*, 1/1: 14–26.

—— (1991b). *Liberal Purposes: Goods, Virtues, and Diversity in the Liberal State* (Cambridge: Cambridge University Press).

—— (2000). 'Civic Education and Political Participation', paper presented at Brown University conference on youth and citizenship, 18 Mar. 2000.

George, R. (1987). 'Who should Bear the Cost of Children?', *Public Affairs Quarterly*, 1: 1–42.

Gilligan, C. (1982). *In a Different Voice: Psychological Theory and Women's Development* (Cambridge, Mass: Harvard University Press).

Glendon, M. A. (1989). *The Transformation of Family Law: State, Law and Family in the United States and Western Europe* (Chicago: University of Chicago).

Goldscheider, F. K., and Waite, L. J. (1991). *New Families, No Families? The Transformation of the American Home* (Berkeley, Calif.: University of California Press).

Goode, W. (1970). *World Revolution and Family Patterns* (New York: Free Press).

Goodin, R., and Gibson, D. (1997). 'Rights, Young and Old', *Oxford Journal of Legal Studies*, 17/2: 185–203.

Greeno, J., and Collins, A. (1996). 'Cognition and Learning', in D. Berliner and R Calfee (eds.), *Handbook of Educational Psychology* (New York: Macmillan Library Reference).

Greven, P. (1977). *The Protestant Temperament* (New York: Knopf).

Griffin, J. (1986). *Well-Being: Its Meaning, Measurement, and Moral Importance* (Oxford: Oxford University Press).

Grotius, Hugo (1925). *De Juri Belli ac Pacis Libri Tres* [1646], tr. Francis W. Kelsey, with the collaboration of Arthur E. R. Boak, Henry A. Sanders, Jesse S. Reeves and Herbert F. Wright, introduction by James Brown Scott (Oxford: Clarendon Press).

Gutmann, A. (1987). *Democratic Education* (Princeton: Princeton University Press).

—— (1989). 'Undemocratic Education', in N. Rosenblum (ed.), *Liberalism and the Moral Life* (Cambridge, Mass.: Harvard University Press), 71–88.

—— (1995). 'Civic Education and Social Diversity', *Ethics*, 105/3: 557–79.

—— and Thompson, D. (1990). 'Moral Conflict and Political Consensus', *Ethics*, 101: 76–86.

Harden, B. (2001). 'Bible Belt Couples Put Asunder More, Despite New Efforts.' *New York Times* (21 May).

Harris, J. (1989). 'The Right to Found a Family', in G. Scare (ed.), *Children, Parents and Politics* (Cambridge: Cambridge University Press).

Hegel, G. W. F. (1967). *Philosophy of Right*, tr. T. M. Knox (Oxford: Oxford University Press).

Hernandez, D. (1993). *America's Children: Resources from Family, Government, and the Economy* (New York: Russell Sage Foundation).

Hewlett, S. A., and West, C. (1998). *The War Against Parents: What we Can Do for America's Beleaguered Moms and Dads* (Boston: Houghton Mifflin Co.).

—— (2000). 'Caring for Crib Lizards', *American Prospect* 12/1: 17–20).

Heyd, D. (1992). *Genethics: Moral Issues in the Creation of People* (Berkeley, Calif.: University of California Press).

Hobbes, T. (1968). *Leviathan* [1651], ed. with an introduction by C. B. Macpherson Harmondsworth: Penguin).

—— (1994). *The Elements of Law, Natural and Politic* [1650], ed. with an introduction by J. C. A. Gaskin (Oxford: Oxford University Press).

Hochschild, A. (1989). *The Second Shift: Working Parents and the Revolution at Home* (New York, Viking).

Holloway, S. D. (1997). *Through My Own Eyes: Single Mothers and the Cultures of Poverty* (Cambridge, Mass.: Harvard University Press).

Holt, J. C. (1975). *Escape from Childhood: The Need and Rights of Children* (Harmondsworth: Penguin).

Houlgate, L. (1998). *Family Ethics: Readings in the Moral Problems of Marriage and Family Life* (Belmont, Calif.: Wadsworth).

Hughes, J. (1989). 'Thinking about Children', in G. Scarre (ed.) *Children, Parents and Politics* (Cambridge: Cambridge University Press), 36–51.

Hurka, T. (1994). 'Indirect Perfectionism: Kymlicka on Liberal Neutrality', *Journal of Political Philosophy*, 3: 36–57.

—— (1997). *Perfectionism* (Oxford: Oxford University Press).

Ignatieff, M. (1984). *The Needs of Strangers* (London: Chatto & Windus).

Jacobs, L. (1997). *An Introduction to Modern Political Philosophy: The Democratic Vision of Politics* (Upper Saddle River, NJ: Prentice-Hall).

Josselson, R. (1980). 'Ego Development in Adolescence', in J. Adelson (ed.), *Handbook of Adolescent Psychology* (New York: John Wiley & Sons).

Kagan, S. (1998). *Normative Ethics* (Boulder, Colo.: Westview Press).

Kamarck, E., and Galston, W. (1990). *Putting Children First: A Progressive Family Policy for the 1990s* (Washington, DC: Progressive Policy Institute).

Kant, I. (1965). *The Metaphysical Elements of Justice*, tr. J. Ladd (Indianapolis: Bobbs-Merrill).

—— (1996). *The Metaphysics of Morals*, tr. and ed. M. Gregor, with an Introduction by Roger J. Sullivan (Cambridge: Cambridge University Press).

Kilpatrick, W. (1992). *Why Johnny Can't Tell Right from Wrong* (New York: Simon & Schuster).

Kohlberg, L. (1969). 'Stage and Sequence: The Cognitive-Developmental Approach to Socialization' in D. Goslin (ed.), *Handbook of Socialization Theory and Research* (Chicago: Rand McNally & Co.).

—— (1976). 'Moral Stages and Moralization: The Cognitive Developmental Approach', in T. Lickona (ed.), *Moral Development and Behavior: Theory, Research, and Social Issues* (New York: Holt, Rinehart, & Wilson).

—— and Gilligan, C. (1979). 'The Adolescent as Philosopher: The Discovery of Self in a Postconventional World', in R. Mosher (ed.), *Adolescents' Development and Education: A Janus Knot* (Berkeley, Calif.: McCutchan Publishing Corporation), 76–8.

Kramer, M. H., Simmonds, N. E., and Steiner H. (eds.) (1998). *A Debate over Rights*: *Philosophical Inquiries* (Oxford: Oxford University Press).

Kristol, Irving (1994). 'Life without Father', *Wall Street Journal* (3 Nov.).

Kymlicka, W. (1989). *Liberalism, Community, and Culture* (Oxford: Oxford University Press).

—— (1990). *Contemporary Political Philosophy: An Introduction* (Oxford: Oxford University Press).

—— (1995). *Multicultural Citizenship: A Liberal Theory of Minority Rights* (Oxford: Oxford University Press).

—— and Norman, W. (1994). 'Return of the Citizen: A Survey of Recent Work on Citizenship Theory', *Ethics*, 104: 352–81.

La Follette, H. (1989). 'Freedom of Religion and Children', *Public Affairs Quarterly*, 3/1: 75–87.

—— (1999). 'Circumscribed Autonomy: Children, Care, and Custody', in U. Narayan and J. Bartkowiak (eds.), *Having and Raising Children: Unconventional Families, Hard Choices, and the Social Good* (Newbury Park, PA: Penn State Press), 137–52.

Lapsley, D. (1996). *Moral Psychology* (Boulder, Colo.: Westview Press).

Larmore, C. (1996). *The Morals of Modernity* (Cambridge: Cambridge University Press).

Larrabee, M. J. (ed.) (1993). *An Ethic of Care: Feminist and Interdisciplinary Perspectives* (New York: Routledge).

Leach, P. (1994). *Children First: What our Society Must Do—and is Not Doing for Our Children Today* (New York: Knopf).

Levinson, M. (1999). *The Demands of Liberal Education* (Oxford: Oxford University Press).

Lipson, M., and Vallentyne, P. (1989). 'Equal Opportunity and the Family', *Public Affairs Quarterly*, 3/4: 27–45.

Locke, J. (1960). *Some Thoughts Concerning Education* [1693], in *The Educational Writings of John Locke*, ed. J. L. Axtell (Cambridge: Cambridge University Press).

—— (1988). *Two Treatises of Government*, Cambridge Texts in the History of Political Thought, ed. Peter Laslett (Cambridge: Cambridge University Press).

Lomasky, L. (1987). *Persons, Rights, and the Moral Community* (New York: Oxford University Press).

MacCormick, N. (1982). *Legal Right and Social Democracy: Essays in Legal and Political Philosophy* (Oxford: Clarendon Press).

Macedo, S. (1995). 'Liberal Civic Education and Religious Fundamentalism: The Case of God v. John Rawls?', *Ethics*, 105: 467–96.

—— (1996). 'Community, Diversity, and Civic Education: Toward a Liberal Political Science of Group Life', in E. Paul, F. Miller, Jr., and J. Paul (eds.), *The Communitarian Challenge to Liberalism* (Cambridge: Cambridge University Press).

—— (2000). *Diversity and Distrust: Civic Education in a Multicultural Society* (Cambridge, Mass.: Harvard University Press).

MacIntyre, A. (1981). *After Virtue: A Study in Moral Theory* (London: Duckworth).

McLanahan, S., and Sandefur, G. (1994). *Growing up with a Single Parent: What Hurts, What Helps* (Cambridge: Harvard University Press).

Macleod, C. (1997). 'Conceptions of Parental Autonomy', *Politics and Society*, 25/1: 117–41.

—— (1998). *Liberalism, Justice and Markets: A Critique of Liberal Equality* (Oxford: Oxford University Press).

McMahan, J. (1998). 'Wrongful Life: Paradoxes in the Morality of Causing People to Exist', in J. L. Coleman and C. W. Morris (eds.), *Rational Commitment and Social Justice: Essays for Gregory Kavka* (New York: Cambridge University Press).

Marcia, J. (1980). 'Identity in Adolescence', in J. Adelson (ed.), *Handbook of Adolescent Psychology* (New York: John Wiley and Sons).

—— (1993a). 'The Ego Identity Status Approach to Ego Identity', in J. Marcia *et al.* (eds.), *Ego Identity: A Handbook for Psychosocial Research* (New York: Springer-Verlag).

—— (1993b). 'The Status of the Statuses: Research Review', in J. Marcia *et al.* (eds.), *Ego Identity: A Handbook for Psychosocial Research* (New York: Springer-Verlag).

Mill, J. S. (1859). *On Liberty* (Indianapolis: Bobbs-Merrill Co.).

Montague, P. (2000). 'The Myth of Parental Rights', *Social Theory and Practice*, 26/1: 47–68.

Montgomery, J. (1988). 'Children as Property?', *Modern Law Review*, 51: 323–42.

Mosher, R., Kenny, Jr., R., and Garrod, A. (1994). *Preparing for Citizenship: Teaching Youth to Live Democratically* (Westport, Conn.: Praeger).

Moshman, D. (1999). *Adolescent Psychological Development: Rationality, Morality, and Identity* (Mahwah, NJ: Lawrence Erlbaum).

Moss, P. and Penn, H. (1996). *Transforming Nursery Education* (London: Paul Chapman).

Munoz-Dardé, V. (1998). 'John Rawls, Justice in the Family and Justice of the Family', *Philosophical Quarterly*, 48/192: 335–52.

—— (1999). 'Is the Family to be Abolished then?', *Proceedings of the Aristotelian Society*, 99: 37–56.

—— (2000). *La Justice sociale: Le Libéralisme égalitaire de John Rawls* (Paris: Nathan Université).

Murray, C. (1993). 'The Time has Come to Put a Stigma Back on Illegitimacy', *Wall Street Journal* (29 Oct.).

Musick, J. (1993). *Young, Poor and Pregnant: The Psychology of Teenage Motherhood* (New Haven, Conn.: Yale University Press).

Nagel, T. (1979). 'Equality', in *Mortal Questions* (Cambridge: Cambridge University Press).

—— (1991). *Equality and Partiality* (Oxford: Oxford University Press).

Narveson, J. (1998). *The Libertarian Idea* (Philadelphia: Temple University Press).

Noggle, R. (1997). 'The Public Conception of Autonomy and Critical Self-Reflection', *Southern Journal of Philosophy*, 35: 495–515.

—— (1999*a*). 'Integrity, the Self, and Desire-Based Accounts of Individual Good', *Philosophical Studies*, 96: 303–31.

—— (1999*b*). 'Kantian Respect and Particular Persons', *Canadian Journal of Philosophy*, 29: 449–78.

Nolin, M., and Chapman, C. (1997). *Adult Civic Involvement in the United States* (Washington, DC: US Department of Education, National Center for Education Statistics).

Nozick, R. (1974). *Anarchy, State, and Utopia* (New York: Basic Books).

—— (1989). *The Examined Life: Philosophical Meditations* (New York: Simon & Schuster).

O'Neill, J. (1994). *The Missing Child in Liberal Theory: Towards a Covenant Theory of Family, Community, Welfare and the Civic State* (Toronto: University of Toronto Press).

O'Neill, O. (1989). 'Children's Rights and Children's Lives', in her *Constructions of Reason, Exploration of Kant's practical philosophy* (Cambridge: Cambridge University Press), 187–205. Originally in *Ethics*, 98 (1988): 445–63.

Okin, S. M. (1989). *Justice, Gender and the Family* (New York: Basic Books).

—— (1998). 'Multiculturalism and Feminism: Some Tensions', *Ethics*, 108/4: 661–84.

—— Cohen, J., Matthew, H., and Nussbaum, M. (1999). *Is Multiculturalism Bad for Women?* (Princeton: Princeton University Press).

Page, E. (1984). 'Parental Rights', *Journal of Applied Philosophy*, 1/2: 187–203.

Parfit, D. (1984). *Reasons and Persons* (Oxford: Oxford University Press).

—— (1986). 'Comments', *Ethics*, 96: 832–72.

Pateman, C. (1988). *Sexual Contract* (Oxford: Polity Press).

Perry, M. (1991). *Love and Power.* (New York: Oxford University Press).

Pico della Mirandola, G. (1998). *On the Dignity of Man*, tr. Charles Glenn Wallis (Indianapolis: Hackett Publishing).

Popenoe, D. (1990). 'Family Decline in America', in D. Blankenhorn, J. B. Elshtain, and S. Bayne (eds.), *Rebuilding the Nest: A New Commitment to the American Family* (Milwaukee: Family Service America).

—— (1992*a*). 'Fostering the New Familism: A Goal for America', *Responsive Community* 2/4

—— (1992*b*). 'The Controversial Truth: The Two-Parent Family is Better', *The New York Times* (26 Oct.).

—— (1996). *Life without Father: Compelling New Evidence that Fatherhood and Marriage are Indispensable for the Good of Children and Society* (New York: Free Press).

Power, F., Higgins, A., and Kohlberg, L. (1989). *Lawrence Kohlberg's Approach to Moral Education* (New York: Columbia University Press).

Purdy, L. (1992). *In their Best Interest? The Case Against Equal Rights for Children* (Ithaca, NY: Cornell University Press).

—— (1996). *Reproducing Persons: Issues in Feminist Bioethics* (Ithaca, NY: Cornell University Press).

Rakowski, E. (1991). *Equal Justice* (New York: Oxford University Press).

Rawls. J. (1971). *A Theory of Justice* (Cambridge, Mass.: Harvard University Press).

—— (1974). 'Reply to Alexander and Musgrave', *Quarterly Journal of Economics*, 88/4: 633–55.

—— (1980). 'Kantian Constructivism in Moral Theory', *Journal of Philosophy*, 77/9: 515–72.

—— (1985). 'Justice as Fairness: Political Not Metaphysical', *Philosophy and Public Affairs*, 14: 223–51.

—— (1993). *Political Liberalism* (New York: Columbia University Press).

—— (1999*a*). *A Theory of Justice*, rev. edn. (Cambridge, Mass.: Harvard University Press).

—— (1999*b*). *Collected Papers*, ed. S. Freeman (Cambridge, Mass.: Harvard University Press).

—— (2001). *Justice as Fairness: A Restatement*, ed. Erin Kelly (Cambridge, Mass.: Harvard University Press).

Raz, J., and Margalit, A. (1995). 'National Self-Determination', in W. Kymlicka (ed.), *The Rights of Minority Cultures* (Oxford: Oxford University Press), 79–92.

Richards, N. (1986). 'A Conception of Personality', *Behaviorism*, 14: 147–57.

Ripstein, A. (1999). *Equality, Responsibility, and the Law* (Cambridge: Cambridge University Press).

Roberts, M. (1998). *Child versus Childmaker: Future Persons and Present Duties in Ethics and the Law* (New York: Rowman & Littlefield).

Robinson, O. F., Fergus, T. D. and Gordon, W. M. (1994). *European Legal History: Sources and Institutions*, 2nd edn. (London: Butterworth).

Rodgers, H. R. (1996). *Poor Women, Poor Children: American Poverty in the 1990s* (Armonk, NY: M. E. Sharpe).

Roemer, J. (1995*a*). 'Equality and Responsibility', *Boston Review*, 1 (April–May): 3–7.

—— (1995*b*). 'Equality of Opportunity: Theory and Examples', (mimeo), (Davis, Calif.: University of California).

—— (1998). *Equality of Opportunity* (Cambridge, Mass.: Harvard University Press).

Rogers, C. M., and Wrightsman, L. S. (1978). 'Attitudes towards Children's Rights: Nurturance of Self-Determination?', *Journal of Social Issues*, 34/2: 59–68.

Rose, S. (1988). *Keeping them Out of the Hands of Satan* (New York: Routledge).

Rosen, H. (1980). *The Development of Sociomoral Knowledge: A Cognitive-Structural Approach* (New York: Columbia University Press).

Ruddick, W. (1980). 'Parents and Life Prospects', in O. O'Neill and W. Ruddick (eds.), *Having Children* (Oxford: Oxford University Press).

—— (1999). 'Parenthood: Three Concepts and a Principle', in L. Houlgate (ed.), *Morals, Marriage, and Parenthood: An Introduction to Family Ethics* (Belmont, Calif.: Wadsworth).

Ryan, K., and Bohlin, K. (1999). *Building Character in Schools: Practical Ways to Bring Moral Instruction to Life* (San Francisco: Jossey-Bass).

Sandel, M. (1982). *Liberalism and the Limits of Justice* (Cambridge: Cambridge University Press).

—— (ed.) (1984). *Liberalism and its Critics* (Oxford: Blackwell).

Sangster, P. (1963). *Pity my Simplicity: The Evangelical Revival and the Religious Education of Children, 1738–1800* (London: Epworth Press).

Scanlon, T. M. (1975). 'Preference and Urgency', *Journal of Philosophy*, 72: 655–69.

—— (1998). *What we Owe to Each Other* (Cambridge, Mass.: Harvard University Press).

Schabas, W. (2000). 'Freedom from Fear and Want', *National Journal of Constitutional Law*, 11/2: 189–211.

Schneider, B., and Stevenson, D. (1999). *The Ambitious Generation: America's Teenagers, Motivated But Directionless* (New Haven, Conn.: Yale University Press).

Shapiro, W. (2001). 'Hype and Glory', *USA Today* (15 June).

Shiffrin, S. V. (1999). 'Wrongful Life, Procreative Responsibility, and the Significance of Harm', *Legal Theory*, 5: 117–48.

Shoeman, F. (1980). 'Rights of Children, Rights of Parents, and the Moral Basis of the Family', *Ethics*, 91: 6–19.

Shorter, E. (1975). *The Making of the Modern Family* (New York: Basic Books).

Skolnick, A. (1994). *Embattled Paradise: The American Family in an Age of Uncertainty* (New York: Basic Books).

Solomon, Andrew (2001). 'Case Study: The Depressed Poor; Location: Washington D.C.; A Cure for Poverty', *The New York Times Magazine* (6 May).

Stacey, J. (1996). *In the Name of the Family: Rethinking Family Values in the Postmodern Age* (Boston: Beacon Press).

Steinbock, B., and McClamrock, R. (1999). 'When is Birth Unfair to the Child', in L. Houlgate (ed.), *Morals, Marriage, and Parenthood: An Introduction to Family Ethics* (Belmont, Calif.: Wadsworth).

Steiner, H. (1994). *An Essay on Rights* (Oxford: Blackwell).

—— (1997). 'Choice and Circumstance', *Ratio*, 10/3: 296–312.

—— (1998). 'Working Rights', in M. Kramer, N. Simmonds, and H. Steiner (eds.), *A Debate over Rights: Philosophical Enquiries* (Oxford: Oxford University Press).

Stephens, S. (1995). 'Children and the Politics of Culture in "Late Capitalism"', in S. Stephens (ed.), *Children and the Politics of Culture* (Princeton: Princeton: University Press), 3–50.

Strawson, G. (1986). *Freedom and Belief* (Oxford: Oxford University Press).

Sumner, L. W. (1987). *The Moral Foundation of Rights* (Oxford: Oxford University Press).

Taylor, C. (1979). 'Atomism', in A Kontos (ed.), *Powers, Possessions and Freedom: Essays in Honour of C. B. MacPherson* (Toronto: University of Toronto Press).

—— (1992). *Multiculturalism and 'The Politics of Recognition'* (Princeton: Princeton University Press).

Thomson, G. (1987). *Needs* (London: Routledge and Kegan Paul).

Thomson, J. J. (1990). *The Realm of Rights* (Cambridge, Mass.: Harvard University Press).

Thorne, B. (ed.) (1992). *Rethinking the Family: Some Feminist Questions* (Boston: Northeastern University Press).

Tierney, B. (1997). *The Idea of Natural Rights* (Atlanta: Scholars Press).

Tomasi, J. (1991). 'Individual Rights and Community Virtues', *Ethics*, 101/2: 521–36.

—— (2001a). *Liberalism beyond Justice: Citizens, Society, and the Boundaries of Political Theory* (Princeton: Princeton University Press).

—— (2001b). 'Civic Education and Ethical Subservience: From *Mozert* to *Sante Fe* and Beyond', in S. Macedo and Y. Tamir (eds.), *NOMOS XLIII: Moral and Political Education* (New York: New York University Press).

Tronto, J. (1993). *Moral Boundaries* (New York: Routledge).

UNICEF (2000). *The State of the World's Children* (Oxford: Oxford University Press).

Vallentyne, P. (1998). 'Critical Notice of G. A. Cohen's *Self-Ownership, Freedom, and Equality*', *Canadian Journal of Philosophy*, 28: 609–26.

—— (2000). 'Introduction: Left-Libertarianism—A Primer', in H. Steiner and P. Vallentyne (eds.), *Left-Libertarianism and its Critics: The Contemporary Debate* (Basingstoke and New York: Palgrave).

—— (2001). 'Self-Ownership', in C. Becker and L. Becker (eds.), *Encyclopedia of Ethics*, 2nd edn. (New York: Garland).

—— (2003). 'Childrearing Rights and Duties', *William and Mary Bill of Rights Journal* 44 (forthcoming).

Van Parijs, P. (1995). *Real Freedom for All* (Oxford: Oxford University Press).

Wald, M. (1979). 'Children's Rights: A Framework for Analysis', *University of California at Davis Law Review*, 12/2: 255–82.

Waldron, J. (1993). 'When Justice Replaces Affection: The Need for Rights', in J. Waldron, *Liberal Rights: Collected Papers* (New York: Cambridge University Press), 370–91.

Waterman, A. (1993). 'Developmental Perspectives on Identity Formation: From Adolescence to Adulthood', in J. Marcia *et al.* (eds.), *Ego Identity: A Handbook for Psychosocial Research* (New York: Springer-Verlag).

Wellman, C. (1997). 'The Growth of Children's Rights', in C. Wellman, *An Approach to Rights* (Dordrecht: Kluwer), 127–40.

Whitehead, B. D. (1993). 'Dan Quayle was Right', *Atlantic Monthly*, 271/4: 47–84.

Wigfield, A., Eccles, J., and Pintrich, P. (1996). 'Development between the Ages of 11 and 25', in D. Berliner and R. Calfee (eds.), *Handbook of Educational Psychology* (New York: Macmillan Library Reference).

Wiggins, D. (1981). 'Public Rationality, Needs and what Needs are Relative to', in P. Hall and D. Bannister (eds.), *Transport and Public Policy* (London: Mansell), 198–219.

—— (1987). 'Claims of Need', in D. Wiggins, *Needs, Values, Truth* (Oxford: Blackwell), 1–57.

—— and Dermen, S. (1987). 'Needs, Need, and Needing', *Journal of Medical Ethics*, 13: 62–8.

Williams, B. (1973). 'The Idea of Equality', in *Problems of the Self* (Cambridge: Cambridge University Press).

—— (1976). 'Persons, Character and Morality', in A. O. Rorty (ed.), *The Identities of Persons* (Berkeley: University of California Press). Reprinted in B. Williams (ed.), *Moral Luck* (Cambridge: Cambridge University Press, 1981).

Wilson, J. Q. (1993). 'The Family Values Debate', *Commentary*, 95/4: 24–31.

Wolff, J. (1998). 'Fairness, Respect and the Egalitarian Ethos', *Philosophy and Public Affairs*, 27/2: 97–122.

Wolgast, E. (1987). 'Wrong Rights', *Hypatia*, 2/1: 25–44.

Wolterstorff, N. (1993). 'The Grace that Shaped My Life', in K. J. Clark (ed.), *Philosophers who Believe* (Downers Grove: Intervarsity Press), 259–75.

Woodward, J. (1986). 'The Non-Identity Problem', *Ethics*, 96: 804–31.

Wuthnow, R. (1997). *Learning to Care: Elementary Kindness in an Age of Indifference* (Oxford: Oxford University Press).

Wyness, M. G. (2000). *Contesting Childhood* (London: Falmer Press).

Wynne, E. (1986). 'The Great Tradition in Education: Transmitting Moral Values', *Educational Leadership*, 43: 4–14.

—— and Ryan, K. (1993). *Reclaiming Our Schools: A Handbook on Teaching Character, Academics, and Discipline* (New York: Macmillian).

Young, I. M. (1994). 'Making Single Motherhood Normal', *Dissent*, 41/1: 88–93.

—— (1995). 'Mothers, Citizenship, and Independence: A Critique of Pure Family Values', *Ethics*, 105: 535–56.

Younis, J., and Yates, M. (1997). *Community Service and Social Responsibility in Youth* (Chicago: University of Chicago Press).

INDEX

Note: Page numbers followed by '*n*' indicate endnotes; for example 28*n* 1 refers to page 28, note 1.

Index